THE MAJOR LANGUAGES OF SOUTH ASIA, THE MIDDLE EAST AND AFRICA

EDITED BY
BERNARD COMRIE

London

First published as part of
The World's Major Languages in 1987 by
Croom Helm Ltd

Reprinted with revisions and additional material in 1990 by
Routledge
11 New Fetter Lane, London EC4P 4EE

British Library Cataloguing in Publication Data
Available on request

ISBN 0-415-05772-8

Typeset in 10 on 12pt Times by Computype, Middlesex
Printed and bound in Great Britain by Mackays of Chatham

Contents

Preface

The text of this book has been extracted from that of *The World's Major Languages* (Routledge, 1987). The aim of that book was to make available information on some fifty of the world's major languages and language families, in a form that would be accessible and interesting both to the layman with a general interest in language and to the linguist eager to find out about languages outside his or her speciality. Not all of those interested in major languages of the world, however, have an interest that includes all parts of the world, and it therefore seemed advisable to publish portions of the original text in a series of paperbacks — *The Major Languages*. Readers interested in only one part of the world now have access to discussion of those languages without having to acquire the whole volume.

Perhaps the most controversial problem that I had to face in the original volume was the choice of languages to be included. My main criterion was admittedly, a very subjective one: what languages did I think the reader would expect to find included? In answering this question I was, of course, guided by more objective criteria, such as the number of speakers of individual languages, whether they are official languages of independent states, whether they are widely used in more than one country, whether they are the bearers of long-standing literary traditions. These criteria often conflict — thus Latin, though long since deprived of native speakers, was included because of its immense cultural importance — and I bear full responsibility, as editor, for the final choice.

The notion of 'major language' is obviously primarily a social characterisation, and the fact that a language was not included implies no denigration of its importance as a language in its own right: every human language is a manifestation of our species' linguistic faculty and any human language may provide an important contribution to our understanding of language as a general phenomenon. In the recent development of general linguistics, important contributions have come from the Australian Aboriginal languages Walbiri (Warlpiri) and Dyirbal (Jirrbal). Other editors might well have come up with different selections of languages, or have used somewhat different criteria. When linguists learned in 1970 that the last speaker of Kamassian, a Uralic language originally spoken in Siberia, had kept her language alive for decades in her prayers — God being the only other speaker of her language — they may well have wondered whether, for this person, *the* world's major language was not Kamassian.

Contributors were presented with early versions of my own chapters on Slavonic languages and Russian as models for their contributions, but I felt it inappropriate to lay down strict guidelines as to how each individual chapter should be written, although I did ask authors to include at least some material on both the structure of their language and its social background. The main criterion that I asked contributors to follow was: tell the reader what you consider to be the most interesting facts about your language. This necessarily meant that different chapters highlight different phenomena, e.g. the chapter on English the role of English as a world language, the chapter on Arabic the writing system, the chapter on Turkish the grammatical system. But I believe that this variety lent strength to the original volume, since within the space limitations of what is quite a sizable book it would have been impossible to do justice in a more comprehensive and homogeneous way to each of over 50 languages and language families.

The criterion for dividing the contents of the original volume among the four new books has been my assessment of likely common and divergent interests: if the reader is interested in language X, then which of the other major languages of the world is he or she likely to be most interested in? In part, my decisions have been governed by consideration of genetic relatedness (for instance, all Romance languages, including Rumanian, are included in *The Major Languages of Western Europe*), in part by consideration of areal interests (so that *The Major Languages of The Middle East, South Asia and Africa* includes the Indo-Iranian languages, along with other languages of the Middle East and South Asia). Inevitably, some difficulties arose in working out the division, especially given the desire not to have too much overlap among volumes, since a reader might want to acquire more than one of the paperback volumes. In fact, the only overlap among the volumes is in the Introduction, substantial parts of which are the same for all volumes, and in the fact that the chapter on Indo-European languages is included in both of the European volumes (given that most of the languages of both western and eastern Europe are Indo-European).

Editorial support in the preparation of my work on the original volume was provided by the Division of Humanities of the University of Southern California, through the research fund of the Andrew W. Mellon Professorship, which I held during 1983–4, and by the Max Planck Institute for Psycholinguistics (Nijmegen, The Netherlands), where I was a visiting research worker in the summer of 1984. I am particularly grateful to

Jonathan Price for his continuing willingness to consult with me on all details of the preparation of the text.

Bernard Comrie
Los Angeles

Abbreviations

abilit.	abilitative
abl.	ablative
abstr.	abstract
acc.	accusative
acr.	actor
act.	active
act.n.	action nominal
adj.	adjective
adv.	adverb
Alb.	Albanian
Am.	American
anim.	animate
aor.	aorist
Ar.	Arabic
Arm.	Armenian
art.	article
Ashk.	Ashkenazi(c)
asp.	aspirated
AT	actor-trigger
athem.	athematic
aux.	auxiliary
Av.	Avestan
ben.	beneficiary
BH	Biblical Hebrew
BN	B-Norwegian
Boh.	Bohemian
BP	Brazilian Portuguese
Br.	British
BT	beneficiary-trigger
c.	common
Cast.	Castilian
Cat.	Catalan
caus.	causative
cc	class concord
Cent.	Central
cl.	class(ifier)
clit.	clitic
comp.	comparative
conj.	conjunction
conjug.	conjugation
conjv.	conjunctive
cont.	contemplated
cop.	copula
cp	class prefix
crs.	currently relevant state
Cz.	Czech
Da.	Danish
dat.	dative
dbl.	double
decl.	declension
def.	definite
dent.	dental
deriv. morph.	derivational morpheme
de-v.	deverbal
dir.	direct
disj.	disjunctive
Dor.	Doric
drc.	directional
DT	dative-trigger
du.	dual
dur.	durative
d.v.	dynamic verb
E.	Eastern
Eng.	English
ENHG	Early New High German
EP	European Portuguese
erg.	ergative
ex.	existential-possessive
f.	feminine
fact.	factive
foc.	focus
Fr.	French
fut.	future
g.	gender
gen.	genitive

ger.	gerund(ive)	neg.	negative
Gk.	Greek	NHG	New High German
Gmc.	Germanic	nm.	nominal
Go.	Gothic	NN	N-Norwegian
gr.	grade	nom.	nominative
GR	Gallo-Romance	noms.	nominalisation
gutt.	guttural	NP	New Persian
H	High	nt.	neuter
Hier. Hitt.	Hieroglyphic Hittite	Nw.	Norwegian
Hitt.	Hittite	O.	Oscan
hon.	honorific	OArm.	Old Armenian
IE	Indo-European	obj.	object
imper.	imperative	obl.	oblique
imperf.	imperfect(ive)	OBs.	Old Burmese
inanim.	inanimate	Oc.	Occitan
incl.	inclusive	OCS	Old Church Slavonic
indef.	indefinite	OE	Old English
indic.	indicative	OFr.	Old French
indir.	indirect	OFri.	Old Frisian
infin.	infinitive	OHG	Old High German
inst.	instrumental	OIc.	Old Icelandic
intr.	intransitive	OIr.	Old Irish
inv.	inversion particle	OIran.	Old Iranian
irr.	irrational	OLat.	Old Latin
It.	Italian	OLith.	Old Lithuanian
IT	instrument-trigger	ON	Old Norse
i.v.	intransitive verb	OP	Old Persian
L	Low	opt.	optative
lab.	labial	OPtg.	Old Portuguese
Lat.	Latin	orig.	original(ly)
Latv.	Latvian	OS	Old Saxon
LG	Low German	OV	object–verb
lig.	ligature	p.	person
lingu.	lingual	pal.	palatal
lit.	literally	part.	participle
Lith.	Lithuanian	pass.	passive
loc.	locative	pat.	patient
m.	masculine	PDr.	Proto-Dravidian
MBs.	Modern Burmese	perf.	perfect(ive)
ME	Middle English	pers.	person
med.	medio-passive	PGmc.	Proto-Germanic
MH	Middle Hebrew	PIE	Proto-Indo-European
MHG	Middle High German	PIt.	Proto-Italic
mid.	middle	Pkt.	Prakrit
MidFr.	Middle French	pl.	plural
ModE	Modern English	Po.	Polish
ModFr.	Modern French	pos.	position
MoH	Modern Hebrew	poss.	possessive
Mor.	Moravian	prep.	preposition
MP	Middle Persian	prepl.	prepositional
n.	noun	pres.	present
necess.	necessitative	pret.	preterit

prim.	primary	st.	standard
prog.	progressive	su.	subject
pron.	pronoun	subj.	subjunctive
PT	patient-trigger	sup.	superlative
Ptg.	Portuguese	s.v.	stative verb
Q	question	SVO	subject–verb–object
rat.	rational	Sw.	Swedish
recip.	reciprocal	tap.	tense/aspect pronoun
refl. pron.	reflexive pronoun	tg.	trigger
rel.	relative	them.	thematic
rep.	reported	Tk.	Turkish
res.	result	Toch.	Tocharian
Ru.	Runic	top.	topic
Rum.	Rumanian	tr.	transitive
Rus.	Russian	transg.	transgressive
Sard.	Sardinian	t.v.	transitive verb
SCr.	Serbo-Croat	U.	Umbrian
sec.	secondary	v.	verb
Seph.	Sephardi(c)	v.n.	verbal noun
sg.	singular	vd.	voiced
S-J	Sino-Japanese	Ved.	Vedic
Skt.	Sanskrit	VL	Vulgar Latin
Slk.	Slovak	vls.	voiceless
SOV	subject–object–verb	VO	verb–object
Sp.	Spanish	voc.	vocative
spec.	species	VSO	verb–subject–object

* The asterisk is used in discussion of historical reconstructions to indicate a reconstructed (non-attested) form. In synchronic discussions, it is used to indicate an ungrammatical item; (*X) means that inclusion of X makes the item ungrammatical; *(X) means that omission of X makes the item ungrammatical.

In the chapters on Tamil and Vietnamese, a subscript numeral *n* after a word in the English translation indicates that that word glosses the *n*th word in the Tamil or Vietnamese example.

INTRODUCTION

Bernard Comrie

1 Preliminary Notions

How many languages are there in the world? What language(s) do they speak in India? What languages have the most speakers? What languages were spoken in Australia, or in California before European immigration? When did Latin stop being spoken, and when did French start being spoken? How did English become such an important world language? These and other similar questions are often asked by the interested layman. One aim of this volume — taking the Introduction and the individual chapters together — is to provide answers to these and related questions, or in certain cases to show why the questions cannot be answered as they stand. The chapters concentrate on an individual language or group of languages, and in this Introduction I want rather to present a linking essay which will provide a background against which the individual chapters can be appreciated.

After discussing some preliminary notions in this section, section 2 of the Introduction provides a rapid survey of the languages spoken in the world today, concentrating on those not treated in the subsequent chapters, so that the reader can gain an overall impression of the extent of linguistic diversity that characterises the world in which we live. Since the notion of 'major language' is primarily a social notion — languages become major (such as English), or stop being major (such as Sumerian) not because of their grammatical structure, but because of social factors — section 3 discusses some important sociolinguistic notions, in particular concerning the social interaction of languages.

1.1 How Many Languages?

Linguists are typically very hesitant to answer the first question posed above, namely: how many languages are spoken in the world today? Probably the best that one can say, with any hope of not being contradicted, is that at a very conservative estimate some 4,000 languages are spoken today. Laymen are often surprised that the figure should be so high, but I would emphasise that this is a conservative estimate. But why is it that linguists are not able to give a more accurate figure? There are several different reasons conspiring to prevent them from doing so, and these will be outlined below.

One is that many parts of the world are insufficiently studied from a linguistic viewpoint, so that we simply do not know precisely what languages are spoken there. Our knowledge of the linguistic situation in remote parts of the world has improved dramatically in recent years — New Guinea, for instance, has changed from being almost a blank linguistic map to the stage where most (though still not all) of the languages can be pinpointed with accuracy: since perhaps as many as one fifth of the world's languages are spoken in New Guinea, this has radically changed any estimate of the total number of languages. But there are still some areas where uncertainty remains, so that even the most detailed recent index of the world's languages, Voegelin and Voegelin (1977), lists several languages with accompanying question marks, or queries whether one listed language might in fact be the same as some other language but under a different name.

A second problem is that it is difficult or impossible in many cases to decide whether two related speech varieties should be considered different languages or merely different dialects of the same language. With the languages of Europe, there are in general established traditions of whether two speech varieties should be considered different languages or merely dialect variants, but these decisions have often been made more on political and social grounds rather than strictly linguistic grounds.

One criterion that is often advanced as a purely linguistic criterion is mutal intelligibility: if two speech varieties are mutually intelligible, they are different dialects of the same language, but if they are mutually unintelligible, they are different languages. But if applied to the languages of Europe, this criterion would radically alter our assessment of what the different languages of Europe are: the most northern dialects and the most southern dialects (in the traditional sense) of German are mutually unintelligible, while dialects of German spoken close to the Dutch border are mutually intelligible with dialects of Dutch spoken just across the border. In fact, our criterion for whether a dialect is Dutch or German relates in large measure to social factors — is the dialect spoken in an area where Dutch is the standard language or where German is the standard language? By the same criterion, the three nuclear Scandinavian languages (in the traditional sense), Danish, Norwegian and Swedish, would turn out to be dialects of one language, given their mutual intelligibility. While this criterion is often applied to non-European languages (so that nowadays linguists often talk of the Chinese languages rather than the Chinese dialects, given the mutual unintelligibility of, for instance, Mandarin and Cantonese), it seems unfair that it should not be applied consistently to European languages as well.

While native speakers of English are often surprised that there should be problems in delimiting languages from dialects — since present-day dialects of English are in general mutually intelligible (at least with some familiarisation), and even the language most closely related genetically to English, Frisian, is mutually unintelligible with English — the native speaker of English would be hard put to interpret a sentence in Tok Pisin, the English-based pidgin of much of Papua New Guinea, like *sapos ol i karamapim bokis bilong yumi, orait bai yumi paitim as bilong ol* 'if they cover our box, then we'll spank them', although each word, except perhaps *i*, is of English origin ('suppose all ?he cover-up-him box belong you-me, all-right by you-me fight-him arse belong all').

In some cases, the intelligibility criterion actually leads to contradictory results, namely when we have a dialect chain, i.e. a string of dialects such that adjacent dialects are readily mutually intelligible, but dialects from the far ends of the chain are not mutually intelligible. A good illustration of this is the Dutch-German dialect complex. One could start from the far south of the German-speaking area and move to the far west of the Dutch-speaking area without encountering any sharp boundary across which mutual intelligibility is broken; but the two end points of this chain are speech varieties so different from one another that there is no mutual intelligibility possible. If one takes a simplified dialect chain A – B – C, where A and B are mutually intelligible, as are B and C, but A and C are mutually unintelligible, then one arrives at the contradictory result that A and B are dialects of the same language, B and C are dialects of the same language, but A and C are different languages. There is in fact no way of resolving this contradiction if we maintain the traditional strict difference between language and dialects, and what such examples show is that this is not an all-or-nothing distinction, but rather a continuum. In this sense, it is impossible to answer the question how many languages are spoken in the world.

A further problem with the mutual intelligibility criterion is that mutual intelligibility itself is a matter of degree rather than a clearcut opposition between intelligibility and unintelligibility. If mutual intelligibility were to mean 100 per cent mutual intelligibility of all utterances, then perhaps no two speech varieties would be classified as mere dialect variants; for instance, although speakers of British and American English can understand most of one another's speech, there are areas where intelligibility is likely to be minimal unless one speaker happens to have learned the linguistic forms used by the other, as with car (or auto) terms like British *boot, bonnet, mudguard* and their American equivalents *trunk, hood, fender*. Conversely, although speakers of different Slavonic languages are often unable to make full sense of a text in another Slavonic language, they can usually make good sense of parts of the text, because of the high percentage of shared vocabulary and forms.

Two further factors enter into the degree of mutual intelligibility between two speech varieties. One is that intelligibility can rise rapidly with increased familiarisation: those who remember the first introduction of American films into Britain often recall that they were initially considered difficult to understand, but increased exposure to American English has virtually removed this problem. Speakers of different dialects of Arabic often experience difficulty in understanding each other at first meeting, but soon adjust to the major differences between their respective dialects, and Egyptian Arabic, as the most widely diffused modern Arabic dialect, has rapidly gained in intelligibility throughout the Arab world. This can lead to 'one-way intelligibility', as when speakers of, say, Tunisian Arabic are more likely to understand Egyptian Arabic than vice versa, because Tunisian Arabic speakers are more often exposed to Egyptian Arabic than vice versa. The second factor is that intelligibility is to a certain extent a social and psychological phenomenon: it is easier to understand when you want to understand. A good example of this is the conflicting assessments different speakers of the same Slavonic language will often give about the intelligibility of some other Slavonic language, correlating in large measure with whether or not they feel well-disposed to speakers of the other language.

The same problems as exist in delimiting dialects from languages arise, incidentally, on the historical plane too, where the question arises: at what point has a language changed sufficiently to be considered a different language? Again, traditional answers are often contradictory: Latin is considered to have died out, although its descendants, the Romance languages, live on, so at some time Latin must have changed sufficiently to be deemed no longer the same language, but a qualitatively different language. On the other hand, Greek is referred to in the same way throughout its attested history (which is longer than that of Latin and the Romance languages combined), with merely the addition of different adjectives to identify different stages of its development (e.g. Ancient Greek, Byzantine Greek, Modern Greek). In the case of the history of the English language, there is even conflicting terminology: the oldest attested stages of English can be referred to either as Old English (which suggests an earlier stage of Modern English) or as Anglo-Saxon (which suggests a different language that is the ancestor of English, perhaps justifiably so given the mutual unintelligibility of Old and Modern English).

A further reason why it is difficult to assess the number of languages spoken in the world today is that many languages are on the verge of extinction. While it has probably been the case throughout mankind's history that languages have died out, the historically recent expansion of European population to the Americas and Australia has resulted in a greatly accelerated rate of language death among the indigenous languages of these areas. Perusal of Voegelin and Voegelin (1977) will show a number of languages as 'possibly extinct' or 'possibly still spoken', plus an even greater number of languages with only a handful of speakers — usually of advanced age — so that a language may well be dying out somewhere in the world as I am writing these words. When a language dies, this is sometimes an abrupt process, such as the death of a fluent speaker who happened to have outlived all other speakers of the language; more typically, however, the community's facility with the language decreases, as more and more functions are taken over by some other language, so that what they speak, in terms of the original language of the community, is only a part of that language. Many linguists working on Australian Aboriginal languages have been forced, in some cases, to do what has come to be called 'salvage linguistics', i.e. to elicit portions of a language from someone who has neither spoken nor heard the language for decades and has perhaps only a vague recollection of what the language was like.

1.2 Language Families and Genetic Classification

One of the basic organisational principles of this volume, both in section 2 of the Introduction and in the arrangement of the individual chapters, is the organisation of languages into language families. It is therefore important that some insight should be provided into what it means to say that two languages belong to the same language family (or equivalently: are genetically related).

It is probably intuitively clear to anyone who knows a few languages that some languages are closer to one another than are others. For instance, English and German are closer to one another than either is to Russian, while Russian and Polish are closer to one another than either is to English. This notion of similarity can be made more precise, as is done for instance in the chapter on the Indo-European languages below, but for the moment the relatively informal notion will suffice. Starting in the late eighteenth century, a specific hypothesis was proposed to account for such similarities, a hypothesis which still forms the foundation of research into the history and relatedness of languages. This hypothesis is that where languages share some set of features in common, these features are to be attributed to their common ancestor. Let us take some examples from English and German.

In English and German we find a number of basic vocabulary items that have the same or almost the same form, e.g. English *man* and German *Mann*. Likewise, we find a number of bound morphemes (prefixes and suffixes) that have the same or almost the same form, such as the genitive suffix, as in English *man's* and German *Mann(e)s*. Although English and

German are now clearly different languages, we may hypothesise that at an earlier period in history they had a common ancestor, in which the word for 'man' was something like *man* and the genitive suffix was something like *-s*. Thus English and German belong to the same language family, which is the same as saying that they share a common ancestor. We can readily add other languages to this family, since a word like *man* and a genitive suffix like *-s* are also found in Dutch, Frisian, and the Scandinavian languages. The family to which these languages belong has been given the name Germanic, and the ancestor language is Proto-Germanic. It should be emphasised that the proto-language is not an attested language — although if written records had gone back far enough, we might well have had attestations of this language — but its postulation is the most plausible hypothesis explaining the remarkable similarities among the various Germanic languages.

Although not so obvious, similarities can be found among the Germanic languages and a number of other languages spoken in Europe and spreading across northern India as far as Bangladesh. These other languages share fewer similarities with the Germanic languages than individual Germanic languages do with one another, so that they are more remotely related. The overall language family to which all these languages belong is the Indo-European family, with its reconstructed ancestor language Proto-Indo-European. As is discussed in more detail in the chapter on Indo-European languages, the Indo-European family contains a number of branches (i.e. smaller language families, or subfamilies), such as Slavonic (including Russian and Polish), Iranian (including Persian and Pashto), and Celtic (including Irish and Welsh). The overall structure is therefore hierarchical: the most distant ancestor is Proto-Indo-European. At an intermediate point in the family tree, and therefore at a later period of history, we have such languages as Proto-Germanic and Proto-Celtic, which are descendants of Proto-Indo-European but ancestors of languages spoken today. Still later in history, we find the individual languages as they are spoken today or attested in recent history, such as English or German as descendants of Proto-Germanic and Irish and Welsh as descendants of Proto-Celtic. One typical property of language change that is represented accurately by this family-tree model is that, as time goes by, languages descending from a common ancestor tend to become less and less similar. For instance, Old English and Old High German (the ancestor of Modern German) were much closer to one another than are the modern languages — they may even have been mutually intelligible, at least to a large extent.

Although the family-tree model of language relatedness is an important foundation of all current work in historical and comparative linguistics, it is not without its problems, both in practice and in principle. Some of these will now be discussed.

We noted above that with the passage of time, genetically related languages will grow less and less similar. This follows from the fact that, once two languages have split off as separate languages from a common ancestor, each will innovate its own changes, different from changes that take place in the other language, so that the cumulative effect will be increasing divergence. With the passage of enough time, the divergence may come to be so great that it is no longer possible to tell, other than by directly examining the history, that the two languages do in fact come from a common ancestor. The best established language families, such as Indo-European or Sino-Tibetan, are those where the passage of time has not been long enough to erase the obvious traces of genetic relatedness. (For language families that have a long written tradition, one can of course make use of earlier stages of the language, which contain more evidence of genetic relatedness). In addition, there are many hypothesised language families for which the evidence is not sufficient to convince all, or even the majority, of scholars. For instance, the Turkic language family is a well-established language family, as is each of the Uralic, Mongolian and Tungusic families. What is controversial, however, is whether or not these individual families are related as members of an even larger family. The possibility of an Altaic family, comprising Turkic, Mongolian, and Tungusic, is rather widely accepted, and some scholars would advocate increasing the size of this family by adding some or all of Uralic, Korean and Japanese.

The attitudes of different linguists to problems of this kind have been characterised as an opposition between 'splitters' (who require the firmest evidence before they are prepared to acknowledge genetic relatedness) and 'clumpers' (who are ready to assign languages to the same family on the basis of quite restricted similarities). I should, incidentally, declare my own splitter bias, lest any of my own views that creep in be interpreted as generally accepted dogma. The most extreme clumper position would, of course, be to maintain that all languages of the world are genetically related, although there are less radical positions that are somewhat more widely accepted, such as the following list of sixteen stocks, where a stock is simply the highest hierarchical level of genetic relatedness (just as a language family has branches, so families would group together to form stocks): Dravidian, Eurasiatic (including, inter alia, Uralic and Altaic), Indo-European, Nilo-Saharan, Niger-Kordofanian, Afroasiatic, Khoisan, Amerind (all indigenous languages of the Americas except Eskimo-Aleut and Na-Dene), Na-Dene, Austric (including Austro-Asiatic, Tai and Austronesian), Indo-Pacific (including all Papuan languages and Tasmanian), Australian, Sino-Tibetan, Ibero-Caucasian (including Basque and Caucasian), Ket, Burushaski – this schema still operates, incidentally, with two language isolates (Ket and Burushaski), i.e. languages not related to any other language, and retains a number of established language families as distinct (Dravidian, Indo-European, Nilo-Saharan, Niger-Kordofanian, Afro-asiatic, Khoisan, Australian, and Sino-Tibetan). In the survey of the distribution of languages of the world in section 2, I have basically retained my own splitter position, although for areas of great linguistic diversity and great controversy surrounding genetic relations (such as New Guinea and South America) I have simply refrained from detailed discussion.

While no linguist would doubt that some similarities among languages are due to genetic relatedness, there are several other possibilities for the explanation of any particular similarity, and before assuming genetic relatedness one must be able to exclude, at least with some degree of plausibility, these other possibilities. Unfortunately, in a great many cases it is not possible to reach a firm and convincing decision. Let us now examine some of the explanations other than genetic relatedness.

First, two languages may happen purely by chance to have some feature in common. For instance, the word for 'dog' in Mbabaram, an Australian Aboriginal language, happens to be *dog*. This Mbabaram word is not, incidentally, a borrowing from English, but is the regular development in Mbabaram of a Proto-Australian form something like **gudaga* (it is usual to prefix reconstructed forms with an asterisk). If anyone were tempted to assume on this basis, however, that English and Mbabaram are genetically related, examination of the rest of Mbabaram vocabulary and grammar would soon quash the genetic relatedness hypothesis, since there is otherwise minimal similarity between the two languages. In comparing English and German, by contrast, there are many similarities at all levels of linguistic analysis. Even sticking to vocabulary, the correspondence *man*: *Mann* can be matched by *wife* : *Weib*, *father* : *Vater*, *mother* : *Mutter*, *son* : *Sohn*, *daughter* : *Tochter*, etc. Given that other languages have radically different words for these concepts (e.g. Japanese *titi* 'father', *haha* 'mother', *musuko* 'son', *musume* 'daugher'), it clearly can not be merely the result of chance that English and German have so many similar items. But if the number of similar items in two languages is small, it may be difficult or impossible to distinguish between chance similarity and distant genetic relatedness.

Certain features shared by two languages might turn out to be manifestations of language universals, i.e. of features that are common to all languages or are inherently likely to occur in any language. Most discussions of language universals require a fair amount of theoretical linguistic background, but for present purposes I will take a simple, if not particularly profound, example. In many languages across the world, the syllable *ma* or its reduplicated form *mama* or some other similar form is the word for 'mother'. The initial syllable *ma* enters into the Proto-Indo-European word for 'mother' which has given English *mother*, Spanish *madre*, Russian *mat'*, Sanskrit *mātā*. In Mandarin Chinese, the equivalent word is *mā*, while in Wiyaw (Harui) (Papua New Guinea) it is *mam*. Once again, examination of other features of Indo-European languages, Chinese and Wiyaw would soon dispel any possibility of assigning Chinese or Wiyaw to the Indo-European language family. Presumably the frequency across languages of the syllable *ma* in the word for 'mother' simply reflects the fact that this is typically one of the first syllables that babies articulate clearly, and is therefore interpreted by adults as the word for 'mother'. (In the South Caucasian language Georgian, incidentally, *mama* means 'father' — and 'mother' is *deda* — so that there are other ways of interpreting baby's first utterance.)

Somewhat similar to universals are patterns whereby certain linguistic features frequently cooccur in the same language, i.e. where the presence of one feature seems to require or at least to foster the presence of some other feature. For instance, the study of word order universals by Greenberg (1963) showed that if a language has verb-final word order (i.e. if 'the man saw the woman' is expressed literally as 'the man the woman saw'), then it is highly probable that it will also have postpositions rather than prepositions (i.e. 'in the house' will be expressed as 'the house in') and that it will have genitives before the noun (i.e. the pattern 'cat's house' rather than 'house of cat'). Thus, if we find two languages that happen to share the features: verb-final word order, postpositions, prenominal genitives, then the cooccurrence of these features is not evidence for genetic relatedness. Many earlier attempts at establishing wide-ranging genetic relationships suffer precisely from failure to take this property of typological patterns into account. Thus the fact that Turkic languages, Mongolian languages, Tungusic languages, Korean and Japanese share all of these features is not evidence for their genetic relatedness (although there may, of course, be other similarities, not connected with recurrent typological patterns, that do establish genetic relatedness). If one were to accept just these features as evidence for an Altaic language family, then the family would have to be extended to include a variety of other languages with the same word order properties, such as the Dravidian languages of southern India and Quechua, spoken in South America.

Finally, two languages might share some feature in common because one of them has borrowed it from the other (or because they have both borrowed it from some third language). English, for instance, borrowed a huge number of words from French during the Middle Ages, to such an extent that an uncritical examination of English vocabulary might well lead to the conclusion that English is a Romance language, rather than a Germanic language. The term 'borrow', as used here, is the accepted linguistic term, although the terminology is rather strange, since 'borrow' suggests a relatively superficial acquisition, one which is moreover temporary. Linguistic borrowings may run quite deep, and there is of course no implication that they will ever be repaid. Among English loans from French, for instance, there are many basic vocabulary items, such as *very* (replacing the native Germanic *sore*, as in the biblical *sore afraid*). Examples from other languages show even more deep-seated loans: the Semitic language Amharic — the dominant and official language of Ethiopia — for instance, has lost the typical Semitic word order patterns, in which the verb precedes its object and adjectives and genitives follow their noun, in favour of the order where the verb follows its object and adjectives and genitives precede their noun; Amharic is in close contact with Cushitic languages, and Cushitic languages typically have the order object-verb, adjective/genitive-noun, so that Amharic has in fact borrowed these word orders from neighbouring Cushitic languages.

It seems that whenever two languages come into close contact, they will borrow features from one another. In some cases the contact can be so intense among the languages in a given area that they come to share a significant number of common features, setting this area off from adjacent languages, even languages that may happen to be more closely related genetically to languages within the area. The languages in an area of this kind are often said to belong to a sprachbund (German for 'language league'), and perhaps the most famous example of a sprachbund is the Balkan sprachbund, whose members (Modern Greek, Albanian, Bulgarian (with Macedonian), Rumanian) share a number of striking features not shared by closely related languages like Ancient Greek, other Slavonic languages (Bulgarian is Slavonic), or other Romance languages (Rumanian is Romance). The most striking of these features is loss of the infinitive, so that instead of 'give me to drink' one says 'give me that I drink' (Modern Greek *ðos mu na pjo*, Albanian *a-më të pi*, Bulgarian *daj mi da pija*, Rumanian *dă-mi să beau*; in all four languages the subject of the subordinate clause is encoded in the inflection of the verb).

Since we happen to know a lot about the history of the Balkan languages, linguists were not deceived by these similarities into assigning a closer genetic relatedness to the Balkan languages than in fact holds (all are ultimately members of the Indo-European family, though from different branches). In other parts of the world, however, there is the danger of mistaking areal phenomena for evidence of genetic relatedness. In South-East Asia, for instance, many languages share very similar phonological and morphological patterns: in Chinese, Thai and Vietnamese words are typically monosyllabic, there is effectively no morphology (i.e. words do not change after the manner of English *dog*, *dogs* or *love*, *loves*, *loved*), syllable structure is very simple (only a few single consonants are permitted word-finally, while syllable-initially consonant clusters are either disallowed or highly restricted), and there is a phonemic tone (thus Mandarin Chinese *mā*, with a high level tone, means 'mother', while *mǎ*, with a falling-rising tone, means 'horse'), and moreover there are a number of shared lexical items. For these reasons, it was for a long time believed that Thai and Vietnamese were related genetically to Chinese, as members of the Sino-Tibetan family. More recently, however, it has been established that these similarities are not the result of common ancestry, and Thai and Vietnamese are now generally acknowledged not to be genetically related to Chinese. The similarities are the results of areal contact. The shared vocabulary items are primarily the result of intensive Chinese cultural influence, especially on

Vietnamese. The tones and simple syllable structures can often be shown to be the result of relatively recent developments, and indeed in one language that is incontrovertibly related to Chinese, namely Classical Tibetan, one finds complex consonant clusters but no phonemic tone, i.e. the similarities noted above are neither necessary nor sufficient conditions for genetic relatedness.

In practice, the most difficult task in establishing genetic relatedness is to distinguish between genuine cognates (i.e. forms going back to a common ancestor) and those that are the result of borrowing. It would therefore be helpful if one could distinguish between those features of a language that are borrowable and those that are not. Unfortunately, it seems that there is no feature that can absolutely be excluded from borrowing. Basic vocabulary can be borrowed, so that for instance Japanese has borrowed the whole set of numerals from Chinese, and even English borrowed its current set of third person plural pronouns (*they*, *them*, *their*) from Scandinavian. Bound morphemes can be borrowed: a good example is the agent suffix *-er* in English, with close cognates in other Germanic languages; this is ultimately a loan from the Latin agentive suffix *-ārius*, which has however become so entrenched in English that it is a productive morphological device applicable in principle to any verb to derive a corresponding agentive noun.

At one period in the recent history of comparative linguistics, it was believed that a certain basic vocabulary list could be isolated, constant across languages and cultures, such that the words on this list would be replaced at a constant rate. Thus, if one assumes that the retention rate is around 86 per cent per millennium, this means that if a single language splits into two descendant languages, then after 1,000 years each language would retain about 86 per cent of the words in the list from the ancestor language, i.e. the two descendants would then share just over 70 per cent of the words in the list. In some parts of the world, groupings based on this 'glottochronological' method still form the basis of the only available detailed and comprehensive attempt at establishing genetic relations. It must be emphasised that the number of clear counter-examples to the glottochronological method, i.e. instances where independent evidence contradicts the predictions of this approach, is so great that no reliance can be placed on its results.

It is, however, true that there are significant differences in the ease with which different features of a language can be borrowed. The thing that seems most easily borrowable is cultural vocabulary, and indeed it is quite normal for a community borrowing some concept (or artifact) from another community to borrow the foreign name along with the object. Another set of features that seem rather easily borrowable are general typological features, such as word order: in addition to the Amharic example cited above, one might note the fact that many Austronesian languages spoken in New Guinea have adopted the word order where the object is placed before the verb, whereas almost all other Austronesian languages place the object after the verb; this change occurred under the influence of Papuan languages, almost all of which are verb-final. Basic vocabulary comes next. And last of all one finds bound morphology. But even though it is difficult to borrow bound morphology, it is not impossible, so in arguments over genetic relatedness one cannot exclude *a priori* the possibility that even affixes may have been borrowed.

2 Languages of South Asia, the Middle East and Africa

In South Asia (the traditional 'Indian subcontinent'), four language families meet. Indo-European languages, more specifically languages of the Indo-Aryan branch of Indo-European, dominate in the north, while the south is the domain of the Dravidian languages (although some Dravidian languages are spoken further north, in particular Brahui, spoken in Pakistan). The northern fringe of the subcontinent is occupied by Sino-Tibetan languages, while the fourth family is Austro-Asiatic (or Munda-Mon-Khmer), whose languages are scattered from central India eastwards into Vietnam. In India itself, the Austro-Asiatic language with the most speakes is Santali, but the major languages of this family, Vietnamese and Khmer (Cambodian), are spoken in South-East Asia, while the major Sino-Tibetan languages are spoken in East and South-East Asia (e.g. Chinese, Burmese). In addition to these four families, there is one language isolate, Burushaski, spoken in northern Pakistan, while the genetic affiliations of the languages of the Andaman Islands remain unclear.

The Middle East is home to two main language families, the Semitic branch of Afroasiatic and the Iranian branch of Indo-European. Iranian languages are spoken over most of Persia, nearly all of Afghanistan, and parts of Soviet Central Asia (especially Tadjikistan), though individual languages are scattered as far west as the Caucasus and as far east as northwestern China. The Afroasiatic family, as its name suggests, is spoken in both Asia and Africa. In Asia its main focus is the Arab countries of the Middle East, although Hebrew and Aramaic are also Afroasiatic languages of Asia, belonging to the Semitic branch of Afroasiatic. In addition Arabic is, of course, the dominant language of North Africa, where Afroasiatic is also represented by a number of other Semitic languages (those of Ethiopia, the major one being Amharic), but also by Berber, the Cushitic languages of the Horn of Africa (including Somali, the official language of Somalia), and the Chadic languages of northern Nigeria and adjacent areas (including Hausa). One branch of Afroasiatic formerly spoken in Africa, Egyptian (by which is meant the language of ancient Egypt, not the dialect of Arabic currently spoken in Egypt), is now extinct.

Until quite recently, ideas on the classification of the languages of sub-Saharan Africa were almost as diffuse as those on the classification of languages of New Guinea or the Americas. One language family, Bantu, was recognised early on, spoken over most of eastern and southern Africa. It was suspected that many of the languages of West Africa might be related to one another, and it was recognised that the Khoisan languages, spoken in the southwestern corner of Africa, were probably a single family. This near chaos was reduced to order in large measure by the efforts of Joseph H. Greenberg, who posited a four-way classification of the languages of Africa: in the north, the Afro-Asiatic family; in the north-east of sub-Saharan Africa, the Nilo-Saharan family; in the south-west corner of Africa, the Khoisan family (with two outliers, Sandawe and Hatsa, in Tanzania) — the Khoisan languages are noted for having click sounds as part of their regular phoneme inventory. The whole of the rest of the continent, from the Atlantic to the Indian Ocean, is covered by the Niger-Kordofanian family (Greenberg 1966); Bantu is a sub-sub-sub-subgroup of this family. In general, Greenberg's classification has gained widespread acceptance, in particular the division into four major families, although some of the details remain controversial (see, for instance, the chapter on Niger-Kordofanian languages for proposed revisions to the internal classification of this family). Falling outside this classification are, of course, Malagasy, the Austronesian language of Madagascar, and languages introduced into Africa by external colonisation (though one such language, Afrikaans, a descendant of colonial Dutch, is a language of Africa by virtue of its geographic distribution).

3 The Social Interaction of Languages

As was indicated in the Preface, the notion of 'major language' is defined in social terms, so it is now time to look somewhat more consistently at some notions relating to the social side of language, in particular the social interaction of languages. Whether a language is a major language or not has nothing to do with its structure or with its genetic affiliation, and the fact that so many of the world's major languages are Indo-European is a mere accident of history.

First, we may look in more detail at the criteria that serve to define a language as being major. One of the most obvious criteria is the number of speakers, and certainly in making my choice of languages to be given individual chapters in this volume number of speakers was one of my main criteria. However, number of speakers is equally clearly not the sole criterion.

An interesting comparison to make here is between Chinese (or even more specifically, Mandarin) and English. Mandarin has far more native speakers than English, yet still English is generally considered a more useful language in the world at large than is Mandarin, as seen in the much larger number of people studying English as a second language than studying Mandarin as a second language. One of the reasons for this is that English is an international language, understood by a large number of people in many different parts of the world; Mandarin, by contrast, is by and large confined to China, and even taking all Chinese dialects (or languages) together, the extension of Chinese goes little beyond China and overseas Chinese communities. English is not only the native language of sizable populations in different parts of the world (especially the British Isles, North America, Australia and New Zealand) but is also spoken as a second language in even more countries, as is discussed in more detail in the chapter on English. English happens also to be the language of some of the technologically most advanced countries (in particular of the USA), so that English is the basic medium for access to current technological developments. Thus factors other than mere number of speakers are relevant in determining the social importance of a language.

Indeed, some of the languages given individual chapters in this volume have relatively few native speakers. Some of them are important not so much by virtue of the number of native speakers but rather because of the extent to which they are used as a lingua franca, as a second language among people who do not share a common first language. Good examples here are Swahili and Malay. Swahili is the native language of a relatively small population, primarily on the coast of East Africa, but its use as a lingua franca has spread through much of East Africa (especially Kenya and Tanzania), and even stretches into parts of Zaire. Malay too is the native language of relatively few people in western Malaysia and an even smaller number in Indonesia, but its adoption as the lingua franca and official language of both countries has raised the combined first and second language speakers to well over a hundred million. In many instances, in my choice of languages I have been guided by this factor rather than by raw statistics. Among the Philippine languages, for instance, Cebuano has more native speakers than Tagalog, but I selected Tagalog because it is both the national language of the Philippines and used as a linga franca across much of the country. Among the Indonesian languages, Javanese has more native speakers than Malay and is also the bearer of an old culture, but in terms of the current social situation Malay is clearly the dominant language of this branch of Austronesian. A number of other Indo-Aryan languages would surely have qualified for inclusion in terms of number of speakers, such as Marathi, Rajasthani, Panjabi, Gujarati, but they have not been assigned individual chapters because in social terms the major languages of the northern part of South Asia are clearly Hindi-Urdu and Bengali.

Another important criterion is the cultural importance of a language, in terms of the age and influence of its cultural heritage. An example in point is provided by the Dravidian languages, where Telugu actually has more speakers than Tamil; Tamil, however, is the more ancient literary language, and for this reason my choice rested with Tamil. I am aware that many of these decisions are in part subjective, and in part dangerous: as I emphasised in the Preface, the thing furthest from my mind is to intend any slight to speakers of languages that are not considered major in the contents of this volume.

Certain languages are major even despite the absence of native speakers, as with Latin and Sanskrit. Latin has provided a major contribution to all European languages, as can be seen most superficially in the extent to which words of Latin origin are used in European languages. Even those languages that have tried to avoid the appearance of Latinity by creating their own vocabulary have often fallen back on Latin models: German *Gewissen* 'conscience', for instance, contains the prefix *ge-*, meaning 'with', the stem *wiss-*, meaning 'know', and the suffix *-en* to form an abstract noun — an exact copy of the Latin *con-sci-entia*; borrowings that follow the structure rather than the form in this way are known as calques or loan translations. Sanskrit has played a similar role in relation to the languages of India, including Hindi. Hebrew is included not because of the number of its speakers — as noted in the chapter on Hebrew, this has never been large — but because of the contribution of Hebrew and its culture to European and Middle Eastern society.

A language can thus have influence beyond the areas where it is the native or second language. A good example to illustrate this is Arabic. Arabic loans form a large part of the vocabulary of many languages spoken by Islamic peoples, even of languages that are genetically only distantly related to Arabic (e.g. Hausa) or that are genetically totally unrelated (e.g. Turkish, Persian and Urdu). The influence of Arabic can also be seen in the adoption of the Arabic writing system by many Islamic peoples. Similarly, Chinese loan words form an important part of the vocabulary of some East Asian languages, in particular Vietnamese, Japanese and Korean; the use of written Chinese characters has also spread to Japan and Korea, and in earlier times also to Vietnam.

It is important to note also that the status of a language as a major language is far from immutable. Indeed, as we go back into history we find many significant changes. For instance, the possibility of characterising English as the world's major language is an innovation of the twentieth century. One of the most important shifts in the distribution of major languages resulted from the expansion of European languages, especially English, Spanish, Portuguese, and to a lesser extent French as a result of the colonisation of the Americas: English, Spanish and Portuguese all now have far more native speakers in the New World than in Britain, Spain or Portugal. Indeed, in the Middle Ages one would hardly have imagined that English, confined to an island off the coast of Europe, would have become a major international language.

In medieval Europe, Latin was clearly the major language, since, despite the lack of native speakers, it was the lingua franca of those who needed to communicate across linguistic boundaries. Yet the rise of Latin to such preeminence — which includes the fact that Latin and its descendants have ousted virtually all other languages from southwestern Europe — could hardly have been foreseen from its inauspicious beginnings confined to the area around Rome. Equally spectacular has been the spread of Arabic, in the wake of Islamic religious zeal, from being confined to the Arabian peninsula to being the dominant language of the Middle East and North Africa.

In addition to languages that have become major languages, there are equally languages that have lost this status. The earliest records from Mesopotamia, often considered the cradle of civilisation, are in two languages: Sumerian and Akkadian (the latter the language of the Assyrian and Babylonian empires); Akkadian belongs to the Semitic branch of Afroasiatic, while Sumerian is as far as we can tell unrelated to any other known language. Even at the time of attested Sumerian inscriptions, the language was probably already approaching extinction, and it continued to be used in deference to tradition (as with Latin in medieval Europe). The dominant language of the period was to become Akkadian, but in the intervening period this too has died out, leaving no direct descendants. Gone too is Ancient Egyptian, the language of the Pharaohs. The linguistic picture of the Mediterranean and Middle East in the year nought was very different from that which we observe today.

Social factors and social attitudes can even bring about apparent reversals in the family-tree model of language relatedness. At the time of the earliest texts from Germany, two distinct Germanic languages are recognised: Old Saxon and Old High German. Old Saxon is the ancestor of the modern Low German (Plattdeutsch) dialects, while Old High German is the ancestor of the modern High German dialects and of the standard language. Because of social changes — such as the decline of the Hanseatic League, the economic mainstay of northern Germany — High German gained social ascendancy over Low German. Since the standard language, based on High German, is now recognised as the standard in both northern and southern Germany, both Low and High German dialects are now considered dialects of a single German language, and the social relations between a given Low German dialect and standard German are in practice no different from those between any High German dialect and standard German.

One of the most interesting developments to have arisen from language contact is the development of pidgin and creole languages. A pidgin language arises from a very practical situation: speakers of different languages need to communicate with one another to carry out some practical task, but do not speak any language in common and moreover do not have the opportunity to learn each other's languages properly. What arises in such a situation is, initially, an unstable pidgin, or jargon, with highly variable structure — considerably simplified relative to the native languages of the people involved in its creation — and just enough vocabulary to permit practical tasks to be carried out reasonably successfully. The clearest examples of the development of such pidgins arose from European colonisation, in particular from the Atlantic slave trade and from indenturing labourers in the South Pacific. These pidgins take most of their vocabulary from the colonising language, although their structures are often very different from those of the colonising language.

At a later stage, the jargon may expand, particularly when its usefulness as a lingua franca is recognised among the speakers of non-European origin, leading to a stabilised pidgin, such as Tok Pisin, the major lingua franca of Papua New Guinea. This expansion is on several planes: the range of functions is expanded, since the pidgin is no longer restricted to uses of language essential to practical tasks; the vocabulary is expanded as a result of this greater range of functions, new words often being created internally to the pidgin rather than borrowed from some other language (as with Tok Pisin *maus gras* 'moustache', literally 'mouth grass'); the structure becomes stabilised, i.e. the language has a well defined grammar.

Throughout all of this development, the pidgin has no native speakers. The next possible stage (or this may take place even before stabilisation) is for the pidgin to 'acquire native speakers'. For instance, if native speakers of different languages marry and have the pidgin as their only common language, then this will be the language of their household and will become the first language of their children. Once a pidgin has acquired native speakers, it is referred to as a creole. The native languages of many inhabitants of the Caribbean islands are creoles, for instance the English-based creole of Jamaica, the French-based creole of Haiti, and the Spanish-and/or Portuguese-based creole Papiamentu (Papiamento) of the Netherlands Antilles (Aruba, Bonaire and Curaçao). At an even later stage, social improvements and education may bring the creole back into close contact with the European language that originally contributed much of its vocabulary. In this situation, the two languages may interact and the creole, or some of its varieties, may start approaching the standard language. This gives rise to the so-called post-creole continuum, in which one finds a continuous scale of varieties of speech from forms close to the original creole (basilect) through intermediate forms (mesolect) up to a slightly regionally coloured version of the standard language. Jamaican English is a good example of a post-creole continuum.

No pidgin or creole language has succeeded in gaining sufficient status or number of speakers to become one of the world's major languages, but pidgin and creole languages provide important insights into the processes that arise from natural language contact. And while it would probably be an exaggeration to consider any of the word's major languages a creole, it is not unlikely that some of the processes that go to create a pidgin or a creole have been active in the history of some of these languages — witness, for instance, the morphological simplification that has attended the development from Old English to Modern English, or from Latin to the modern Romance languages.

A few centuries ago, as we saw above, it would have been difficult to predict the present-day distribution of major languages in the world. It is equally impossible to predict the future. In terms of number of native speakers, it is clear that a major shift is underway in favour of non-European languages: the rate of population increase is much higher outside Europe than in Europe, and while some European languages draw some benefit from this (such as Spanish and Portuguese in Latin America), the main beneficiaries are the indigenous languages of southern Asia and Africa. It might well be that a later version of this volume would include fewer of the European languages that are restricted to a single country, and devote more space to non-European languages. Another factor is the increase in the range of functions of many non-European languages: during the colonial period European languages (primarily English and French) were used for most official purposes and also for education in much of Asia and Africa, but the winning of independence has meant that many countries have turned more to their own languages, using these as official language and medium of education. The extent to which this will lead to increase in their status as major languages is difficult to predict — at present, access to the frontiers of scholarship and technology is still primarily through European languages, especially English; but one should not forget that the use of English, French and German as vehicles for science was gained only through a prolonged struggle against what then seemed the obvious language for such writing: Latin. (The process may go back indefinitely: Cicero was criticised for writing philosophical treatises in Latin by those who thought he should have used Greek.) But at least I hope to have shown the reader that the social interaction of languages is a dynamic process, one that is moreover exciting to follow.

Bibliography

The most comprehensive and up-to-date index of the world's languages, with genetic classification, is Grimes (1988), which supersedes Voegelin and Voegelin (1977). A recent valuable work on genetic classification of the world's languages is Ruhlen (1987).

References

Greenberg, J. H. 1963. 'Some Universals of Grammar with Particular Reference to the Order of Meaningful Elements', in J. H. Greenberg (ed.), *Universals of Language* (MIT Press, Cambridge, Mass.), pp. 73–112

Greenberg, J. H. 1966. *The Languages of Africa* (Indiana University, Bloomington and Mouton, The Hague)
Grimes, B. F. (ed.). 1988. *Ethnologue: Languages of the World* (11th edition) (Summer Institute of Linguistics, Dallas)
Ruhlen, M. 1987. *A Guide to the World's Languages, Volume 1: Classification* (Stanford University Press, Stanford)
Voegelin, C. F. and F. M. 1977. *Classification and Index of the World's Languages* (Elsevier, New York)

1 INDO-ARYAN LANGUAGES

George Cardona

1 Introduction

Indo-Aryan languages, the easternmost group within Indo-European, are spoken by approximately five hundred million persons in India, Pakistan, Bangladesh, Nepal and other parts of the Himalayan region, as well as in Sri Lanka. Gypsy (Romany) dialects of the USSR, the Middle East and North America are also of Indo-Aryan origin. Indo-Aryan is most closely related to Iranian, with which it forms the Indo-Iranian subgroup, speakers of which shared linguistic and cultural features, including a name they called themselves (Sanskrit *ārya-*, Avestan *airya-*). Among the innovations that characterise Indo-Iranian is the merger of Proto-Indo-European *ĕ*, *ŏ*, *ă* into *ă*: Skt. *asti* 'is', *pati-* 'master, husband', *ajati* 'leads', *dadhāti* 'puts, makes', *dadāti* 'gives', *mātr̥-* 'mother': Av. *asti*, *paiti-*, *azaiti*, *dadāiti* ('puts, makes, gives'), *mātar-*: Gk. *estì*, *pósis*, *ágei*, *títhēsi*, *dídōsi*, *mā́tēr* (Dor.). Two major phonological features distinguish Indo-Aryan from the rest of Indo-European, including Iranian. One of these is an inherited property: Indo-Aryan retains voiced aspirated stops, as in Skt. *gharma-* 'warmth', *dadhāti*, *bharati* 'carries'. The other is an innovation: Indo-Aryan languages distinguish dental and retroflex stops. Originally, retroflex *-ḍ-*, *-ḍh-* arose through sound changes, as in Skt. *nīḍa-* 'resting place, nest', *mīḍha-* 'reward', with *-īḍ-*, *-īḍh-* from *-iẓḍ-*, *-iẓḍh-* (< *-izd-*, *-izdh-*). Such developments resulted in contrastive retroflex stops, albeit restricted, and the compass of such consonants was extended through borrowings from Dravidian languages. Most Indo-Aryan languages still have voiced aspirates and retroflex stops, although in certain ones, abutting on non-Indo-Aryan languages, these contrasts have been reduced: Sinhalese (Sinhala) has no aspirated stops, Kashmiri lacks voiced aspirates and Assamese (Asamiya) has no retroflex stops.

Old Indo-Aryan is represented in numerous sources (see the chapter on Sanskrit). The earliest preserved Middle Indo-Aryan documents are Aśoka's edicts (third century BC), in various dialects. Middle Indo-Aryan languages were also used for other literary, philosophical and religious works. The Buddhist canon and later treatises of Theravada Buddhism are in Pāli, the Jaina canon in Ardhamāgadhī; Jainas also used Jaina Māhārāṣṭrī and Śaurasenī in works. The literary exemplar of Middle Indo-Aryan, however, is Māhārāṣṭrī, and the most advanced stages of Middle Indo-Aryan developments are found in Apabhraṁśa dialects, used as literary vehicles from before the sixth century. All Middle Indo-Aryan varieties can be subsumed under the label Prakrit (Skt. *prākr̥ta-*, Pkt. *pāia-* 'stemming from the original, natural'), referring to vernaculars in contrast to the polished language called *saṁskr̥ta*. Traditionally, most Indian commentators and grammarians of Prakrits derive these from Sanskrit, but there are formations in Prakrits found in Vedic sources but not in Classical Sanskrit. Thus, as Classical Sanskrit is not derivable from a single attested Vedic dialect, so the Prakrits cannot be derived from Classical Sanskrit. In the present sketch, I use *Prakrit* in a narrow sense, of Middle Indo-Aryan languages other than Aśokan dialects, Pāli or Apabhraṁśa. There are abundant literary sources for New Indo-Aryan languages from the twelfth century on, some materials from earlier times.

Several scripts have been and currently are used for Indo-Aryan languages. In ancient times, two major scripts were used on the subcontinent: Kharoṣṭhī, written from right to left, was predominantly used in the north-west, Brāhmī, written from left to right, elsewhere. Most scripts used for Indo-Aryan languages stem from Brāhmī, including Devanāgarī (see section 2 of the chapter on Sanskrit), widely employed for Sanskrit and now the official script for Hindi, Marathi, Nepali. The Arabic script, with modifications, is used for some Indo-Aryan languages, including Urdu.

2 Phonological and Grammatical Developments

In the following, I sketch major phonological and grammatical developments that characterise Middle and New Indo-Aryan, using Old Indo-Aryan as a point of reference (see sections 1.2, 2 of the chapter on Sanskrit).

2.1 Phonology

In Middle Indo-Aryan, word-final consonants other than *-m*, which developed to *-ṁ* with shortening of a preceding vowel, were lost: Skt. *putrāt* (abl. sg.) 'son', *putrās* (nom. pl.), *putram* (acc. sg.): Pāli *puttā*, *puttaṁ*. Interior clusters of dissimilar consonants were generally eliminated through assimilation (as in *puttā*) or epenthesis: Skt. *sakthi-* 'thigh', *varga-* 'group', *agni-* 'fire', *śukla-* 'white', *pakva-* 'cooked, ripe', *satya-* 'true', *adya* 'today': Pāli *satthi-*, *vagga-*, with assimilation of the first consonant to the second, *aggi-*, *sukka-*, *pakka-*, with the second consonant assimilated to the first, and *sacca-*, *ajja-*, with palatalisation; similarly, Skt. *rājnā* (inst. sg.) 'king', *rājñas* (gen. sg.): *rāññā*, *rañño* in the Girnār version of Aśoka's first rock edict, but *lājinā*, *lājine*, with epenthesis, in the Jaugaḍa version. Generally, a nasal remains unassimilated before an obstruent: Skt. Pāli *danta-* 'tooth'. Metathesis applies in clusters of *h* with nasals or *y*, *v*: Skt. *cihna-* 'mark', *sahya-* 'to be endured', *jihvā-* 'tongue': Pāli *cinha-*, *sayha-*, *jivhā-*. Clusters of voiceless spirants with obstruents develop to obstruent sequences with aspiration: Skt. *paścāt* 'afterwards', *hasta-* 'hand': Pāli *pacchā*, *hattha-*. Further, clusters with voiceless spirants and nasals show voice assimilation and metathesis, resulting in nasals followed by *h*: Skt. *tr̥ṣṇā-* 'thirst, longing': Pāli *taṇhā-*. Initial clusters changed in the same ways, with subsequent simplification: Skt. *prathama-* 'first', *tyajati* 'abandons', *skandha-* 'shoulder', *snāti* 'bathes': Pāli *paṭhama-*, *cajati*, *khandha-*, *nhāyati*. In compounds and preverb-verb combinations where the assimilated cluster was intervocalic, it was retained, resulting in alternations such as Pāli *pamāṇa-* 'measure': *appamāṇa-* 'without measure, endless' (Skt. *pramāṇa-*, *apramāṇa-*). In early Middle Indo-Aryan, word-internal single consonants were retained, as shown in examples cited. Later, as exemplified in Māhārāṣṭrī, non-labial non-retroflex unaspirated obstruents were generally deleted, and *p*, *b* changed to *v*: *loa-* 'world, people', *naa-* 'mountain', *paura-* 'ample', *gaa-* 'elephant', *viāṇa-* 'awning', *savaha-* 'oath': Skt. *loka-*, *naga-*, *pracura-*, *gaja-*, *vitāna-*, *śapatha-*. Presumably, an intermediate step prior to loss involved the voicing of consonants, and some dialects reflect this; for example, in Śaurasenī intervocalic dentals were voiced (*ido* 'hence', *tadhā* 'thus': Skt. *itas*, *tathā*), and *thūbe* 'stupa' (Skt. *stūpas*) occurs in Aśokan. The loss of consonants resulted in word-internal sequences of vowels that were not found in Old Indo-Aryan, though such vowels were separated by *y*, *v* in some dialects. Intervocalic non-retroflex aspirates generally changed to *h*, but *-ṭ-*, *-ṭh-* were voiced, and *-ḍ-* developed to *-ḷ-*, whence *-l-*: Pkt. *sāhā-* 'branch', *meha-* 'cloud', *naḍa-* 'actor', *maḍha-* 'cloister' (Skt. *śākhā-*, *megha-*, *naṭa-*, *maṭha-*), Skt. *krīḍati* 'plays': Pāli *kīḷati*, Pkt. *kīlai*. The spirantal system of Old Indo-Aryan was also generally simplified. On the evidence of Aśokan documents, dialects of the extreme north-west retained *ś ṣ s*, as in Shāhbāzgaṛhī *paśucikisa* 'medical treatment for cattle', *vaṣeṣu* (loc. pl.) 'years'. But elsewhere the sibilants merged to *s*, and later in the east, as represented by Māgadhī, one has *ś* (e.g. *keśeśu* (loc. pl.) 'hair', *śahaśśa-* 'thousand': Skt. *keśeṣu*, *sahasra-*). In Apabhraṁśa, *-s(s)-* developed to *-h-*, as in *taho* 'of that' (Pāli *tassa*, Skt. *tasya*), and intervocalic nasals lost their occlusion, resulting in nasalisation, as in *gāũ* 'village' (Pkt. *gāmo*, Skt. *grāmas*), *pasāẽ* 'through the grace of' (Pkt. *pasāeṇa*, Skt. *prasādena*).

The Middle Indo-Aryan vowel system also shows major developments. As shown, word-internal vowel sequences not permitted earlier now occurred. Conversely, overheavy syllables — with long vowels followed by consonant clusters — permissible in Old Indo-Aryan, were eliminated, through shortening of vowels or reduction of clusters. Moreover, as -V̄C- and -V̆CC- were prosodically equivalent, one has either as reflex of earlier -V̄C-, -V̆CC-. For example: Skt. *lākṣā-* 'lac', *dīrgha-* 'long', *śvaśrū-* 'mother-in-law', *sarṣapa-* 'mustard seed': Pāli *lākha-*, *dīgha-*, *sassū-*, *sāsapa-*: Pkt. *lakkhā-*, *diggha-/dīgha-*, *sāsū-*, *sāsava-*. In addition, vocalic *r̥* is replaced by various vowels; *ai*, *au*, were monophthongised to *e*, *o*; *-aya-*, *-ava-* developed to *-e-*, *-o-*; and short *ĕ*, *ŏ* arose through shortening before clusters: Skt. *r̥kṣa-* 'bear', *vr̥ścika-* 'scorpion', *pr̥cchati* 'asks', *taila-* 'oil', *jayati* 'is victorious', *prekṣate* 'looks', *aurasa-* 'legitimate', *bhavati* 'is', *maulya-* 'price': Pāli *accha-*, *vicchika-*, *pucchati*, *tela*, *jeti*, *pekkhati*, *orasa-*, *hoti*, *molla-*. Moreover, many of the complex morphophonemic alternations that applied in Old Indo-Aryan across word boundaries (see section 1.2 of the chapter on Sanskrit) were eliminated. Certain phonological developments also characterised major dialect areas. As noted, the extreme north-west retained different sibilants. In addition, at Aśoka's time the extreme west and east respectively were characterised by having *r*, consonant assimilation and *-o* for earlier *-as* and its variants as opposed to *l*, a tendency to epenthesis and *-e*: *rāñño* versus *lājine*.

Some of the tendencies observed earlier continue in evidence into New Indo-Aryan. Thus, the resolution of -V̆CC- to -V̄C- takes place in some areas: Gujarati *pākū̃* 'ripe', *lāḍu* 'a sweet': Hindi *pakkā*, *laḍḍu*. Though *ai*, *au* are retained well into the modern period and still found, they are also monophthongised, as in Hindi *hɛ* 'is', *cɔthā* 'fourth' (spelled *hai*, *cauthā*). Middle Indo-Aryan *ḍ*, *ḍh* develop to flaps (but the etymological spellings are retained) except in initial position and after nasals; e.g., Hindi *sāḍī* 'sari' (Pkt. *sāḍiā-*). In the north-west, assimilation affects a sequence of a nasal with an obstruent: Panjabi *dand* 'tooth' versus Hindi *dā̃t*. On the other hand, the widespread loss of earlier final vowels results in word-final consonants, although in certain areas the final vowels are retained; e.g. Panjabi *dand*, Hindi *dā̃t*, but Sindhi *Dandu*. The last has an initial imploded stop, characteristic of Sindhi and some adjacent languages. Dialectal developments have resulted in other phonological features not found in Middle Indo-Aryan. For example, Panjabi developed a tonal system; Kashmiri has developed pharyngealised consonants; in languages of the south-west there are two sets of affricates, as in Marathi *c* (= *ts*) versus *č*; and languages of the extreme east have rounded the vowel *a*, as in Bengali (Bangla), where one also finds limited vowel harmony.

2.2 Morphology and Syntax

The grammatical system of Middle Indo-Aryan is characterised by a general reduction of complexities in comparison with Old Indo-Aryan. The dual is eliminated as a category distinct from the plural. The trend to replace variable consonant stems with single stems ending in vowels, already evident in Old Indo-Aryan (e.g. Skt. *danta-* 'tooth', earlier *dant-/dat-*), continues: Pāli *gacchanta-* 'going' (masc. nom. sg. *gacchanto*, gen. pl. *gacchantānaṁ*) as against Skt. *gacchant-/gacchat-* (see section 2.2.2 of the chapter on Sanskrit). The loss of final consonants also contributed to the steady elimination of consonant stems, e.g. Pāli *āpā-* 'emergency', *sappi-* 'butter': Skt. *āpad-*, *sarpis-*. The nominal case system too is reduced. At an early stage, the dative is replaced by the genitive except in expressing a goal or purpose: Pāli *etesaṁ pi abhayam dammi* 'I grant (*dammi*) them too (*etesaṁ pi*) security' has a genitive *etesaṁ* construed with *dammi*, and Jaina Māhārāṣṭrī *namo tāṇaṁ purisaṇaṃ* 'homage to those men' has a genitive in construction with *namo*. Formal datives occur in examples like Aśokan *etāya atthāya idaṁ lekhāpitaṁ* 'this (*idaṁ*) has been caused to be written (*lekhapitaṁ*) for this purpose (*etāya atthāya*)', Pāli *jhassu rūpaṁ apunabbhavanāya* 'give up (*jhassu*) your body (*rūpaṁ*) so as not to be born again (*apunabbhavanāya*)'. In addition, nominal and pronominal types are less strictly segregated, as can be seen from *etāya*, *tāṇaṁ* (Skt. *etasmai*, *teṣām*) in examples cited.

Although early Middle Indo-Aryan retains middle forms, the contrast between active and medio-passive in the verb system is generally obliterated. Thus, Pāli has *maññati* 'thinks', *jāyati* 'is born' and passives of the type *vuccati* 'is said', with etymologically active endings; contrast Skt. *manyate*, *jāyate*, *ucyate*. The contrast between two kinds of future formations is absent in Middle Indo-Aryan, which has the type Pāli *hossati* 'will be'. Further, the distinction among aorist, imperfect and perfect is obliterated. With few exceptions, the sigmatic aorist supplies the productive preterit. Thus, Pāli has several preterital formations, but the productive one is sigmatic and based on the present stem, not on the root as in Old Indo-Aryan: *ahosi* 'was' (3 sg.), *ahosuṁ* 'were' (pres. *hoti honti*), *agacchi*, *agacchisuṁ* (*gacchati*, *gacchanti*). In later Middle Indo-Aryan, verbally inflected preterits are generally given up in favour of participial forms, as in Śaurasenī *mahārāo vi āado* 'the king (*mahārāo*) also (*vi*) has arrived (*āado*)', where *āado* agrees in case, number and gender with *mahārāo*. The participle of a verb that takes a direct object shows object agreement: in Jaina Māhārāṣṭrī *teṇa vi savvaṁ siṭṭhaṁ* 'he too has told everything', *teṇa* (inst. sg.) refers to the agent, and *siṭṭhaṁ* 'told' agrees with *savvaṁ* (nom. sg. nt.) 'everything'. If no object is explicitly referred to, the neuter nominative singular of a participle is used; e.g., Jaina Māhārāṣṭrī *pacchā raṇṇā cintiyaṁ* 'afterwards, the king (inst. sg. *raṇṇā*) thought (*cintiyaṁ*)'.

Alternations of the type Skt. *asti–santi* (see section 2.2.3 of the chapter on Sanskrit) are eliminated in Middle Indo-Aryan, where the predominant present formation involves a single stem: Pāli *eti* 'goes' *enti* 'go', *sakkoti–sakkonti* (*sak* 'be able'), *chindati–chindanti* (*chid* 'cut'). Stems like *chinda-* reflect a generalisation, based on a reanalysis of third plural forms, of stems with *-a*. The elimination of strictly athematic presents with variable stems allowed the use of the second singular imperative *-hi* in a domain wider than this had in Old Indo-Aryan; e.g., Pāli *jīvāhi* 'live' (Skt. *jīva*). Similarly, optatives with *-e-* and *-yā-* are not sharply segregated; a form like Pāli *bhaveyya* (3 sg.) shows a blend of the two. Middle Indo-Aryan continues to use morphological causatives with *-i-/-e-* (Pāli 3 sg. pres. *kāreti*), but the type in *-āpe-* (Pkt. *-āve-*) is extended beyond its earlier domain, as in Pāli *vasāpeti* 'has ... stay'.

Nominal forms of the Middle Indo-Aryan verb system are of the same types as in Old Indo-Aryan: present and past participles (see above), gerundives (Pāli *kātabba-* 'to be done', *dassanīya-* 'worthy of being seen'), gerunds, infinitives, with some innovations. For example, Pāli *nikkhamitvā* 'after leaving' has *-tvā-* after a compound, and *pappotuṁ* has *-tuṁ* added to the present stem, not the root. Contrast Skt. *niṣkramya*, *prāptum*.

The late Middle Indo-Aryan stage represented in Apabhraṁśa foreshadows New Indo-Aryan in several ways. Forms of the nominal system with *-au*, *-aũ*, *-ī* presage the modern oppositions among masculine, neuter and feminine types such as Gujarati *navo*, *navũ*, *navī* 'new', Hindi *nayā*, *naī* (m., f.). The case system of Apabhraṁśa is at a more advanced stage of disintegration than found earlier. For example, instrumental and locative plurals are now formally identical, and etymologically instrumental singular forms like *dāhiṇabhāẽ* are used in locatival function: *dāhiṇabhāẽ bharahu thakku* 'Bharata is located (*thakku*) in the southern division'. The paucity of distinct forms is evident in personal pronouns, where, for example, *maĩ*, *paĩ* (1st, 2nd person sg.) have functions equivalent to older accusative, instrumental and locative forms. Although Apabhraṁśa has some presents like *hoi* 'is', stems in *-a* of the type *kara-* 'do, make' (3 sg. *karai*) predominate. The Apabhraṁśa causative type *karāva-* (*karāvai*) is comparable to New Indo-Aryan formations (e.g. Gujarati *karāvɛ chɛ* 'has... do'). Moreover, Apabhraṁśa has causative formations found in modern languages but not attested earlier in Middle Indo-Aryan; e.g. *bhamāḍ-a-* 'cause to turn' (Gujarati *bhamāḍ-*).

The gender system of earlier Indo-Aryan is retained in some modern languages (e.g. Gujarati, see above), but is reduced in others (e.g. Hindi, with masculine and feminine only); some languages (e.g. Bengali) have eliminated systematic gender distinctions. Various inflectional forms are retained (e.g. Gujarati agentive *mɛ̃* 'I'), but the prevalent modern nominal system involves stems and postpositions or, much less commonly, prepositions. Over a large area of New Indo-Aryan, one finds variable nominals with direct and oblique forms, the former used independently, the latter with postpositions and other clitic elements. For example, Gujarati has singular direct forms in *-o* (m.), *-ũ* (nt.), *-ī* (f.), oblique forms in *-ā* (m.-nt.), *-ī*. Some languages (e.g. Hindi) distinguish direct and oblique in the plural, others (e.g. Gujarati) do not. There are also nominals without these variations. Combinations of stems and postpositions serve the functions of inflected forms in earlier Indo-Aryan. Different languages have different postpositions for the same functions; e.g. Hindi *-ko*, Gujarati *-ne* mark definite direct objects, regularly animate, and indirect objects. Adjectives in general are formally like nouns, which they regularly precede in attributive constructions, and, with few exceptions, postpositions follow such phrases, not individual components; e.g. Gujarati *mẽ tamārā dikrā-ne joyo* 'I saw your son'. Second person pronouns in New Indo-Aryan are differentiated essentially according to distinctions of deference, distance and familiarity, not according to number; e.g. Hindi *āp* has plural agreement but can refer to one person. Languages of the south-west also distinguish between first person inclusive and exclusive forms; e.g. Gujarati *ame* (exclusive), *āpṇe*. In demonstrative and relative pronouns, languages differ with regard to gender distinctions made; e.g. Marathi relative singular *jo* (m.), *je* (nt.), *ji* (f.), Gujarati *je* for all genders. They also differ in the deictic distinctions made.

The tendency to incorporate nominal forms in the verb system, evident in earlier times, continues into New Indo-Aryan. For example, Hindi has a contrast comparable to that of Bengali *korchi* 'am doing', *kori* 'do', both verbally inflected, but instead uses nominally inflected forms: *kar rahā/rahī hū̃* 'am doing', *kartā/kartī hū̃* 'do'. Gujarati lacks the contrast, but has verbally inflected presents (*karū̃ chū̃* 'do, am doing') and nominally inflected preterits (*karto hato, kartī hatī*). Temporal auxiliaries like Hindi *hū̃*, Gujarati *chū̃* show verbal inflection, as do imperatives and some other forms. Person-number distinctions accord with the use of pronouns, but some languages (e.g. Bengali) have given up number distinctions in the verb. Future formations also show areal differences. Some languages have futures with *-š-* or *-h-* (e.g. Gujarati *kariš* 'I will do'), but *-b-* is characteristic of the east (e.g. Bengali *jabe* 'will go') and there are future formations that include gender distinctions, as in Hindi *jāegā* 'he will go', *jāegī* 'she will go'. The perfective of many New Indo-Aryan languages is semi-ergative, reflecting earlier participial constructions. For example, Gujarati *ghɛr gayo/gaī* 'he/she went home' has masculine *gayo*, feminine *gaī*, depending on whether the agent is a man or a woman, but in *mẽ tamārā dīkrā-ne joyo* 'I saw your son' agreement (m. sg. *joyo*) is determined by the object (*dīkrā-ne* 'son'). Some languages (e.g. Hindi) suspend agreement if an object nominal takes a postposition, so that the construction is no longer strictly passive. A formal passive such as *nahī bulāyā jāegā* (m. sg.) 'will not be invited' in an example like Hindi *baccõ-ko nahī bulāyā jāegā* 'children will not be invited' is also construed with a noun phrase containing an object marker (*baccõ-ko*), so that this construction too is different from the passive of earlier Indo-Aryan. Moreover, formal passives normally are used in sentences without agent expressions except under particular semantic conditions; e.g. Gujarati *mārā-thī nahi jawāy* 'I (agentive *mārā-thī*) won't be able to go', with the passive *jaw-ā-y* (3 sg. pres.). As shown, formal passives are also not restricted to transitive verbs, and in some languages they are formed with a suffix, in others they are periphrastic formations.

Examples cited illustrate the usual unmarked word order of most New Indo-Aryan languages: subject (including agentive forms), object (with attributive adjectives, including number words, before this and preceded by possessives), verb (with auxiliaries). Adverbials can precede sentences or the verb. Relative clauses generally precede correlative clauses. A notable exception to the above, at least in its superficial order, is Kashmiri, where the verb occurs in second position.

Bibliography

Cardona and Emmerick (1974) contains a survey of Indo-Aryan on pages 439b–457a, including a table of languages and a map. Bloch (1965) is a general and masterful survey of the historical developments, while Varma (1972–6) is a handy summary of Grierson's survey of the modern languages, still valuable, though in serious need of updating. Turner (1966–9) is an indispensable reference work for lexicon, and includes an index by D.R. Turner.

References

Bloch, J. 1965. *Indo-Aryan from the Vedas to Modern Times* (Adrien-Maisonneuve, Paris; translation by A. Master, with revisions, additions and an index, of *L'Indo-Aryen du véda aux temps modernes*, Adrien-Maisonneuve, Paris, 1934)

Cardona, G. and R.E. Emmerick. 1974. 'Indo-Aryan Languages', in *The New Encyclopaedia Britannica: Macropaedia*, 15th ed., pp. 439b–457a (Encyclopaedia Britannica, Chicago)

Turner, R.L. 1966–9. *A Comparative Dictionary of the Indo-Aryan Languages*, 2 vols. (Oxford University Press, London)

Varma, S. 1972–6. *G.A. Grierson's Linguistic Survey of India, a Summary*, 3 vols. (Vishveshvaranand Institute, Panjab University, Hoshiarpur)

2 *Sanskrit*

George Cardona

1 Background

1.1 Introduction

Sanskrit (*saṁskr̥ta-* 'adorned, purified') refers to several varieties of Old Indo-Aryan, whose most archaic forms are found in Vedic texts: the *Rigveda* (*R̥gveda*), *Sāmaveda*, *Atharvaveda*, *Yajurveda*, with various branches. Associated with these are groupings of explicatory and speculative works (called *brāhmaṇas*, *āraṇyakas*, *upaniṣads*) as well as texts concerning the performance of rites (*kalpa-* or *śrauta-sūtras*), treatises on phonetics, grammar proper, etymological explanations of particular words, metrics and astrology. Early Vedic texts are pre-Buddhistic — the composition of the *Rigveda* is plausibly dated in the mid-second millennium BC — although their exact chronology is difficult to establish. Brāhmaṇas and early sūtra works can properly be called late Vedic. Also of the late Vedic period is the grammarian Pāṇini (not later than early fourth century BC), author of the *Aṣṭādhyāyī*, who distinguishes between the language of sacred texts (*chandas*) and a more usual language of communication (*bhāṣā*, from *bhāṣ* 'speak'), tantamount to Classical Sanskrit. Epic Sanskrit is so called because it is represented principally in the two epics, *Mahābhārata* and *Rāmāyaṇa*. The date of composition for the core of early epic is considered to be in the first centuries BC. It is in the *Rāmāyaṇa* that the term *saṁskr̥ta-* is encountered probably for the first time with reference to the language. Classical Sanskrit is the language of major poetical works, dramas, tales and technical treatises on grammar, philosophy and ritual. It was not only used by Kalidasa and his predecessors but continued in use after Sanskrit had ceased to be a commonly used mother tongue. Sanskrit is a language of learned treatises and commentaries to this day. It has also undergone a literary revival, and original works are still being composed in this language. Indeed, Sanskrit is used as a lingua franca by paṇḍitas from different parts of India, and several thousand people claim it as their mother tongue.

1.2 Diachronic Changes Within Sanskrit

Linguistic changes are discernible in Sanskrit from earliest Vedic down to the language Pāṇini describes. The nominative plural masculine in *-āsas* (*devāsas* 'gods'), which has a counterpart in Iranian, is already less frequent in the *Rigveda* than the type in *-ās* (*devās*), and continues to lose ground; in Brāhmaṇas, *-ās* is the norm. The *Rigveda* has examples of an archaic genitive plural in *-ām* to *a*-stems, but the form in *-ānām* prevails here and is the only one used later. The instrumental singular of *a*-stems has both *-ā* and *-ena* (originally a pronominal type) in the *Rigveda* (*vīryā*/*vīryeṇa* 'heroic might, act'), but the latter is already prevalent and becomes the norm later. The Rigvedic nominative-accusative dual masculine of *a*-stems ends in *-ā* or *-au* (*mitrāvaruṇā*/*-varuṇau* 'Mitra and Varuṇa'), distributed according to phonological environments in early parts of the *Rigveda*, but *-au* steadily gains the upper hand and finally ousts *-ā* completely. For the nominative-accusative plural of neuter *a*-stems, the *Rigveda* has forms in *-ā* and *-āni*: *bhīmāni āyudhā* 'fearful weapons'. The former predominates in the *Rigveda*, but the situation is reversed in the *Atharvaveda*; later, *-āni* is the norm. Early Vedic had derivate *ī*-stems of two types, as in *vr̥kīs* 'she wolf', *devī* 'goddess' (nom. sg.), *vr̥kyas, devīs* (nom. pl.). The type *vr̥kī-* is gradually eliminated as an independent formation, but leaves traces incorporated into the *devī* type (e.g. nom. pl. *devyas*). Rigvedic feminine *i*- and *u*-stems have instrumental singular forms of the type *ūtī* 'with, for help', *jātū* 'by nature' in addition to forms with *-ā* (*ūtyā*, *dhenvā* 'cow'). Even in the *Rigveda*, *u*-stems usually have forms of the type *dhenvā*, and the type *ūtyā* also becomes the norm later. Masculine and neuter stems in *-i*, *-u* have Rigvedic instrumental singulars with *-ā* (*pavyā*, *paśvā* to *pavi-* 'felly', *paśu-* 'animal') and *-nā* (*agninā* 'fire, Agni', *paśunā*). The latter predominate in the *Atharvaveda* and ultimately take over except for a few nouns (*patyā* 'husband', *sakhyā* 'friend'). The *Rigveda* has *avyas*, *madhvas*, genitive singulars of *avi-* 'sheep', *madhu-* 'honey'; the regular later forms are *aves*, *madhunas* (also *madhos* in Vedic). Endingless locatives like *ahan* (*ahan-* 'day') are also gradually eliminated in favour of forms with the ending *-i*: *ahani*/*ahni*. Early Vedic has pronominal forms not found in Classical Sanskrit: *asme*, *yuṣme* (loc. pl.) from the first and second person pronouns, replaced by *asmāsu*, *yuṣmāsu*; *āvos* (1st person gen.-loc. du.), *mahya* (1st person dat. sg.), replaced by *āvayos*, *mahyam*. Pāṇini expressly classes such earlier Vedic forms as belonging to the language of sacred texts.

The verbal system shows comparable differences. Early Vedic had modal forms from several stems: present, aorist, perfect. For example, the Rigvedic imperatives *śr̥ṇudhi*, *śr̥ṇuhi*, *śr̥ṇu* (2 sg.) and the Atharvavedic optative *śr̥ṇuyāt* (3 sg.) are formed to the present stem *śr̥ṇu-* of *śru* 'hear, listen', but the Rigvedic imperative *śrudhi* (2 sg.) and optative *śruyās* (3 sg.) are formed to the aorist stem. In later Sanskrit, imperatives and optatives regularly are formed from present stems. The first plural primary active ending *-masi* (*bharāmasi* 'we carry'), which has an equivalent in Iranian, predominates over *-mas* in the *Rigveda*, but not in the *Atharvaveda*, and later *-mas* is the rule. Early Vedic forms like *ās* 'was' (3 sg. imperfect of *as*) and *avāṭ* (3 sg. aorist of *vah* 'transport') show the effects of the simplification of word-final clusters. Such forms are replaced by the types *āsīt*, *avākṣīt*, with *-īt* (2 sg. *-īs*), in which endings are clearly shown. Aorist forms made directly from verb roots are also replaced by forms from stems in *-a* or sigmatic stems, the latter especially in the medio-passive. Thus, the *Rigveda* has 1 sg. *akaram*, 2 sg. *akar* (< *akar-s*), 3 sg. *akar* (< *akar-t*), but the *Atharvaveda* has 2 sg. *akaras*, 3 sg. *akarat*, from *kr̥* 'make, do', and the *Rigveda* has not only a root aorist third plural middle *ayujran* but also a sigmatic form *ayukṣata* 'they yoked'. Commentators like Patañjali (mid-second century BC) and the etymologist Yāska before him used the sigmatic form *akr̥ṣata* (3 pl. middle) in paraphrasing a Vedic verse with the root aorist form *akrata*. Early Vedic forms of the type *śaye* 'is lying' are gradually replaced by the type *śete*, with *te*, which is explicitly marked for person.

Early Vedic distinguishes among the aorist, imperfect and perfect. The aorist is commonly used to refer to something that has recently taken place, and the imperfect is a narrative tense form used of acts accomplished or states prevailing at a past time not close at hand. For example, *úd u jyótir ... savitā́ aśret* 'Savitr̥ has set up (*úd ... aśret*) the light (*jyótis*)', spoken at dawn, has the aorist *úd ... aśret*, but *ná mr̥tyúr āsīd amŕ̥taṁ ná tárhi ná rā́tryā áhna āsīt praketáḥ* 'then (*tárhi*) was there (*āsīt*) not (*ná*) death (*mr̥tyús*) or deathlessness (*amŕ̥tam*), nor was there the mark (*praketás*) of night (*rā́tryās*) or day (*áhnas*)' has the imperfect *āsīt*. The perfect originally signified, as in early Greek, a state of being; e.g. *bibhāya* '... is afraid'. From the earliest Vedic texts, however, this is not always the use of the perfect, which came to be used as a narrative tense. For example, the following Brāhmaṇa passage has both perfect and imperfects: *yajño vai devebhya ud akrāman na vo'ham annaṁ bhaviṣyāmīti/ neti devā abruvan annam eva no bhaviṣyasīti/ taṁ devā vimethire ... te hocur devā na vai na itthaṁ vihr̥to'laṁ bhaviṣyati hantemaṁ yajñaṁ saṁ bharāmeti/ tatheti taṁ saṁ jabhruḥ* 'the sacrifice (*yajñas*) fled (*ud akrāmat*) from the gods (*devebhyas*), saying (citation particle *iti*), "I will not be (*na bhaviṣyāmi*) food (*annam*) for you (*vas*)"; the gods (*devās*) said (*abruvan*), "No, you will be (*bhaviṣyasi*) food for us (*nas*)"; the gods tore it apart (*taṁ vi methire*) ... the gods said (*ūcus*), "Truly (*vai*), it will not be sufficient (*na ... alaṁ bhaviṣyati*) for us thus (*ittham*) torn apart (*vihr̥tas*), so let us put this sacrifice together (*imaṁ yajñaṁ saṁ bharāma*)"; they agreed (*tatheti* 'yes') and put it together (*taṁ saṁ jabhrus*)'. The imperfect *ud akrāmat, abruvan* and the perfect *vi methire, saṁ jabhrus* occur in similar contexts. This passage also illustrates the normal later combination of preverbs and verbs: preverbs immediately precede the verb stems with which they are connected; in earlier Vedic, tmesis was common — as in *úd ... aśret* of the Rigvedic passage cited earlier.

In addition, the augment became obligatory, as it had not been before, in imperfect and aorist forms.

The Brāhmaṇa passage just quoted also contains the future forms *bhaviṣyāmi*, *bhaviṣyasi*, *bhaviṣyati*, from the verb *bhū*, with the augmented suffix *-iṣya*. This and the unaugmented suffix *-sya* (*dāsya-* 'will give') are used from earliest Vedic on, but there is also a composite type, originally formed from an agent noun of the type *kartṛ́-* (nom.sg. *kartā́*) followed, except in the third person, by forms of the verb 'be': *kartāsmi* 'I will do', *kartāsi* 'you will do', *kartā* 'he will do'. This formation, which was in common use at Pāṇini's time, was rare in early Vedic. The perfect also has a periphrastic formation, for derived verbs such as causatives; e.g. *gamayāñ cakāra* (3 sg.) 'made to go' (3 sg. present *gamayati*), formed with the accusative singular of an action noun (*gamayā-*) and the perfect of *kṛ* 'do'. This type first appears in the *Atharvaveda* (form cited), and gains currency; Pāṇini recognises it not only as the regular perfect for derived verbs but also for some primitive verbs. Corresponding to future forms such as *bhariṣyati* 'will carry', there were, from earliest Vedic, secondary augmented forms like *abhariṣyat* 'was going to carry', and these are later to become the regular verbal constituents in contrary-to-fact conditional sentences.

Early Vedic has a category that goes out of use later: the injunctive, formally an unaugmented secondary form; for example, *bhūt*, *carat* are third person singular injunctives corresponding to the aorist *abhūt* and the imperfect *acarat*. In a *Rigveda* passage such as *agníh sáptiṁ vājambharáṁ dadāti* ... *agnī́ ródasī ví carat* 'Agni (*agnís*) gives (*dadāti*) a horse (*sáptim*) that carries away prizes (*vājambharám*) ... Agni wanders through (*ví carat*) the two worlds (*ródasī*)', the injunctive *ví carat* and the present *dadāti* are juxtaposed, both used of general truths. In such statements, Vedic also uses subjunctives, characterised by the vowel *-a-* affixed to a present, aorist or perfect stem, as in Rigvedic *ná duṣṭutī́ mártyò vindate vásu ná srédhantaṁ rayír naśat* 'a mortal (*mártyas*) does not find (*ná vindate*) treasure (*vásu*) through bad praise (*duṣṭutī́*), nor does wealth (*rayís*) come to (*naśat*) one who faulters in the performance of rites (*srédhantam*)', where the present *vindate* is juxtaposed with the aorist subjunctive *naśat* 'reach'. In addition, subordinate clauses such as *pūṣā́ no yáthā* ... *ásad vṛdhé rakṣitā́* 'so that (*yáthā*) Pūṣan be (*ásat*) our protector in order that we might grow (*vṛdhé*)' use the subjunctive, which also occurs in requests; e.g. *devó devébhir ā́ gamat* 'may the god come (*ā́ gamat*) with the gods (*devébhis*)'. In negative commands, the injunctive is used with the particle *mā*, as in *mā́ no vadhīḥ* ... *mā́ párā dāḥ* 'do not kill (*mā́ vadhīs*) us (*nas*), do not forsake (*mā́ párā dās*) us', with the second person singular aorist injunctives *vadhīs*, *parā dās*. The regular negative particle used with a subjunctive, however, is *na*: e.g. *sá jáno ná reṣan máno yó asya* ... *ā vívāsāt* 'that person (*sá jánas*) does not suffer ill (*ná reṣat*), who seeks to win (*yás ā vívāsāt*) his (*asya*) spirit (*mánas*)' has the aorist subjunctive *reṣat* and the subjunctive of the present desiderative stem *ā vivāsa-* (*-sāt* < *-sa-a-t*). Later, the injunctive is retained only in negative commands of the type *mā vadhīs*, 3 sg. *mā vadhīt*. The subjunctive also steadily loses ground until it is no longer current; for Pāṇini, subjunctive forms belong to the language of sacred texts. Only the first person type *karavāṇi* 'I may do, let me do', incorporated into the imperative system, is retained. The functions of the subjunctive are taken over by the optative and the future. For example, in Vedic a subordinate clause introduced by *yathā* may have a subjunctive or an optative, but *yadi* 'if' is regularly used with a subjunctive in early Vedic. Thus, a passage cited above has *yathā* ... *asat*, and *yáthā bhávema mīḷhúṣe ánāgāḥ* 'that we may be (*yáthā bhavema*) sinless (*ánāgās*) towards the gracious one (*mīḷhúṣe*)' has the optative *bhavema*, but *ā́ gha gamad yádi śrávat* 'let him come (*ā́* ... *gamat*) if he hear (*yádi śrávat*)' has the aorist subjunctive *śravat*. In later Vedic, however, *yadi* is used with an optative, as in *yádi bibhīyā́d duścármā bhaviṣyāmī́ti somapauṣṇáṁ śyāmám ā́ labheta* 'if he fear (*yádi bibhīyā́t*) that he might be (*bhaviṣyāmī́ti* 'I will become') stricken by a skin disease (*duścármā* 'bad-skinned'), let him immolate (*ā́ labheta*) a black goat (*śyāmám* 'black') dedicated to Soma and Pūṣan'.

Nominal forms within the verbal system of early Vedic are numerous. The Rigveda has derivatives with *-ya*, *-tva* that function as gerundives: *vācya-* 'to be said' (root *vac*), *kartva-* 'to be done' (*kṛ*). In addition, the *Atharvaveda* has forms with *-(i)tavya*, *-anīya*: *hiṁsitavya-* 'to be harmed', *upajīvanīya-* 'to be subsisted upon'. By late Vedic, the type with *-tva* has lost currency, and for Pāṇini the regular formations are of the types *kārya-*, *kartavya-*, *karaṇīya-*. In Indo-Aryan from Vedic down to modern times, gerunds are used with reference to the earlier of actions performed in succession, usually by the same agent ('after doing A, ... does B', '... does A before doing B'); e.g. *yuktvā́ háribhyāṁ úpa yāsad arvā́k* 'let him yoke his bay horses to his chariot (*yuktvā* 'after yoking') and come hither (*upa yāsad arvāk*) with them (*haribhyām* 'with two bay horses')', *gūḍhvī́ támo* ... *abodhi* '(dawn) has awakened (*abodhi*) after hiding away (*gūḍhvī*) the darkness (*támas*)', *piba niṣadya* 'sit down (*niṣadya* 'after sitting down') and drink (*piba*)'. The *Rigveda* has gerunds with *-tvā*, *-tvāya -tvī*, *-(t)ya*, but these are ultimately reduced to two main types: *-tvā* after simple verbs or verbs with the negative prefix *a*(*n*)-, *-ya* after compounds with preverbs. Early Vedic uses a variety of case forms of action nouns, including root nouns, as what western grammarians traditionally call infinitives; e.g. dat. sg. *vṛdhe* (root noun *vṛdh-* 'growing'), *-tave* (*dātave* 'to give'), gen. sg. *-tos* (*dātos*), the last two from a derivative in *-tu* which also supplies the accusative *-tum* (*dātum*). There are other Vedic types, but nouns in *-tu* are noteworthy in that for later Vedic the accusative with *-tum* and the genitive in *-tos*, the latter construed with *īś* or *śak* 'be able', become the norm. According to Pāṇini, forms in *-tum* and datives of action nouns are equivalent in sentences like *bhoktum/ bhojanāya gacchati* '...is going (*gacchati*) in order to eat'.

1.3 Sanskrit Dialects

That some formations fell into disuse in the course of Old Indo-Aryan is no surprise: the developments sketched above represent chronological and dialectal changes. Such changes were recognised by grammarians who spoke the language. Patañjali notes that second plural perfect forms like *cakra* or *ūṣa* (*vas* 'dwell) were not used in his time; instead, one used participial forms such as *kr̥tavantas, ūṣitās* (nom. pl. m.). Grammarians also recognised that various dialects existed. Pāṇini takes note of forms used by northerners, easterners and various dialectal usages described by other grammarians. The etymologist Yāska notes, as does Patañjali, that finite forms of the verb *dā* 'cut' were used in the east, while in the north the verb occurred in the derivative *dātra-* 'sickle'. Earlier documents also afford evidence of dialect differences. The major dialect of the *Rigveda* is one in which Proto-Indo-European *l* merged with *r* (e.g., *pūrṇa-* 'full'), but other dialects developed *l*, and one finds doublets such as *rohita-/lohita-* 'red'. The development of retroflex liquids *-ḷ-*, *-ḷh-* from intervocalic *-ḍ-* *-ḍh-* is another characteristic of some areas, among them the major dialect of the *Rigveda*.

1.4 Sanskrit and Other Languages

Classical Sanskrit represents a development of one or more such Old Indo-Aryan dialects, accepted as standard, at a stage when archaisms such as those noted (section 1.2) had largely been eliminated. It is plausible to accept that both Classical Sanskrit and earlier dialects of Indo-Aryan coexisted with vernaculars that were removed from these by changes which characterise Middle Indo-Aryan, just as in later times Sanskrit and vernaculars were used side by side under particular circumstances. There is evidence to support this view, particularly in Patañjali's *Mahābhāṣya*, where he discusses the use of 'correct speech forms' (*śabda*) and 'incorrect speech forms' (*apaśabda*), considered corruptions (*apabhraṁśa*) of the former. Patañjali speaks of *śiṣṭas*, model speakers, who are characterised as much by moral qualities as by their speech. They are Brāhmaṇas who reside in Āryāvartta, the land of the Āryas in north-central India, who at any time have only as much grain as will fit in a small pot, who are not greedy, who behave morally without ulterior motives and who attain full knowledge of traditional learning with consummate ease, not having to be taught. These model speakers are those one should imitate and, it is assumed, the models Pāṇini followed in composing his grammatical rules. However, even learned men did not avoid vernaculars, as Patañjali also points out. He remarks that a restriction such that correct speech forms should be used to the exclusion of others is absolute only in respect of rituals. To illustrate, Patañjali speaks of sages who said *yar vā ṇaḥ* 'what is ours', *tar vā ṇaḥ* 'that is ours' instead of *yad vā naḥ, tad vā naḥ* but did not use such forms in the course of ritual acts. Now, forms like *yar* instead of *yad* reflect an Indo-Aryan tendency to eliminate obstruence for non-initial retroflex and dental stops; the particular change in question is seen also in Prakrit *bāraha* as opposed to Sanskrit *dvādaśa* 'twelve'. Moreover, Patañjali must have been, if not a native speaker of Sanskrit in the strictest sense, at least one fully fluent in the language, with authority concerning its usage. For he explicitly distinguishes between what is desirable — that is, what is required by accepted usage — and what obtains by grammatical rules. At Patañjali's time, then, Sanskrit must have been a current vehicle of communication in certain circles and under particular social and religious conditions, used concurrently with vernaculars. Much the same picture is painted for later periods, when Sanskrit was doubtless revived. Thus, in his *Kāmasūtra*, Vātsyāyana notes that to be held in high esteem a man-about-town should use neither Sanskrit nor a local language exclusively. Indeed, the coexistence of Middle Indo-Aryan and Sanskrit speech is to be envisaged even for the time when very early texts were given their final redactions. The *Rigveda* has forms like *vikaṭa-* 'deformed' and *jyotis-* 'light'. The former is a Middle Indo-Aryan form of *vikr̥ta-*, with *-aṭ-* for *-r̥t-*, comparable to Aśokan *kaṭa-* 'made' (Skt. *kr̥ta*), and the latter had *jy-* for *dy-*. It has been suggested, plausibly in my estimation, that there was an archaic Middle Indo-Aryan contemporaneous with early Vedic.

Sanskrit was also subject to non-Aryan influence from early on. In the sixth century BC Darius counted Gandhara as a province of his kingdom, and Alexander the Great penetrated into the north of the subcontinent in the fourth century. From Iranian come terms such as *lipi-* 'writing, script', *kṣatrapa-* 'satrap', and Greek is the source of such words as *kendra-* 'centre', *jāmitra-* 'diameter', *horā-* 'hour'. At a later time borrowings entered from Arabic and other sources. But long before this Sanskrit was influenced by Dravidian, from which it borrowed terms such as *kāla-* 'black', *kuṭī-* 'hut' (cf. Tamil *kaṟ* 'blackness', *kuṭi*) and the influence of which contributed to the spread of retroflex consonants (see section 1 of the chapter on Indo-Aryan). It is not certain in every instance, however, that borrowing proceeded from Dravidian to Indo-Aryan, since Dravidian languages also freely borrowed from Indo-Aryan. For example, some scholars maintain that Skt. *kaṭu-* 'sharp, pungent' is a Dravidian borrowing, but others treat it as a Middle Indo-Aryan development of **kr̥tu-* 'cutting' (root **kr̥t* 'cut'). Whatever be the judgement on any individual word, nevertheless, it is clear that Sanskrit and other Indo-Aryan dialects borrowed from Dravidian sources.

2 Brief Description of Classical Sanskrit

2.1 Sound System and Script

The sounds of Sanskrit are shown in table 2.1. In the present context, it is not necessary to take a particular stand about which sounds should be considered 'basic', 'underlying' or 'phonemic'. Suffice it to note that sounds

Table 2.1: The Sounds of Sanskrit

Vowels			
	i ī		u ū
	e		o
		a	
		ā	
	r̥ [r̥̄] [l̥]		ai au

Consonants	*Obstruents* Voiceless		Voiced		*Nasals*	*Semi-vowels*	*Liquid*	*Tap*	*Spirants* Voiceless	Voiced
Pharyngeal									[ḥ]	h
Velar	k	kh	g	gh	[ṅ]				[χ]	
Palatal	c	ch	j	jh	[ñ]	y			ś	
Retroflex	ṭ	ṭh	ḍ	ḍh	ṇ			r*	ṣ	
Alveolar								r*		
Dental	t	th	d	dh	n		l		s	
Labio-dental						v				
Labial	p	ph	b	bh	m [ṁ]				[φ]	

Note: *Some ancient authorities say *r* is retroflex, others say it is alveolar.

of table 2.1 within square brackets have restricted distributions. *r̥̄* occurs only in accusative or genitive plurals of *r̥*-stems (*pitr̥̄n* 'fathers', *mātr̥̄s* 'mothers', gen. pl. *pitr̥̄ṇām*, *mātr̥̄ṇām*, rare nom.-acc. pl. nt. *kartr̥̄ṇi* 'which do'); *l̥* is found only in forms of *kl̥p* 'be fit, arrange, imagine' (past participle *kl̥pta-*). Due to the reduction of word-final clusters, *-ṇ* occurs in words such as *prāṅ* (nom. sg.) 'directed forward, toward the east', but otherwise *ṇ* and *ñ* are found before velar and palatal stops, respectively, though not necessarily as replacements of *n* or *m* at morph boundaries. The nasal off-glide *ṁ* occurs word-internally before spirants at morph boundaries as the final segment of items that have *-n* or *-m* before vowels and in word-final position before spirants and semi-vowels or stops, where it varies with nasalised semi-vowels and nasal stops homorganic with following stops. *ḥ* is a word-final segment in prepause position or before voiceless spirants, velars and labials. *χ φ* are alternants to *-ḥ* before velars and labials. Like *ṅ* and *ñ*, *ṇ* is not the initial sound of lexical items. It occurs in word-final position, though rarely except before nasals as the final sound of a morph that has a non-nasal retroflex stop before vowels, but intervocalic *-ṇ-* is found in words like *kaṇa-* 'grain, atom', that do not contain sounds which condition retroflexion.

The vowels *i*, *u* and *ī*, *ū* differ essentially in duration: short vowels last one mora (*mātrā*), long vowels two morae; however, in accepted modern pronunciations, *i* and *u* can be lower than their long counterparts. *e*, *o* are monophthongs of two morae, though they derive historically from diphthongs and alternate with *ay*, *av* before vowels. *ai*, *au* are diphthongs for which ancient phoneticians and grammarians recognised dialect variants: for example, the first segment of each was a closer vowel in some dialects than in others. Prosodically, however, *ai*, *au* behave in the manner of simple long vowels, and there are good reasons for not treating them as combinations of *ā* with *i, u*. *r̥* is also a complex sound, consisting of *r* surrounded by vowel segments, according to a fairly old description, but this also behaves prosodically as a single vowel. In north-central India, *r̥* is pronounced as *r* followed by short *i*. *a*, *ā* behave as a pair of short and long vowels, but they are also qualitatively different, as shown. Vowels can be unnasalised or nasalised. They also have pitch differences such that they are called *anudātta*, *udātta* and *svarita*. Pāṇini's statements concerning these are best understood as reflecting a system in which an anudātta vowel is low-pitched, an udātta vowel is high-pitched, and a svarita vowel has a combination of both pitches: *a*, *á*, *à*. According to Pāṇini, a svarita vowel is high-pitched for the duration of half a mora from its beginning, low-pitched for its remainder, but there were dialectical variations, as can be seen from other ancient descriptions. There are also differences in Vedic traditions of recitation concerning the relative pitches of the vowels in question.

Sanskrit generally does not allow word-final clusters, although -*r*C is permitted if both consonants belong to the same element; e.g. *ūrk* (nom. sg.) 'strength' (acc. sg. *ūrj-am*). Sanskrit also has a fairly complex system of morphophonemic adjustments (*sandhi*) across grammatical boundaries, at word boundaries if the items in question are pronounced in close juncture (*saṁhitāyām*). Some of these adjustments are illustrated in examples given; e.g. in the Brāhmaṇa passage cited in section 1.2: *yajño vai* ← *yajnas vai*, *devebhya ud* ← *devebhyas ud*, *akrāman na* ← *akrāmat na*, *voham* ← *vas aham*, *annaṁ bhaviṣyāmīti* ← *annam bhaviṣyāmi iti*, *neti* ← *na iti*, *devā abruvan* ← *devās abruvan*, *no bhaviṣyasi* ← *nas bhaviṣyasi*, *taṁ devā vi methire* ← *tam devās vi methire*, *hocur devā na* ← *ha ūcus devās na*, *tatheti* ← *tathā iti*, *taṁ saṁ jabhruḥ* ← *tam sam jabhrus*, the last with -*ḥ* instead of -*s in pausa*. These adjustments also affect vowel pitches. The particular place of a high-pitched vowel in an underived base is not predictable. In general, a syntactic word has one high-pitched vowel only — but may have none — and a finite verb form following a term that is not a finite verb has no high-pitched vowel except in particular collocations. Further, a low-pitched vowel following a high-pitched one shifts to a svarita vowel, as in *ā́ gàmat* ← *ā́ gamat*. There are other accentual adjustments that involve considerable complexity and dialectal variation.

Sanskrit was and continues to be written in various scripts in different areas, but the most widely recognised is the Devanāgarī script, the symbols of which are shown in table 2.2. These are traditionally arranged as follows: symbols for vowels, then for consonants; the latter are subdivided into: stops (five groups of five), semi-vowels, voiceless spirants, *h*. In addition, there are symbols for *ḷ* and *ḥ*. *ṁ* is designated by a dot (*bindu*) over a consonant or a

Table 2.2: Devanāgarī Symbols and their Transliterations

Vowels (*svarāḥ*)

अ	आ	इ	ई	उ	ऊ	ऋ	ॠ	ऌ	ए	ऐ	ओ	औ
a	ā	i	ī	u	ū	ṛ	ṝ	ḷ	e	ai	o	au

Consonants (*vyañjanāni*)

Stops (*sparśāḥ*)					*Semi-vowels* (*antaḥsthāḥ*)	*Spirants* (*ūṣmāṇaḥ*)	*Others*
क	ख	ग	घ	ङ		ह	ः
k	kh	g	gh	ṅ		h	ḥ
च	छ	ज	झ	ञ	य	श	
c	ch	j	jh	ñ	y	ś	
ट	ठ	ड	ढ	ण	र	ष	ळ
ṭ	ṭh	ḍ	ḍh	ṇ	r	ṣ	ḷ
त	थ	द	ध	न	ल	स	
t	th	d	dh	n	l	s	
प	फ	ब	भ	म	व		
p	ph	b	bh	m	v		

Examples of combinations

का	काँ	कि	की	कु	कू	कृ	कॄ	कॢ	क्त	क्र	क्ष	ज्ञ	त्र	त्व	द्य
kā	kāṁ	ki	kī	ku	kū	kṛ	kṝ	kḷ	kta	kra	kṣa	jña	tra	tva	dya

द्र	द्व	प्त	ब्द	र्क	र्कं	श्च	श्र	श्व	स्त	स्य	स्र	स्व	ह्म
dra	dva	pta	bda	rka	rkaṁ	śca	śra	śva	sta	sya	sra	sva	hma

ह्य	ह्र	ह्ल	ह्व	र्त्स्न्य
hya	hra	hla	hva	rtsnya

Numerals

१	२	३	४	५	६	७	८	९	०
1	2	3	4	5	6	7	8	9	0

Note: I have adopted the most generally accepted order of symbols and the subgroupings most widely accepted traditionally; the usual Sanskrit terms for sound classes are given in parentheses.

vowel symbol, nasalisation by a dot within a half-moon (*ardhacandra*) over a symbol; χ φ are designated by ᳵ before symbols for voiceless velars and labials.

In referring to vowels, one pronounces the sounds in question; e.g. '*a*' denotes the vowel *a*. Consonants in general are referred to by a combination of the sounds and a following *a*: e.g., '*ka*' denotes *k*. In addition, a sound name is formed with suffixed *-kāra*; e.g., '*akāra*', '*kakāra*' refer to *a*, *k*.

Certain sounds, however, have particular names: *r ḥ ṁ χ φ*, respectively, are called *repha*, *visarjanīya* (or *visarga*), *anusvāra*, *jihvāmūlīya*, *upadhmānīya*.

Consonant symbols, except those for *ḥ ṁ χ φ*, without any appended element, denote consonants followed by *a*. Other consonant-vowel combinations are designated by consonant symbols with appended vowel symbols, which may precede, follow, or come under the former, as illustrated in table 2.2. There are also ligatures for consonant combinations, some of which are illustrated in table 2.2. Finally, there is a set of Devanāgarī numerals. Variants of symbols are found in different areas.

2.2 Grammar

2.2.1 Introduction

Although many archaic features of earlier Vedic dialects have been eliminated in Sanskrit, the grammatical system nevertheless remains quite rich. Singular, dual and plural forms are distinguished in both the nominal and the verbal systems, and ablaut variations are maintained in many types of formations.

2.2.2 Nominal system

Eight cases can be distinguished, although the vocative does not have a syntactic status comparable to the others: nominative (nom.), vocative (voc.), accusative (acc.), instrumental (inst.), dative (dat.), ablative (abl.), genitive (gen.), locative (loc.), according to traditional western terminology. All eight are formally distinguished in the singular of masculine *a*-stems; e.g. *deva-* 'god': nom. *devas*, voc. *deva*, acc. *devam*, inst. *devena*, dat. *devāya*, abl. *devāt*, gen. *devasya*, loc. *deve*. Otherwise, there are homophonous forms as follows. All stems: dual nom.-voc.-acc., inst.-dat.-abl., gen.-loc.: *deva-*: *devau*, *devābhyām*, *devayos*; *phala-* (nt.) 'fruit': *phale*, *phalābhyām*, *phalayos*; *senā-* (f.) 'army': *sene*, *senābhyām*, *senayos*; *agni-* (m.) 'fire': *agnī*, *agnibhyām*, *agnyos* (similarly *kr̥ti-* (f.) 'deed'); *vāri-* (nt.) 'water': *vāriṇī*, *vāribhyām*, *vāriṇos*; *vāyu-* (m.) 'wind': *vāyū*, *vāyubhyām*, *vāyvos* (similarly *dhenu-* (f.) 'cow'); *madhu-* (nt.) 'honey': *madhunī*, *madhubhyām*, *madhvos*; *devī-* 'goddess': *devyau*, *devībhyām*, *devyos*; *vadhū-* 'bride': *vadhvau*, *vadhūbhyām*, *vadhvos*; *sakhi-* (m.) 'friend': *sakhāyau*, *sakhibhyām*, *sakhyos*; *pitr̥-* 'father': *pitarau*, *pitr̥bhyām*, *pitros* (similarly *mātr̥-* 'mother'); *kartr̥-* 'doer, maker': *kartārau* (m.) *kartr̥ṇī* (nt.), *kartr̥bhyām*, *kartros*; *go-* 'ox, cow': *gāvau*, *gobhyām*, *gavos*; *rājan-* 'king': *rājānau*, *rājabhyām*, *rājños*; *vāc-* (f.) 'voice, speech': *vācau*, *vāgbhyām*, *vācos*; *sraj-* (f.) 'garland': *srajau*, *sragbhyām*, *srajos*; nom.-voc. pl.: *devās*, *phalāni*, *senās*, *agnayas*, *kr̥tayas*, *vārīṇi*, *vāyavas*, *dhenavas*, *madhūni*, *devyas*, *vadhvas*, *sakhāyas*, *pitaras*, *mātaras*, *kartāras* *kartr̥̄ṇi*, *gāvas*, *rājānas*, *vācas*, *srajas*. All stems except personal pronouns:

dat.-abl. pl.: *devebhyas*, *phalebhyas*, *senābhyas* etc. (with *agni-* etc. and *-bhyas*), *rājabhyas*, *vāgbhyas*, *sragbhyas*, but dat. *asmabhyam* 'us', *yuṣmabhyam* 'you', abl. *asmat, yuṣmat*. Nom.-acc. of all numbers for neuter stems: sg. *phalam*, *vāri*, *madhu*, *kartṛ*; for dual and plural see above. Abl.-gen. sg. except for masculine and neuter *a*-stems and personal pronouns: *senāyās*, *agnes*, *kṛtes*/*kṛtyās*, *vāriṇas*, *dhenos*/*dhenvās*, *madhunas*, *devyās*, *vadhvās*, *sakhyus*, *pitus*, *mātus*, *kartus*, *gos*, *rājñas*, *vācas*, *srajas*, but *devāt devasya* (similarly for *phala-*), *mat mama*, *tvat tava*. The accusative plural of feminine *ā*-stems and consonant stems is homophonous with the nominative and vocative plural (see above), but other stems make a distinction: *devān*, *agnīn*, *kṛtīs*, *vāyūn*, *dhenūs*, *devīs*, *vadhūs*, *sakhīn*, *pitṝn*, *mātṝs*, *kartṝn*, *rājñas*. In the singular, a few stems make no distinction between nominative and vocative (e.g. *gaus*, *vāk*, *śrīs* 'splendour, wealth'), but the two are usually distinguished: *devas*, *deva*; *senā*, *sene*; *agnis*, *agne*; *kṛtis*, *kṛte*; *vāri*, *vāre*/*vāri*; *vāyus*, *vāyo*; *dhenus*, *dheno*; *madhu*, *madho*/*madhu*; *devī*, *devi*; *vadhūs*, *vadhu*; *sakhā*, *sakhe*; *pitā*, *pitar* (similarly *mātṛ-*, *kartṛ-*); *rājā*, *rājan*. As can be seen, certain endings have variants according to stems, and this is true of the genitive plural, which has *-ām* after consonant stems (*rājñām*, *vācām*, *srajām*) and some vowel stems (e.g. *śriyām*, *gavām*) but *-nām* after most vowel stems, with lengthening of short vowels before this ending: *devānām*, *phalānām*, *senānām*, *agnīnam* etc.; however, personal pronouns have *-kam* (*asmākam*, *yuṣmākam*), and other pronominals have *-sām* (e.g. *teṣām* 'of them').

Endings are divisible into two groups with respect to phonological and grammatical alternations; nominative, vocative, accusative singular and dual and nominative plural for non-neuter stems as well as the nominative and accusative plural for neuter stems are strong endings, others are weak endings. Consonant-initial weak endings behave phonologically as though they were separated from stems by a word boundary; for example, *as*-stems have variants with *-o* before *-bhyām* (inst.-dat.-abl. du.), *-bhis* (inst. pl.), *-bhyas* (dat.-abl. pl.), *-aḥ* before *-su* (loc. pl.): *manas-* 'mind, spirit': nom.-acc. sg. *manas*, inst. sg. *manasā* but *manobhyām*, *manobhis*, *manaḥsu*.

Stems show variation that in part reflects Proto-Indo-European ablaut alternation. For example: *agni*/*agne-* (*agnay-* before vowels), *vāyu-*/*vāyo-* (*vāyav-*), *sakhi-*/*sakhe-*/*sakhāy*/*sakhā-*, *pitṛ-*/*pitar-*/*pitā-*, *kartṛ-*/*kartar-*/*kartār-*/*kartā-*, *rājan-*/*rājān-*/*rājā-*/*rājñ-* (before vocalic weak endings)/*rāja-* (before consonantal weak endings). There are also heteroclitic stems such as *asthi-*/*asthan-* (nt.) 'bone': nom.-acc. sg. *asthi*, du. *asthinī*, pl. *asthīni*, inst.-dat.-abl. du. *asthibhyām*, etc., with *asthi-* before consonantal weak endings, but inst. sg. *asthnā* etc., with *asthn-* before vocalic weak endings, and loc. sg. *asthani*/*asthni*. Due to the palatalisation of *k*, *g* to *c*, *j* before front vowels prior to the merger of *ĕ* with *ă* and to analogic realignments, there are stems with palatals before vocalic endings and velars elsewhere; e.g. *vāc-*, *sraj-* (see above).

Adjectives generally pattern in the manner of comparable nouns. For example, *śukla-*, *śuklā-* 'white', *śuci-* 'bright', *guru-* 'weighty, heavy', *paṅgū-* 'lame' inflect in the same way as noun stems in *-a*, *-ā*, *-i*, *-u*, *-ū*. There are also consonant stem adjectives with ablaut alternation; e.g. *sant-/sat-* 'being' (m. nom. sg. *san*, nom.-acc. du. *santau*, nom. pl. *santas*, acc. sg. *santam*, acc. pl. *satas*, inst. sg. *satā*, inst.-dat.-abl. du. *sadbhyām*, etc.), *gacchant-/gacchat-* 'going' (*gacchan*, *gacchantau*, *gacchantas*, *gacchantam*, *gacchatas*, *gacchatā*, *gacchadbhyām*, etc.), *vidvans-/vidvāns-/viduṣ-/vidvad-* 'one who knows' (*vidvān*, *vidvan* (voc. sg.), *vidvāṁsau*, *vidvāṁsas*, *vidvāṁsam*, *viduṣā*, *vidvadbhyām*, etc.). In addition, there are adjectives that inflect pronominally. For example, nom. pl. *sarve*, dat. sg. *sarvasmai* (m.-nt.), *sarvasyai* (f.), gen. pl. *sarveṣām*, *sarvāsām*, from *sarvǎ-* 'whole, all', are comparable to *te*, *tasmai*, *tasyai*, *teṣām*, *tāsām* from *tǎ-* 'this, that'.

Personal pronouns not only have variants but also distinguish between independently accented and enclitic forms: acc. sg. *mā tvā*, dat. sg. *me te*, acc.-dat.-gen. du. *nau vām*, acc.-dat.-gen. pl. *nas vas* are enclitics corresponding to sg. acc. *mām tvām*, dat. *mahyam tubhyam*, gen. *mama tava*, du. acc. *āvām yuvām*, dat. *āvābhyām yuvābhyām*, gen. *āvayos yuvayos*, pl. acc. *asmān yuṣmān*, dat. *asmabhyam yuṣmabhyam*, gen. *asmākam yuṣmākam*. Demonstrative pronouns distinguish various degrees of proximity and distance: *etad* 'this here', *idam* 'this', *tad* 'this, that', *adas* 'that yonder' (all nom.-acc. sg. nt.). Interrogative and relative pronouns respectively have *kǎ-*, *yǎ-*, which inflect like pronominal *a*-stems except in the nominative and accusative singular neuter of the former (*kim yad*).

The Sanskrit system of number words is a familiar Indo-European one in that terms for 'one' to 'four' show inflectional and gender variation, but it also differs from the system of other ancient Indo-European languages in that higher number words also inflect; e.g. inst. pl. *pañcabhis* 'five', *ṣaḍbhis* 'six', *saptabhis* 'seven', *aṣṭābhis* 'eight', *navabhis* 'nine', *daśabhis* 'ten'.

Sanskrit is also like other older Indo-European languages in using suffixes for deriving what are traditionally called comparatives and superlatives, with two kinds of suffixes. For example, *garīyas-* 'quite heavy', *gariṣṭha-* 'exceedingly heavy' have *-īyas* and *-iṣṭha* following *gar-*, a form of the base that appears in the adjectival derivative *guru-*, but *-tara* and *-tama* follow adjectival stems, as in *madhumattara-* 'quite sweet', *madhumattama-* 'exceedingly sweet', from the stem *madhumat-*. It is noteworthy that *-tara*, *-tama* are used not only in derivates like *uttara-* 'upper, superior', *uttama-* 'highest', from *ud* 'up', but also in derivates from terms like *na* 'not' and finite verb forms: *natarām* 'the more not so (in view of an additional argument)', *natamām* 'all the more not so', *pacatitarām* 'cooks quite well', *pacatitamām* 'cooks exceedingly well'.

Derived nominal bases formed directly from verb roots include action nouns like *gati-* 'going', *pāka-* 'cooking', agent nouns such as *kartṛ-*, *kāraka-* 'doer, maker', object nouns like *karman-* 'deed, object', instrument nouns such as *karaṇa-* 'means', participles like *gata-* 'gone', *kṛta-* 'done, made', gerunds, gerundives and abstract nouns that function as infinitives (see section 1.2). Bases with secondary derivate affixes (*taddhita* affixes) are of several types. There is a large group of derivates that correspond to phrases of the type *X-E Y-*, with which they alternate, where the values of *X-E* are case forms of particular nominals and *Y* stands for a nominal whose meaning is attributable to the derivational affix. For example, there are patronymics such as *dākṣi-* 'son of Dakṣa': any case form of *dākṣi-* corresponds to and alternates with a phrase containing the genitive *dakṣasya* 'of Daksa' and a form of *putra-* 'son' or a synonym. Other derivatives are formed from a more restricted set of nominals — predominantly pronominals — and correspond to particular case forms; e.g. *tatas* 'from that, thence', *tatra* 'in that, there' correspond respectively to ablative and locative forms of *tad-* 'this, that', with which they alternate. There are also redundant affixes. For example, *aśvaka-* 'nag' differs in meaning from *aśva-* 'horse', but *avika-* and *avi-* 'sheep' show no such semantic difference. Moreover, some taddhita affixes form derivates which do not alternate with forms or phrases containing items to which they are added. Thus, *kṛtrima-* 'artificial' has a suffix *-ma*, but *kṛtrima-* does not alternate with a phrase containing a form of *kṛtri-*, since there is no such action noun: once *-tri* is affixed to *kṛ*, then, *-ma* is obligatory.

Compounds are of four general types: tatpuruṣa (determinative), dvandva (copulative), bahuvrīhi (exocentric), and a type that is usually invariant (avyayībhava). The first member of a tatpuruṣa compound is generally equivalent to a case form other than a nominative. For example, *tatpuruṣas* (nom. sg. m.) 'his man, servant' is equivalent to *tasya puruṣas*, with which it can alternate. Similarly, *grāmagatas* 'gone to the village' is equivalent to *grāmaṁ gatas*, with the accusative *grāmam* 'village'. There is a subtype of tatpuruṣa compounds in which the first member is coreferential with the second, which it modifies, as in *nīlotpalam* 'blue (*nīla-*) lotus', equivalent to *nīlam utpalam*, with two nominatives. Copulative compounds are equivalent to phrases with *ca* 'and'; e.g. *mātāpitarau* 'mother and father' alternates with *mātā pitā ca*. The term *bahuvrīhi* is an example of a bahuvrīhi compound: *bahuvrīhis* is equivalent to *bahur vrīhir asya*, used with reference to someone who has (*asya* 'of this') much (*bahus*) rice (*vrīhis*); similarly: *prāptodaka-* '(somewhere) that water (*udaka-*) has reached (*prāpta-*)', *ūḍharatha-* '(an animal) by which a chariot (*ratha-*) has been drawn (*ūḍha-*)'. There are also exocentric compounds which, for technical reasons, belong to the tatpuruṣa group; e.g. *pañcagava-* 'a group of five cows', a member of the subgroup of tatpuruṣas called *dvigu*. Avyayībhava compounds are generally, though not always, invariant; e.g. *upāgni* 'near the fire', *anujyeṣṭham* 'according to (*anu*) seniority (*jyeṣṭha-* 'oldest')'. Compounds like *upāgni* do not have alternative phrases containing the members of the derivate.

2.2.3 Verbal System

The basic elements on which the Sanskrit verbal system is built are the verb base or root, either primary or derived, and the present-imperfect stem. The root is the base for the present-imperfect stem, for various aorist stems and future formations, the perfect, the conditional and the precative. The present-imperfect stem is the basis not only for present and imperfect forms but also for imperative and optative forms. Although Sanskrit has eliminated quite a few complexities found in Vedic, its verbal system is still varied.

There is a systematic contrast between active and medio-passive. Some verbs take only active endings in agentive forms, others only middle endings. For example, the present *asmi*, *asi*, *asti* (1, 2, 3 sg.), *svas*, *sthas*, *stas* (1, 2, 3 du.), *smas*, *stha*, *santi* (1, 2, 3 pl.) and the imperfect *āsam āsīs āsīt*, *āsva āstam āstām*, *āsma āsta āsan* have only active endings with *as* 'be', and *āse āsse āste*, *āsvahe āsāthe āsāte*, *āsmahe ādhve āsate*, *āsi āsthās āsta*, *āsvahi āsāthām āsātām*, *āsmahi ādhvam āsata* have middle endings with *ās* 'be seated'. Other verbs take either active or middle endings in agentive forms, depending on a semantic contrast: if the result of the act in question is intended for the agent, middle endings are used, if not, active endings occur. For example, *kurute* is used with reference to someone making something for himself, *karoti* of one making something for another. Medio-passive endings alone are used in passives; e.g. *kaṭaḥ kriyate* 'a mat (*kaṭas*) is being made', with *-te* after the passive stem *kriya-*. Sanskrit also has formally passive forms comparable to the impersonal middle found in other Indo-European languages (the type Latin *itur* 'it is gone' i.e. 'one goes'), but it allows an agent to be signified with an instrumental in construction with such forms; e.g. *devadattena supyate* 'Devadatta is sleeping', with the formally passive *supyate* (act. *svapiti*) and the agentive instrumental *devadattena*. In both active and middle sets, three groups of endings are distinguished, which, following usual western terminology, I shall call primary, secondary and perfect endings. Although comparative evidence shows that certain primary endings were originally complexes with a particle, analogic developments have obscured this relation in some instances. The contrast between primary and secondary endings has been illustrated above: primary active; *-mi*, *-si* (*asi* < *as-si*), *-ti*; *-vas*, *-thas*, *-tas*; *-mas*, *-tha*, *-anti*/*ati* (e.g. *juhvati* 'they offer oblations'); secondary active: *-am*, *-s*, *-t* (augmented *-īs -īt*); *-va*, *-tam*, *tām*; *-ma*, *-ta*, *-ant*/*us* (e.g. *ajuhavus* 'they offered oblations', *adus* 'they have given', *akārṣus* 'they have made'); primary medio-passive: *-e*, *-se*, *-te*; *-vahe*, *-āthe*, *-āte*; *-mahe*, *-dhve* (*ādhve* < *ās-dhve*), *-ate*/*ante* (e.g. *edhante* 'they thrive'); secondary medio-passive: *-i*, *-thās*, *-ta*; *-vahi*, *-āthām*, *-ātām*; *-mahi*, *-dhvam*, *-ata*/*anta*. Certain endings are particular to the perfect, as can be seen from the following (*kṛ*): active: *cakăr-a*, *cakar-tha*, *cakār-a*; *cakṛ-va*, *cakr-athus*, *cakr-atus*; *cakṛ-ma*, *cakr-a*, *cakṛ-us*; medio-passive: *cakr-e*, *cakṛ-ṣe*, *cakr-e*; *cakṛ-vahe*, *cakr-āthe*, *cakr-āte*; *cakṛ-*

mahe, *cakr̥ḍhve*, *cakr-ire*.

There is also a contrast between augmented and unaugmented stems. Indicative imperfect and aorist forms, as well as those of the conditional, have augmented stems. The augment is *a* for consonant-initial bases, *ā* for vowel-initial bases; e.g. imperfect *akarot*, aorist *akārṣīt*, conditional *akariṣyat* from *kr̥*, imperfect *āsit* (3 pl. *āsan*) from *as*.

Present-imperfect stems may be considered according to two major criteria. Some stems consist simply of verb roots, others have affixes; some stems exhibit grammatical alternation (ablaut), others do not. Stems that do not show grammatical alternation regularly have suffixes with *-a*: root-accented *bhav-a-* 'be, become' (*bhavāmi*, *bhavasi*, *bhavati*; *bhavāvas*, *bhavathas*, *bhavatas*; *bhavāmas*, *bhavatha*, *bhavanti*); *edh-a-* 'thrive' (*edhe*, *edhase*, *edhate*; *edhāvahe*, *edhethe*, *edhete*; *edhāmahe*, *edhadve*, *edhante*); *dīv-ya-* 'gamble' (*dīvyāmi* etc.); suffix-accented *tud-a-* 'goad, wound' (*tudāmi* etc.), passive *kri-ya-*. Such stems have *-ā* (< **o* by 'Brugmann's Law') before *-v-*, *-m-* of endings and *-e-* in second and third dual medio-passive forms. Root presents generally exhibit ablaut variation: full-grade in the singular active indicative, zero-grade elsewhere. For example: *as-ti*, *s-tas*, *s-anti*; *han-ti*, *ha-tas*, *ghn-anti* (*han* 'kill'); *dveṣ-ṭi*, *dviṣ-ṭas*, *dviṣ-anti*; *dviṣ-ṭe*, *dviṣ-āte*, *dviṣ-ate* (*dviṣ* 'hate'); *dog-dhi*, *dug-dhas*, *duh-anti*; *dug-dhe*, *duh-āte*, *duh-ate* (*duh* 'milk'). On the other hand, *ad* 'eat' has an invariant root stem (*at-ti at-tas ad-anti*) due in the first instance to phonologic developments (e.g. 3 du. **tas* < *ttas* < *d-tas*) that led to remodelling, and bases in *-ā* generalised this vowel in root presents, as in *yāti*, *yātas*, *yānti* (*yā* 'go, travel'). Moreover, there are some verbs with inherited invariant root presents, such as *ās*, *vas* 'have on, wear' (*vas-te*, *vas-āte*, *vas-ate*), *śī* 'lie, recline' (*śe-te*, *śay-āte*, *śe-rate*). Further, root presents of verbs in *-u* have *-au* instead of *-o* in alternation with *-u*; e.g. *stau-ti*, *stu-tas*, *stuv-anti* (*stu* 'praise'). There are also reduplicated stems, as in *juho-ti*, *juhu-tas*, *juhv-ati* (*hu* 'offer oblations'). In addition, ablauting present-imperfect stems are formed with suffixes and an infix. Thus, *śakno-/śaknu-* (*śak* 'be able'), *cino-/cinu-* (*ci* 'gather, heap'), *suno-/sunu-* (*su* 'press juice out of something') have a suffix *-no-/-nu-* (*-nv-* before vowels, *-nuv-* if the root ends in a consonant): *śaknoti*, *śaknutas*, *śaknuvanti*; *cinoti*, *cinutas*, *cinvanti*, *cinute*, *cinvāte*, *cinvate*; *sunoti*, *sunute*, etc. But *chi-na-d-/chi-n-d-* (*chinatti*, *chinttas*, *chindanti*; *chintte*, *chindāte*, *chindate*) shows an infix *-na-/-n-* added to *chid* 'cut'. Stems such as *pu-nā-/pu-nī-/pu-n-* 'purify' (*punāti*, *punītas*, *punanti*, *punīte*, *punāte*, *punate*), with short root vowels (contrast *pū-ta-* 'purified'), reflect an inherited formation with an infix added to a laryngeal base (Proto-Indo-European **-ne-H-/-n-H-*), but the types *krī-ṇā-*... 'buy' (*krīṇāti krīṇite* etc.), *badh-nā-*... 'tie up' (*badhnāti* etc.), with *-nā* etc. after a long vowel (cf. *krī-ta-* 'bought') or a consonant, show that this has been reanalysed as a suffix comparable to *-no-/-nu-*. Historical developments led to the creation of a stem *karo-/kuru-* (*karoti*, *kurutas*, *kurvanti*, *kurute*, *kurvāte*, *kurvate*) from *kr̥*, in addition to the earlier *kr̥ṇo-/kr̥ṇu*, which allowed the abstraction of a suffix *-o/-u-*, as in *tano-/tanu-* (*tanoti*, *tanute* etc.), comparable to *śakno-/śaknu-*, from *tan* 'stretch', although originally this was the same suffix as in the type *śakno-/śaknu-*, only with bases in *-n* (*tano-/tanu-* < **tn̥-neu-/tn̥-nu-*).

Third person active and medio-passive imperative forms respectively have *-u*, *ām* instead of *-i*, *-e* of present indicatives; e.g. *as-tu*, *s-antu*; *ās-tām*, *ās-ātām*, *ās-atām*. However, second singular active imperatives of stems in *-a* have no overt ending: *bhav-a*, *dīv-ya*, *tud-a*. The same is true of the type *ci-nu*. However, if *-u* of the suffix *-nu-* follows a cluster, the imperative retains the ending *-hi*: *śaknuhi*; and this ending has a variant *-dhi* after *juhu-* and consonant-final stems: *juhudhi*, *chindhi* (< *chinddhi*). In addition, following consonant-final stems one has *-āna-* for presents with *-nā-*: *punīhi*, *krīṇīhi*, but *badhāna*. Second singular middle imperatives have a suffix *-sva*: *āssva*, *edhasva*, *cinuṣva*. First person imperative forms are historically subjunctives (see section 1.2): *bhavāni*, *bhavāva*, *bhavāma*; *edhai*, *edhāvahai*, *edhāmahai*. Other forms simply have secondary endings. In addition, there is an imperative with *-tāt* for both second and third singular, which, according to Pāṇini's description, was used in wishing someone well, as in *jīvatāt* 'may you/he live long'.

Stems in *-a* form optatives with *-ī-/-īy-*; other stems have optatives with *-yā-/-y-* in active forms and *-ī-/-īy-* in medio-passive forms. Optatives have the usual secondary endings except for active third plural *-us*, middle first singular *-a*, third plural *-ran*. For example: *bhaveyam*, *bhaves*, *bhavet*, *bhaveva*, *bhavetam*, *bhavetām*, *bhavema*, *bhaveta*, *bhaveyus*; *edheya*, *edhethās*, *edheta*, *edhevahi*, *edheyāthām*, *edheyātām*, *edhemahi*, *edhedhvam*, *edheran*; *syām*, *syās*, *syāt*, *syāva*, *syātam*, *syātām*, *syāma*, *syāta*, *syus* (*as* 'be'); *āsīya*, *āsīthās*, *āsīta*, *āsīvahi*, *āsīyāthām*, *asīyātām*, *āsimahi*, *āsīdhvam*, *āsīran*. Although synchronically the types *bhavet*, *edheta* are analysable as containing *-īy-/-ī-* (*-ey-* < *-a-īy-*, *-e-* < *-a-ī-*), these correspond to optatives elsewhere in Indo-European that point to **-oi-*. In addition, the use of *-yā-* in active and *-ī-* in medio-passive forms represents a redistribution of ablaut variants of an original single affix.

Aorists are either radical or formed with suffixes. Unreduplicated root aorists are rare in Classical Sanskrit as compared with earlier Vedic. Except for the third person singular passive aorist type *akāri* 'has been made' — which is freely formed to any verb, but is not necessarily to be analysed as a root aorist — only active forms of bases in *-ā* (e.g. *dā* 'give': *adāt*, *adātām*, *adus*) and of *bhū* 'be, become' (*abhūt*, *abhūtām*, *abhūvan*) regularly belong to this type, although some middle forms of root aorists have been incorporated into the sigmatic system. There are also stems in *-a*, such as *agama-* (*agamat*, *agamatām*, *agaman*: *gam* 'go'), *aghasa-* (*ghas* 'eat'), *aśaka-* (*śak* 'be able'). In addition, a reduplicated stem in *-a* regularly corresponds to a causative (see below) and supplies aorist forms to a few other verbs; e.g. *adudruva-* (*dru* 'run'). However, the productive Sanskrit aorist formation is sigmatic, of four subtypes: *-s-*, *-iṣ*, *-siṣ-*, *-sa-*. The last developed from the middle of the *s*-aorist of *duh* (e.g. 1 sg. *adhukṣi*, 3 sg. du. pl. *adugdha*, *adhukṣātām*, *adhukṣata*), as can be seen from the earliest usage in Vedic, from the fact that *s*-forms are indeed incorporated into the *sa*-paradigm (e.g. mid. 1 sg. *adhukṣi*, 3 sg. *adugdha/adhukṣata*), and from the fact that this aorist is formed only with verbs that have penultimate *i*, *u*, *ṛ* and final consonants which give *-kṣ-* in combination with the *-s-* of the suffix. The *s*-aorist itself is characterised by particular variants of roots preceding the suffix. Verbs with *-ĭ*, *-ŭ*, *-ṛ* have alternants with *-ai*, *-au*, *-ār* before *-s-* in active forms, and verbs with *-ĭ*, *-ŭ* have variants with *-e*, *-o* in medio-passive forms; e.g. *ci*: *acaiṣīt*, *acaiṣṭām*, *acaiṣus*, *aceṣṭa*, *aceṣātām*, *aceṣata*; *hu*: *ahauṣīt*, *kṛ*: *akārṣīt* (but middle *akṛta akṛṣātām akṛṣata*). Verbs with medial vowels also have alternants with vṛddhi vowels in active forms, but they have medio-passives with *-a-*, *-i-*, *-u-*, *-ṛ-*; e.g. *pac* 'cook': *apākṣīt*, *chid*: *achaitsit*, *rudh* 'obstruct': *arautsit*, *mṛṣ* 'suffer, allow': *amārṣīt* versus *apakta*, *achitta*, *aruddha*, *amṛṣṭa*. Forms such as *akṛta*, *adita* (*dā* 'give') beside *akṛṣātām*, *adiṣātām* etc. and active *adāt* etc. reflect the incorporation of root aorist forms into the productive sigmatic system. The *iṣ*-aorist is probably best considered originally an *s*-formation to verbs with *-i* from a laryngeal, then spread well beyond these limits. This also has vṛddhi vowels in forms such as *apāvīt*, *apāviṣṭām*, *apāviṣus* (*pū*), but in general not for consonant-final bases; e.g. *div* 'gamble': *adevīt*. The *siṣ*-aorist, obviously a combination of *-s-* and *-iṣ-*, is of very limited compass, predominantly from verbs in *-ā*; e.g. *ayāsīt* (*yā*).

Although scholars disagree concerning the historical origins of the precative, the place of the forms in question within the Sanskrit system viewed synchronically is fairly clear. The active precative type *bhuyāt*, *bhuyāstām*, *bhuyāsus* 'may... be, prosper' is radical, and the middle type *edhiṣīṣta*, *edhiṣīyāstām*, *edhiṣīran* 'may... thrive' is sigmatic.

The semantically unmarked future of Sanskrit has a suffix *-(i)ṣya* after a root. In addition, there is a future used with reference to a time beyond the day of reference. In origin, this is a periphrastic formation (see section 1.2), but synchronically it cannot be treated as such in view of forms like *edhitāhe*, *edhitāsve*, *edhitāsmahe* (1 sg. du. pl. mid.), since *as* does not regularly have middle inflection. The future in *-(i)ṣya* (e.g., *bhaviṣyati*, *edhiṣyate*) is the basis for the Sanskrit conditional, of the type *abhaviṣyat*, *aidhiṣyata* — with augment and secondary endings — used in both the protasis and the apodosis of contrary-to-fact conditional sentences.

The Sanskrit perfect is generally characterised not only by particular endings but also by reduplication (see above). Yet one inherited perfect, which in Sanskrit functions as a present, lacks reduplication: *veda*, *vidatus*, *vidus* 'know(s)'. As can be seen, perfect stems show the same kind of grammatical alternation as found in present and aorist stems. However, for verbs of the structure C*a*C, in which *-a-* is flanked by single consonants the first of which is not subject to modification in a reduplicated syllable, instead of -CC- preceded by a reduplicated syllable, one has C*e*C alone; e.g. *tan*: *tatāna*, *tenatus*, *tenus*; *śak*: *śasāka*, *śekatus*, *śekus* (contrast *gam*: *jagāma*, *jagmatus*, *jagmus*). This represents the spread of a particular form from verbs like *yam* 'extend' (*yayāma*, *yematus* (< *ya-ym-*) ...), *sad* 'sit' (*sasada*, *sedatus* (< *sa-zd-*) ...). There is also a periphrastic perfect, which in Sanskrit has been extended to some primary verbs; e.g. *hu*: *juhavāñ cakāra* beside *juhāva*.

As can be seen from what has been said, it is not possible in Sanskrit to predict an aorist formation from the present-imperfect stem of a verb. There are instances where totally separate roots are used suppletively in different formations. Thus, *as* supplies only a present-imperfect stem; other forms are from *bhū* 'be, become': aorist *abhūt*, future *bhaviṣyati*, perfect *babhūva*, infinitive *bhavitum*, past participle *bhūta-* etc. Similarly: *han* 'strike, kill': aorist *avadhīt*, precative *vadhyāt*, *ad* 'eat': aorist *aghasat*, *i*: aorist *agāt*.

Derived verbs are deverbative or denominative. Causatives are formed with *-i-*/*-e-*; e.g. *kr̥*: *kār-i* 'have ... do, make' (*kār-ay-a-ti*, *kār-ay-ate*), *pac*: *pāc-i*, *chid*: *ched-i*, *yuj-* 'connect, yoke': *yoj-i*. Certain verbs have augmented variants before the causative suffix. For example, many verbs with *-ā* take the augment *-p*, as in *dāp-i* 'have ... give' (*dā*). The causative is also connected with a particular active aorist formation, a reduplicated *a*-aorist; e.g. *kār-i*: *acīkarat* etc. (but medio-passive *akārayita*, *akārayiṣātām*, etc.). Desideratives are formed with *-sa-*, which conditions reduplication; e.g. *kr̥*: *cikīrṣa-* (*cikīrṣati*, etc.). Desiderative forms alternate with phrases consisting of a verb meaning 'wish' and infinitives; e.g. *cikīrṣati* = *kartum icchati* '... wishes to do, make'. Intensives are formed with *-ya-*, which also conditions a particular type of reduplication; further, intensives have middle inflection; e.g. *kr̥*: *cekrīya-* (*cekrīyate*) 'do intensely, repeatedly', *chid*: *cechidya-*, *yuj*: *yoyujya-*, *pac*: *pāpacya-*. Derived verbs form periphrastic perfects, as in *gamayāñ cakāra*, *cekrīyāñ cakre*. Moreover, such deverbative formations can involve suppletion; e.g. *ad*: desiderative *jighatsa-*, *i*: *jigamiṣa-*. Denominatives are formed with several suffixes, principal among which is *-ya-*, and have a broad range of meanings. For example, *putrīyati* (*putrīya-*) corresponds to *putram icchati* '... desires a son', *putram ivācarati* '... behaves (*ācarati*) towards ... as though he were his son (*putram iva*)'; *śyenāyate* corresponds to *śyena ivācarati* 'behaves like a falcon (*śyena iva*)', *tapasyati* is equivalent to *tapaś carati* 'carries out (*carati*) ascetic acts (*tapas*).' Especially noteworthy in view of the later Indo-Aryan causative type in *-āv-e-* (see section 2.2 of the chapter on Indo-Aryan) is the denominative type *satyāpi-* (*satyāpayati*) 'say something is true (*satya*)', known already to Pāṇini, which involves *-āp-* and the suffix *-i-*/*-e-*.

2.2.4 Syntax

In major aspects of syntax Sanskrit is a fairly conservative Indo-European language, although it exhibits specifically Indic features. Examples given in the following sketch are based on Pāṇinian sources, reflecting usage that antedates classical literary works, but every construction illustrated has a counterpart in Vedic (see section 1.2) and literary texts of later times.

The seven cases of the nominal system excluding the vocative (section 2.2.2) are used with reference to various roles participants play in respect of what is signified by verbs in general or by particular verbs. Typical roles and case forms linked with them are illustrated by the following. In *devadattaḥ kaṭaṁ karoti* 'Devadatta is making (*karoti*) a mat (*kaṭam*)', *devadatto grāmaṁ gacchati* 'Devadatta is going (*gacchati*) to the village (*grāmam*)', the accusatives *kaṭam, grāmam* refer to objects, the latter specifically to a goal of movement. Such a goal is alternatively signified by a dative: *devadatto grāmāya gacchati*. In addition, an object can be designated by a genitive in construction with an agent noun; e.g. *sa kumbhānāṃ kartā* 'he (*sa*) (is) a maker (*kartā*) of pots (*kumbhānām*)'. In the passive sentence *devadattena kaṭaḥ kriyate* 'a mat is being made (*kriyate*) by Devadatta', the instrumental *devadattena* refers to an agent, as does the same form in *devadattena supyate* (section 2.2.3). The instrumental *dātreṇa* 'sickle' of *dātreṇa lunāti* '...cuts (*lunāti*) with a sickle', on the other hand, refers to a means of cutting. A dative can be used with references not only to a goal of movement but also to a desired object, in construction with *spr̥h* 'yearn for': *puṣpebhyaḥ spr̥hayati* '... yearns for flowers (*puṣbebhyas*)'. More generally, dative forms designate indirect objects, as in *māṇavakāya bhikṣāṁ dadāti* '... gives (*dadāti*) alms (*bhikṣām*) to the lad (*māṇavakāya*)'. Ablatives can be used to signify points of departure, as in *grāmād ā gacchati* '...is coming (*ā gacchati*) from the village', but they have other functions as well; for example, in *vr̥kebhyo bibheti* '... is afraid (*bibheti*) of wolves', *vr̥kebhyas* refers to wolves as sources of fear. Locative forms are used of loci where agents and objects are while they are involved in whatever a verb signifies; e.g. *devadattaḥ sthālyāṁ gr̥ha odanaṁ pacati* 'Devadatta is cooking (*pacati*) rice (*odanam*) in a pot (*sthālyām*) in the house (*gr̥he*)'.

There are also relations that do not directly involve verb meanings, so that syntactically one has nominals directly linked with each other. The typical case form for such relations is the genitive; e.g. *vr̥kṣasya śākhā-* 'branch (*śākhā-*) of a/the tree (*vr̥kṣasya*)' in *vr̥kṣasya śākhāṁ paraśunā chinatti* '... is cutting a branch (*śākhām*) of the tree with an axe (*paraśunā*)'. Particular nominals, however, co-occur with other case forms. For example, *namo devebhyaḥ* '(let there be) homage (*namas*) to the gods' has the dative *devebhyas* in construction with *namas*. Moreover, pre- and postposed particles take part in such constructions: *sādhur devadatto mātaraṁ prati* 'Devadatta (is) good (*sadhus*) towards his mother (*mātaraṁ prati*)', *putreṇa sahāgataḥ* 'he came (*āgatas*) with his son (*putreṇa saha*)', *māṣān asmai tilebhyaḥ prati dadāti* '... gives (*dadāti*) this man (*asmai*) māṣa-beans (*māṣān*) in exchange for sesame seeds (*tilebhyaḥ prati*)', *ā pāṭaliputrād varṣati* 'it is raining (*varṣati*) up to Pāṭaliputra (*ā pāṭaliputrāt*)', have the accusative *mātaram* linked to *prati*, the instrumental *putreṇa* connected to *saha*, and the ablatives *tilebhyas*, *pāṭaliputrāt* construed with *prati* and *ā*.

There are different kinds of complex sentences. Some involve related finite verb forms, others finite forms connected with particular nominal derivates, infinitival and participial. For example, optatives are used in conditional sentences such as *mriyeya* ... *na syās tvaṁ yadi me gatiḥ* 'I would die (*mriyeya*) if (*yadi*) you (*tvam*) were (*syās*) not (*na*) my (*me*) refuge (*gatis*)', but *edhān āhartum gacchati* '... is going (*gacchati*) in order to fetch (*āhartum*) firewood (*edhān*)' has *gacchati* linked to the infinitive *āhartum*, itself connected with the accusative *edhān*. There is an elliptical version of the second sentence type, with a dative referring to the direct object in question: *edhebhyo gacchati* '... is going for firewood'. Present participle forms occur in complex sentences such as *pacantaṁ devadattam paśyati* '... is watching (*paśyati*) Devadatta cook', in which *pacantam* 'cooking' agrees with *devadattam*, or *grāmaṁ gacchatā devadattena bhuktam* 'Devadatta ate on his way to the village', where the participial form *gacchatā* 'going' agrees with the agentive instrumental *devadattena*, both construed with *bhuktam* 'eaten'. In addition, Sanskrit has absolute constructions, the prevalent one being a locative absolute, as in *goṣu duhyamānāsu gataḥ* 'he left (*gatas*) while the cows were being milked': the present participle *duhyamānāsu* (loc. pl. f.) agrees with *goṣu* 'cows', both used absolutely. Where two or more verbs signify sequentially related acts or states, Sanskrit subordinates by using gerunds; e.g. *bhuktvā vrajati* '... eats before going out', with the gerund *bhuktvā* 'after eating', *piba niṣadya* (see section 1.2).

Examples cited illustrate the agreement features of Sanskrit. Finite verb forms — which themselves signal person and number differences — agree in person and number with nominals that function as grammatical subjects used in referring to agents or objects. Participial forms and other adjectivals, whether attributive or predicative, agree in gender and number with the nominals to which they are complements. The examples also illustrate the most common aspects of Sanskrit word order. What may be called the neutral word order in prose, where metrical constraints are not at play, generally has the verb in last position. However, a sentence does not necessarily have an overt verb: Sanskrit has nominal sentences, in which a third person present form of a verb meaning 'be' is not overtly expressed. There are few restrictions on word order that are strictly formal, but the position of certain particles is fixed: particles like *vai* 'as is known, truly', *ced* 'if ' occupy second position, as does *ca* 'and' used as a sentence connective. Similarly, the enclitic pronouns *mā*, *tvā* etc. (section 2.2.2) are excluded from sentence-initial position.

An aspect of overall sentence prosody is worth noting in this context. A sentence-internal vocative generally has no high-pitched vowel. Under certain conditions, however, the vowels of an utterance are all pronounced monotone, except for the last vowel, which is then not only high-pitched but also prolated. For example, in *ā gaccha bho māṇavaka devadatta* 'come along (*ā gaccha*), Devadatta my boy (*bho māṇavaka devadatta*)', used in calling Devadatta from afar, all the vowels up to the *-a* of the vocative *devadatta* are uttered without pitch variations, but this last vowel is prolated and udātta.

Bibliography

Burrow (1965) is a summary of the prehistory and history of Sanskrit, including Vedic, with references to Middle Indo-Aryan; somewhat personal views are given in places, but the work remains valuable. For a good summary of views on the dialects of Old Indo-Aryan, with discussion of theories proposed and references, see Emeneau (1966).

The standard reference grammar is Whitney (1889). Renou (1956) is an insightful summary of the grammar, vocabulary and style of different stages of Sanskrit, including Vedic, with text selections and translations. Wackernagel (1896–) is the most thorough reference grammar of Sanskrit, but remains incomplete: the published volumes are: I (*Lautlehre*), reissued with a new 'Introduction générale' by L. Renou and 'Nachträge' by A. Debrunner (1957); II, 1 (*Einleitung zur Wortlehre, Nominalkomposition*), 2nd ed. with 'Nachträge' by A. Debrunner (1957); II, 2 (*Die Nominalsuffixe*), by A. Debrunner (1954); III (*Nominalflexion – Zahlwort – Pronomen*) (1930); there is also a *Register zur altindischen Grammatik von J. Wackernagel und A. Debrunner* by R. Hauschild (1964).

References

Burrow, T. 1965. *The Sanskrit Language*, 2nd ed. (Faber and Faber, London)

Emeneau, M.B. 1966. 'The Dialects of Old Indo-Aryan', in H. Birnbaum and J. Puhvel (eds.), *Ancient Indo-European Dialects* (University of California Press, Berkeley and Los Angeles), pp. 123–38.

Renou, L. 1956. *Histoire de la langue sanskrite* (IAC, Paris)

Wackernagel, J. 1896–. *Altindische Grammatik* (Vandenhoek and Ruprecht, Göttingen)

Whitney, W.D. 1889. *Sanskrit Grammar, Including Both the Classical Language and the Older Dialects, of Veda and Brahmana*, 2nd ed. (Harvard University Press, Cambridge, Mass.)

3 *Hindi-Urdu*

Yamuna Kachru

1. Introduction

Hindi is a New Indo-Aryan language spoken in the north of India. It belongs to the Indo-Iranian branch of the Indo-European family of languages. It is spoken by more than two hundred million people either as a first or second language in India, and by peoples of Indian origin in Trinidad, Guyana, Fiji, Mauritius, South Africa and other countries. Along with English, it is the official language of India. In addition, it is the state language of Bihar, Haryana, Himachal Pradesh, Madhya Pradesh, Rajasthan and Uttar Pradesh.

Urdu, a language closely related to Hindi, is spoken by twenty-three million people in India and approximately eight million people in Pakistan as a mother tongue. It is the official language of Pakistan and the state language of the state of Jammu and Kashmir in India.

It is difficult to date the beginnings of the New Indo-Aryan languages of India. Scholars generally agree that the development of Indo-Aryan languages of India took place in three stages. The Old Indo-Aryan stage is said to extend from 1500 BC to approximately 600 BC. The Middle Indo-Aryan stage spans the centuries between 600 BC and AD 1000. The Middle Indo-Aryan stage is further subdivided into an early Middle Indo-Aryan stage (600–200 BC), a transitional stage (200 BC–AD 200), a second Middle Indo-Aryan stage (AD 200–600), and a late Middle Indo-Aryan stage (AD 600–1000). The period between AD 1000–1200/1300 is designated the Old New Indo-Aryan stage because it is at this stage that the changes that began at the Middle Indo-Aryan stage became established and the New Indo-Aryan languages such as Hindi, Bengali, Marathi etc. assumed distinct identities.

Before proceeding with a description of Hindi-Urdu, it may be useful to sketch briefly the sociolinguistic situation of Hindi-Urdu in the Indian subcontinent (Rai 1984).

The name Hindi is not Indian in origin; it is believed to have been used by the Persians to denote the peoples and languages of India (Verma 1933). Hindi as a language is said to have emerged from the patois of the market place and army camps during the period of repeated Islamic invasions and establishment of Muslim rule in the north of India between the eighth and tenth centuries AD. The speech of the areas around Delhi, known as *khaṛī bolī*, was adopted by the Afghans, Persians and Turks as a common language of interaction with the local population. In time, it developed a variety called *urdū* (from Turkish *ordu* 'camp'). This variety, naturally, had a preponderance of borrowings from Arabic and Persian. Consequently, it was also known as *rextā* 'mixed language'. The speech of the indigenous population, though influenced by Arabic and Persian, remained relatively free from large-scale borrowings from these foreign languages. In time, as Urdu gained some patronage at Muslim courts and developed into a literary language, the variety used by the general population gradually replaced Sanskrit, literary Prakrits and Apabhraṁśas as the literary language of the midlands (*madhyadeśa*). This latter variety looked to Sanskrit for linguistic borrowings and Sanskrit, Prakrits and Apabhraṁśas for literary conventions. It is this variety that became known as Hindi. Thus, both Hindi and Urdu have their origins in the *khaṛī bolī* speech of Delhi and its environs although they are written in two different scripts (Urdu in Perso-Arabic and Hindi in Devanāgarī). The two languages differ in minor ways in their sound system, morphology and syntax. These differences are pointed out at appropriate places below.

Hindi and Urdu have a common form known as Hindustani which is essentially a colloquial language (Verma 1933). This was the variety that was adopted by Mahatma Gandhi and the Indian National Congress as a symbol of national identity during the struggle for freedom. It, however, never became a language of literature and high culture (see Bhatia 1987 for an account of the Hindi-Urdu-Hindustani controversy in the late nineteenth and early twentieth centuries).

Both Urdu and Hindi have been in use as literary languages since the twelfth century. The development of prose, however, begins only in the eighteenth century under the influence of English, which marks the emergence of Hindi and Urdu as fully-fledged literary languages.

2 Phonology

The segmental phonemes of Hindi-Urdu are listed in table 3.1. The phonemes that occur only in the highly Sanskritised or highly Persianised varieties are given in parentheses. The two noteworthy features of the inventory of consonant phonemes are the following: Hindi-Urdu still retains the original Indo-European distinction between aspirated and unaspirated voiced plosives (cf. Indo-European **ghr̥dho* and Hindi *ghər* 'house'). It retains the distinction between aspirated and unaspirated voiceless plosives that emerged in Indo-Aryan, i.e. the distinction between *kal* 'time' and *khal* 'skin'. Another Indo-Aryan feature, that of retroflexion, is also retained in Hindi-Urdu, cf. *tota* 'parrot' and *ṭoṭa* 'lack'. These two features, i.e. those of aspiration and retroflexion, are mainly responsible for why Hindi-Urdu sounds so different from its European cousins.

Table 3.1: Phonemes of Hindi-Urdu

Vowels

	Front	*Centre*	*Back*
High	i		u
	ɪ		ʊ
Mid High	e		o
Mid Low	ɛ	ə	ɔ
Low		a	

Consonants

			Labial	*Dental*	*Retro-flex*	*Alveo-Palatal*	*Velar*	*Back Velar*
Stop	vls.	unasp.	p	t	ṭ	č	k	(q)
		asp.	ph	th	ṭh	čh	kh	
	vd.	unasp.	b	d	ḍ	ǰ	g	
		asp.	bh	dh	ḍh	ǰh	gh	
Nasal			m	n	(ṇ)	(ñ)	(ŋ)	
Flap	vd.	unasp.			ṛ	r		
		asp.			ṛh			
Lateral						l		
Fricative	vls.		(f)	s	(ṣ)	š	(x)	
	vd.			(z)		(ž)	(γ)	
Semi-vowels			w (v)			y		

Note: Oral and nasal vowels contrast, e.g. *ak* 'a plant' and *ãk* 'draw, sketch'; hence, nasalisation is distinctive. Short and long consonants contrast, e.g. *pəta* 'address', *pətta* 'leaf'; hence, length is distinctive.

The contrast between aspirated and unaspirated consonants is maintained in all positions, initial, medial and final. The distinction between tense *i* and lax *ɪ* and tense *u* and lax *ʊ*, however, is lost in the final position except in very careful and formal speech in the highly Sanskritised variety.

Stress is not distinctive in Hindi-Urdu; words are not distinguished on the basis of stress alone. For instance, a word such as *kəla* 'art', whether stressed as *'kəla* or *kə'la*, means the same. The tense vowels are phonetically long and in pronunciation the vowel quality as well as length is maintained irrespective of the position of the vowel or stress in the word. For instance, the word *mʊskərahəṭ* 'smile' can either be stressed as *'mʊskərahəṭ* or *mʊskə'rahəṭ*, in either case, the vowel quality and length in the syllable *-ra-*

remains unaffected. Words such as *ǰamata* 'son-in-law' are pronounced with three successive long vowels although only the first or the second syllable is stressed. Stressing and destressing of syllables is tied to syllable weight in Hindi-Urdu. Syllables are classified as one of the three measures of weight: light (syllables ending in a lax, short vowel), medium (syllables ending in a tense, long vowel or in a lax, short vowel followed by a consonant) and heavy (others). Where one syllable in a word is of greater weight than others, the tendency is to place the word stress on it. Where more than one syllable is of maximum weight in the word (i.e. there is a succession of medium or heavy syllables), usually the last but one bears the word stress. This stress pattern creates the impression of the staccato rhythm that speakers of English notice about Hindi-Urdu.

The predominant pattern of penultimate stress in Hindi-Urdu is inherited from an earlier stage of Indo-Aryan, i.e. the Middle Indo-Aryan stage. Old Indo-Aryan had phonemic accent of the pitch variety and there is evidence for three pitches in Vedic: *udātta* 'high, raised', *anudātta* 'low, unraised' and *svarita* 'high falling, falling' (see section 2.1 of the chapter on Sanskrit). At a later stage of Old Indo-Aryan, Classical Sanskrit does not record accent. By late Old Indo-Aryan, pitch accent seems to have given way to stress accent. There are different opinions about stress accent in Middle Indo-Aryan. It is generally believed that stress occurred on the penultimate syllable of the word, if long, or on the nearest preceding syllable if the penultimate was not long; in words with all short syllables, stress occured on the initial syllable.

Syllable boundaries in Hindi-Urdu words fall as follows: between successive vowels, e.g. *pa-e* 'legs', *a-ɪ-e* 'come' (hon.), *nə-i* 'new' (f.), *so-ɪ-e* 'sleep' (hon.); between vowels and following consonants, e.g. *ro-na* 'to cry', *pə-ta* 'address', *ū-ča* 'tall, high'; between consonants, e.g. *səṛ-kẽ* 'roads', *pət-la* 'thin', *hɪn-di* 'Hindi language'.

As has already been said, Hindi is written in the Devanāgarī script, which is the script used by Sanskrit, Marathi and Nepali also. On the basis of the evidence obtained from the ancient inscriptions, it is clear that Devanāgarī is a descendant of the Brāhmī script. Brāhmī was well established in India some time before 500 BC. Despite some controversy regarding the origin of the Brāhmī script, it is generally believed that its sources lie in the same Semitic script which later developed into the Arabic, Hebrew, Greek, Latin scripts etc. The scripts used for the New Indo-Aryan and the Dravidian languages of India are believed to have developed from the northern and southern varieties of Brāhmī.

There are minor differences between the scripts used for Hindi, Sanskrit, Marathi and Nepali. For instance, Hindi does not have the retroflex lateral ळ or the retroflex vowels ॠ, ऌ and ॡ. It uses the retroflex vowel symbol ऋ and the symbol for weak aspiration : only in words borrowed from Sanskrit. Although written as ऋ, the vowel is pronounced as a combination of *r* and *ɪ*.

In general, there is a fairly regular correspondence between the script and the pronunciation. The one notable exception is the pronunciation of the inherent vowel *ə*. The Devanāgarī script is syllabic in that every consonant symbol represents the consonant plus the inherent vowel *ə*, thus, the symbol क represents the sound *k* plus *ə*, or *kə*. Vowels are represented differently according to whether they comprise entire syllables or are parts of syllables, i.e. are immediately preceded by a consonant: thus, the symbol ई represents the syllable *i*, but in the syllable *ki*, it has the shape ी which is adjoined to the symbol for *k*, resulting in की. Even though each consonant symbol represents a consonant plus the inherent vowel, a word written as कल, i.e. *kələ*, is not pronounced as *kələ*, it is pronounced as *kəl* 'yesterday, tomorrow'. That is, all the final inherent vowels are dropped in pronunciation. The rules regarding the realisation of the inherent vowel in pronunciation are as follows; in two or three syllable words, the penultimate inherent vowel is pronounced when the final one is dropped, and in words of four syllables, both the final and the antepenultimate inherent vowels are dropped while the others are pronounced. Thus, *səməǰhə* is pronounced as *səməǰh* 'understanding', *mehənətə* is pronounced as *mehnət* 'hard work'. These general principles, however, do not apply to words containing medial *h*, loanwords, compounds and words formed with derivational suffixes. For instance, *səməǰh* with the inflectional suffix of perfective *-a* is pronounced as *səmǰha* 'understood', but with the derivational agentive suffix *-dar* is pronounced *səməǰhdar* 'sensible' (see Ohala (1983) for details of *ə*-deletion).

Although most derivational and inflectional morphology of Hindi is affixal in nature (i.e. Hindi mostly utilises prefixes and suffixes), there are remnants of the morphophonemic ablaut alternation of vowels of the *guṇa* and *vrddhi* type in a substantial number of verbal roots and nominal compounds in Hindi. These are the most frequent and regular of vowel changes for derivation as well as inflection in Sanskrit. A *guṇa* vowel differs from a simple vowel by a prefixed *a*-element which is combined with the other according to the usual rules; a *vrddhi* vowel, by the further prefixation to a *guṇa* vowel. *a* is its own *guṇa* and *ā* remains unchanged for both *guṇa* and *vrddhi*. The series of corresponding degrees is as follows (Kellogg 1875):

Simple vowels:	a	ā	i	ī	u	ū	r̥	l̥
guṇa vowels:	a	ā	e		o		ar	al
vr̥ddhi vowels:	ā		ai		au		ār	

The *guṇa* increment is an Indo-European phenomenon, the *vr̥ddhi* increment is specifically Indian in origin. These processes are still utilised to some extent in coining new compounds of borrowings from Sanskrit for modernising Hindi. Some examples of the verbal roots that exemplify these processes are pairs such as *khʊl* 'open' (intr.) and *khol* 'open' (tr.); *kəṭ* 'cut' (intr.) and *kaṭ* 'cut' (tr.), *dɪkh* 'be visible' and *dekh* 'see'; and some examples of nominal compounds are *pərəmə* + *išvərə* = *pərəmešvər* 'Supreme God'; *məha* + *išə* = *məheš* 'Great God' (a name of Šiva); *səda* + *evə* = *sədɛv* 'always'. Some examples of modern vocabulary coined on the same principles are *sərvə* + *udəyə* = *sərvodəy* 'universal welfare', *mətə* + *ɛkyə* = *mətɛky* 'unanimity of opinion', *šʊbhə* + *ɪččhʊ* = *šʊbheččhʊ* 'well wisher'.

Table 3.2 gives the Devanāgarī script as used for Hindi:

Table 3.2: Chart of Devanāgarī Alphabet

Vowels
Independent

अ	आ	इ	ई	उ	ऊ	ऋ
ə	a	ɪ	i	ʊ	u	rɪ
ए	ऐ	ओ	औ	अं	अः	
e	ɛ	o	ɔ	əm	əh	

Following Consonant

ा	ि	ी	ु	ू	े	ै	ो	ौ	ं	ः
a	ɪ	i	ʊ	u	e	ɛ	o	ɔ	əm	əh

Consonants

क	ख	ग	घ	ङ			
kə	khə	gə	ghə	ŋə			
च	छ	ज	झ	ञ			
čə	čhə	ǰə	ǰhə	ñə			
ट	ठ	ड	ढ	ण			
ṭə	ṭhə	ḍə	ḍhə	ṇə			
त	थ	द	ध	न			
tə	thə	də	dhə	nə			
प	फ	ब	भ	म			
pə	phə	bə	bhə	mə			
य	र	ल	व	श	ष	स	ह
yə	rə	lə	və	šə	ṣə	sə	hə
क़	ख़	ग़	ज़	फ़			
qə	xə	ɣə	zə	fə			

To the extent that it shares a basic vocabulary with Hindi, the *guṇa* and *vr̥ddhi* phenomena are applicable to Urdu as well. The Urdu writing system, however, is based on the Perso-Arabic script. As is clear from table 3.3, the script lacks adequate vowel symbols but has an overabundance of consonant symbols for the language. Table 3.3 lists the independent forms only (see also the discussion of script in the chapters on Arabic and Persian).

Table 3.3: The Urdu Alphabet

Letter	*Pronunciation*	*Urdu Name*
ا	a*	əlyf
ب	b	be
پ	p	pe
ت	t	te
ٹ	ṭ	ṭe
ث	s	se
ج	ǰ	ǰim
چ	č	če
ح	h	he [/bəṛi he/]
خ	x	xe
د	d	dal
ڈ	ḍ	ḍal
ذ	z	zal
ر	r	re
ڑ	ṛ	ṛe
ز	z	ze
ژ	ž	že
س	s	sin
ش	š	šin
ص	s	swad
ض	z	zwad
ط	t	to, toe
ظ	z	zo, zoe
ع	*	əyn
غ	γ	γəyn
ف	f	fe
ق	q	qaf
ک	k	kaf
گ	g	gaf
ل	l	lam
م	m	mim
ن	n	nun
و	v	vao
ہ	h	he [/choṭi he/]
ی	y	ye

Note: əlyf is pronounced as *ā* following a consonant; əyn is either not pronounced at all or given the value of *a* or *ā* following a consonant. It is pronounced as a glottal stop only in High Urdu.

3 Morphology

A brief description of Hindi-Urdu nominal and verbal morphology follows (for a detailed discussion of derivational and inflectional morphology, see McGregor (1972), Sharma (1958) and Bailey (1956)).

3.1 Nominal

Forms of Hindi-Urdu nouns undergo changes in order to indicate number, gender and case. There are two numbers, singular and plural; two genders, masculine and feminine; and three cases, direct, oblique and vocative. Nouns are declined differently according to the gender class and the phonological property of the final segment in the word. Given here are paradigms of the major classes of masculine and feminine nouns.

Paradigm of Masculine Nouns Ending in *-a*

	Sg.	*Pl.*
Dir.	ləṛka 'boy'	ləṛke
Obl.	ləṛke	ləṛkõ
Voc.	ləṛke	ləṛko

Ending in *-i*

Dir.	mali 'gardener'	mali
Obl.	mali	malıyõ
Voc.	mali	malıyo

Ending in *-u*

Dir.	saṛhu 'wife's sister's husband'	saṛhu
Obl.	saṛhu	saṛhʊõ
Voc.	saṛhu	saṛhʊo

Ending in a consonant

Dir.	nɔkər 'servant'	nɔkər
Obl.	nɔkər	nɔkərõ
Voc.	nɔkər	nɔkəro

Certain masculine nouns ending in *-a* such as *rağa* 'king' and kinship terms such as *pıta* 'father', *čača* 'father's younger brother', *mama* 'mother's brother' are exceptions in that they do not change for direct plural and oblique singular in modern standard Hindi.

Paradigm of Feminine Nouns Ending in *-i*

	Sg.	*Pl.*
Dir.	ləṛki 'girl'	ləṛkıyã
Obl.	ləṛki	ləṛkıyõ
Voc.	ləṛki	ləṛkıyo

Ending in *-a*

Dir.	mata 'mother'	mataẽ
Obl.	mata	mataõ
Voc.	mata	matao

Ending in *-u*

Dir.	bəhu 'daughter-in-law'	bəhʊẽ
Obl.	bəhu	bəhʊõ
Voc.	bəhu	bəhʊo

Ending in a consonant

Dir.	bəhən 'sister'	bəhnẽ
Obl.	bəhən	bəhnõ
Voc.	bəhən	bəhno

In Perso-Arabic borrowings, High Urdu keeps the Perso-Arabic plural markers, e.g. *kaγəz* 'paper': *kaγzat* 'papers'.

The oblique case forms are used whenever a noun is followed by a postposition, e.g. *ləṛke ko* 'to the boy', *ghərõ mẽ* 'in the houses', *ləṛkɪyõ ke sath* 'with the girls' etc.

The adjectives occur before the noun and agree with their head noun in number, gender and case. They do not, however, exhibit the full range of forms. This can be seen in the paradigm of *əččhA* 'good' (*A* is a cover symbol for the various inflections).

əččhA 'good'

	Masculine		*Feminine*	
	Sg.	Pl.	Sg.	Pl.
Dir.	əččha	əččhe	əččhi	əččhi
Obl.	əččhe	əččhe	əččhi	əččhi
Voc.	əččhe	əččhe	əččhi	əččhi

The adjectives that end in a consonant, e.g. *sʊndər* 'beautiful', and in a vowel other than *-a*, e.g. *nəkli* 'false, artificial', are invariant, e.g. *sʊndər ləṛka/ləṛki* 'handsome boy/beautiful girl', *nəkli dãt* (m.)/*bãh* (f.) 'artificial teeth/arm'.

The main postpositions that indicate case relations such as accusative, dative, instrumental etc. are the following: *ne* 'agentive, marker of a transitive subject in the perfective', *ko* 'accusative/dative', *se* 'instrumental/ablative/comitative', *mẽ*, *pər* 'locative', *kA* 'possessive/genitive', and *ke lɪye* 'benefactive'. There are several other postpositions that indicate location, direction, etc. such as *ke pas* 'near', *ki or* 'toward', *ke samne* 'in front of', *ke pĭche* 'behind', *ke bahər* 'out (of)', *ke əndər* 'inside', *ke par* 'across', *ke bɪna* 'without', *ke sath* 'with' and *ke hath/dvara* 'through'.

The pronouns have more case forms than the nouns, as is clear from the following paradigm:

	1st		*2nd*		*3rd*	
	Sg.	Pl.	Sg.	Pl.	Sg.	Pl.
Dir.	mɛ̃	həm	tu	tʊm	yəh/vəh	ye/ve
Obl.	mʊǰh	həm	tʊǰh	tʊm	ɪs/ʊs	ɪn/ʊn
Poss.	merA	həmarA	terA	tʊmharA	ɪs/ʊs kA	ɪn/ʊn kA

The third person pronominal forms are the same as the proximate and remote demonstratives, *yəh* 'this' and *vəh* 'that', and their inflected forms.

The possessive form of the pronouns behaves like an adjective and agrees with the possessed noun in number, gender and case, e.g. *mere beṭe ko* 'to my son', *tʊmhari kɪtabõ mẽ* 'in your books', *ʊnki bəhnõ ke sath* 'with their sisters' etc. The oblique forms are used with the postpositions except that the first and second person pronouns are used in their direct case forms with the agentive postposition *ne*. The third person plural pronouns have special combined forms when they are followed by the agentive postposition, e.g. *ɪn + ne = ɪnhõne* and *ʊn + ne = ʊnhõne*. All the pronouns listed above have special contracted forms when followed by the accusative/dative postposition, e.g. *mʊǰh + ko = mʊǰhe, tʊǰh + ko = tʊǰhe, ɪs/ʊs + ko = ɪse/ ʊse, həm + ko = həmẽ, tʊm + ko = tʊmhẽ, ɪn/ʊn + ko = ɪnhẽ/ʊnhẽ*.

In addition to the pronouns listed above, Hindi-Urdu has a second person honorific pronoun *ap* which is used with both singular and plural reference for both male and female addressees. The honorific pronoun has the same form in all numbers and cases, i.e. it is invariant. The possessive is formed by adding the postposition *kA* to *ap*. To make the plural reference clear, the item *səb* 'all' or *log* 'people' may be added to the form *ap*, e.g. *ap səb/log*.

Hindi-Urdu also has a reflexive pronoun *ap* 'self ' which has an oblique form *əpne* and a possessive form *əpnA*. The form *ap* is used for all persons. There is a reduplicated form of *ap*, i.e. *əpne ap*, which is also used as the reflexive pronoun in Hindi-Urdu, e.g. *ram ne əpne ko/əpne ap ko šiše mẽ dekha* 'Ram looked at himself in the mirror'.

The two interrogative pronouns, *kɔn* and *kya* are used for human and non-human respectively. The oblique forms of these pronouns are *kɪs* in the singular and *kɪn* in the plural. The possessive is formed by adding the possessive postposition *kA* to the oblique. Similar to the third person pronouns, these pronouns also have combined forms such as *kɪnhõne*, *kɪse* and *kɪnhẽ*.

The devices of reduplication and partial reduplication or echo-compounding are used for expressing various meanings. For instance, reduplication of adjectives has either an intensive or a distributive meaning, e.g. *lal-lal saṛi* 'very red saree', *taza-taza dudh* 'very fresh milk', *kale-kale bal* 'jet-black hair', *ũče-ũče pəhaṛ* 'tall mountains', etc. Echo-compounding of adjectives, nouns and verbs has the meaning 'and the like', e.g. *sʊndər-vʊndər* 'pretty and such', *čay-vay* 'tea and other such things', *mɪlna-vɪlna* 'meeting and other such things' etc. The echo-compounding usually tones down the meaning of the adjective; it, however, adds to the meaning of other word classes. For instance, *čay-vay* means not only tea but snacks that go with tea, *pəṛhna-vəṛhna* means not only reading but other activities that go with studying.

In addition to reduplication and echo-compounding, another device used extensively is that of compounding two words with related meanings, e.g. *hə̃si-xuši* 'laughter and happiness' (pleasant state or occasion), *dʊkh-taklif* 'sorrow and pain' (state full of sorrow), *šadi-byah* 'wedding' etc. Note that in all these examples, one item is from Indic sources, the other from Perso-Arabic sources. This is extremely common, though not absolutely obligatory.

In Hindi-Urdu, the possessor normally precedes the possessed and the possessive postposition *kA* agrees with the possessed in number, gender and case, e.g. *ləṛke ki kıtab* 'the boy's book', *ləṛke ke sır pər* 'on the boy's head' etc. High-Urdu has an alternative construction where the possessed precedes the possessor following the convention of the ezafe-construction in Persian (see page 117), e.g. *šer-e-kəšmir* 'the lion of Kashmir', *qəvaıd-e-ʊrdu* 'grammar of Urdu', etc.

3.2 Verbal

Two most noticeable things about Hindi-Urdu verbs are their occurrence in morphologically related sets and in series. The first phenomenon is known as causal verbs and the second as compound verbs. Whereas the causative is inherited from Old Indo-Aryan, the development of compound verbs in New Indo-Aryan is recent — it became frequent only in the period between AD 600 and 1000.

Some examples of causal verbs can be seen in the chart given here.

Causal Verbs

Intr.	*Tr.*	*Dbl. tr.*	*Caus.*
ʊṭh 'rise'	ʊṭha 'raise'	–	ʊṭhva 'cause to rise/raise'
kəṭ 'be cut'	kaṭ 'cut'	–	kəṭva 'cause to (be) cut'
–	sʊn 'hear'	sʊna 'recite/narrate'	sʊnva 'cause to hear/narrate'
–	kha 'eat'	khıla 'feed'	khılva 'cause to eat/feed'

Examples of compound verbs are *gır ǰana* 'fall go = fall down', *kha lena* 'eat take = eat up', *pəṛh lena* 'read take = read to oneself ', *pəṛh dena* 'read give = read out loud to someone'.

Hindi-Urdu verbs occur in the following forms: root, e.g. *kha* 'eat', *a* 'come', imperfect stem, e.g. *khatA*, *atA*, perfect stem, e.g. *khayA*, *ayA*, and infinitive, *khanA*, *anA*. The stems behave like adjectives in that they agree with some noun in the sentence in number and gender. The imperfect and perfect participles, which are made up of the imperfect and perfect stems followed by the perfect stem of the verb *ho* 'be', i.e. *hʊA*, agree in case also. This means that the stem final *-A* changes to *-e* or *-i* for agreement. Whereas the imperfect and perfect aspectual distinction is expressed by suffixation, the continuous aspect is indicated by an independent lexical item, *rəhA*. This marker follows the root and behaves like the imperfect and perfect stems with regard to gender and number agreement.

The tense distinction of present versus past is expressed with the forms of the auxiliary verb, the present auxiliary *hE* and the past auxiliary *thA*. These are the present and past forms of the stative verb *honA* 'be'. As in all Indo-

European languages, the verb 'be' is irregular in Hindi. It has the following forms: root *ho*, imperfect stem *hotA*, perfect stem *hʊA*, infinitive *honA*, stative present *hE*, stative past *thA*. The stem-final *-A* changes to *-e*, *-i* or *-ī* for number and gender agreement and the final *-E* changes to various vowels to indicate person, number and gender agreement. The forms of the verb *honA* in stative present are as follows: 1st person sg. *hũ*, 2nd and 3rd person sg. *hɛ*, 2nd person pl. *ho*, and 1st and 3rd person pl. and 2nd hon. *hɛ̃*.

In addition to tense and aspect distinctions, the verbal forms express mood distinctions as well. There is no distinction made between indicative and interrogative, i.e. in assertions as well as questions, the verbal forms are made up of the stems and auxiliaries described above. Historically, Old Indo-Aryan did not make a distinction between these two moods either. The moods in Old Indo-Aryan were indicative, imperative, optative and subjunctive. In Hindi-Urdu, the optative forms are made up of the root and the following suffixes: 1st person sg. *-ũ*, 2nd and 3rd person sg. *-e*, 1st and 3rd pl. and 2nd honorific *-ẽ*, and 2nd pl. *-o*. The future tense is formed by adding the suffix *-gA* to the optative forms, e.g. *ǰa-ũ-ga* 'I (m.) will go', *ǰaogi* 'you (f.) will go' etc. The following are the imperative forms: root form of the verb (intimate or rude), 2nd pl. optative (familiar), root with the suffix *-ɪye* (honorific, polite), root with the suffix *-ɪye* followed by the suffix *-ga* (remote, therefore, extra polite) and the infinitive form of the verb (remote imperative, therefore even when used with second plural, polite). Thus, the imperative forms of the verb *kha* are *(tu) kha* 'you (intimate) eat', *tʊm khao* 'you (familiar) eat', *(ap) khaɪye* 'you (honorific) eat', *(ap) khaɪyega* 'you (honorific) please eat (perhaps later?)', *(tʊm) khana* 'you (familiar, polite) eat' or 'you (familiar) eat (perhaps later?)'.

The paradigm of the verb *ghumna* 'to take a walk' illustrates the full range of the forms discussed above.

Paradigm of Verb Forms

Root: ghum 'take a walk'
Imperfect stem: ghumtA
Perfect stem: ghumA
Infinitive: ghumnA
Optative: ghumũ (1st sg.), ghumo (2nd pl.), ghume (2nd and 3rd sg.), ghumẽ (1st and 3rd pl., 2nd honorific)
Imperative: ghum (2nd sg., intimate/rude), ghumo (2nd pl., familiar), ghumɪye (2nd honorific, polite), ghumɪyega (2nd honorific, extra polite)

Future

	1st		*2nd*		*3rd*	
	M.	F.	M.	F.	M.	F.
Sg.	ghumunga	ghumungi	ghumega	ghumegi	ghumega	ghumegi
Pl.	ghumenge	ghumengi	ghumoge	ghumogi	ghumenge	ghumengi
Hon.	–	–	ghumenge	ghumengi	ghumenge	ghumengi

Present imperfect

		Sg.	*Pl.*	*Hon.*
1st	M.	ghumta hũ	ghumte hẽ	–
	F.	ghumti hũ	ghumti hẽ	–
2nd	M.	ghumta hɛ	ghumte ho	ghumte hẽ
	F.	ghumti hɛ	ghumti ho	ghumti hẽ
3rd	M.	ghumta hɛ	ghumte hẽ	ghumte hẽ
	F.	ghumti hɛ	ghumti hẽ	ghumti hẽ

Past imperfect: ghumta tha, ghumte the, ghumti thi, ghumti thī, etc.
Present perfect: ghuma hũ, ghumi hũ, etc.
Past perfect: ghuma tha, ghumi thi, etc.
Present continuous: ghum rəha hũ, ghum rəhi hũ, etc.
Past continuous: ghum rəha tha, ghum rəhi thi, etc.

In general, Urdu speakers use the masculine plural form as undifferentiated for gender in the first person, e.g. *həm kəl kəlkətte ǰa rəhe hẽ* 'We (m./f.) are going to Calcutta tomorrow.'

The contingent, past contingent and presumptive tenses are formed with the imperfect and perfect stems and the continuous form followed by the auxiliaries *ho* 'contingent', *hotA* 'past contingent', and *hogA* 'presumptive'. Roughly, these three are translatable into English as follows: *ata ho* '(he) may be coming', *aya ho* '(he) may have come', *ata hota* 'had (he) been coming', *aya hota* 'had (he) come', *ata hoga* '(he) must be coming', *aya hoga* '(he) must have come'.

Hindi-Urdu verbs are very regular, which means that once we know the infinitive form of the verb, we can isolate the root and derive the imperfect and perfect stems by suffixing *-tA* and *-A* respectively. Thus, from *hə̃sna* 'laugh', we get the imperfect stem *hə̃stA* and perfect stem *hə̃sA*. Note that when the root ends in a vowel and the perfect stem-forming suffix *-A* is added to it, a semi-vowel is inserted to separate the two vowels. If the root ends in *-i*, *-a* or *-o*, a *-y-* is inserted, if the root ends in *-u*, a *-v-* is inserted, e.g. *kha* + *-A* = *khaya* 'ate (m.)', *ro* + *-A* = *roya* 'cried (m.)', *pi* + *-A* = *pɪya* 'drank (m.)', *čhu* + *-A* = *čhʊva* 'touched (m.)'.

One verb, *čahɪye*, is completely irregular in that it has only this form. It takes a dative subject and means 'to need' or 'want'. The following have irregular perfect stems: *kər* 'do' – *kɪya*, *le* 'take' – *lɪya*, *de* 'give' – *dɪya*, *ǰa* 'go' – *gəya*. The following have irregular polite imperative forms: *kər* 'do' = *kiǰɪye*, *le* 'take' = *liǰɪye*, *de* 'give' = *diǰɪye*, *pi* 'drink' = *piǰɪye*.

Hindi-Urdu has two types of compound verbs: those that involve verbs in a series and those that involve a nominal and a verbal. Some examples of the former have already been given (see page 63), a few examples of the latter follow: *svikar kərna* 'acceptance do' or 'to accept', *pəsənd hona* 'liking be' or 'to like' (non-volitional), *pəsənd kərna* 'liking do' or 'to like' (volitional), *təng ana* 'torment come' or 'to be fed up'.

In the verbs-in-series type of compound verbs, usually the meaning of the whole is derived from the meaning of the first, or main, verb; the second, or explicator, verb performs the function of either restricting, or adding some specific shade of meaning to, the meaning of the main verb. Also, the explicator verb necessarily expresses the meaning 'a one-shot action or process'. For instance, *marna* can mean either 'hit' or 'kill', *mar ḍalna* 'hit/kill pour' means only 'kill'; *lɪkhna* means 'write', *lɪkh marna* 'write hit' means 'to dash off a few lines in a hurry/thoughtlessly'; *rəkhna* means 'keep, put', *rəkh čhoṛna*', 'keep leave' means 'save'. The main explicator verbs are the following and they roughly signify the meanings described below:

ana 'come' occurs with intransitive verbs of motion and indicates that the action of the main verb is oriented towards a focal point which may be a person or which may be set in time or space; e.g. *vəh siṛhɪyā čəṛh ai* 'she came up the steps' and *vəh siṛhɪyō se utər ai* 'she came down the steps'.

ǰana 'go' occurs with intransitive verbs of motion and other change-of-state verbs and indicates motion away from the focal point; with dative subject verbs, it indicates definitive meaning; and with transitive verbs, it indicates hurried, compulsive action; e.g. *vəh siṛhɪyā čəṛh gəi* 'she went up the steps', *raǰu ko kɪtab mɪl gəi* 'Raju got the book', *vəh gusse mẽ ǰane kya-kya lɪkh gəya* 'who knows what he dashed off in his anger!'

lena 'take' occurs with affective (see page 68) (transitive) verbs and indicates completive meaning; with other transitive verbs, it indicates a self-benefactive meaning; and with certain intransitive verbs, it indicates internal expression; e.g. *ʊsne kam kər lɪya* '(s)he completed (his/her) job', *mɛ̃ ne thik soč lɪya hɛ* 'I have made a decision'.

dena 'give' occurs with transitive verbs other than affective verbs and indicates that the action is directed towards a beneficiary other than the agent of the action denoted by the main verb; and with intransitive verbs of expression, it indicates external expression; e.g. *ʊsne sara rəhəsy bəta dɪya* 'he divulged the whole secret', *sima zorõ se hə̃s di* 'Sima laughed loudly'.

ʊṭhna 'rise' occurs with intransitive and transitive verbs of punctual action and indicates suddenness; e.g. *vəh mʊǰhe dekhte hi ro ʊṭhi* 'she suddenly began to cry when she saw me'.

bɛṭhna 'sit' occurs with certain transitive verbs and indicates impudence; e.g. *vəh əpne 'bas' se ləṛ bɛtha* 'he fought with his boss'.

pəṛna 'fall' occurs with intransitive change-of-state verbs, and certain verbs of expression, and indicates suddenness; e.g. *ləṛki bərf pər phɪsəl kər gɪr pəri* 'the girl slipped and fell on the ice'.

ḍalna 'pour' occurs with transitive verbs that express violent action and certain transitive verbs (*kər* 'do', *pərh* 'read', *lɪkh* 'write') and indicates violence; e.g. *ǰəldi se pətr lɪkh dalo!* 'write the letter quickly (get it over with)!'

rəkhna 'keep' occurs with certain transitive verbs and indicates a temporary state resulting from the action of the main verb; e.g. *mɛ̃ ne khana pəka rəkha hɛ* 'I have cooked (and saved) the food'.

čhoṛna 'leave' occurs with certain transitive verbs and indicates dissociation of the agent with the result of the action; e.g. *pɪtaǰi ne meri pəṛhai ke lɪye pɛse rəkh čhoṛe hɛ̃* 'father has put aside money for my education'.

marna 'hit' occurs with very few verbs and indicates rash action; e.g. *kʊčh bhi lɪkh maro!* 'just write something!'

dhəməkna 'thump' occurs with *ana* 'come' and *ǰana* 'go' and indicates unwelcome arrival; e.g. *vəh sʊbəh-sʊbəh a dhəmka, mʊǰhe nəhane tək ka mɔka nəhi mɪla* 'he showed up very early, I did not even have time to shower'.

pəhʊ̃čna 'arrive' occurs with *ana* 'come' and *ǰana* 'go' and indicates arrival rather than motion; e.g. *šyam dɪlli ǰa pəhʊ̃ča* 'Shyam arrived in Delhi'.

nikəlna 'emerge' indicates sudden emergence from some enclosed space — real or imaginary; e.g. *uski ãkhõ se ãsu bəh nɪkle* 'tears began to flow from her eyes'.

4 Syntax

In this brief section on syntax, I will discuss mainly the verbal syntax of Hindi-Urdu after a few remarks on word order. The reason for this will become clearer as the discussion progresses.

Hindi-Urdu is a verb final language, i.e. the order of words in a sentence is subject, object and verb. Actually, the position of the verb is relatively more fixed than the position of any other constituent. Since most grammatical functions of nouns are indicated by the postpositions following them, the nominal constituents can be moved around freely for thematic purposes. The position of the verb is changed only in poetic or extremely affective style. Historically, word order was relatively free in Old Indo-Aryan, but became more fixed in Middle Indo-Aryan between AD 200 and 600.

In existential sentences, the locational/temporal adverbial comes first: *mez pər kıtab hɛ* 'there is a book on the table', *kəl bəṛi ṭhəṇḍ thi* 'it was very cold yesterday'. The verb agrees with the unmarked noun in the sentence. In intransitive and non-perfective transitive sentences, where the subject is unmarked, the verb agrees with the subject, e.g. *ləṛke bɛṭhe* 'the boys sat', *ləṛki səmačar sʊn rəhi hɛ* 'the girl is listening (f.) to the news (m.)', *raǰu čay pita hoga* 'Raju (m.) must be drinking (m.) tea (f.)'. In transitive sentences in the perfective, where the subject is followed by the postposition *ne*, the verb does not agree with the subject. It agrees with the object if it is unmarked; if the object is followed by the postposition *ko*, the verb remains in its neutral form, i.e. third person singular masculine: cf. *raǰu ne kıtab pəṛhi* 'Raǰu (m.) read (f.) the book (f.)', *əfsərõ ne əpni pətnıyõ ko bʊlaya* 'the officers called (3rd sg. m.) their wives'. Not all transitive verbs require that their subjects be marked with the agentive postposition *ne*: e.g. *bolna* 'speak', *lana* 'bring' do not take *ne, səməǰhna* 'understand' can occur either with or without *ne*: *mɛ apki bat nəhī səmǰha* 'I do not understand you', *ap ne kya səmǰha?* 'what did you understand?' In the case of compound verbs, only if both the main and the explicator verbs require *ne* does the compound verb require *ne*: *šila ne dudh pıya* 'Sheila drank the milk', *šila ne dudh lıya* 'Sheila took the milk', *šila ne dudh pi lıya* 'Sheila drank up the milk', but *šila dudh pi gəi* 'Sheila drank up the milk' since the intransitive verb *ǰa* 'go' is not a *ne* verb.

Semantically, Hindi-Urdu makes a distinction between volitional versus non-volitional verbs and affective versus non-affective verbs. A verb is volitional if it expresses an act that is performed by an actor/agent. A verb is affective if the act expressed by the verb is directed towards the actor/agent, i.e. it is self-benefactive. Ingestive verbs such as *khana* 'eat', *pina* 'drink' etc. are good examples of affective verbs in that it is the actor/agent of eating, drinking etc. who benefits from these acts. Verbs such as 'work', 'write' etc., on the other hand may be either self-benefactive or directed toward some other beneficiary. Typically, the explicator verb *lena* 'take' occurs with an affective verb, the explicator *dena* 'give' does not, i.e. sentences such as the following are ungrammatical in Hindi-Urdu: *ʊsne khana kha dıya* 'he/she ate for someone else' because *khana* 'eat' is an ingestive verb whereas the explicator *dena* 'give' indicates that the beneficiary is someone other than the actor/agent of the main verb. Verbs such as *girna* 'fall', *ǰana* 'go' etc. express self-directed actions, hence are affective.

These distinctions are important for the verbal syntax of Hindi-Urdu. Transitivity, volitionality and affectiveness do not necessarily coincide. For instance, *sona* 'sleep' is intransitive, volitional and affective, *sikhna* 'learn' is transitive, volitional and affective, *gırna* 'fall' is intransitive, non-volitional and affective, *ǰana* 'go' is intransitive, volitional and affective. Only the affective verbs participate in the compound verbal construction with *lena* 'take' as the explicator, only volitional verbs occur in the passive construction (Kachru 1980; 1981).

In many cases, verbs in Hindi-Urdu come in related forms so that the stative versus active and volitional versus non-volitional meanings can be expressed by varying the syntactic constructions. For instance, the verb *mɪlna* can mean both 'to run into someone' (accidental meeting) or 'to go see someone' (deliberate meeting). In the first case, the verb is used with a dative subject and the object of meeting is unmarked, in the second case, the subject is unmarked and the object is marked with a comitative postposition *se*, e.g. *kəl bazar ǰate hʊe mʊǰhe ram mɪla tha* 'yesterday while going to the market I ran into Ram', *kəl mɛ̃ ram se ʊske dəftər mẽ mɪla tha* 'yesterday I met Ram in his office'. In a large number of cases, the intransitive verb denotes non-volitional action and if the actor is to be expressed, it is expressed with the instrumental postposition *se*, e.g. *apka šiša mʊǰhse ṭuṭ gəya* 'your mirror got broken by me'. The deliberate action is expressed with the related transitive verb in the agentive construction, e.g. *ɪs šərarti bəčče ne apka šiša toṛ ḍala* 'this naughty child broke your mirror'. Most intransitive and all dative subject verbs are either stative or change-of-state verbs and are non-volitional. Hindi-Urdu has sets of stative, change-of-state and active verbs of the following types:

Stative	*Change-of-state*	*Active*
khʊla hona 'be open'	khʊlna	kholna
krʊddh hona 'be angry'	krodh ana	krodh kərna
yad hona 'remember'	yad ana	yad kərna
pəsənd hona 'like'	pəsənd ana	pəsənd kərna

Note that the stative verbs are usually made up of an adjective or past participle and the verb 'be', the change-of-state verbs are either lexical verbs or compounds made up of a nominal and the verb 'become' or 'come', and the active is either a causal verb morphologically derived from the intransitive or a compound made up of a nominal and the verb 'do' (or a small set of other active transitive verbs).

This, however, does not mean that all intransitive verbs in Hindi are of the above types. There are active intransitive verbs such as the verbs of motion (*ǰa* 'go', *čəl* 'move' etc.), verbs of expression (*hə̃s* 'laugh', *ro* 'cry' etc.) and others. Note that verbal compounding is also exploited to reduce volitionality of verbs, e.g. *ro pəṛna* 'cry + fall = to burst out crying', *bol ʊṭhna* 'speak + rise = to blurt out' etc.

The non-volitional intransitive sentence above (*apka šiša mʊǰhse ṭuṭ gəya* 'your mirror got broken by me') has been translated into English with the passive; it is, however, not a passive construction in Hindi-Urdu. The passive in Hindi-Urdu is formed by marking the agent of the active sentence, if retained, with the instrumental postposition *se* and using the perfect stem of the verb and the auxiliary *ǰa* 'go' which takes all the tense-aspect endings: e.g. *ram ne khana nəhī khaya* 'Ram did not eat' vs. *ram se khana nəhī khaya gəya* 'Ram was not able to eat'. The translation equivalent of the Hindi-Urdu passive in English points to an interesting fact about this construction. If the agent is retained and marked with the instrumental postposition, the passive sentence is usually interpreted as a statement about the capability of the agent; if, however, the agent is deleted, the passive sentence has a meaning similar to that of English. That is, the sentence is interpreted as being about the object in the active sentence and the agent is either unknown or not important enough to be mentioned (Guru 1920; Kachru 1980).

In addition to the present and past participles, there are two other participles in Hindi which are used a great deal: the conjunctive participle which is formed by adding the form *kər* to the root of the verb and the agentive participle which is formed by adding the suffix *-vala* to the oblique form of the verbal noun, e.g. *lɪkhnevala* 'writer', *ǰanevala* 'one who goes', *sonevala* 'one who sleeps', *ʊgnevala* 'that which rises or grows', etc. This suffix has become a part of the English lexicon in the form *wallah* and is used extensively in Indian English and the native varieties of English, especially in the context of topics related to India. Forms such as *Congresswallah* ('one belonging to the Indian National Congress'), *Bombaywallah* ('one from Bombay') are common in literature dealing with India.

The syntax of Hindi-Urdu differs from that of English most noticeably in the use of the participles. For instance, the preferred constructions for modifying nouns or conjoining clauses are the participles: the present, past and agentive for modifying nouns and the conjunctive participle for conjoining clauses. Compare the following Hindi sentences with their English translations: *vəh gẽd khelte hʊe bəččõ ko dekh rəha tha* 'he was observing the children (who were) playing ball'; *tʊmhẽ mohən ki likhi hʊi kəvɪtaẽ pəsənd hɛ̃?* 'do you like the poems written by Mohan?'; *mʊǰhe bat bat pər ronewale bəčče bɪlkʊl pəsənd nəhī* 'I do not like children who cry at every thing'; *vəh ghər a kər so gə ya* 'he came home and went to sleep'. Both the present and the past participles are used adjectivally as well as adverbially, cf. *mã ne rote hʊe bəčče ko god mẽ ʊṭha lɪya* 'Mother picked up the child who was crying' vs. *vəh rote hʊe bhag gəya* 'he ran away, crying' and *mɛ̃ vəhã bɛṭhi hʊ ləṛki ko nəhī ǰanti* 'I don't know the girl seated over there' vs. *ləṛki vəhã bɛṭhi (hui) pətr lɪkh rəhi hɛ* 'the girl is writing a letter sitting there'. The agentive participle is used both as an agentive noun, e.g. *(gaṛi) cəlanevala* 'driver (of a vehicle)' and as an adjective, e.g. *bharət se anevale čhatr* 'the students who come from India'. The conjunctive participle is used to express the meanings of sequential action, related action, cause-effect relationship and purpose adverbial, e.g. *vəh hɪndi pəṛh kər khelne ǰaega* 'he will go to play after studying Hindi', *vəh kud kər upər a gəi* 'she jumped and came up', *həm ne ʊse pɛse de kər xuš kər lɪya* 'we pleased him by giving him money', *ǰəldi se bazar ǰakər dudh le ao* 'go quickly to the market and bring some milk' (Kachru 1980).

Although the participial constructions are preferred in Hindi-Urdu, there are linguistically determined environments where full relative and other types of subordinate and conjoined clauses are used. The relative clause, unlike in English, is not a constituent of the noun phrase. It may either precede or follow the main clause as in the following: *ǰo ləṛka vəhã bɛṭha hɛ vəh mera bhai hɛ* or *vəh ləṛka mera bhai hɛ ǰo vəhã bɛṭha hɛ* 'the boy who is seated there is my brother'. Note that, depending upon the order of the relative and the main clause, either the noun in the subordinate or the main clause is deleted, i.e. the above are the results of deleting the noun in parentheses in the following: *ǰo ləṛka vəhã bɛṭha hɛ vəh (ləṛka) mera bhai hɛ* or *vəh ləṛka mera bhai hɛ ǰo (ləṛka) vəhã bɛṭha hɛ*. The relative marker *ǰo* (obl. sg. *ǰɪs*, obl. pl. *ǰɪn*, special forms with *ne* and *ko*, *ǰɪnhõne* and *ǰɪnhẽ*) and the correlative marker *vəh*, which is identical to the remote demonstrative/third person pronoun, function like a determiner to their respective head nouns. Both the head nouns may be retained in the case of an emphatic construction; in normal speech/writing, however, the second instance is deleted. Under the influence of Persian and later, English, the relative clause is sometimes positioned following the head noun, e.g. *vəh ləṛka ǰo vəhã bɛṭha hɛ mera bhai hɛ*; in this case, the second instance of the noun (following *ǰo*) must be deleted.

Earlier, it has been said that the nominal constituents of a sentence in Hindi-Urdu can be moved around freely for thematic purposes. Usually, the initial element in a sentence in Hindi coincides with the theme. The focus position in Hindi is identified with the position just before the main verb. In addition to manipulating the word order, heavy sentence stress and certain particles are used to indicate focus, e.g. *'ram' ne mohən ko piṭa* 'it was Ram who hit Mohan', *šila hi ne yəh bat kəhi thi* 'it was Sheila who had said this', *sima to čəli gəi*, 'as for Sima, she has left', where the item in quotes in the first sentence and the items followed by the particles *hi* and *to* in the second and the third sentence respectively are under focus. As the initial position is not the favoured device for indicating focus, the interrogative pronouns in Hindi-Urdu do not necessarily occur sentence-initially; compare the Hindi-Urdu sentences with their English equivalents, *ap kya pəṛh rəhe hɛ̃?* 'what are you reading?', *vəh kəl kəhã gəya tha?* 'where did he go yesterday?', *ɪn mẽ se ap ko kɔn si kɪtab pəsənd hɛ?* 'which of these books do you like?'.

To sum up, Hindi-Urdu differs from its European cousins typologically in several respects. Phonologically, aspiration, retroflexion, nasal vowels and lack of distinctive stress mark Hindi-Urdu as very different from English. Morphologically, the gender and case distinctions and the devices of reduplication and echo-compounding exemplify the major differences between the two languages. Syntactically, the word order differences are striking. So is the fact that Hindi-Urdu makes certain semantic distinctions which are not made as clearly in English, viz. volitionality and affectiveness. These distinctions result in a closer correspondence between semantic and syntactic grammatical roles that nominal constituents have in a sentence, e.g. all agentive (*-ne*-marked) subjects are agents, all dative (*ko*-marked) subjects are experiencers, and so on. Many of these characteristics of Hindi-Urdu are shared by not only the other Indo-Aryan but also the Dravidian and other languages of India.

Bibliography

The standard reference grammar for modern standard Hindi is Guru (1920). Other reference grammars are Sharma (1958) and McGregor (1972), the latter directed to the needs of learners of Hindi. Kellogg (1875) describes Hindi and the major dialects of the Hindi area, and contains a good introduction to Hindi prosody; data are drawn mostly from literary texts of the period and the work is hence dated. For Urdu, see Bailey (1956). For an account of the parallel development of Hindi-Urdu see Rai (1984).

Ohala (1983) is a phonological description of Hindi, while Kachru (1980) describes syntactic constructions of Hindi in non-technical language. Verma (1933) is a brief sketch of the history of the Hindi language. Kachru (1981) contains a supplement on transplanted varieties of Hindi-Urdu and one on transitivity in Hindi-Urdu. Bhatia (1987) discusses the native and non-native grammatical tradition.

References

Bailey, T.G. 1956. *Teach Yourself Urdu* (English Universities Press, London)

Bhatia, T.K. 1987. *A History of Hindi (Hindustani) Grammatical Tradition* (E.J. Brill, Leiden)

Guru, K.P. 1920. *Hindi vyākaraṇ* (Kashi Nagri Pracharini Sabha, Banaras)

Kachru, Y. 1980. *Aspects of Hindi Grammar* (Manohar Publications, New Delhi)

—— 1981. 'Dimensions of South Asian Linguistics', *Studies in the Linguistic Sciences*, vol. 11, no. 2

Kellogg, S.H. 1875. *A Grammar of the Hindi Language* (Routledge and Kegan Paul, London)

McGregor, R.S. 1972. *Outline of Hindi Grammar* (Oxford University Press, London)

Ohala, M. 1983. *Aspects of Hindi Phonology* (Motilal Banarsidass, Delhi)

Rai, A. 1984. *A House Divided* (Oxford University Press, Delhi)

Sharma, A. 1958. *A Basic Grammar of Modern Hindi* (Government of India, Ministry of Education and Scientific Research, Delhi)

Verma, Dh. 1933. *Hindi bhaṣa ka itihas* (Hindustani Academy, Allahabad)

4 Bengali

M. H. Klaiman

1 Historical and Genetic Setting

Bengali, together with Assamese and Oriya, belongs to the eastern group within the Magadhan subfamily of Indo-Aryan. In reconstructing the development of Indo-Aryan, scholars hypothetically posit a common parent language from which the modern Magadhan languages are said to have sprung. The unattested parent of the Magadhan languages is designated as Eastern or Magadhi Apabhraṁśa, and is assigned to Middle Indo-Aryan. Apart from the eastern languages, other modern representatives of the Magadhan subfamily are Magahi, Maithili and Bhojpuri.

Within the eastern group of Magadhan languages, the closest relative of Bengali is Assamese. The two share not only many coincidences of form and structure, but also have in common one system of written expression, on which more details will be given later.

Historically, the entire Magadhan group is distinguished from the remaining Indo-Aryan languages by a sound change involving sibilant coalescence. Specifically, there occurred in Magadhan a falling together of three sibilant elements inherited from common Indo-Aryan, dental /s/, palatal /š/ and retroflex /ṣ/. Among modern Magadhan languages, the coalescence of these three sounds is manifested in different ways; e.g. the modern Assamese reflex is the velar fricative /x/, as contrasted with the palatal /š/ of Modern Bengali.

The majority of Magadhan languages also show evidence of historical regression in the articulation of what was a central vowel /ă/ in common Indo-Aryan; the Modern Bengali reflex is /ɔ/.

Although the Magadhan subfamily is defined through a commonality of sound shifts separating it from the rest of Indo-Aryan, the three eastern languages of the subfamily share one phonological peculiarity distinguishing them from all other modern Indo-Aryan languages, both Magadhan and non-Magadhan. This feature is due to a historical coalescence of the long and short variants of the high vowels, which were distinguished in common Indo-Aryan. As a result, the vowel inventories of Modern Bengali, Assamese and Oriya show no phonemic distinction of /ĭ/ and /ī/, /ŭ/ and /ū/.

Moreover, Assamese and Bengali are distinguished from Oriya by the innovation of a high/low distinction in the mid vowels. Thus Bengali has /æ/ as well as /e/, and /ɔ/ as well as /o/. Bengali differs phonologically from Assamese principally in that the latter lacks a retroflex consonant series, a fact which distinguishes Assamese not just from Bengali, but from the majority of modern Indo-Aryan languages.

Besides various phonological characteristics, there are certain grammatical features peculiar to Bengali and the other Magadhan languages. The most noteworthy of these features is the absence of gender, a grammatical category found in most other modern Indo-Aryan languages. Bengali and its close relative Assamese also lack number as a verbal category. More will be said on these topics in the section on morphology, below.

Writing and literature have played no small role in the evolution of Bengali linguistic identity. A common script was in use throughout eastern India centuries before the emergence of the separate Magadhan vernaculars. The Oriya version of this script underwent special development in the medieval period, while the characters of the Bengali and Assamese scripts coincide with but a couple of exceptions.

Undoubtedly the availability of a written form of expression was essential to the development of the rich literary traditions associated not just with Bengali, but also with other Magadhan languages such as Maithili. However, even after the separation of the modern Magadhan languages from one another, literary composition in eastern India seems to have reflected a common milieu scarcely compromised by linguistic boundaries. Although vernacular literature appears in eastern India by AD 1200, vernacular writings for several centuries thereafter tend to be perceived as the common inheritance of the whole eastern area, more so than as the output of individual languages.

This is clearly evident, for instance, in the case of the celebrated Buddhist hymns called the *Caryāpada*, composed in eastern India roughly between AD 1000 and 1200. Though the language of these hymns is Old Bengali, there are reference works on Assamese, Oriya and even Maithili that treat the same hymns as the earliest specimens of each of these languages and their literatures.

Bengali linguistic identity is not wholly a function of the language's genetic affiliation in the Indo-Aryan family. Eastern India was subjected to Aryanisation before the onset of the Christian era, and therefore well before the evolution of Bengali and the other Magadhan languages. Certain events of the medieval era have had a greater significance than Aryanisation in the shaping of Bengali linguistic identity, since they furnished the prerequisites of Bengali regional and national identity.

Among these events, one of the most crucial was the establishment of Islamic rule in the early thirteenth century. Islamisation led to six hundred years of political unity in Bengal, under which it was possible for a distinctly national style of literary and cultural expression to evolve, more or less unaffected by religious distinctions. To be sure, much if not all early popular literature in Bengali had a sacred basis; the early compositions were largely translations and reworkings of Hindu legends, like the Krishna myth cycle and the *Rāmāyaṇa* religious epic. However, this material seems to have always been looked upon more as a product of local than of sectarian tradition. From the outset of their rule, the Muslim aristocracy did little to discourage the composition of literature on such popular themes; on the contrary, they often lent their patronage to the authors of these works, who were both Muslim and Hindu. Further, when in the sixteenth and seventeenth centuries Islamic writers ultimately did set about creating a body of sectarian, didactic vernacular literature in Bengali, they readily adapted the originally Hindu motifs, themes and stories that had become part of the local cultural tradition.

The relative weakness of religious identity in Bengali cultural institutions is perhaps best interpreted in light of a major event which occurred concomitant to the rise of Islamic rule. This event was a massive shift in the course of the Ganges River between the twelfth and sixteenth centuries AD. Whereas it had earlier emptied into the Bay of Bengal nearly due south of the site of present-day Calcutta, the river gradually approached and eventually became linked with the Padma River system in the territory today called Bangladesh. The shift in the Ganges has been one of the greatest influences upon material history and human geography in eastern India; for, prior to the completion of the river's change of course, the inhabitants of the eastern tracts had been virtually untouched by civilisation and sociocultural influences from without, whether Islamic or Hindu. Over the past four centuries, it is the descendants of the same people who have come to make up the majority of speakers of the Bengali language; so that the basis of their Bengali identity is not genetic and not religious, but linguistic. That the bulk of the population perceives commonality of language as the principal basis of its social unity is clear from the name taken by the new nation-state of eastern Bengal following the 1971 war of liberation. In the proper noun *Bangladesh* (composed of *bāṅglā* plus *deśa*, the latter meaning 'country'), the first part of the compound does not mean the Bengali people or the territory of Bengal; the term *bāṅglā* specifically refers, rather, to the Bengali language.

The Muslim aristocracy that ruled Bengal for some six centuries was supplanted in the eighteenth century by new invaders, the British. Since the latter's withdrawal from the subcontinent in 1947, the community which identifies itself as Bengali has been divided between two sovereign political entities. However, the Bengali language continues to be spoken throughout Bengal's traditional domains, and on both sides of the newly-imposed international boundary. Today, Bengali is one of the official regional speeches of the Indian Union, a status which is also enjoyed by the other eastern Magadhan languages, Oriya and Assamese. Among the three languages, the one which is currently in the strongest position is Bengali, since it alone also has the status of a national language outside India's present borders. In India, about eight per cent of the overall population, or some 55 million people per 1981 census figures, speak Bengali. The great bulk of these speakers reside in West Bengal, the Indian state contiguous to Bangladesh. At the same time, in Bangladesh, 1980 census figures report a population of nearly ninety million, of whom over 95 per cent are Bengali speakers. Thus the combined community of Bengali speakers in India and Bangladesh approaches 145 million, a larger body of native speakers than currently exists for French.

2 Orthography and Sound System

The writing system of Modern Bengali is derived from Brāhmī, an ancient Indian syllabary. Brāhmī is also the source of all the other native Indian scripts (including those of the modern South Indian languages) as well as of Devanāgarī, a script associated with classical Sanskrit and with a number of the modern Indo-Aryan languages.

The scripts of the modern eastern Magadhan languages (Oriya, Assamese and Bengali) are based on a system of characters historically related to, but distinct from, Devanāgarī. The Bengali script is identical to that of Assamese except for two characters; while the Oriya script, though closely related historically to the Bengali-Assamese script, is quite distinctive in its appearance.

Like all Brāhmī-derived scripts, Bengali orthography reads from left to right, and is organised according to syllabic rather than segmental units.

Table 4.1: Bengali Script

Vowel Segments

Special name of character, if any	*Independent form*	*Combining form (shown with the sign kɔ)*	*Transliteration*
	অ	ক	ɔ
	আ	কা	a
hrɔsso i	ই	কি	i
dirgho i	ঈ	কী	ī
hrɔsso u	উ	কু	u
dirgho u	ঊ	কূ	ū
ri	ঋ	কৃ	ri
	এ	কে	e
	ঐ	কৈ	oy
	ও	কো	o
	ঔ	কৌ	ow

Consonant Segments

	Ordinary form	*Special form(s)*	*Transliteration (so-called 'inherent vowel' not represented)*
	ক		k
	খ		kh
	গ		g
	ঘ		gh
	ঙ	ং	ṅ
	চ		c
	ছ		ch
	জ		j
	ঝ		jh
	ঞ		ñ
	ট		ṭ
	ঠ		ṭh
	ড		ḍ
	ড়		ṛ
	ঢ		ḍh
	ঢ়		ṛh
	ণ		ṇ
	ত	ৎ	t
	থ		th
	দ		d
	ধ		dh
	ন		n
	প		p
	ফ		ph
	ব		b
	ভ		bh
	ম		m
ɔntostho jɔ	য		j
ɔntostho ɔ	য়	্য	y, w
	র	্র র্	r
	ল		l
talobbo sɔ	শ		ś
murdhonno sɔ	ষ		ṣ
donto sɔ	স		s
	হ	ঃ	h
Special diacritics			
cɔndrobindu	ঁ		˜
hɔsonto	্		

Accordingly, a special diacritic or character is employed to represent a single consonant segment in isolation from any following vowel, or a single vowel in isolation from any preceding consonant. Furthermore, the writing system of Bengali, like Devanāgarī, represents characters as hanging from a superimposed horizontal line and has no distinction of upper and lower cases.

Table 4.1 sets out the Bengali script according to the traditional ordering of characters, with two special diacritics listed at the end. Most Bengali characters are designated according to the pronunciation of their independent or ordinary form. Thus the first vowel character is called *ɔ*, while the first consonant character is called *kɔ*. The designation of the latter is such, because the corresponding sign in isolation is read not as a single segment, but as a syllable terminating in /ɔ/, the so-called 'inherent vowel'. Several Bengali characters are not designated by the pronunciation of their independent or ordinary forms; their special names are listed in the leftmost column of table 4.1. Among the terms used in the special designations of vowel characters, *hrɔsso* literally means 'short' and *dirgho* 'long'. Among the terms used in the special designations of consonant characters, *talobbo* literally means 'palatal', *murdhonno* 'retroflex', and *donto* 'dental'. These terms are used, for historical reasons, to distinguish the names for the three sibilant characters. The three characters (transliterated *ś*, *ṣ* and *s*) are used to represent a single non-obstruent sibilant phoneme in Modern Bengali. This phoneme is a palatal with a conditioned dental allophone; further discussion will be given below. It might be pointed out that another Bengali phoneme, the dental nasal /n/, is likewise represented in orthography by three different characters, which are transliterated *ñ*, *ṇ*, and *n*.

In Bengali orthography, a vowel sign normally occurs in its independent form only when it is the first segment of a syllable. Otherwise, the combining form of the vowel sign is written together with the ordinary form of a consonant character, as illustrated in table 4.1 for the character *kɔ*. There are a few exceptional cases: for instance, the character *hɔ* when written with the combining form of the sign *ri* appears not as হৃ , but as হৃ (pronounced [hri]). The character *rɔ* combined with *dirgho u* is written not as রূ , but as রূ [ru]. The combination of *talobbo sɔ* with *hrɔsso u* is optionally represented either as শু or as শু (both are pronounced [šu]), while *gɔ*, *rɔ* and *hɔ* in combination with *hrɔsso u* yield the respective representations গু [gu], রু [ru], and হু [hu].

Several of the consonant characters in Bengali have special forms designated in table 4.1; their distribution is as follows. The characters *ṅɔ* and *tɔ* occur in their special forms when the consonants they represent are the final segments of phonological syllables. Thus /baṅla/ 'Bengali language' is written বাংলা , while /šɔt/ 'true' is written সৎ .

The character *ɔntostho ɔ* has a special form listed in table 4.1; the name of this special form is *jɔ phɔla*. Generally, *jɔ phɔla* is the form in which *ɔntostho ɔ* occurs when combined with a preceding ordinary consonant sign, as in ত্যাগ [tæg] 'renunciation'. When combined with an ordinary consonant sign in non-initial syllables, *jɔ phɔla* tends to be realised as gemination of the consonant segment, as in গ্রাম্য [grammo] 'rural'. The sign *ɔntostho ɔ* in its ordinary form is usually represented intervocalically, and generally realised phonetically as a front or back high or mid semi-vowel. Incidentally, the character *ɔntostho ɔ* in its ordinary form is not to be confused with the similar looking character that precedes it in table 4.1, the *ɔntostho jɔ* character. This character has the same phonemic realisation as the consonant sign *jɔ* (listed much earlier in table 4.1), and is transliterated in the same way. While *jɔ* and *ɔntostho jɔ* have the same phonemic realisation, they have separate historical sources; and the sign *ɔntostho jɔ* occurs today in the spelling of a limited number of Bengali lexemes, largely direct borrowings from Sanskrit.

The sign *rɔ* exhibits one of two special forms when written in combination with an ordinary consonant sign. In cases where the ordinary consonant sign represents a segment which is pronounced before /r/, then *rɔ* appears in the combining form *rɔ phɔla*; to illustrate: প্রেত [pret] 'ghost, evil spirit'. In cases where the sound represented by the ordinary consonant sign is realised after /r/, *rɔ* appears in the second of its combining forms, which is called *reph*; as in অর্থ [ɔrtho] 'value'.

The sign *hɔ* has a special form, listed in table 4.1, which is written word-finally or before a succeeding consonant in the same syllable. In neither case, however, is the special form of *hɔ* very commonly observed in Bengali writing.

Two special diacritics are listed at the end of table 4.1. The first of these, *cɔndrobindu*, represents the supersegmental for nasalisation, and is written over the ordinary or combining form of any vowel character. The other special diacritic, called *hɔsonto*, is used to represent two ordinary consonant signs as being realised one after another, without an intervening syllabic, in the same phonological syllable; or to show that an ordinary consonant sign written in isolation is to be realised phonologically without the customary 'inherent vowel'. Thus: বাক্ [bak] 'speech', বাক্‌শক্তি [bakšokti] 'power of speech'. In practice, the use of this diacritic is uncommon, except where spelling is offered as a guide to pronunciation; or where the spelling of a word takes account of internal morpheme boundaries, as in the last example.

Table 4.1 does not show the representation of consonant clusters in Bengali orthography. Bengali has about two dozen or so special *sоṅjukto* (literally 'conjunct') characters, used to designate the combination of two, or sometimes three, ordinary consonant signs. In learning to write Bengali, a person must learn the *soṅjukto* signs more or less by rote.

Before considering the sound system of Bengali, it should be mentioned that the spelling of Bengali words is well standardised, though not in all cases a strict guide to pronunciation. There are two especially common areas of inconsistency. One involves the representation of the sound [æ]. Compare the phonetic realisations of the following words with their spellings and transliterations: [æto] এত (transliterated *etɔ*) 'so much, so many'; [bæsto] ব্যস্ত (transliterated *byɔstɔ*) 'busy'; and [læj] ল্যাজ (transliterated *lyajɔ*) 'tail'. The sound [æ] can be orthographically represented in any of the three ways illustrated, and the precise spelling of any word containing this sound must accordingly be memorised.

Another area of inconsistency involves the realisation of the 'inherent vowel'. Since, as mentioned above, the diacritic *hɔsonto* (used to indicate the absence of the inherent vowel) is rarely used in practice, it is not always clear whether an unmodified ordinary consonant character is to be read with or without the inherent vowel. Compare, for example, [kɔto] কত (transliterated *kɔtɔ*) 'how much/how many' with [mɔt] মত (transliterated *mɔtɔ*) 'opinion'. This example makes it especially clear that Bengali spelling is not an infallible guide to pronunciation.

The segmental phonemes (oral vowels and consonants) of the standard dialect of Bengali are set forth in table 4.2. As table 4.2 makes clear, the feature of aspiration is significant for obstruents and defines two phonemically distinct series, the unaspirates and the aspirates. Though not represented in the table since it is non-segmental, the feature of nasalisation is nonetheless significant for vowels and similarly defines two phonemically distinct series. Thus in addition to the oral vowels as listed in table 4.2, Bengali has the corresponding nasalised vowel phonemes /ɔ̃/, ã/, /æ̃/, /õ/, /ẽ/, /ũ/ and /ĩ/.

Table 4.2: Segmental Phonemes of Bengali

Consonants

	Labial	*Dental*	*Retroflex*	*Palatal*	*Velar*	*Post-velar*
Obstruents						
voiceless:						
unaspirated	p	t	ṭ	c	k	
aspirated	ph	th	ṭh	ch	kh	
voiced:						
unaspirated	b	d	ḍ	j	g	
aspirated	bh	dh	ḍh	jh	gh	
Nasals	m	n			ṅ	
Flaps		r	ṛ			
Lateral		l				
Spirants				s		h

Vowels

	Front		*Back*
High	i		u
High mid	e		o
Low mid	æ		ɔ
Low		a	

The phonemic inventory of modern standard Bengali marks it as a fairly typical Indo-Aryan language. The organisation of the consonant system in terms of five basic points of articulation (velar, palatal, retroflex, dental and labial) is characteristic, as is the stop/flap distinction in the retroflex series.

(Hindi-Urdu, for instance, likewise has several retroflex stop phonemes and retroflex flaps.) Also typically Indo-Aryan is the distinctive character of voicing in the Bengali obstruent inventory, along with the distinctive character of aspiration. The latter feature tends, however, to be suppressed preconsonantally, especially in rapid speech. Moreover, the voiced labial aspirate /bh/ tends to be unstable in the pronunciation of many Bengali speakers, often approximating to a voiced labial continuant [v].

In the consonant inventory, Bengali can be regarded as unusual only in having a palatal sibilant phoneme in the absence of a dental sibilant. The historical background of this has been discussed in the preceding section. The phoneme in question is realised as a palatal [š] in all environments, except before the segments /t/, /th/, /n/, /r/, and /l/, where it is realised as a dental, i.e. as [s]. For simplicity, this Bengali sibilant is represented as *s* in the remainder of this chapter.

Nasalisation as a distinctive non-segmental feature of the vowel system is typical not only of Bengali but of modern Indo-Aryan languages generally. In actual articulation, the nasality of the Bengali nasalised vowel segments tends to be fairly weak, and is certainly not as strong as the nasality of vowels in standard French.

The most interesting Modern Bengali phonological processes involve the vowel segments to the relative exclusion of the consonants. One process, Vowel Raising, produces a neutralisation of the high/low distinction in the mid vowels, generally in unstressed syllables. Given the stress pattern of the present standard dialect, which will be discussed later, Vowel Raising generally applies in non-word-initial syllables. Evidence for the process is found in the following alternations:

mɔl	'dirt'	ɔmol	'pure'
sɔ	'hundred'	ækso	'one hundred'
æk	'one'	ɔnek	'many'

A second phonological process affecting vowel height is very significant because of its relationship to morphophonemic alternations in the Bengali verbal base. This process may be called Vowel Height Assimilation, since it involves the assimilation of a non-high vowel (other than /a/) to the nearest succeeding vowel segment within the phonological word, provided the latter has the specification [+high]. Outside the area of verbal morphophonemics, the evidence for this process principally comes from the neutralisation of the high/low distinction in the mid vowels before /i/ or /u/ in a following contiguous syllable. Some alternations which illustrate this process are:

æk	'one'	ekṭi	'one' (plus classifier -ṭi)
lɔjja	'shame'	lojjito	'ashamed'
nɔṭ	'actor'	noṭi	'actress'
æk	'one'	ekṭu	'a little, a bit'
tɔbe	'then'	tobu	'but (then)'

At this point it will be useful to qualify the observation drawn earlier that Bengali is — phonologically speaking — a fairly typical Indo-Aryan language. It is true that most of the segments in the Modern Bengali sound system can be traced more or less directly to Old Indo-Aryan. However, the retroflex flap /ṛ/ of the former has no counterpart in the latter, and its presence in modern standard Bengali (and in some of its sisters) is due to a phonological innovation of Middle Indo-Aryan. Furthermore, while the other retroflex segments of Modern Bengali (/ṭ/, /ṭh/, /ḍ/, /ḍh/) have counterparts in the Old Indo-Aryan sound system, their overall frequency (phonetic load) in Old Indo-Aryan was low. On the other hand, among the modern Indo-Aryan languages, it is Bengali (along with the other Magadhan languages, especially the eastern Magadhan languages) which demonstrates a comparatively high frequency of retroflex sounds. Some external, i.e. non-Aryan influence on the diachronic development of the Bengali sound system is suggested. Such a hypothesis ought logically to be tied in with the observation in the earlier section of this essay that the numerical majority of Bengali speakers represents what were, until recent centuries, culturally unassimilated tribals of eastern Bengal, about whose prior linguistic and social history not much is known.

Further evidence of probable non-Aryan influence in the phonology is to be found in the peculiar word stress pattern of Modern Bengali. Accent was phonemic only in very early Old Indo-Aryan, i.e. Vedic (see page 39). Subsequently, however, predictable word stress has typified the Indo-Aryan languages; the characteristic pattern, moreover, has been for the stress to fall so many morae from the end of the phonological word. Bengali word stress, though, is exceptional. It is non-phonemic and, in the standard dialect, there is a strong tendency for it to be associated with word-*initial* syllables. This pattern evidently became dominant after AD 1400, or well after Bengali acquired a linguistic identity separate from that of its Indo-Aryan sisters. What this and other evidence may imply about the place of Bengali within the general South Asian language area is an issue to be further pursued toward the end of this essay.

3 Morphology

Morphology in Modern Bengali is non-existent for adjectives, minimal for nouns and very productive for verbs. Loss or reduction of the earlier Indo-Aryan adjective declensional parameters (gender, case, number) is fairly typical of the modern Indo-Aryan languages; hence the absence of adjectival morphology in Modern Bengali is not surprising. Bengali differs from many of its sisters, however, in lacking certain characteristic nominal categories. The early Indo-Aryan category of gender persists in most of the modern languages, with the richest (three-gender) systems still to be found in some of the western languages, such as Marathi. Early stages of the

Magadhan languages (e.g. Oriya, Assamese and Bengali) also show evidence of a gender system. However, the category is no longer productive in any of the modern Magadhan languages. In Modern Bengali, it is only in a few relic alternations (e.g. the earlier cited pair *nɔṭ* 'actor'/*noṭi* 'actress') that one observes any evidence today for the system of nominal gender which once existed in the language.

The early Indo-Aryan system of three number categories has been reduced in Modern Bengali to a singular/plural distinction which is marked on nouns and pronouns. The elaborate case system of early Indo-Aryan has also been reduced in Modern Bengali as it has in most modern Indo-Aryan languages. Table 4.3 summarises the standard Bengali declension for full nouns (pronouns are not given). Pertinent parameters not, however, revealed in this table are animacy, definiteness and determinacy. Generally, the plural markers are added only to count nouns having animate or definite referents; otherwise plurality tends to be unmarked. Compare, e.g. *jutogulo dɔrkar* 'the (specified) shoes are necessary' versus *juto dɔrkar* '(unspecified) shoes are necessary'. Further, among the plurality markers listed in table 4.3, *-gulo* (nominative), *-guloke* (objective), *-gulor* (genitive) and *-gulote* (locative-instrumental) are applicable to nouns with both animate and inanimate referents, while the other markers cooccur only with animate nouns. Hence: *chelera* '(the) boys', *chelegulo* '(the) boys', *jutogulo* 'the shoes', but **jutora* 'the shoes'.

Table 4.3: Bengali Nominal Declension

	Singular	*Plural*
Nominative	Ø	-ra/-era; -gulo
Objective	-ke	-der(ke)/-eder(ke); -guloke
Genitive	-r/-er	-der/-eder; -gulor
Locative-Instrumental	-te/-e *or* -ete	-gulote

The Bengali case markers in table 4.3 which show an alternation of form (e.g. *-r/-er, -te/-e* or *-ete, -der(ke)/-eder(ke)*, etc.) are phonologically conditioned according to whether the forms to which they are appended terminate in a syllabic or non-syllabic segment respectively. Both *-eder(ke)* and *-ete* are, however, currently rare. The usage of the objective singular marker *-ke*, listed in table 4.3, tends to be confined to inanimate noun phrases having definite referents and to definite or determinate animate noun phrases. Thus compare *kichu (*kichuke) caichen* 'do you want something?' with *kauke (*kau) caichen* 'do you want someone?'; but: *pulis caichen* 'are you seeking a policeman/some policemen?' versus *puliske caichen* 'are you seeking the police?'.

Bengali subject-predicate agreement will be covered in the following section on syntax. It bears mentioning at present, however, that the sole parameters for subject-verb agreement in Modern Bengali are person (three are distinguished) and status. Inflectionally, the Bengali verb is marked for three status categories (despective/ordinary/honorific) in the second person and two categories (ordinary/honorific) in the third. It is notable that the shapes of the honorific inflectional endings are modelled on earlier Indo-Aryan plural inflectional markers. Table 4.4 lists the verbal inflection of modern standard Bengali.

Table 4.4: Bengali Verbal Inflection

	1st person	*2nd person despective*	*2nd person ordinary*	*3rd person ordinary*	*Honorific (2nd, 3rd persons)*
Present imperative	–	Ø	-o	-uk	-un
Unmarked indicative and *-(c)ch-* stems	-i	-is	-o	-e	-en
-b- stems	-o	-i	-e	-e	-en
-t- and *-l-* stems	-am	-i	-e	-o	-en

The most interesting area of Bengali morphology is the derivation of inflecting stems from verbal bases. Properly speaking, a formal analysis of Bengali verbal stem derivation presupposes the statement of various morphophonological rules. However, for the sake of brevity and clarity, the phenomena will be outlined below more or less informally.

But before the system of verbal stem derivational marking can be discussed, two facts must be presented concerning the shapes of Bengali verbal bases, i.e. the bases to which the stem markers are added.

First, Bengali verbal bases are all either monosyllabic (such as *jan-* 'know') or disyllabic (such as *kamṛa-* 'bite'). The first syllabic in the verbal base may be called the root vowel. There is a productive process for deriving disyllabic bases from monosyllabics by the addition of a stem vowel. This stem vowel is *-a-* (post-vocalically *-oa-*) as in *jana-* 'inform'; although, for many speakers, the stem vowel may be *-o-* if the root vowel (i.e. of the monosyllabic base) is [+high]; e.g. *jiro-*, for some speakers *jira-* 'rest'. Derived disyllabics usually serve as the formal causatives of their monosyllabic counterparts. Compare: *jan-* 'know', *jana-* 'inform'; *oṭh-* 'rise', *oṭha-* 'raise'; *dækh-* 'see', *dækha-* 'show'.

Second, monosyllabic bases with non-high root vowels have two alternate forms, respectively called low and high. Examples are:

	Low alternate base	*High alternate base*
'know'	jan-	jen-
'see'	dækh-	dekh-
'sit'	bɔs-	bos-
'buy'	ken-	kin-
'rise'	oṭh-	uṭh-

When the root vowel is /a/, /e/ is substituted to derive the high alternate base; for bases with front or back non-high root vowels, the high alternate base is formed by assimilating the original root vowel to the next higher vowel in the vowel inventory (see again table 4.2). The latter behaviour suggests an extended application of the Vowel Height Assimilation process discussed in the preceding section. It is, in fact, feasible to state the rules of verb stem derivation so that the low/high alternation is phonologically motivated; i.e. by positing a high vowel (specifically, /i/) in the underlying shapes of the stem-deriving markers. In some verbal forms there is concrete evidence for the /i/ element, as will be observed below. Also, Vowel Height Assimilation must be invoked in any case to account for the fact that, in the derivation of verbal forms which have zero marking of the stem (that is, the present imperative and unmarked (present) indicative), the high alternate base occurs before any inflection containing a high vowel. Thus *dækh-* 'see', *dækho* 'you (ordinary) see', but *dekhi* 'I see', *dekhis* 'you (despective) see', *dekhun* (honorific) 'see!', etc. That there is no high-low alternation in these inflections for disyllabic bases is consistent with the fact that Vowel Height Assimilation only applies when a high syllabic occurs in the immediately succeeding syllable. Thus *oṭha-* 'raise (cause to rise)', *oṭhae* 'he/she raises', *oṭhai* (**uṭhai*) 'I/we raise', etc.

The left-hand column of table 4.4 lists the various Bengali verbal stem types. Two of the verbal forms with Ø stem marking, the present imperative and present indicative, were just discussed. It may be pointed out that, in this stem type, the vowel element /u/ of the third person ordinary inflection *-uk* and of the second/third person honorific inflection *-un*, as well as the /i/ of the second person despective inflection *-is*, all disappear post-vocalically (after Vowel Height Assimilation applies); thus (as above) *dekhis* 'you (despective) see' but (from *hɔ-* 'become') *hok* 'let him/her/it/them become!'; *hon* 'he/she/you/they (honorific) become!'; *hos* 'you (despective) become'.

A verbal form with Ø stem marking not so far discussed is the denominative verbal form or verbal noun. The verbal noun is a non-inflecting form and is therefore not listed in table 4.4. In monosyllabic bases, the marker of this form is suffixed *-a* (*-oa* post-vocalically); for most standard dialect speakers, the marker in disyllabics is *-no*. Thus *oṭh-* 'rise', *oṭha* 'rising', *oṭha-* 'raise', *oṭhano* 'raising'; *jan-* 'know', *jana* 'knowing', *jana-* 'inform', *janano* 'informing'; *ga-* 'sing', *gaoa* 'singing', *gaoa-* 'cause to sing', *gaoano* 'causing to sing'.

Continuing in the leftmost column of table 4.4, the stem-deriving marker *-(c)ch-* signals continuative aspect and is used, independent of any other derivational marker, to derive the present continuous verbal form. The element (*c*) of the marker *-(c)ch-* deletes post-consonantally; compare *khacche* 'is eating' (from *kha-*) with *anche* 'is bringing' (from *an-*). In forming the verbal stem with *-(c)ch-* the high alternate base is selected, unless the base is disyllabic or is a monosyllabic base having the root vowel

/a/. Compare the last examples with *uṭhche* 'is rising' (from *oṭh-*), *oṭhacche* 'is raising' (from *oṭha-*). In a formal treatment of Bengali morphophonemics, the basic or underlying form of the stem marker could be given as *-i(c)ch-*; in this event, one would posit a rule to delete the element /i/ after Vowel Height Assimilation applies, except in a very limited class of verbs including *ga-* 'sing', *sɔ-* 'bear' and *ca-* 'want'. In forming the present continuous forms of these verbs, the element /i/ surfaces, although the element (*c*) of the stem marker tends to be deleted. The resulting shapes are, respectively: *gaiche* 'is singing' (*gacche* is at best non-standard); *soiche* (**socche*) 'is bearing'; *caiche* 'is wanting' (*cacche* does, however, occur as a variant).

The stem-deriving marker *-b-* (see table 4.4) signals irrealis aspect and is used to derive future verbal forms, both indicative and imperative (except for the imperative of the second person ordinary, which will be treated after the next paragraph). In Bengali, the future imperative, as well as the present imperative, may occur in affirmative commands; however, the future imperative, never the present imperative, occurs in negative commands.

In forming the verbal stem with *-b-*, the high alternate base is selected except in three cases: where the base is disyllabic, where the monosyllabic base has the root vowel /a/ and where the monosyllabic base is vowel-final. Thus: *uṭhbo* 'I/we will rise' (from *oṭh-*), but *oṭhabo* 'I/we will raise' (from *oṭha-*); *janbo* 'I/we will know' (from *jan-*), *debo* 'I/we will give' (from *de-*). Compare, however, *dibi* 'you (despective) will give', where Vowel Height Assimilation raises the root vowel. It is possible, again, to posit an underlying /i/ in the irrealis stem marker's underlying shape (i.e. *-ib-*), with deletion of the element /i/ applying except for the small class of verbs noted earlier; thus *gaibo* (**gabo*) 'I/we will sing', *soibo* (**sobo*) 'I/we will bear', *caibo* (**cabo*) 'I/we will want'.

The future imperative of the second person ordinary takes the termination *-io*, which can be analysed as a stem formant *-i-* followed by the second person ordinary inflection *-o* (which is also added to unmarked stems, as table 4.4 shows). When combining with this marker *-i-*, all monosyllabic bases occur in their high alternate shapes; e.g. *hoio* 'become!' (from *hɔ-*). The *-i-* marker is deleted post-consonantally, hence *uṭho* 'rise!' (from *oṭh-*); it also deletes when added to most monosyllabic bases terminating in final /a/, for instance: *peo* 'get!' (**peio*) (from *pa-* 'receive'); *geo* 'sing!' (from *ga-* 'sing'). Bengali disyllabic bases drop their final element /a/ or /o/ before the future imperative stem marker *-i-*. Vowel Height Assimilation applies, hence *uṭhio* 'you must raise!' (from *oṭha-*), *dekhio* 'you must show!' (from *dækha-*), *kamṛio* 'you must bite!' (from *kamṛa-*).

Continuing in the left-hand column of table 4.4, the stem-deriving marker *-t-* signals non-punctual aspect and appears in several forms of the Bengali verb. The Bengali infinitive termination is invariant *-te*, e.g. *jante* 'to know' (from *jan-*) (as in *jante cai* 'I want to know'). The marker *-t-* also occurs in the finite verbal form used to express the past habitual and perfect conditional, e.g. *jantam* 'I/we used to know' or 'if I/we had known'. The high alternate of monosyllabic bases cooccurs with this marker except in those bases containing a root vowel /a/ followed by a consonant. To illustrate, the infinitive of *oṭh-* 'rise' is *uṭhte*; of *oṭha-* 'raise', *oṭhate*; of *de-* 'give', *dite*; of *hɔ-* 'become', *hote*; of *kha-* 'eat', *khete*; of *an-* 'bring', *ante* (**ente*). Similarly, *uṭhtam* 'I/we used to rise' or 'if I/we had risen'; *oṭhatam* 'I/we used to raise' or 'if I/we had raised', etc. As before, evidence for an /i/ element in the underlying form of the marker *-t-* (i.e. *-it-*) comes from the earlier noted class of verbs 'sing', etc.; for example, *gaite* (**gate*) 'to sing', *gaitam* (**gatam*) 'I/we used to sing' or 'if I/we had sung'; *soite* (**sote*) 'to bear', *soitam* (**sotam*) 'I/we used to bear' or 'if I/we had borne'; *caite* (**cate*) 'to want', *caitam* (**catam*) 'I/we used to want' or 'if I/we had wanted', etc.

The stem-deriving marker *-l-* signals anterior aspect and appears in two verbal forms. The termination of the imperfect conditional is invariant *-le*, e.g. *janle* 'if one knows' (from *jan-*). The marker *-l-* also occurs in the ordinary past tense verbal form, e.g. *janlam* 'I/we knew'. The behaviour of monosyllabic verbal bases in coocurrence with this marker is the same as their behaviour in cooccurrence with the marker *-t-* discussed above. Thus *uṭhle* 'if one rises', *oṭhale* 'if one raises', *dile* 'if one gives', *hole* 'if one becomes', *khele* 'if one eats', *anle* 'if one brings'; *uṭhlam* 'I/we rose', *oṭhalam* 'I/we raised'; and, again, *gaile* (**gale*) 'if one sings', *soile* (**sole*) 'if one bears', *caile* (**cale*) 'if one wants'; *gailam* 'I/we sang', and so on.

To complete the account of the conjugation of the Bengali verb it is only necessary to mention that certain stem-deriving markers can be combined on a single verbal base. For instance, the marker *-l-* combined with the uninflected stem in *-(c)ch-* yields a verbal form called the past continuous. Illustrations are: *uṭhchilam* 'I was/we were rising' (from *oṭh-*), *oṭhacchilam* 'I was/we were raising' (from *oṭha-*), *khacchilam* 'I was/we were eating' (from *kha-*).

It is also possible to combine stem-deriving markers on the Bengali verbal base in the completive aspect. The marker of this aspect is *-(i)e-*, not listed in table 4.4 because it is not used in isolation from other stem-forming markers to form inflecting verbal stems. Independently of any other stem-forming marker it may, however, be added to a verbal base to derive a non-finite verbal form known as the conjunctive participle (or gerund). An example is: *bujhe* 'having understood' from *bujh-* 'understand' (note that the element (*i*) of *-(i)e-* deletes post-consonantally). When attached to the completive aspect marker *-(i)e-*, all monosyllabic bases occur in their high alternate shapes; disyllabic bases drop their final element /a/ or /o/; and in the latter case, Vowel Height Assimilation applies. Thus: *uṭhe* 'having risen' (from *oṭh-*); *jene* 'having known' (from *jan-*); *diye* 'having given' (from *de-*); *uṭhie* 'having raised' (from *oṭha-*), *janie* 'having informed' (from *jana-*). Now the stem-deriving marker *-(c)ch-* may combine with the verbal stem in *-(i)e-*, yielding a verbal form called the present perfect; the combining shape of the

Bengali Verbal Conjugation Types

	pa- 'receive'		*an- 'bring'*		*bɔs- 'sit'*		*bɔsa- 'seat'*	
Verbal noun	paoa	'receiving'	ana	'bringing'	bɔsa	'sitting'	bɔsano	'seating'
Present indicative	pae	'receives'	ane	'brings'	bɔse	'sits'	bɔsae	'seats'
Present imperative	pak	'let him/her/ them receive!'	anuk	'let him/ her/them bring!'	bosuk	'let him/ her/them sit!'	bɔsak	'let him/her/ them seat!'
Present continuous	pacche	'is receiving'	anche	'is bringing'	bosche	'is sitting'	bɔsacche	'is seating'
Future indicative/ future imperative	pabe	'will receive'/ 'must receive!'	anbe	'will bring'/ 'must bring!'	bosbe	'will sit'/ 'must sit!'	bɔsabe	'will seat'/ 'must seat!'
Infinitive	pete	'to receive'	ante	'to bring'	boste	'to sit'	bɔsate	'to seat'
Perfect conditional/ past habitual	peto	'would receive'	anto	'would bring'	bosto	'would sit'	bɔsato	'would seat'
Imperfect conditional	pele	'if one receives'	anle	'if one brings'	bosle	'if one sits'	bɔsale	'if one seats'
Ordinary past	pelo	'received'	anlo	'brought'	boslo	'sat'	bɔsalo	'seated'
Past continuous	pacchilo	'was receiving'	anchilo	'was bringing'	boschilo	'was sitting'	bɔsacchilo	'was seating'
Conjunctive participle	peye	'having received'	ene	'having brought'	bose	'having sat'	bosie	'having seated'
Present perfect	peyeche	'has received'	eneche	'has brought'	boseche	'has sat'	bosieche	'has seated'
Past perfect	peyechilo	'had received'	enechilo	'had brought'	bosechilo	'had sat'	bosiechilo	'had seated'

former marker in such cases is invariably *-ch-*. This is to say that the element *(c)* of the marker *-(c)ch-* not only deletes post-consonantally (see the earlier discussion of continuous aspect marking), but also following the stem-deriving marker *-(i)e-*. Some examples are: *dekheche* 'has seen' (from monosyllabic *dækh-*), *dekhieche* 'has shown' (from disyllabic *dækha-*), *diyeche* 'has given' (from *de-* 'give'). The verbal stem in *-(i)e-* followed by *-(c)ch-* may further combine with the anterior aspect marker *-l-* to yield a verbal form called the past perfect; e.g. *dekhechilam* 'I/we had seen', *dekhiechilam* 'I/we had shown'.

Examples of conjugation for four Bengali verbal bases are given in the chart of verbal conjugation types. The inflection illustrated in the chart is the third person ordinary.

4 Syntax

The preceding discussion of declensional parameters (case and number for nouns, person and status for verbs) ties in naturally with the topic of agreement in Bengali syntax. A number of modern Indo-Aryan languages (see, for example, the chapter on Hindi-Urdu) demonstrate a degree of ergative patterning in predicate-noun phrase agreement; and Bengali, in its early historical stages, likewise showed some ergative patterning (i.e. sentential verb agreeing with subject of an intransitive sentence but with object, not subject, of a transitive sentence). However, this behaviour is not characteristic today of any of the eastern Magadhan languages.

Thus in Modern Bengali, sentences normally have subjects in the nominative or unmarked case, and the finite predicates of sentences normally agree with their subjects for the parameters of person and status. There are, however, two broad classes of exceptions to this generalisation. The passive constructions exemplify one class. Passive in Modern Bengali is a special variety of sentence nominalisation. When a sentence is nominalised, the predicate takes the verbal noun form (discussed in the preceding section) and the subject is marked with the genitive case. Under passivisation, a sentence is nominalised and then assigned to one of a small set of matrix predicates, the most common being *hɔ-* 'become' and *ja-* 'go'; and when the latter is selected, the subject of the nominalised sentence is obligatorily deleted. Examples are: *tomar jɔtheṣṭo khaoa hoyeche?* (your enough eating has-become) 'have you eaten enough?' (i.e. has it been sufficiently eaten by you?) and *oke paoa gælo* (to-him getting it-went) 'he was found' (i.e. him was found). In a passive sentence, the matrix verb (*hɔ-* or *ja-*) lacks agreement with any noun phrase. In particular, it cannot agree with the original subject of the active sentence — this noun phrase has become marked with the genitive case under nominalisation, or deleted altogether. This is to say that the Modern Bengali passive construction lacks a formal subject; it is of a type referred to in some grammatical literature as the 'impersonal passive'. These constructions form one class of exceptions to the characteristic pattern of Bengali subject-verb agreement.

The other class of exceptions comprises certain expressions having subjects which occur in a marked or oblique case. In Bengali there are a few complex constructions of this type. Bengali also has several dozen predicates which regularly occur in non-complex constructions with marked subjects. These constructions can be called indirect subject constructions, and indirect subjects in Modern Bengali are invariably marked with the genitive case. (At an earlier historical stage of the language, any of the oblique cases could be used for the marking of the subject in this sort of construction.) In the Modern Bengali indirect subject construction, the finite predicate normally demonstrates no agreement. An example is: *maer tomake pɔchondo hɔy* (of-mother to-you likes) 'Mother likes you'. Bengali indirect subject predicates typically express sensory, mental, emotional, corporal and other characteristically human experiences. These predicates constitute a significant class of exceptions to the generalised pattern of subject-finite predicate agreement in Modern Bengali.

The remainder of this overview of Bengali syntax will be devoted to the topic of word order, or the relative ordering of major constituents in sentences. In some literature on word order types, Bengali has been characterised as a rigidly verb-final language, wherein nominal modifiers precede their heads; verbal modifiers follow verbal bases; the verbal complex is placed sentence-finally; and the subject noun phrase occupies the initial position in a sentence. In these respects Bengali is said to contrast with earlier Indo-Aryan, in which the relative ordering of sentential constituents was freer, notwithstanding a statistical tendency for verbs to stand at the ends of their clauses.

It is true that the ordering of sentential elements is more rigid in Modern Bengali than in Classical Sanskrit. However, the view that Bengali represents a 'rigid' verb-final language does not adequately describe its differences from earlier Indo-Aryan word order patterning.

Word order within the Modern Bengali noun phrase is, to be sure, strict. An adjective or genitive expression is always placed before the noun it modifies. By contrast, in earlier Indo-Aryan, adjectives showed inflectional concord with their modified nouns and consequently were freer in their positioning; more or less the same applied to the positioning of genitive expressions with respect to nominal heads. Not only is the ordering of elements within the noun phrase more rigid in Modern Bengali, but the mutual ordering of noun phrases within the sentence is strict as well, much more so than in earlier Indo-Aryan. The subject noun phrase generally comes first in a Modern Bengali sentence, followed by an indirect object if one occurs; next comes the direct object if one occurs; after which an oblique object noun phrase may be positioned. This strictness of linear ordering can be ascribed to the relative impoverishment of the Modern Bengali case system in comparison with earlier Indo-Aryan. Bengali case markers are, nonetheless, supplemented by a number of postpositions, each of which may govern nouns declined in one of two cases, the objective or genitive.

We will now consider word order within the verb phrase. At the Old Indo-Aryan stage exemplified by Classical Sanskrit, markers representing certain verbal qualifiers (causal, desiderative, potential and conditional) could be affixed to verbal bases, as stem-forming markers and/or as inflectional endings. Another verbal qualifier, the marker of sentential negation, tended to be placed just before the sentential verb. The sentential interrogative particle, on the other hand, was often placed at a distance from the verbal complex.

In Modern Bengali, the only verbal qualifier which is regularly affixed to verbal bases is the causal. (See the discussion of derived disyllabic verbal bases in section 3 above.) The following pair of Bengali sentences illustrates the formal relationship between non-causative and causative constructions: *cheleṭi ciṭhiṭa poṛlo* (the-boy the-letter read) 'the boy read the letter'; *ma cheleṭi-ke diye ciṭhiṭa pɔṛalen* (mother to-the-boy by the-letter caused-to-read) 'the mother had the boy read the letter'. It will be noted that in the second example the non-causal agent is marked with the postposition *diye* 'by' placed after its governed noun, which appears in the objective case. Usually, when the verbal base from which the causative is formed is transitive, the non-causal agent is marked in just this way. The objective case alone is used to mark the non-causal agent when the causative is derived either from an intransitive base, or from any of several semantically 'affective' verbs — transitive verbs expressing actions whose principal effect accrues to their agents and not their undergoers. Examples are: 'eat', 'smell', 'hear', 'see', 'read' (in the sense of 'study'), 'understand' and several others.

It was mentioned above that the modalities of desiderative and potential action could be marked on the verbal form itself in Old Indo-Aryan. In Modern Bengali, these modalities are usually expressed periphrastically; i.e. by suffixing the infinitive marker to the verbal stem, which is then followed by a modal verb. To illustrate: *uṭhte cae* 'wants to rise', *uṭhte pare* 'can rise'.

Conditional expressions occur in two forms in Modern Bengali. The conditional clause may be finite, in which case there appears the particle *jodi*, which is a direct borrowing from a functionally similar Sanskrit particle *yadi*. To illustrate: *jodi tumi kajṭa sarbe (tɔbe) eso* (if you the-work will-finish (then) come) 'if/when you finish the work, (then) come over!'. An alternate way of framing a conditional is by means of the non-finite conditional verbal form (imperfect conditional), which was mentioned in section 3. In this case no conditional particle is used; e.g. *tumi kajṭa sarle (tɔbe) eso* (you the-work if-finish (then) come) 'if/when you finish the work, come over!'.

The particle of sentential negation in Bengali is *na*. In independent clauses it generally follows the sentential verb; in subjoined clauses (both finite and non-finite), it precedes. Thus: *boslam na* (I-sat not) 'I did not sit'; *jodi tumi na bɔso* (if you not sit) 'if you don't sit'; *tumi na bosle* (you not if-sit) 'if you don't sit'. Bengali has, it should be mentioned, two negative verbs. Each of them is a counterpart to one of the verbs 'to be'; and in this connection it needs to be stated that Bengali has three verbs 'to be'. These are respectively the predicative *hɔ-* 'become'; the existential verb 'exist', having independent/subjoined clause allomorphs *ach-/thak-*; and the equational verb or copula, which is normally Ø but in emphatic contexts is represented by *hɔ-* placed between two arguments (compare, for example, non-emphatic *ini jodu* (this-person Ø Jodu) 'this is Jodu' versus emphatic *ini hocchen jodu* (this-person is Jodu) 'this (one) is Jodu'). While the predicative verb 'to be' has no special negative counterpart (it is negated like any other Bengali verb), the other two verbs 'to be' each have a negative counterpart. Moreover, for each of these negative verbs, there are separate allomorphs which occur in independent and subjoined clauses. The respective independent/subjoined shapes of the negative verbs are existential *nei/na thak-* (note that the verb *nei* is invariant) and equational *nɔ-/na hɔ-*. It bears mentioning, incidentally, that negative verbs are neither characteristic of modern nor of earlier Indo-Aryan. They are, if anything, reminiscent of negative copulas and other negative verbs in languages of the Dravidian (South Indian) family, such as Modern Tamil.

The Modern Bengali sentential interrogative particle *ki* is inherited from an earlier Indo-Aryan particle of similar function. The sentential interrogative *ki* may appear in almost any position in a Bengali sentence other than absolute initial; however, sentences vary in their presuppositional nuances according to the placement of this particle, which seems to give the most neutral reading when placed in the second position (i.e. after the first sentential constituent). To illustrate, compare: *tumi ki ekhane chatro?* (you interrogative here student) 'are you a student here?'; *tumi ekhane ki chatro?* (you here interrogative student) 'is it here that you are a student?'; *tumi ekhane chatro (na) ki?* (you here student (negative) interrogative) 'oh, is it that you are a student here?'.

To complete this treatment of word order, we may discuss the relative ordering of marked and unmarked clauses in Bengali complex sentences. By 'marked clause' is meant either a non-finite subordinate clause or a clause whose function within the sentential frame is signalled by some distinctive marker; an instance of such a marker being *jodi*, the particle of the finite conditional clause. As a rule, in a Bengali sentence containing two or more clauses, marked clauses tend to precede unmarked. This is, for instance, true of conjunctive participle constructions; e.g. *baṛi giye kapoṛ cheṛe ami can korlam* (home having-gone clothes having-removed I bath did) 'going home and removing my clothes, I had a bath'. Relative clauses in Bengali likewise generally precede main clauses, since they are marked (that is, with relative pronouns); Bengali, then, exhibits the correlative sentential type which is well attested throughout the history of Indo-Aryan. An illustration of this construction is: *je boiṭa enecho ami seṭa kichu din rakhbo* (which book you-brought I it some days will-keep) 'I shall keep the book you have brought for a few days'. Finite complement sentences marked with the complementiser *bole* (derived from the conjunctive participle of the verb *bɔl-* 'say') likewise precede unmarked clauses; e.g. *apni jacchen bole ami jani* (you are-going complementiser I know) 'I know that you are going'.

An exception to the usual order of marked before unmarked clauses is exemplified by an alternative finite complement construction. Instead of clause-final marking (with *bole*), the complement clause type in question has an initial marker, a particle *je* (derived historically from a complementiser particle of earlier Indo-Aryan). A complement clause marked initially with *je* is ordered invariably after, not before, the unmarked clause; e.g. *ami jani je apni jacchen* (I know complementiser you are-going) 'I know that you are going'.

5 Concluding Points

In this final section the intention is to relate the foregoing discussion to the question of Bengali's historical development and present standing, both within the Indo-Aryan family and within the general South Asian language area. To accomplish this, it is useful to consider the fact of lectal differentiation in the present community of Bengali speakers. Both vertical and horizontal varieties are observed.

Vertical differentiation, or diglossia, is a feature of the current standard language. This is to say that the language has two styles used more or less for complementary purposes. Of the two styles, the literary or 'pundit language' (*sadhu bhasa*) shows greater conservatism in word morphology (i.e. in regard to verbal morphophonemics and the shapes of case endings) as well as in lexis (it is characterised by a high frequency of words whose forms are directly borrowed from Sanskrit). The less conservative style identified with the spoken or 'current language' (*colti bhasa*) is the everyday medium of informal discourse. Lately it is also gaining currency in more formal discourse situations and, in written expression, has been encroaching on the literary style for some decades.

The institutionalisation of the *sadhu-colti* distinction occurred in Bengali in the nineteenth century, and (as suggested in the last paragraph) shows signs of weakening today. Given (1) that the majority of Bengali speakers today are not Hindu and cannot be expected to maintain an emotional affinity to Sanskritic norms, plus (2) the Bangladesh government's recent moves to enhance the Islamic character of eastern Bengali society and culture and (3) the fact that the colloquial style is overtaking the literary even in western Bengal (both in speech and writing), it remains to be seen over the coming years whether a formal differentiation of everyday versus 'pundit' style language will be maintained.

It should be added that, although throughout the Bengali-speaking area a single, more or less uniform variety of the language is regarded as the standard dialect, the bulk of speakers have at best a passing acquaintance with it. That is, horizontal differentiation of Bengali lects is very extensive (if poorly researched), both in terms of the number of regional dialects that occur and in terms of their mutual divergence. (The extreme eastern dialect of Chittagong, for instance, is unintelligible even to many speakers of other eastern Bengali dialects.) The degree of horizontal differentiation that occurs in the present Bengali-speaking region is related to the ambiguity of Bengali's linguistic affiliation, i.e. areal as contrasted with genetic. It is to be noted that the Bengali-speaking region of the Indian subcontinent to this day borders on or subsumes the domains of a number of non-Indo-Aryan languages. Among them are Malto (a Dravidian language of eastern Bihar); Ahom (a Tai language of neighbouring Assam); Garo (a Tibeto-Burman language spoken in the northern districts of Bengal itself); as well as several languages affiliated with Munda (a subfamily of Austro-Asiatic), such as Santali and Mundari (both of these languages are spoken within as well as outside the Bengali-speaking area).

It has been pointed out earlier that modern standard Bengali has several features suggestive of extra-Aryan influence. These features are: the frequency of retroflex consonants; initial-syllable word stress; absence of grammatical gender; negative verbs. Though not specifically pointed out as such previously, Bengali has several other formal features, discussed above, which represent divergences from the norms of Indo-Aryan and suggest convergence with the areal norms of greater South Asia. These features are: post-verbal negative particle placement; clause-final complement sentence marking; relative rigidity of word order patterning in general, and sentence-final verb positioning in particular; proliferation of the indirect subject construction (which was only occasionally manifested in early Indo-Aryan).

In addition to the above, it may be mentioned that Bengali has two lexical features of a type foreign to Indo-Aryan. These features are, however, not atypical of languages of the general South Asian language area (and are even more typical of South-East Asian languages). One of these is a class of reduplicative expressives, words such as: *kickic* (suggesting grittiness), *miṭmiṭ* (suggesting flickering), *ṭɔlmɔl* (suggesting an overflowing or fluid state). There are dozens of such lexemes in current standard Bengali. The other un-Aryan lexical class consists of around a dozen classifier words, principally numeral classifiers. Examples are: *du jon chatro* (two human-classifier student) 'two students'; *tin khana boi* (three flat-thing-classifier book) 'three books'.

It is probable that the features discussed above were absorbed from other languages into Bengali after the thirteenth century, as the language came to be increasingly used east of the traditional sociocultural centre of Bengal. That centre, located along the former main course of the Ganges (the present-day Bhagirathi-Hooghley River) in western Bengal, still sets the standard for spoken and written expression in the language. Thus standard Bengali is defined even today as the dialect spoken in Calcutta and its environs. It is a reasonable hypothesis nevertheless, as suggested above in section 1, that descendants of non-Bengali tribals of a few centuries past now comprise the bulk of Bengali speakers. In other words, the vast majority of the Bengali linguistic community today represents present or former inhabitants of the previously uncultivated and culturally unassimilated tracts of eastern Bengal. Over the past several centuries, these newcomers to the Bengali-speaking community are the ones responsible for the language's having acquired a definite affiliation within the South Asian linguistic area, above and beyond the predetermined and less interesting fact of its genetic affiliation in Indo-Aryan.

Bibliography

Chatterji (1926) is the classic, and indispensable, treatment of historical phonology and morphology in Bengali and the other Indo-Aryan languages. A good bibliographical source is Čižikova and Ferguson (1969). For the relation between literary and colloquial Bengali, see Dimock (1960).

The absence of a comprehensive reference grammar of Bengali in English is noticeable. Ray et al. (1966) is one of the better concise reference grammars. Chatterji (1939) is a comprehensive grammar in Bengali, while Chatterji (1972) is a concise but thorough treatment of Bengali grammar following the traditional scheme of Indian grammars. Two pedagogical works are also useful: Dimock et al. (1965), a first-year textbook containing very lucid descriptions of the basic structural categories of the language, and Bender and Riccardi (1978), an advanced Bengali textbook containing much useful information on Bengali literature and on the modern literary language. For individual topics, the following can be recommended: on phonetics-phonology, Chatterji (1921) and Ferguson and Chowdhury (1960); on the morphology of the verb, Dimock (1957), Ferguson (1945) and Sarkar (1976); on syntax, Klaiman (1981), which discusses the syntax and semantics of the indirect subject construction, passives and the conjunctive participle construction in modern and earlier stages of Bengali.

References

Bender, E. and T. Riccardi, Jr. 1978. *An Advanced Course in Bengali* (South Asia Regional Studies, University of Pennsylvania, Philadephia)

Chatterji, S.K. 1921. 'Bengali Phonetics', in *Bulletin of the School of Oriental and African Studies*, vol. 2, pp. 1–25

—— 1926. *The Origin and Development of the Bengali Language*, 3 vols. (Allen and Unwin, London)

—— 1939. *Bhāṣāprakāśa bāṅgālā byākaraṇa* (Calcutta University, Calcutta)

—— 1972. *Sarala bhāṣāprakāśa bāṅgālā byākaraṇa*, revised ed. (Bāk-sāhitya, Calcutta)

Čižikova, K.L. and C.A. Ferguson. 1969. 'Bibliographical Review of Bengali Studies', in T. Sebeok (ed.), *Current Trends in Linguistics*, vol. 5: *Linguistics in South Asia* (Mouton, The Hague), pp. 85–98

Dimock, E.C., Jr. 1957. 'Notes on Stem-vowel Alternation in the Bengali Verb', *Indian Linguistics*, vol. 17, pp. 173–7

—— 1960. 'Literary and Colloquial Bengali in Modern Bengali Prose', *International Journal of American Linguistics*, vol. 26, no. 3, pp. 43–63

—— et al. 1965. *Introduction to Bengali*, part 1 (East-West Center, Honolulu; reprinted South Asia Books, Columbia, Mo., 1976)

Ferguson, C.A. 1945. 'A Chart of the Bengali Verb', *Journal of the American Oriental Society*, vol. 65, pp. 54–5

—— and M. Chowdhury. 1960. 'The Phonemes of Bengali', *Language*, vol. 36, pp. 22–59

Klaiman, M.H. 1981. *Volitionality and Subject in Bengali: A Study of Semantic Parameters in Grammatical Processes* (Indiana University Linguistics Club, Bloomington)

Ray, P.S., et al. 1966. *Bengali Language Handbook* (Center for Applied Linguistics, Washington, DC)

Sarkar, P. 1976. 'The Bengali Verb', *International Journal of Dravidian Linguistics*, vol. 5, pp. 274–97

5 IRANIAN LANGUAGES

J. R. Payne

The approximate present distribution of the Iranian languages is illustrated in the attached sketch-map. The languages currently spoken, according to their genetic relations within Iranian (see below) are:

South-West Iranian: Persian (Iran, Persian Gulf); Dari (Afghanistan); Tajiki (USSR); Luri and Bakhtiari (nomadic, Iran); Kumzari (Persian Gulf); non-Persian dialects of Fars province, centred on Shiraz, Kazerun, Sivand and Lar (Iran); Tati (USSR).

North-West Iranian: Kurdish (Turkey, Iran, Iraq, Syria, USSR); Talishi (USSR, Iran); Balochi (Pakistan, Iran, Afghanistan, USSR, Persian Gulf); Gilaki (Iran); Mazandarani (Iran); Zaza (Turkey); Gurani (Iran, Iraq); Bashkardi (Iran); Parachi (Afghanistan); Ormuri (Afghanistan, Pakistan); Semnani and related dialects (Iran); 'Tat' dialects, centred on Tabriz, Zanjan, Qazvin and Saveh (Iran); Vafsi and Ashtiyani (Iran); dialects of central Iran, centred on Kashan, Esfahan, Yazd, Kerman and the Dashte-Kavir (Iran).

South-East Iranian: Pashto (Afghanistan, Pakistan); Yazgulami (USSR); Shughni (USSR, Afghanistan); Roshani (USSR, Afghanistan); Bartangi (USSR); Oroshori (USSR); Sarikoli (China); Ishkashmi (Afghanistan, USSR); Sanglechi (Afghanistan); Zebaki (Afghanistan); Wakhi (Afghanistan, USSR, Pakistan, China); Munji (Afghanistan); Yidgha (Pakistan).

North-East Iranian: Ossete (USSR), Yaghnobi (USSR).

It will be noted that the names of the genetic groups do not always accurately reflect the geographic location of the modern languages. In particular, Ossete, which belongs to the North-East group, is spoken in the Caucasus, which represents the north-west of the present Iranian language area, and Balochi, which belongs to the North-West group, is located in the extreme south-east on either side of the Iran-Pakistan border. In fact, the geographic nomenclature is more closely tied to the distribution of extinct Iranian languages from the Old Iranian (up to the fourth/third centuries BC) and Middle Iranian (from the fourth/third centuries BC to the eighth/ninth centuries AD) periods.

The oldest attested forms of Iranian are Old Persian, known from the cuneiform inscriptions of the Achaemenid emperors, in particular Darius the Great (521–486 BC) and Xerxes (486–465 BC), and Avestan, the language of the Avesta, a collection of sacred Zoroastrian texts. The oldest parts of the Avesta, the Gathas or songs attributed to the prophet Zoroaster himself, reflect a slightly more archaic stage of development than the Old Persian inscriptions, and must therefore be dated to the sixth century BC or earlier, although the first manuscripts are from the thirteenth and fourteenth centuries AD. Genetically, Old Persian can be clearly associated with the South-West Iranian group, the Achaemenid empire being centred on the province of Persis in the south-west of modern Iran, and must be considered a direct precursor of forms of Middle and Modern Persian. The position of Avestan is, however, complex and disputed, as might be expected of an orally transmitted religious text. The focus of Zoroastrian conversion is held to be Bactria, south of the Oxus river in the east, and the Gathas do indeed show some east Iranian characteristics, notably a tendency to voice clusters which appear as *-ft-* and *-xt-* in West Iranian (see below). A possible explanation for the occurrence of some West Iranian forms is the subsequent spread of Zoroastrianism towards Media in the north-west. It is clear, nevertheless, that Avestan shows none of the features characteristic of South-West Iranian.

From archaeological and textual evidence, it can be deduced that Iranian languages at the time of the Achaemenid empire had a wider geographical distribution than at present, extending from the steppes of southern Russia in the west to areas of Chinese Turkestan (Sinkiang) in the east. Old Persian and Avestan are the main linguistic sources from this period; however, proper names and toponyms provide some information about Median, the language of the province of Media centred on Ecbatana (modern Hamadan in north-west Iran), and about the language of the Scythian and Sarmatian tribes of the south Russian steppes. The Median dialect, which belongs genetically to the North-West group, was originally the language of the Median empire (eighth to sixth centuries BC), and some of its influence can be seen in the Old Persian inscriptions. Knowledge of the Scythian and Sarmatian dialects is based on the analysis of proper names and toponyms in inscriptions from the Greek colonies of the period and by comparison with forms of Ossete, the only modern descendant.

By comparison, the Middle Iranian period provides a wealth of materials.

Map 5.1: Approximate Distribution of Iranian Languages

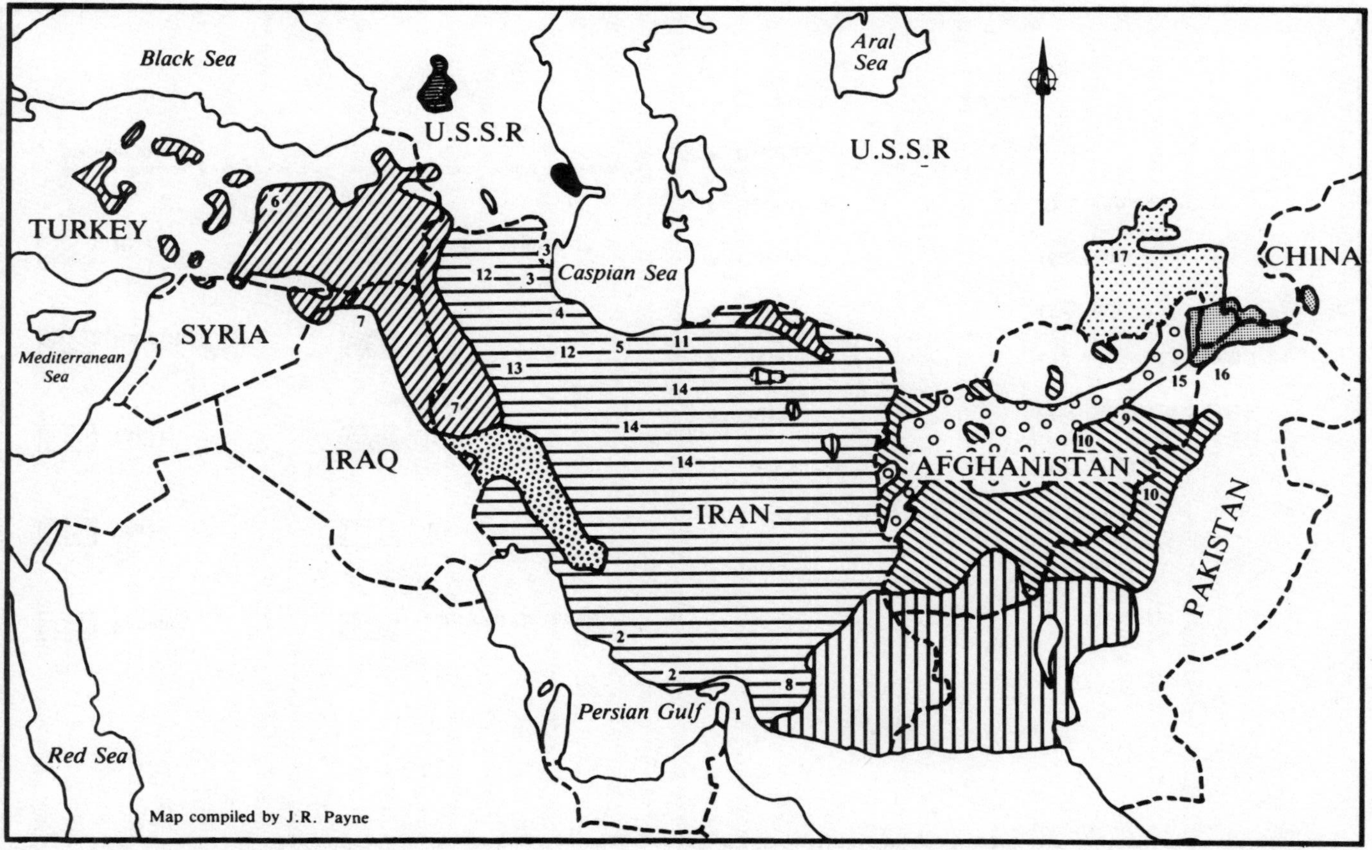

Map compiled by J.R. Payne

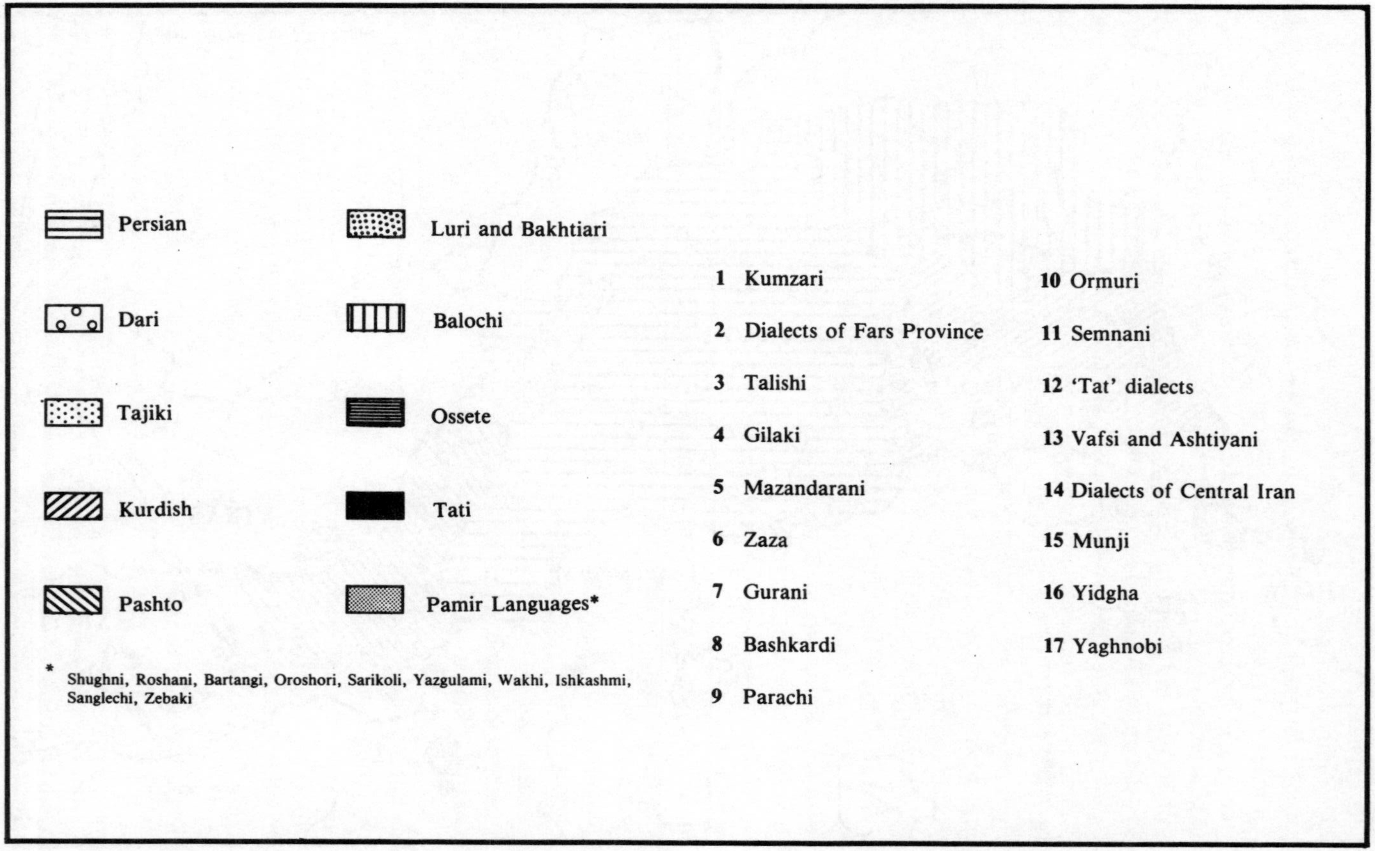

Persian

Dari

Tajiki

Kurdish

Pashto

Luri and Bakhtiari

Balochi

Ossete

Tati

Pamir Languages*

* Shughni, Roshani, Bartangi, Oroshori, Sarikoli, Yazgulami, Wakhi, Ishkashmi, Sanglechi, Zebaki

1 Kumzari
2 Dialects of Fars Province
3 Talishi
4 Gilaki
5 Mazandarani
6 Zaza
7 Gurani
8 Bashkardi
9 Parachi
10 Ormuri
11 Semnani
12 'Tat' dialects
13 Vafsi and Ashtiyani
14 Dialects of Central Iran
15 Munji
16 Yidgha
17 Yaghnobi

To the South-West group belongs Middle Persian, the direct descendant of Old Persian and the precursor of Modern Persian. Although the earliest documents, inscriptions on coins, date from the second century BC, the main corpus illustrates the language of the Sassanid empire (third to seventh centuries AD), centred on the province of Fars (ancient Persis), but by the time of the Arab conquest (seventh/eighth centuries AD) extending over a wide area of present-day Iran, Afghanistan and Central Asia. It includes both secular and Zoroastrian documents written in the Pahlavi script, which is based on the Aramaic and does not show short vowels. The term *Pahlavi* itself is the adjective from the noun *Pahlav* < *Parθava* 'Parthia'. Middle Persian is also represented by a large corpus of Manichean texts found in Turfan, Chinese Turkestan (Sinkiang), and dating mainly to the eighth and ninth centuries AD, although the earliest documents go as far back as the time of Mani (AD 216–74), the founder of the religion. These latter are written mostly in the Manichean script, another derivative of Aramaic, but are also found in Sogdian and Runic Turkic forms.

To the North-West group, apart from Median, belongs Parthian, the source of the Middle Persian script. Parthian itself is more sparsely documented than Middle Persian, but was the language of the province of Parthia which flourished at the time of the Arsacid dynasty (third century BC) to the south-east of the Caspian Sea. It is known through Parthian versions of Sassanid inscriptions and Manichean texts, as well as through minor documents from the first century BC and ostraca from ancient Nisa, located near Ashkhabad in modern Soviet Turkmenia.

For the North-East group there are two representatives. Sogdian, the lingua franca of an extensive area centred on Samarkand and the silk route to China, is known in a number of forms and scripts. In the Sogdian script proper are letters from the fourth century AD, an archive of secular documents dating to the eighth century AD from Mt. Mugh in the Zeravshan area of Tajikistan, as well as a number of Buddhist texts of the same period. There is also an extensive corpus of Manichean and Christian texts, some of the latter written in the Syriac script. The modern descendant of Sogdian is Yaghnobi, spoken until very recently by a small group in one of the high valleys of the Zeravshan, but now dissipated to more lowland areas. Also important as a representative of North-East Iranian in the Middle Iranian period is Khwarezmian, located in a region centred on modern Khiva, and attested in documents and inscriptions in a type of Aramaic script dating mainly to the third to eighth centuries AD. Later fragments of Khwarezmian have survived in Islamic texts of the eleventh to fourteenth centuries AD.

Finally, to the South-East group belong Saka, the language of eastern Scythian tribes from Khotan (Chinese Sinkiang), and Bactrian, the language of the Kushan kingdom of Bactria. The former is known through an extensive corpus of Buddhist texts in the Brahmi script, and dating primarily to the fifth to tenth centuries AD, while the latter is represented mainly by an inscription of twenty-five lines in a variant of the Greek script, found at the temple of Surkh Kotal in northern Afghanistan.

Within the Indo-European family, the Iranian languages are satem languages, e.g. Proto-Indo-European ***k̂m̥tom* 'hundred', Avestan *satəm*, and show a very close relationship to the Indo-Aryan (and Dardic) branches. Three common phonological developments separate Iranian and Indo-Aryan from the rest of Indo-European: (1) the collapse of Proto-Indo-European **a*, **e*, **o*, **n̥*, **m̥* into *a*, and correspondingly of **ā*, **ē*, **ō*, **n̥̄*, **m̥̄* into *ā*, e.g. Proto-Indo-European **dek̂m̥* 'ten' > Avestan *dasa*, Sanskrit *dáśa*, but Old Church Slavonic *desętь*, Latin *decem*; (2) the development of Proto-Indo-European **ə* into *i*, e.g. Proto-Indo-European **pətē(r)* 'father' > Old Persian *pitā*, Sanskrit *pitā́*, but Latin *pater*; (3) the development of Proto-Indo-European **s* into *š* or *ṣ* after **i*, **u*, **r*, **k*, e.g. Proto-Indo-European **u̯eks-* 'grow' > Old Persian and Avestan *vaxš-*, Sanskrit *vakṣ-*, but German *wachs-*, English *wax*; Proto-Indo-European **sed-* 'sit' > Old Persian *ni-šad-*, Sanskrit *ni-ṣīd-* (with additional prefix), but Latin *sed-*, English *sit*. In addition, Iranian and Indo-Aryan inherit from Proto-Indo-European strikingly similar verbal conjugations and nominal declensions. Compare for example the following forms of the first person singular pronoun 'I': (a) nominative: Old Persian *adam*, Avestan *azəm*, Sanskrit *ahám*; (b) accusative: Old Persian *mām*, Avestan *mām*, Sanskrit *mā́m*; (c) genitive: Old Persian *manā*, Avestan *mana*, Sanskrit *máma*; (d) enclitic accusative: Old Persian *-mā*, Avestan *-mā*, Sanskrit *-mā*; (e) enclitic genitive: Old Persian *-maiy*, Avestan *-mōi*, Sanskrit *-mē*; (f) enclitic ablative: Old Persian *-ma*, Avestan *-maṯ*, Sanskrit *-mát*.

In total, according to a recent count, the number of isoglosses linking Iranian with Indo-Aryan is 57, compared with 27 between Indo-Aryan and Greek, 24 between Indo-Aryan and Slavonic and 22 between Indo-Aryan and Baltic. These linguistic facts, in conjunction with shared cultural features such as the name *arya-* 'Aryan', suggest that the Iranian and Indo-Aryan tribes represent a single ethnic and linguistic group within the Indo-European family. Opinions differ, however, as to the dates and routes of migration which led both Iranians and Indo-Aryans away from the Indo-European homeland into the Iranian plateau, Central Asia and India. Since the Rigveda, composed no earlier than the middle of the second millennium BC, already places the Indo-Aryans in India, this date sets a *terminus ante quem* for the loss of Indo-Iranian unity. According to the traditional view, the Aryans must have been in close contact for some time after the break-up of Indo-European, migrating together during the third millennium BC towards Central Asia and the Hindukush. Central Asia then became the focus for the later expansion of Indo-Aryans into India (middle of second millennium BC) and eventually of Iranians into Iran and further west (beginning of first millennium BC). An alternative view, based primarily on archaeological evidence and inscriptions from Mesopotamia, suggests that the Indo-Aryans split from the Iranians by migrating through the Caucasus at the beginning of the second millennium BC, at a time when both groups were still in contact with other Indo-European groups in southern Russia. Iranian tribes would have maintained this contact, in particular with Greek and Armenian, until they too (at least the western Iranian precursors of the Medes and Persians) entered Iran from the north through the Caucasus at the turn of the first millennium BC.

The main linguistic features characterising the split of Iranian and Indo-Aryan are: (1) Indo-Iranian voiced aspirates **bh*, **dh*, **gh* (< Proto-Indo-European **bh*, **dh*, **gh*) are preserved in Indo-Aryan but converted to *b*, *d*, *g* in Iranian, e.g. Sanskrit *bhrắtar*, Old Persian and Avestan *brātar*; (2) Indo-Iranian voiceless aspirates **ph*, **th*, **kh* (< Proto-Indo-European **ph*, **th*, **kh* primarily) are preserved in Indo-Aryan but converted to voiceless fricatives *f*, *θ*, *x* in Iranian, or unaspirated stops *p*, *t*, *k* after *s*, e.g. Sanskrit *path-* 'path', Old Persian and Avestan *paθ-*, Sanskrit *sthā-* 'stand', Old Persian and Avestan *stā-*; (3) Indo-Iranian voiceless **p*, **t*, **k* (< Proto-Indo-European **p*, **t*, **k*) become *f*, *θ*, *x* in Iranian when initial in a consonant cluster, e.g. Sanskrit *putrá-* 'son', Avestan *puθra-*, Old Persian *puça-* (with subsequent *θr* > *ç*), but Wakhi, one of the most archaic languages phonologically, preserves the cluster *-tr-*, e.g. *pətr* 'son'; (4) Indo-Iranian palatals **ć*, **ȷ́*, **ȷ́h* (< Proto-Indo-European **k̂*, **ĝ*, **ĝh*) are realised as *s*, *z*, *z* or *θ*, *d*, *d* in Iranian, but *ś*, *j*, *h* in Indo-Aryan, e.g. Sanskrit *hasta-* 'hand', Avestan *zasta-*, Old Persian *dasta-*; (5) Indo-Iranian **s* is preserved in Indo-Aryan, but converted in Iranian, except before **p*, **t*, **k*, into *h*, e.g. Sanskrit *ásmi* '(I) am', Avestan *ahmi*, Old Persian *amiy* (where the *h* is not written). This isogloss *s* > *h*, shared by Greek and Armenian, is used in support of the hypothesis that Iranian tribes entered Iran via the Caucasus rather than from the east.

By the time of the Achaemenids in the middle of the first millenium BC, it is clear that the dialectal divisions are already established which give rise to the modern genetic groupings within Iranian. The basic division between East and West Iranian is characterised by the following correspondences: (1) West Iranian preserves *b*, *d*, *g*, but these are mainly converted in East Iranian into the corresponding voiced fricatives *β* (*v*, *w*), *δ*, *γ*, e.g. Old Persian *brātar* 'brother', Modern Persian *berādar*, Balochi *brās*, but Sogdian *βr't*, Yaghnobi *virōt*; Avestan *dasa* 'ten', Modern Persian *dah*, Bakhtiari *deh*, Zaza *däs*, but Sogdian *δs'*, Shughni *δīs*; Old Persian *gauša* 'ear', Modern Persian *gōš*, Gurani *goš*, Kurdish *goh*, but Sogdian *γwš*, Ossete *γos*, Bartangi *γu*; (2) West Iranian preserves *č*, but this is mainly converted into *c* in East Iranian, e.g. Middle Persian *čahār* 'four', Balochi *čār*, but Khwarezmian *cf'r*/*cβ'r*, Shughni *cavōr*; (3) the consonantal clusters *-ft-* and *-xt-* are preserved in West Iranian, but converted into the voiced counterparts *-vd-* and *-γd-* in East Iranian, equally originally voiced clusters of this type tend to be preserved in East Iranian but devoiced in West

Iranian, e.g. **hafta* 'seven' > Middle Persian *haft*, Kurdish *häft*, but Khwarezmian *'βd*, Ossete *avd*, Yazgulami *uvd*; **duγdar* 'daughter' > Modern Persian *doxtar*, Gilaki *duxtər*, but Avestan *dugədā*, Khwarezmian *δγd*, Wakhi *δəγ̌d*.

Further phonological characteristics separate the South-West and North-West groups. The South-West Iranian languages, in particular, represent a close-knit group sharing a number of features which distinguish them not only from North-West Iranian but also from East Iranian. The earliest of these, characteristic of the Old Iranian period, is the correspondence North-West, East *s*, *z* = South-West *θ*, *d*, both deriving from the original palatal series (see above), e.g. Avestan *masišta* 'longest', Parthian *msyšt*, but Old Persian *maθišta* 'biggest', Middle Persian *mahist* (with subsequent *θ* > *h*); Avestan *zān-* 'know', Parthian *z'n-*, Gurani *zān-*, Kurdish *zan-*, but Old Persian *dān-*, Modern Persian *dān-*, Tati *dan-*. Later changes *ǰ* > North-West *ǰ-/ž-*, South-West *z-*, and *dv-* > North-West *b-*, South-West *d-*, also clearly differentiate the groups, e.g. Parthian *ǰn* 'woman', Zaza *ǰan*, but Middle Persian *zan*, Modern Persian *zan*; Parthian *br* 'door', Zaza *bär*, but Middle Persian *dar*, Modern Persian *dar*. Further subclassification within the North-West group is complicated by the fragmented nature of much of the material and the influence of Persian on many of the dialects, but Gurani and Balochi both preserve archaic characteristics.

Within the East Iranian group, subdivision into South-East and North-East Iranian is based on both phonological and morphological features. The morphological feature characterising the North-East group is the development of a plural marker in *-t* from a suffix originally deriving abstract nouns. Examples of this marker are Sogdian *'wt'k* 'place', plural *'wt'kt*, Yaghnobi *pōda* 'foot', plural *pōdō-t*, and Ossete *sər* 'head', plural *sər-tə*. The South-East group, on the other hand, shows a variety of voiced continuants in place of invervocalic *-š-*, e.g. Yaghnobi *γuš* 'ear', but Shughni *γůγ̌*, Munji *γūy*, as well as a tendency to develop retroflex consonants (though these are lacking in the Shughni-Roshani subgroup of Pamir languages). Within the South-East group, Shughni, Roshani, Bartangi, Oroshori and Sarikoli (and more distantly Yazgulami) form a genetic subgroup, as do Ishkashmi, Zebaki and Sanglechi, and Munji and Yidgha. Munji and Yidgha share with Pashto the development of *d* > *l* (see the chapter on Pashto).

All Iranian languages of the Middle and Modern periods exhibit some common characteristics. The unmarked word order is typically verb-final, and the tense system is invariably based on two verb stems, present and past. Whereas the present stem continues the Old Iranian present, inherited directly from Indo-European, the past stem is based on a participial form of the verb ending in *-ta*. This participle had an active orientation for intransitive verbs, but was originally passive in the transitive paradigm, as in Old Persian *hamiçiyā hagmatā* (rebels (nom.) assembled (nom. m. pl.)) 'the rebels assembled', *ima tya manā kartam* (this what me (gen.) done (nom. nt.

sg.)) 'this is what was done by me'. The subsequent reanalysis of the passive participle as an active verb leads to ergative past tenses, preserved in a number of languages including Kurdish and Pashto, e.g. Kurdish (Kurmanji dialect) *ez ket-im* (I (abs.) fell (1 sg.)) 'I fell', but *min çîrok xwend* (I (obl.) story (abs.) read (3 sg.)) 'I read a story'. The majority of the modern Iranian languages exhibit various stages in the decay of the past tense ergative system into a nominative one, as preserved in the tenses based on the present stem. Modern Persian is typical here of the final stage, with no traces of ergativity except the form of the first person singular pronoun *man* 'I' (< Old Persian genitive *manā*).

Bibliography

The fullest and most detailed general survey available is Rastorgueva (1979–); planned in five volumes, four have appeared so far: 1 (*Drevneiranskie jazyki*) on Old Iranian (1979), 2 (*Sredneiranskie jazyki*) on Middle Iranian (1981), 3 (*Novoiranskie jazyki: zapadnaja gruppa, prikaspijskie jazyki*) on the South-West Iranian and Caspian languages (1982), 4 (*Novoiranskie jazyki; vostočnaja gruppa*) on the East Iranian languages (1987). Spuler (1958) is the only comprehensive handbook in a language other than Russian, although Payne (1981) gives a short survey of linguistic properties of Iranian languages of the USSR. Oranskij (1963) includes annotated specimens of many of the languages and a useful map. Among bibliographical resources, MacKenzie (1969) is a short survey of Iranian studies and full basic bibliography; Oranskij (1975) is a very thorough bibliographical guide to the Iranian languages of the USSR; Redard (1970) is a comprehensive survey of the study of minor Iranian languages, with full bibliography.

References

MacKenzie, D.N. 1969. 'Iranian Languages', in T.A. Sebeok (ed.), *Current Trends in Linguistics*, vol. 5 *Linguistics in South Asia* (Mouton, The Hague), pp. 450–77.

Oranskij, I.M. 1963. *Iranskie jazyki* (Izd-vo Vostočnoj Literatury, Moscow)

—— 1975. *Die neuiranischen Sprachen der Sowjetunion*, 2 vols. (Mouton, The Hague)

Payne, J.R. 1981. 'Iranian languages', in B. Comrie, *The Languages of the Soviet Union* (Cambridge University Press, Cambridge), pp. 158–79

Rastorgueva, V.S. (ed.) 1979–. *Osnovy iranskogo jazykoznanija* (Nauka, Moscow)

Redard, G. 1970. 'Other Iranian Languages', in T.A. Sebeok (ed.), *Current Trends in Linguistics*, vol. 6 *Linguistics in Southwest Asia and North Africa* (Mouton, The Hague), pp. 97–135

Spuler, B. (ed.) 1958. *Handbuch der Orientalistik. Abt. I, Bd. IV, 1, Iranistik* (Brill, Leiden)

6 *Persian*

Gernot L. Windfuhr

1 Historical Background

1.1 Dialectology

Within the Iranian branch of Indo-European, Persian is a member of the West Iranian group, together with the Iranian languages and dialects spoken in Iran and others spoken also outside of Iran, such as Kurdish and Balochi. Within West Iranian, Persian is a member of the South-Western branch, together with other dialects spoken mainly in the southwestern province of Fars, such as Luri and Bakhtiari.

Persian has various dialects. The three major representatives of these are the Persian of Iran in the west, the Persian of Afghanistan now called Dari in the east and the Persian spoken in Soviet Tajikistan in Central Asia in the north-east. Each again has its own dialectal divisions. The number of speakers in each country is approximately: Iran 30 million, Afghanistan five million, USSR 2.2 million.

Iran is a multi-lingual country. While Persian is the official language of Iran, it is the mother tongue of only about 50 per cent of the population. Speakers of non-Persian Iranian dialects constitute some 25 per cent. The remainder speak non-Iranian languages. Besides Arabic, New Aramaic, Armenian, Georgian and Gypsy, Turkic dialects are the most widely spoken, such as Azerbaidjani in the north-west, the archaic Khalaj in the centre of Iran, Turkmenian in the north-east and Qashqa'i in the south-west. Turkic dialects have virtually erased Iranian in northern Afghanistan and Central Asia except for the Tajiki enclave. The Turkisation of much of these areas began before the end of the first millennium AD and does not seem to have halted yet. (Incidentally, those are the same areas where Iranians first took hold on the plateau some 2,000 years earlier.)

1.2 Origins

The evolution of Persian as the culturally dominant language of the eastern Near East, from Iran to Central Asia to northwestern India until recent centuries, began with the political domination of these areas by dynasties originating in the southwestern province of Iran, Parsa, later Arabicised to Fars: first the Achaemenids (559–331 BC) whose official language was Old Persian; then the Sassanids (c. AD 225–651) whose official language was Middle Persian. Hence, the entire country used to be called '*persē*' by the Ancient Greeks, a practice continued to this day. The more general designation 'Iran(-shahr)' derives from Old Iranian *aryānām* (*khshathra*) '(the realm) of the Aryans'.

The dominance of these two dynasties resulted in Old and Middle Persian-speaking colonies throughout the empire, most importantly for the course of the development of Persian, in the north-east, i.e. what is now Khorasan, northern Afghanistan and Central Asia, as documented by the Middle Persian texts of the Manicheans found in the oasis city of Turfan in Chinese Turkestan (Sinkiang). This led to a certain degree of regionalisation.

1.3 The Formative Period

None of the known Middle Persian dialects is the direct predecessor of New Persian. There are indications that New Persian developed between the seventh to ninth centuries, the period of the Muslim conquest of Iran and later of the high culture of the Arabic-speaking Abbasid court in Baghdad (c. 750–850), to which Iranians contributed so decisively. The first preserved documents come from the eastern regions: three brief inscriptions dating from the middle of the eighth century found in eastern Afghanistan. They were written in Hebrew characters, indicating the early use of the new vernacular by minorities less dominated by the written standards of the time, i.e. Arabic, Middle Persian or local languages such as East Iranian Sogdian.

It was in the north-east, more distant from the caliphate in Baghdad, where Iranian nationalism reasserted itself by the eleventh century. Persian became the universally accepted language first in poetic diction. The major document of this period is the *Shāh-nāmah* 'The Book of Kings', the monumental epic by Firdausi of Tus in Khorasan about the Iranian glory from creation to the Muslim conquest, written in the early eleventh century in an archaising language which used comparatively few Arabic words. It soon became also accepted as the language of official communication and of prose writing vis-à-vis Arabic, the sacred language of the Qur'an and the 'Latin' of the Muslim Near East. For example, the philosopher Ibn-e Sina, Latinised Avicenna, d. 1047, while mostly writing in Arabic, chose to write his *Metaphysics* in Persian for which he created his own Persian terminology.

The 'Persianists' won over the 'Arabists'. Muslim religious propaganda began to contribute considerably to the ever-extending use of Persian through popularising texts such as commentaries on the Qur'an, lives of saints, edificational and moral and religious treatises.

Until the Mongol conquests in the middle of the thirteenth century, the north-east, with cultural centres such as Samarkand, Bukhara, Balkh, Merv, Herat and Nishapur, continued to be the major area of New Persian and its literature. Thereafter, the focus shifted to the west, a major centre being the city of Shiraz in Fars with its most famous poets Sa'di (d. 1292) and Hafiz (d. 1390), from where it shifted to the north, first to Isfahan, the splendid capital of the Safavids (1501–1731), then, from the first half of the nineteenth century, to Tehran, the new capital of the Qajars (1779–1924).

1.4 Standardisation

Persian appears fairly standardised first in early poetic diction, which shows few dialectal variations by the tenth century. (This may be partially due to standardisation by copyists.) Nevertheless, the peculiarities of the eastern poets, especially in their lexicon, led to the compilation of dictionaries explaining those in 'common' Persian, such as the dictionary by Asadi from the middle of the eleventh century.

The formative period for prose writing lasted until the end of the twelfth century. The utilitarian religious texts, just as scientific, historical, geographic, philosophical and mystical writings, naturally paid less attention to high style than to reaching the local public. They retained a considerable degree of local features (in spite of the hands of copyists). Most of the preserved texts originate in the eastern regions, and as such exhibit a fair degree of linguistic homogeneity.

By the thirteenth century, the beginning of Classical Persian, the regionally marked features had largely disappeared in both poetry and prose. This process is concomitant not only with the expansion of Persian, but also with the shift of cultural centres to the west, specifically to Fars. The literary standard was achieved not only through the efforts of poets and writers but, perhaps most importantly, through the efforts of the court chanceries where guides and textbooks on style and rhetoric were compiled from the tenth century.

The dominance of Classical Persian continued to a considerable degree until the beginning of the nineteenth century. At that time new political, economic and cultural conditions, not least under influence from Europe, sponsored gradual simplifications of style. With it came the acceptance in writing of features of the educated spoken language that had developed in the capital Tehran, at first in journalism, then in prose and finally in poetry. Thus emerged contemporary standard Persian. At the same time, Tajikistan under Russian and Soviet rule developed its own literary language which is based on local dialects and written in the Russian alphabet. Iranian Persian ceased to be the accepted standard. It is still the norm in Afghanistan, but decreasingly so as the official language beside East Iranian Pashto.

1.5 Colonial Persian

Persian was cultivated at the courts of the Ottoman rulers, several of whom are known for composing Persian poetry. Literary Ottoman Turkish is a virtual amalgam of Turkish and Persian (with all of the latter's Arabic loan elements). Similarly, Urdu, '(the language of the) military camp', developed under heavy Persian influence. Persian first entered India with the conquest of north-west India by Ghaznavid armies in the eleventh century. Four centuries later, Persian in its classical form was chosen as the court language of the Mogul kings (1530–1857), who were major patrons of Persian literature and poets from Iran, unlike the contemporary Safavids in Iran. It was at the courts of India and Turkey where many of the major traditional dictionaries of Persian were compiled from the fifteenth to the eighteenth centuries, many with grammatical treatises. Simultaneously, there developed in India a Persian vernacular, and it was from the Indian scribes and secretaries that the English officers of the East India Company, many of whom wrote grammars of Persian, learned their Persian, with all its local idiosyncrasies. Persian was abolished in its last official bastion — the courts of law — in 1837 by the authorities of the East India Company.

2 Phonology

2.1 Sound System

The sound system of contemporary standard Persian is quite symmetric. Its 29 segmental phonemes consist of four pairs of stops and four pairs of fricatives, two nasals and two liquids, three glides, and three pairs of vowels.

Table 6.1: The Persian Phoneme System

Stops	tense/voiceless	p	t	č	k
	lax/voiced	b	d	ǰ	g
Fricatives	tense/voiceless	f	s	š	x
	lax/voiced	v	z	ž	q
Nasals		m	n		
Liquids		l	r		
Glides		y	h	'	
Vowels	tense/long	i	ā	u	
	lax/short	e	a	o	

2.2 Writing System

The Persian writing system uses the Arabic alphabet, which is a consonantal system (see the chapter on Arabic). Vowels are written as follows: long vowels are represented by the letter of the consonant nearest in pronunciation. Thus, the letter <y> represents both /y/ and /i/, <w> both /v/ and /u/, and <alef> both the glottal stop /'/ and /ā/. Short vowels may be, but are usually not, represented by diacritics which ultimately derive from the same letters <w>, <y>, and <alef>. The main innovations in Persian are two: unlike Arabic, short vowels are always represented by consonantal letters in final position, final /o/ by <w>, and final /e/ and /a/ by <h>. Also, 'Persian' letters were created for the four Persian consonants /p/, /č/, /g/, /ž/ by adding three dots to the 'Arabic' letters ‹b›, ‹j›, ‹k›, ‹z› (the dots merged into an oblique stroke in the case of ‹g›). The Persian alphabet is given in table 6.2.

Table 6.2: The Persian Alphabet

Alone	*End*	*Middle*	*Initial*			*Name*
ا	ـا	ـا	ا	'		alef
ب	ـب	ـبـ	بـ	b		be
پ	ـپ	ـپـ	پـ	p	P	pe
ت	ـت	ـتـ	تـ	t		te
ث	ـث	ـثـ	ثـ	s	A	se-ye senokte
ج	ـج	ـجـ	جـ	j		ǰim
چ	ـچ	ـچـ	چـ	c	P	če
ح	ـح	ـحـ	حـ	h	A	he-ye ǰimi
خ	ـخ	ـخـ	خـ	x		xe
د	ـد	ـد	د	d		dāl
ذ	ـذ	ـذ	ذ	z	A	zāl
ر	ـر	ـر	ر	r		re
ز	ـز	ـز	ز	z		ze
ژ	ـژ	ـژ	ژ	ž	P	že
س	ـس	ـسـ	سـ	s		sin
ش	ـش	ـشـ	شـ	š		šin
ص	ـص	ـصـ	صـ	s	A	sād
ض	ـض	ـضـ	ضـ	z	A	zād
ط	ـط	ـطـ	طـ	t	A	tā
ظ	ـظ	ـظـ	ظـ	z	A	zā
ع	ـع	ـعـ	عـ	'	A	'eyn
غ	ـغ	ـغـ	غـ	q		qeyn
ف	ـف	ـفـ	فـ	f		fe
ق	ـق	ـقـ	قـ	q		qāf
ک	ـک	ـکـ	کـ	k		kāf
گ	ـگ	ـگـ	گـ	g	P	gāf
ل	ـل	ـلـ	لـ	l		lām
م	ـم	ـمـ	مـ	m		min
ن	ـن	ـنـ	نـ	n		nun
و	ـو	ـو	و	v		vāv
ه	ـه	ـهـ	هـ	h		he-ye dočašm
ی	ـی	ـیـ	یـ	y		yā
ءا	أ	ـئـ	أ	'		hamze

A=letters occurring mostly in Arabic loanwords; P=letters found in Persian only.

The Arabic orthography, the pharyngeal consonants of which are not phonemically distinct in Persian, is retained in all Arabic loans. Other than in Arabic loans, the orthography of Persian is basically phonemic, except for the writing of short vowels discussed above, only rarely using a pharyngeal letter such as <ṣ> in <ṣad> /sad/ 'hundred'.

2.3 Features

In spite of systemic simplicity, there remains considerable debate about the features distinguishing both individual phonemes and sets of phonemes, and about their development. A particularly interesting point is the degree of integration of the foreign loan component, most importantly Arabic, into the system inherited from Middle Persian.

Consonant gemination is a distinctive characteristic of Arabic, whereas in Persian it is a marginal feature. While probably retained in Classical Persian, and still in poetry, it is eliminated in the standard pronunciation of today; for example, Persian *matté* 'drill', Arabic *talaffóz* 'pronunciation' today are pronounced /mate/, /talafoz/.

The highly developed consonantal system of Arabic is considerably reduced in Persian. The non-strident interdental fricatives *θ* and *ð* merged with the respective strident fricatives *s* and *z*. Similarly, the distinctively Arabic pharyngeals merged with non-pharyngeals. Two of the more complex mergers are the following.

The phoneme *q* is intriguing because of its diverse origins and its present articulation and conditioned variation. On the one hand, it originates in an indigenous Persian/Iranian voiced velar fricative with limited functional load. On the other hand, it originates in loans. It represents the merger of the Arabic uvular voiceless stop *q* with the uvular voiced fricative (represented by the respective Arabic letters *qaf* and *ɣeyn*), as well as the voice-neutral back velar stop before back vowels in Turkish (represented by *either* of the Arabic letters). Its peculiar Persian articulation appears like a virtual compromise of its origins: intervocalically it is a voiced fricative; in initial and final position it is partially or fully devoiced, following the devoicing rule, and may have an affricate-like voiced release before vowels (varying with the speaker).

In Persian, glottalic vocalic onset is an automatic feature before initial vowels and in hiatus and as such was originally not phonemic. Arabic, however, has a phonemic voiced pharyngeal ʿ (represented by the letter *ʿeyn*) and a glottal stop ' (represented by <alef> or the diacritic <hamze>), which may occur in any position. It is the latter which represents the Persian glottal stop and hiatus in writing, e.g. onset *'in* /'in/ 'this', hiatus *pā'íz* /pā'iz/ 'autumn', affixal hiatus *xāné-i* /xāne-'i/ 'a house', *qahve-í* /qahve-'í/ 'brown (coffee-ish)'. Phonemically, in Persian the pharyngeal merged with the glottal and with vocalic onset.

2.4 Syllable Structure

The syllable structure of Middle Persian generally reflected that of Old Iranian. This included initial consonantal clusters, which were broken up in Early New Persian by the insertion of a vowel, e.g. MP *brādar* > NP *barādár* 'brother', or by initial vowel, e.g. MP *brū-g* > NP *abrú* 'brow' (so mostly if initial sibilant; note modern loans like *estudiyó* 'studio'). This structure thus agrees with that of the Arabic loan component which has only initial CVC. Since the automatic onset before initial vowel has become phonemic, all Persian syllables now have initial CV, e.g. *in* → /'in/ 'this'.

Vowels may be followed by none, one or two consonants, i.e. CV, CVC, CVCC. This makes syllabic boundaries predictable: in any sequence, the consonant immediately preceding a vowel begins a new syllable. This structure has also implications for the status of the two diphthongs of Persian, formerly *ai*, *au*, today assimilated to *ey*, *ow*. Since these are never followed by two consonants like the other vowels, they must be interpreted as a sequence of short vowel + glide, e.g. *dowr* 'turn' as CVCC. They have thus no independent phonemic status, just as in Arabic.

2.5 Stress

The basic stress pattern of Persian is predictable and non-phonemic. Word stress is progressive, i.e. on the last non-enclitic syllable. Phrase stress is regressive. This is evident in pseudo-pairs like *bāz-kón* 'opener' : *bā́z kon* 'open!' (*kon* 'to make, do'), where the compound noun has final stress and the verb phrase has stress on the initial member. The third rule, continued from Indo-European, is that stress is on the initial syllable of the vocative noun or phrase, e.g. *xā̀nandé-y-e azìz* → *xā́nandè-y-e azìz* 'Dear reader!'

2.6 Morphophonemic Alternation

Unlike Eastern Iranian languages such as Pashto, the rules of morphophonemic alternation of Old Iranian had already ceased to be productive in Persian by the end of the Achaemenid period (c. fourth century BC). This alternation is fossilised in the present and past stems of the so-called irregular verbs and in root nouns. Of course, other changes have long since distorted the regular alternation. Moreover, many such verbs have become regularised and their old past stems lost, a process which has been especially observable in recent centuries.

A considerable portion of the morphophonology of Arabic has been borrowed together with the lexicon. Most complex is that of the verbal system as reflected in verbal nouns and participles borrowed into Persian; to cite only a few frequent forms of the root *n-z-r* 'see, watch': *nazár* 'view', *nazír* 'similar, like', the passive participle *manzúr* 'considered, intended', also 'viewpoint, opinion', the verbal noun of the Arabic eighth formation *èntezā́r* 'expectation' with the participle *mòntazér* 'expecting, waiting'.

Probably the most conspicuous part of borrowing is the Arabic plural. Its complex morphophonology has generally been accepted as an integral part of Persian. The many classes of broken plurals are retained to a considerable degree, varying with the word, certainly with style and possibly with semantic field. The extent of such borrowing has induced the authors of many grammars of Persian to include a considerable section on Arabic morphophonology. However, unlike English which has reanalysed Romance to a certain degree (e.g. 'to **re**-do'), in Persian Arabic morphophonology only applies to Arabic loans and it is not productive, certainly not with the uneducated speaker, rarely affecting Persian words, other than those borrowed early into Arabic and then borrowed back, e.g. *gauhár* > Ar. *ǰauhár* 'essence, jewel', pl. *ǰàvāhír*, and was then borrowed back into Persian.

3 Morphology and Syntax

In terms of morphology Persian with its dialects may be called the most atypical Iranian language. It is to Iranian what English is to Germanic. Unlike East Iranian Pashto and many smaller dialects, it has almost completely lost the inherited synthetic nominal and verbal inflection and their inflectional classes, and thus the *inflectional* distinction of case, number and gender as well as of tense, mood, aspect and verbal gender. This process began already in late Old Persian times. Person and number are, however, distinguished, so is human and non-human gender. The pronouns and endings are shown in the chart given here.

	Singular			*Plural*		
Pronouns	1	2	3	1	2	3
Independent	man	to	u	mā	šomá	išắn/ān-há
Suffixed	-am	-at	-aš	-emān	-etān	-ešān
Endings						
Present stem	-am	-i	-ad	-im	-id	-and
Past stem	-am	-i	-Ø	-im	-id	-and
Perfect stem/'to be'	-am	-i	-ast	-im	-id	-and

The second person singular imperative ending is zero, the second person plural ending is *-id*.

The independent and suffixed pronouns alternate in dependent noun constructions, e.g. *ketắb-e man*/*ketắb-am* 'my book'. The three sets of personal endings differ only in the third person singular. The third set is in fact the substantive verb 'to be', which is always enclitic, as opposed to the existential *hast-* 'to be (there)', which takes the endings of the past stem.

Pronouns and endings distinguish between human and non-human. All independent pronouns refer to humans only. Thus *u* only means 'he/she', *išắn* has become almost exclusively used for third person singular in polite phraseology and has been replaced as a plural by the unmarked *ān-há*. Non-human items are referred to by the use of the demonstratives *in*/*ān* 'this/that'. There is no equivalent of 'it' in Persian. This distinction is also found in the interrogative and indefinite pronouns, *ki* 'who' : *če* 'what', *hár-ki* 'whoever' : *hár-če* 'whatever'. Moreover, non-human plurals do not require plural pronouns or endings; their plural marking seems to imply individuation.

3.1 Nouns and Noun Phrases

3.1.1 Nominals

Nouns are simple or compound, based on nominal or verbal stems, e.g. *sāhéb* 'owner', *xāné* 'house', *sāhèb-xāné* 'landlord', *hāvā́* 'air' *-peymā́* 'to transverse', *-bar* 'to carry', [*havà-peymà*]-*bár* '[aircraft] carrier'; or are nominalised noun and verb phrases, e.g. *ràft-o-āmád* 'traffic', past stems of *raft-án* 'to go' and *āmad-án* 'to come', *bād be-zán* 'fan' lit. 'hit wind'.

There are numerous derivational suffixes. The two semantically least restricted ones, which can be freely added even to phrases are: the abstract suffix *-í*, e.g. *mard-í* 'man-liness', *bozorg-í* 'great-ness', *malèk-o-š-šo'arā-í* 'the status of being poet laureate', and the homophonous denominal relational suffix *-í*, e.g. *ìrān-í* 'Iran-ian', [*zèdd-e irān*]-*í* '[anti-Iran]-ian'.

The comparative suffix is *-tár*, e.g. *bozorg-tár* 'great-er'; the ordinal suffix is *-óm*, e.g. [*paǰàh-o yek*]-*óm* 'fifty-first' (except for Arabic *avvál* 'first' and *āxár* 'last').

3.1.2 Noun Phrases

The basic structure of the noun-adjective phrase and the noun-noun phrase is as follows (N = noun, A = Adjective):

NA: *in* – Measure, Number, Kind–Noun–*hā́*–*e*–Adjective–*i*
      ān
NN: NA^1–*e*–NA^2
      NA–Personal Suffixes

The general plural marker is *-hā́*, and *-ā́n* for adjectival and indefinite pronominal human plurals, e.g. *bozorg-ā́n* 'the elder (people), leaders', *digar-ā́n* 'the others'. The latter is also used for human and human-related plural in literary registers. In addition, there are the plurals of the Arabic loan component which tend to function as a marker of a complex unit. Thus, the plural of *taráf* 'side, direction', *atrā́f*, has developed the connotation 'surroundings, about', the plural of *vaqt* 'time', *owqā́t*, generally means 'humour, mood', the loaned feminine-abstract plural *-āt* generalises, e.g. *deh-ā́t* 'the rural area' vis-à-vis the Persian plural *deh-hā́* 'villages'.

The indefinite marker for both singular and plural is *-i*, e.g. *ketā́b-i*/*ketāb-*

hā́-i 'a book/(certain) books'. It follows the adjective, but often the noun in the presence of more than two adjectives.

Measure, numbers and kind precede the noun and in turn are preceded by the demonstratives *in*/*ān* 'this/that', e.g. *sé* (*tā*) *ketȁb* 'three (items) of books', *ín do now' qālì* 'these two kinds of carpet'.

Dependent nominals follow the head noun and are connected by *-e*, e.g. *ketā́b-e bozorg-tàr* 'a larger book'. The general function of this construction with dependent nouns and noun phrases, traditionally called *ezāfe* 'addition', is the identification of class and item, the latter ranging from persons, to names and names of species, to numbers, e.g. *ketȁb-e mán* 'the book of me/my book'; *xānòm-e J̌avādí* 'Mrs Javadi', *hasàn-e mokrí* 'Hassan Mokri', *gòl-e róz* 'the rose(-flower)', *sā́'àt-e sé* 'three o'clock', *dàrs-e haft-óm* 'the seventh lesson'.

3.1.3 Topicalisation

The unmarked sequence head–*e*–dependent is inverted to dependent–Ø–head by topicalisation, most prominently with noun–adjective, noun–comparative, and noun–ordinal, e.g. *kȁr* [*-e xúb*]*-i* → [*xúb*] *kȁr-i* 'good work', *fìlm* [*-e beh-tár*] → [*beh-tar-ín*] *fìlm* 'the best film' (the so-called superlative), *sāl-gàrd* [*-e sad-óm*] → [*sad-om-ín*] *sāl-gàrd* 'the hundredth anniversary'.

3.2 Single Clauses

Subjects are formally unmarked, indirect objects are in general marked by the preposition *be*, direct objects are marked by the postposition *rā* if specific, adverbial phrases are marked by the prepositions *az* 'from, by, than', *bā* 'with', *tā* 'till, than (comparing clauses)', *dar* 'in/into', *be* 'to' and other functions. The latter two may be elided. These combine with nouns to give numerous adverbial phrases such as *ba-rā́-y-e* 'for the reason of, for', (*be*/*dar*) *rú-y-e* '(to/on) the face of, on, onto' largely supplanting *bar* 'on'.

Persian is an SOV language. The unmarked sequence of the parts of speech in all clauses is subject–adverb–object–verb. Interrogatives do not change this sequence, but occur where the respective answer would be, e.g. (*to*) *ketȁb-rā be kí dād-i* lit. 'you the book to whom gave?'. Inversions only occur through topicalisation. In general, sentence-initial and preverbal positions are topical, e.g. *be ù ǰavā́b dād-am*/*ǰavȁb be ú dād-am* 'I gave him an answer/I gave an answer to him'.

3.3 Categories

In spite of the relative simplicity of the formal aspects of the noun phrase, the syntactic-semantic aspects present problems many of which have not yet been solved. The major ones involved are genericity, definiteness, specificity and reference.

3.3.1 Genericity and Plural

Any unmodified noun in Persian may be generic and imply single or more items, whether subject, predicative complement, direct object or other, e.g. *man ketấb lāzèm dār-am* 'I need a book/books', *ketàb mofíd ast* 'a book is/ books are useful', *àn ketấb ast* 'that is a book/those are books' (note the singular pronoun *ān*). This function is exploited in c mpound verbs (see discussion below), where the verbal content is expressed by a noun followed by a small set of function verbs, e.g. *kàr kard-án* 'work-doing/working', *tarǰomè kard-án* 'translation-making/translating'.

Accordingly, plural is not obligatory when more than one item is implied, unlike English, and plurals in Persian have a more restricted function. The condition for plural marking is restriction of genericity, by reference to specific items or simply by qualifying attributes, as in *u mehmấn dār-ad* 'he has a guest/guests' vs. *u mehm ān-hà-y-e āmrikā-í dār-ad* 'he has American guests'. This applies, of course, to covert reference as well, as is seen in the pair *ān-hà mo'allém–Ø hast-and* 'they are teachers' vs. *ān-hà mo'allem-hấ hast-and* 'they are **the** teachers'. This distinction is, however, neutralised after numbers, where plural is never marked.

The basic function of *hā* is not plural, but 'amplification'. While this is interpreted as plural with count nouns, it expresses increase or extent with mass mouns, e.g. *āb-hấ* 'waters, all kinds of waters, plenty of water', and generalisation with adverbs, e.g. *bālā-hấ-y-aš* 'somewhere up there'. This function is most conspicuous with generic objects which remain unmarked, as mentioned. In that case, the presence of *hā* does not express plural, even with count nouns (for specific objects see discussion below), but amplification, e.g. *mà mehmấn–Ø dār-im* 'we have guests' vs. *mà mehmān-hấ dār-im* 'we have lots of, all kinds of guests'.

3.3.2 Genericity and Indefiniteness

Persian distinguishes between genericity and indefiniteness, which latter is marked by the clitic *i*. It occurs with count and mass nouns as well as with singular and plural. As such, it marks restrictive selection out of a generic unit or out of a plurality, e.g. *ketấb-i* 'some/a book' and *ketāb-hấ-i* 'some books', *āb-ǰów-i* 'some, a beer' and *āb-ǰow-hấ-i* 'some kinds of beer'. This function is clearly evident in compound verbs where the presence of *i* eliminates genericity, as in the pair *kấr mi-kon-am* 'I am working' vs. *kấr-i mi-kon-am* 'I am doing something/some work, I am working some/a little'. The restrictive-selective function of *i* is distinct from that of *yek* 'a, one', which counts an item or a group of items. Unlike English 'a' and 'one', both are compatible in Persian, e.g. *yek ketấb-i be-deh* 'give me a (one, some) book'.

There is, however, the similarity between the two languages in that indefiniteness may refer either to specific items known to the speaker or to non-specific items, e.g. *dombàl-e apārtemấn-i mi-gard-am* 'I am looking for an apartment' may either imply a specific apartment (which I read about in the papers), or any apartment (that will do). In either case indefiniteness is opposed to genericity, as in *dombāl-e apārtemấn mi-gard-am* 'I am apartment-hunting'.

3.3.3 *Rā*

Unlike indefiniteness, definiteness is not formally marked in Persian and is only evident in the presence of inherent definites such as demonstratives, personal pronouns, superlatives and ordinal numbers, proper names etc. Thus, the sentence just cited as generic may likewise be interpreted as definite in another context: 'I am looking for **the** apartment'. Until recently it was assumed that there is at least one marker of definiteness, if only with definite direct objects, viz. the postposition *rā*, which was said to be obligatory with such objects. However, not only are there definite direct objects without *rā*, but *rā* is also compatible with indefinite *i*. What is marked by *rā* is not definiteness, but topicalisation or specificity. Thus, since all definite direct objects are normally, but not necessarily specific-referential, they are normally marked by *rā*. It also follows that *rā* is compatible with the indefinite marker *i*, if the latter is specific and implies a unique referent 'a certain, some'. For example, one of the environments where an indefinite is likely to refer to specifics is in sentences with past verbs, as in *xāné-i-rā ātèš zad-and* 'they burned a (certain) house' as opposed to *xāné-i ātèš zad-and* 'they burned a house'. (The sequence indefinite *i* – topicalising *rā* may be roughly compared to the indefinite-specific use of 'this' in colloquial English as in 'they burned **this** house, you know', which refers to a house only known to, or seen by, the speaker.)

While *rā* overwhelmingly topicalises direct objects, it is not confined to them. Thus, it occurs with adverbial phrases of temporal and spatial extension, e.g. *em-šáb-rā in-ǰấ bāš* 'be/stay here (for) tonight', *hamé-y-e šàhr-rā gàšt* 'he walked all around the city'. Neither with such adverbial phrases nor with direct objects is *rā* obligatory unless topicalisation is involved. This explains why *rā* may be absent in spite of definiteness in sentences like *pà tu káfš kard o ràft* 'she put (her) feet ('foot') in her shoes ('shoe') and left' vs. topicalised *pa-hấ-aš-rā tu kàfš kard o ràft* 'she put **her** feet in her shoes and left' and *èšq né-mi-fahm-ad* 'he does not understand love' vs. *éšq-rā né-mi-fahm-ad* 'he does not understand the notion of love/what love is'.

The topicalising function is also found in highly literary registers, where *rā* may occur in initial phrases, such as [*došmán-rā*] ... *hamé darb-hầ-rā be ru-ye ù mí-band-im* 'as to the enemy, we will close all doors except ...' (note the direct object *darb-hā-rā*). The initial phrase *došman-rā* here may well be interpreted as indirect object 'for the enemy'. In fact, there is a small number of verbs where the indirect object is marked by *rā*, such as *má-rā dād* 'he gave (it to) me' side by side *be mán dād*. *Rā* as opposed to *be* appears thus to topicalise these indirect objects as well.

3.3.4 Personal Suffixes

The personal suffixes express not only the experiencing indirect object, but also any direct object: in opposition to topicalised definite direct objects marked by *rā* they express definite non-topical direct objects, e.g. *man ù-rā díd-am → díd-am-aš* 'I saw him'. In fact, the independent personal pronouns are always topical. Thus, it follows that independent possession always requires the independent pronoun, e.g. *màl-e mán* 'mine' lit. 'possession of mine'. By contrast, the corresponding suffixes are always non-topical. In addition to the cases mentioned, they function as non-topical objects of prepositions, e.g. *az ù porsíd-am → àz-aš porsíd-am* 'I asked (of) him', and as possessors in noun phrases, e.g. *ketàb-e ú → ketáb-aš* 'his book'.

In the latter function, they also participate in a remarkable noun phrase inversion, possessor topicalisation: the dependent noun, i.e. the possessor of the subject phrase, is replaced by the respective unstressed suffix, and is itself placed in clause-initial position assuming primary stress so that both bracket the head noun, e.g. *èsm*[*-e ín āqā*] *číst →* [*ín āqā*] *èsm*[*-aš*] *číst* 'what is the name of this gentleman'. With pronouns, there is a threefold gradation: *pedàr*[*-am*] *ostád ast → pedàr*[*-e mán*] *ostád ast →* [*mán*] *pedàr*[*-àm*] *ostád ast* 'my father/mý father/me, my father is a professor'.

The [non-topical:topical] function of the pronouns is most widely utilised in the colloquial language where, for example, the indirect construction is expanding. More widely than in the standard language, it functions as the non-topical correlate of direct active constructions, e.g. *gárm* [*hast-*]*am* 'I am warm' → *gárm-am ast* 'I feel warm' lit. 'to me it is warm'. Pragmatically this gives the speaker the option to describe himself as the 'object' of such mental and bodily sensations which are 'coming or happening to him' without his doing, or as the 'subject' with his active involvement.

Similarly, the possessive construction with *dāšt-án* 'to have' may alternate in colloquial speech with the suffixal construction, as long as no true possession is implied, e.g. 'he is two years old' may be expressed as *ù dó sāl dār-ad* 'he has two years' or as *dó sāl-eš e* (← *ast*) 'two years are to him'.

It is evident, then, that the personal suffixes have the general function of what may be called non-topical 'oblique case'.

3.4 The Verb Phrase

The basic verb system of contemporary Persian may be as given in the chart using the verb *rav/raft* 'go' in the third person singular with negation. As is evident, several of these verb forms have double function.

	Indicative	*Non-Indicative*	
Imperfective:			
Present	né-mi-rav-ad	bé-rav-ad/ná-rav-ad	Subjunctive
Past	né-mi-raft	né-mi-raft	Counterfactual
Inferential Past	né-mi-raft-e ast	né-mi-raft-e ast	Counterfactual
Aorist:	ná-raft	ná-raft	Subjunctive

Perfective:

Present	ná-raft-e ast	ná-raft-e bāš-ad	Subjunctive
Past	ná-raft-e bud	ná-raft-e bud	Counterfactual
Inferential Past	ná-raft-e bud-e ast	ná-raft-e bud-e ast	Counterfactual

The stative verb *bud-án* 'to be' has only an imperfective subjunctive without *be-*, *bā̆́š-ad*, and no past perfect, but a literary present *mi-bā̆́š-ad*. *Dāšt-án* 'to hold, keep, have' has only a perfective subjunctive, *dāšt-é bāš-ad*. Neither has *mi-* when used as imperfective past and counterfactual. This restriction does not apply to the use of *dāšt-án* in compound verbs.

The verb forms are based on three stems: present, aorist and perfect, the last regularly derived from the aorist stem by *-e*. All perfect forms are periphrastic with forms of the verb 'to be'. The imperfective prefix *mi-* occurs with all three stems, while the subjunctive prefix *be-* occurs only with the present stem and is mutually exclusive with negation.

The nominal forms are the three stems and the verbal noun, called 'infinitive', marked by *-an* as in *raft-án* 'to go, going'.

3.4.1 Categories

This verb system used to present considerable problems. Until very recently a good many grammars and textbooks omitted some of the more complex forms, while others postulated non-existing, usually obsolete, forms. And if the complex forms were mentioned, their function was mostly only circumscribed.

3.4.2 Aspect and Tense

The key to the understanding of the system is the recognition of the functions of the forms marked by *mi-*, of the forms marked by the perfect stem in *-e* and, most importantly, of the aorist *raft* which used to be identified as (simple) past or preterit for the obvious reason that this is the general form used in simple past narrative. With the 'past' *raft* opposed to the present *mí-rav-ad*, there appeared to be a system based on tense distinction, quite similar to Western European systems, notably the French system as traditionally understood. This was reinforced by the pair of the present and past perfects *raft-é ast* and *raft-é bud* and the imperfect *mí-raft*.

However, aspect is as basic a categorical vector of the system as is tense. *Mi-* is the marker of imperfectivity. As such it may express habitual action, progressive-ingressive action, as well as future action in the present and past, e.g. present *hamišè/al'ằn/fardằ kā̆́r mi-kon-am* 'I always work/I am working (right) now/I will work, will be working tomorrow', past *hamišè/dirùz/fārdà kā̆́r mi-kard* 'he was always working, would always work/he was working yesterday (when I came)/(he thought:) he would work, would be working the next day', the latter in contexts such as anticipation in an interior monologue.

The perfect forms are not simply perfective, but resultative-stative. This is most evident with change-of-state verbs, e.g. *hasán ān-jā̀ nešast-è ast/bud* 'Hasan has/had sat down there' = 'Hasan is/was sitting there', *Maryàm lebā̀s-e qašáng-i pušid-è ast/bud* 'Maryam has/had put on a nice dress' = 'Maryam is/was wearing a nice dress'. Both occur also in a future context, e.g. *fardā̀ sā'at-e sè raft-é am/raft-é bud-am* 'by three o'clock tomorrow I will be gone/by three o'clock the next day I would be gone', the latter again in anticipation in the past.

Most instructively, the aorist is not confined to past contexts, but occurs in present and future contexts as well, most evident with verbs implying motion, e.g. in a past context *hasán diruz be bāzā́r raft va ín-rā xarid* 'Hasan went to the market yesterday and bought this', in a present context *to bā́š-i, man ráft-am* 'you stay here, I am on my way/am going now', which may be said when still seated, or in a future context *šā̀yad mā́ ham raft-im* 'we will most likely go, too', said after hearing that someone will go to see an exhibition. The future use of this form is largely confined to the colloquial language. In educated registers a formation with *xāh*, the unmarked present stem of *xāst-án* 'to want, will', is used followed by the uninflected form, *ná-xāh-ad raft* 'he will not go'.

The aorist does thus certainly not indicate past tense; rather, it is tense-neutral and it is the context which identifies time. It is a member of both the present and past subsystems, and therefore is called here 'aorist'.

3.4.3 Inferential Past

The complex forms *mí-raft-e ast*, which combines imperfective *mi-* with the perfect *-e*, and *raft-é bud-e ast*, a double perfect, express remote past in the literary register. However, they are not confined to literary style, but are as frequent in the colloquial language without referring to remote past. What they express is the category of inference, that is mainly second-hand knowledge, conclusion and reminiscence. In this they are joined by the perfect form *raft-é ast* which also functions as the inferential aorist. All three forms of the inferential past are thus derived from the perfect as is the case in a good number of other languages which have that category. To give one example: *zāher-án nevisandé, vàqt-i ān nāmè-rā mi-nevešt-é* (*ast*), *xód-aš-rā bā ín āmpúl-i, ke ruz-e qàbl xarid-è bud-é* (*ast*), *košt-é* (*ast*) 'apparently, the writer killed (*košt-e ast*) himself with this injection, which he had bought (*xarid-é bud-e ast*) the day before, while he was writing (*mí-nevešt-e ast*) that letter'. The non-inferential past forms in this context would imply a fact or be at least uncommitted.

The tense opposition [present:[past:inferential past]] is therefore likewise a fundamental vector of the system. Future, however, is not a tense, but at best a modality. As is evident in the examples above, all present and past forms may be used in a future context.

3.4.4 Mood

The basic function of the subjunctive is to express potential action. As such it functions as adhortative, e.g. *bé-rav-ad* 'he should go/let him go'. It is obligatory after verbs with potential connotations such as modal verbs and expressions and verbs like 'to fear/be afraid to', 'to hope to' etc., e.g. *bà-y-ad bé-rav-ad* 'he must go', *mì-tars-ad bé-rav-ad* 'he is afraid to go'. (The infinitive-verbal noun is strictly nominal and expresses 'the going' rather than 'to go'.)

The basic function of the counterfactual is to express actions or states which are unlikely to, or did not, come about. As such it functions in wishes and hypothetical statements. It is thus tense-neutral, and the distinction is strictly one of aspect, e.g. *kàš mí-raft* may be interpreted as 'if he would only go' or 'if he had only gone'. Similarly, the perfective, e.g. *kàš raft-é bud* is either 'if he were only gone' or 'if he had only left'.

In connection with necessity, it also expresses an action which should have, but did not, happen, as well as an action which had to be done instead of another, e.g. *bà-y-ad fardā́ mi-resid* 'he should arrive, have arrived tomorrow (but now they say...)', *tāzè qàbl-aš ham bà-y-ad mí-raft-im qazā́ be-xor-im* 'we first had to go to have some food (and thus did not come)'.

3.4.5 Causation

The causal suffix is *ān*, e.g. *xor* 'to eat' vs. *xor-ā́n* 'to make eat, feed', *rav* 'to go, leave' vs. *rān* 'to drive' (< *rav-ān*). Today, this suffix appears to be increasing in productivity, perhaps due to increased linguistic consciousness of writers. But it had been on the decline along with the general tendency, beginning in Early New Persian, to replace simple verbs by compound verb constructions consisting of a nominal followed by a relatively small set of verbs, the most frequent of which are *kard-án* 'to do, make' and *šod-án* 'to become' (originally 'to go'). These two function as markers of causality. Three stages of causation are distinguished: in simple inherently causative verbs, agent mentioned is expressed actively, agent implied by the third person plural ending, agent not implied by the perfect participle + *šod-án*, e.g. *dár-rā bàst* 'he closed the door', *dár-rā bàst-and* 'they/someone closed the door', *dàr bast-é šod* 'the door closed/was closed'. In compound verbs, *kard-án* assumes the causative function, e.g. *ù-rā bidā́r kard* 'he woke him up', *ù-rā bidā́r kard-and* 'they/someone woke him up', *bidā́r šod* 'he woke up'.

The non-agentive construction with *šod-án* has generally been identified as passive, since with inherently causative verbs it appears like a Western European passive, e.g. *košt-é šod* 'he got killed' is assumed to be a equivalent to 'he was killed'. The Persian passive, however, is strictly agentless: unlike English (*he was killed* ***by X***), it excludes the expression of a known agent. Moreover, it is confined to causal verbs, which may imply a change of state, such as *košt-án* 'to kill', creation, such as *nevešt-án* 'to write', *sāxt-án* 'to build', movement of an object, such as *āvard-án* 'to bring', and observation, such as *nešān dād-án* 'to show'. Its function as a non-agentive construction is utilised pragmatically whenever the speaker wishes not to mention the agent, as is often the case in bureaucratic jargon and in polite phraseology so typical for Persian.

3.5 Subordinate Clauses

3.5.1 Relative Clauses

Relative clauses are introduced by the general relative pronoun *ke* 'that'. The head noun is taken up again in the relative clause by the respective independent or suffixed pronoun, e.g. *àn márd ke māšín-rā [az u] xaríd-i* 'that man, from whom you bought the car'. This pronoun is optional if *ke* functions as the subject or direct object of the relative clause.

Restrictive relative clauses are marked by *-i*, e.g. *àn márd-i ke māšín-rā az-aš xarid-í* 'that man from whom you bought the car' (not the other one etc.). This *-i* merges with the homophonous indefinite *-i*, e.g. *márd-i ke zan ná-dār-ad tanhấ ast* 'a man who has no wife is lonely'.

3.5.2 Sequence of Clauses

The basic rule for the sequence of main and subordinate clauses in contemporary Persian may be stated as follows: subordinate clauses with actions or states which logically or temporally precede others, i.e. cause, time and condition, precede the main clause; those whose actions and states logically or temporally follow others, i.e. explanation, sudden interruption, time of potential or factual completion and exception, follow the main clause.

This basic rule is seen in the pattern of the most frequent adverbial clauses.

Preceding			*Following*		
Cause	čun	'because'	Explanation	zí-rā	'(that is) because'
Time	váqt-i	'when'	Interruption	ke	'when (suddenly)'
Point/	tā	'as soon as'	End point	tā	'until, so that'
Stretch		'as long as'			
Condition	ág^(a)ar	'if'	Exception	mág^(a)ar	'unless, if not'

The semantically neutral enclitic conjunction *ke* may be substituted for the conjunctions of preceding clauses, e.g. *čun/váxt-i/tā/ág^(a)ar pul nà-dār-ám, né-mi-rav-am* 'because/when/as long as/if I have no money I will not go', all → *púl-ke nà-dār-am, né-mi-rav-am*. In addition to these, there are numerous adverbial conjunctival phrases either with nouns, such as *(dar) mowqé-i ke āmád* '(at) the moment (that) he came', or with adverbs, such as *piš az ín ke be-rav-ád* 'before (this that) he left'. Their general structure shows that syntactically they are relative clauses, restrictive relative clauses with nouns, [N-*i ke*], and non-restrictive with adverbs, [- *in ke*]. Since adverbs are strictly prenominal they require a 'dummy' noun to introduce the dependent clause, either *in* 'this' or less frequently *ān* 'that'.

Object, subject and complement clauses, which express facts or possibilities depending on the main clause, follow the main clause, e.g. object *díd-am* (*ke*) *ān-jā̀ níst* 'I saw that he is not there', subject *ma'lúm ast ke u níst* 'it is obvious that he is not here', complement *hàqq-aš ín ast ke pùl ná-dār-am* 'the truth of it is (this) that I have no money'. As is evident, the conjunction *ke* is optional with object clauses, but obligatory with subject and complement clauses.

Syntactically, these clauses are relative clauses as well, as seen most clearly by topicalising inversion: *ín ke u níst ma'lúm ast* '(this) that he is not here is obvious', *ín ke u ān-jā níst díd-am* '(this) that he was not there I noticed'.

3.5.3 Verbal Categories

The 'logic' of the sequence of clauses is paralleled by the 'logic' of the verbal categories. All subordinate clauses, including relative clauses, strictly follow the semantics of tense, aspect and mood.

Factual actions and states are in the indicative, even in conditional clauses, e.g. [*àgar mí-xāh-i*], *mí-rav-im* 'if you (really) want to, we will go'. Potential actions and states are in the subjunctive in clauses with potential connotation such as final, concessive and conditional clauses, as well as in temporal and relative clauses with implicit condition, therefore also including those with conjunctions like 'before', 'without', e.g. *ráft* [*tā az ù bé-pors-ad*] 'he went in order to ask him', [*àgar/vàqt-i be-rav-ád*] *kàs-i digàr níst* 'if/when he goes there will be no one left', *fárš-i* [*ke gere-hā̀-y-aš riz-tàr bāš-ád*] *beh-tár ast* 'a carpet the knots of which are finer is better', [*pìš az ín ke bè-rav-í*] *telefón kon* 'before you go, call'. Unlikely or impossible actions or states are in the counterfactual.

Similarly, aspect. Incomplete actions are expressed by the imperfective, resulting states by the stative and completed perfective actions by the aorist. This is true for both the indicative and the non-indicative. Most instructive in this context is the use of the aorist in explicitly or implictly conditional contexts. There it expresses the potential completion as a condition for another action, in contrast with the imperfective subjunctive, e.g. subjunctive [*àgar hasàn be-rav-ád*] *be màn telefón kon* 'if Hassan leaves/should he leave, give me a call', aorist: [*àgar hasàn-rā did-í*] *be màn telefón kon*, [*àgar na-búd*] *yād-dā́št-i bè-nevis* 'if/as soon as you find Hassan, give me a call; if he is not there, write a note'.

Finally, tense. Most instructive in this context are object clauses expressing observed facts, including reported speech. Not only do these require the indicative, but also the imperfective or stative present if the action or state is simultaneous with the time of the main verb (whereas in

English the tense of the main verb has to be 'mapped' onto the dependent verb), e.g. *vàqt-i resid-ím šeníd-im* [*ān-jà čand ruz-è bārắn mi-ā-y-ad*] 'when we arrived we heard that it had been raining there for several days', *gòft* [*ke né-mi-ā-y-ad*] 'he said he would not come'. On the other hand, completed past action is obligatorily expressed by the past perfective, e.g. *fàsl-i* [*ke ferestād-è bud-íd*] *resíd* 'the chapter you sent has just arrived' (note the simple past in English).

3.6 Continuity and Innovation

The following is a brief summary of the diachronic development of the forms and categories of Persian and of the main divergences between the three main dialects of Persian. Both reflect the continuity of earlier categorical distinctions as well as the process of ever-increasing differentiation after the collapse of the Old Iranian inflectional system.

3.6.1 Gender

The Old Iranian distinction between masculine, feminine and neuter gender had been lost in late Old Persian. Subsequent stages developed various means of distinguishing between animate and inanimate, as in the case of contemporary Persian, described above.

3.6.2 Noun Phrase

Categories. The history of noun phrase morphosyntax is the history of the foregrounding of genericity, indefiniteness and specificity. Already in Old Persian, the singular could be used generically. However, it was restricted to non-human. This still held in Early New Persian where human plural was marked in predicative position, e.g. *havā-šenās*[*-ān*] *bud-and* 'they were meteorologists'. In contemporary Persian, genericity is generalised.

The indefinite marker *-i* originates in the Old Iranian prenominal number *aiwa* 'one'. In Middle Persian it developed the secondary function of indefiniteness if following the noun. In Early New Persian this use was generalised to singular and plural nouns, but it was still immediately attached to the noun. Today, it generally follows the adjective with a few marked exceptions.

The history of *rā* and of the pronominal suffixes is the coming into syntactic-semantic prominence of the direct object and specificity. *Rā* originates in the Old Persian postposition *rādi* 'by reason of, concerning', cf. Latin *ratiōne*. Thus in Middle Persian *rā* expressed cause, purpose and reference (partially like English '(as) for'). By extension of the implicit directional meaning its range began to include occasional use with indirect and direct objects in Late Middle Persian, a range continued in Early New Persian.

In Early New Persian, *rā* had a similar range, but was not obligatory with either direct or indirect objects. The reduction of its range towards specificity may be shown with the following examples. *rā* marked indirect objects which could be: (a) the beneficiary of an action, alternating with the preposition *ba* 'to'; (b) the possessor, alternating with the verb *dāšt-an* 'to have'; and (c) the experiencer in indirect constructions expressing mental and bodily sensations such as hunger and liking, alternating with the personal suffixes. In contemporary Persian, a virtual semantic-syntactic split has occurred. The three indirect objects are now distinctively marked by the alternates, e.g. *man ō-rā mē-gōy-am* > *man be u mi-gu-y-am* 'I am telling him', *ō-rā du pisar bud-and* 'to him were two sons' > *u do pesar dār-ad* 'he had two sons', *az an ma-rā xwaš āmad* > *az ān xoš-am āmad* 'I liked it'. In the Persian of today, for most other uses *rā* has been preserved in, and was replaced by, the prepositional phrase *ba-rā-y-e X* 'for X'.

Nominal Subordination. The function of nominal subordination to express class-item, among which possession is only one, continues an Old Iranian formation, verbless appositional phrases introduced by the generalised relative pronoun Old Persian *haya*/Avestan *yat* > *-e*. This progressive subordination, NN^1-*e* NN^2, is typically South-Western Iranian in terms of dialectology. The marked topical inversions in Persian are the unmarked ones in North-Western Iranian, and can in part be understood as originally marked borrowed features.

The range of the general conjunction *ke* is the result of the merger in New Persian of three Middle Persian conjunctions, *kē* 'who, which', *kā* 'when' and *kū* 'where'. The use of *-i* to introduce restrictive relative clauses, and thus the marking of restrictiveness of relative clauses in contemporary Persian, is the result of a similar generalisation. It originates in the indefinite marker *-ē*, and was exclusively used in Early New Persian with indefinite head nouns.

3.6.3 Verb Phrase

The endings of the aorist continue the Middle Persian substantive verb 'to be', thus MP *h-am* > NP *-am*. The infinitive-verbal noun continues the Old Iranian verbal noun marked by *-tan-*. The endings of the present continue Old Iranian, and ultimately Indo-European endings, as is evident in the endings of the third persons *-ad* < *-a-t-i*, *-and* < *-a-nt-i*, as is the case with the endingless imperative of the second person singular and the initial stress in the imperative and the vocative.

Aspect. The functions of the three stems of the verb reflect their history. Present stems originate in the Old Persian 'present', i.e. imperfective, stems (e.g. OP *bar-a-* > NP *bar-* 'to carry, bear', *da-dā* > NP *dah-* 'to give', *kr-nu-* > NP *kon* 'to do, make'). 'Past', i.e. aorist, stems originate in the Old

Persian perfect participle in *-ta* (e.g. OP *bṛ-tá* > NP *bord*, *dā-tá* > NP*dād*, *kṛ-tá* > NP *kard*). Functionally, constructions with this participle and the copula served as the successor of the older inflectional forms of the Old Iranian 'perfect' and 'aorist' systems, a process that had begun already in Old Iranian. This construction lost its 'perfect' function in Middle Iranian, and a new perfect stem developed in New Persian and a regionally confined number of other dialects, which is derived from the aorist stem by the substantive suffix *-e* (< *-ag* < *-ak-a*).

Similarly, the history of *mi-* reflects the evolution of aspect. *Mi-* originates in the Old Iranian adverb *hama-aiwa-da* 'at the same time, place'. Middle Persian *hamē(w)* 'always, continuously', besides its adverbial function, was also used to express durative action or state, which was extended to iterative and distributive function in Early New Persian.

At that stage, habitual action in past and present, as well as counterfactual action, were expressed by *-ē(d)*, which originates in the generalised third person singular optative *hait* 'may it be' in Old Iranian, where optatives had already a secondary habitual past function. This clitic was virtually lost in Classical Persian, and both habitual and counterfactual functions were taken over by *mē-*, by then strictly an aspectual prefix, with the secondary function of counterfactuality together with the past perfect, as is the case in contemporary Persian.

4 Dialectology

The three main dialects of Persian in Iran, Afghanistan and Tajikistan have diverged in their phonology, most prominently in their vocalic systems. The developments in their morphosyntax is the history of the increasing differentiation prominently in their verb systems by the development of new formations expressing aktionsarten, mood and causation, partially under the influence of Turkic.

The development of the vowels is shown in the diagram given here.

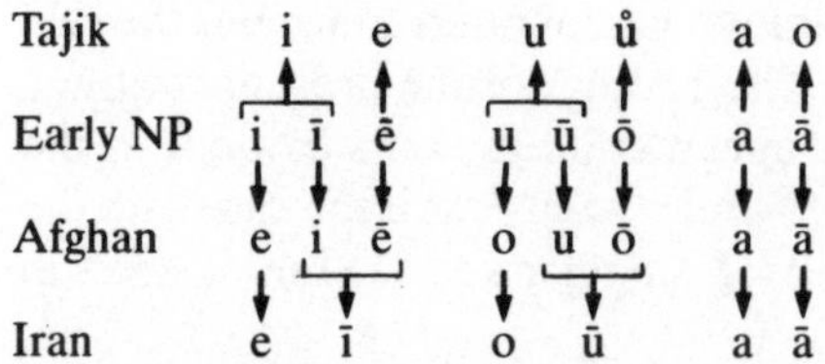

Compared with Early New Persian, Afghan Persian is the least changed, lowering the short high vowels as in Iran to mid vowels, which are now opposed to the retained long mid vowels, while the old long high vowels lose their length distinction. Tajiki is the most changed, losing the length distinction, most likely under the influence of Turkic, by the merger of the short and long high vowels and the rounding of long *a*.

In terms of nominal syntax, the marked inversion of possessor head noun, *pedar-e man* > [*man*] *pedar* [*-am*] 'my father', has become the unmarked construction in Tajiki, again under the influence of Turkic. The colloquial language in Iran has developed a focalising suffix *-é*, e.g. *sag-é* 'the dog mentioned'.

Inference is found in both Afghan and Tajik Persian. Similar forms are found in Early New Persian prose texts, most of which originate in the east, as mentioned, but they disappeared as regionally marked features in Classical Persian. Their appearance in early texts, as well as their reappearance in contemporary standard Persian of Iran, can again be explained by inteference from Turkic where inference is marked by *emiš*. Unlike Turkic, inference is not tense-neutral in Persian, but confined to the past. In Tajiki, however, *mi-raft-e ast* has already become tense-neutral.

The verb forms of Turkic are mostly based on participles. In Tajiki, this has resulted in the development of participial formations with so-called con-verbs, where the participial main verb is followed by a varied set of verbs whose meaning is generalised to express various aktionsarten. For example, *šud-an* 'to become' expresses completion, *bar-omad-an* 'to come out of' thorough completion, and *guzašt-an* 'to pass through, by' completion after a prolonged action, as in [*kitob-ro xond-a*] *šud/bar-omad/guzašt* 'he completed reading the book/he completed reading through the book/he completed the book after prolonged reading'.

Similarly, in Tajiki the progressive is a participial formation with *istod-an* 'to stand', as in [*kitob-ro xond-a*] *istod-a ast* 'he is reading the book'. This development has progressed less in Afghan Persian, which has developed two participial formations, the progressive marked by the con-verb *raft-an* 'to go', as in [*ketāb-ra xānd-a*] *mē-rav-ad* 'he is reading the book', and the dubitative based on the particle *xāt* < *xāh-ad* 'it will/may (be)', as in [*zad-a*] *xat bud-om* 'I might hit'.

In contrast, in the formations developing in Iranian colloquial Persian both verbs are inflected as seen in the progressive based on *dāšt-an* 'to keep, hold, have', as in *dār-ad* [*ketāb-rā mi-xān-ad*] 'he is reading/is about to read the book', in the potential progressive in Tehrani based on *raft-an* 'to go' + subjunctive, as in *mi-rav-ad* [*be-suz-ad*] '(the motor) is about to burn', or in the formation expressing sudden action based on *zad-an* 'to hit', as in *zad-and* [*raft-and*] 'off they went'. Similarly, a new causative formation, 'have-other-do', based on *dād-an* 'to give', inflects both causer and caused, as in *raft va dād* [*šāx-hā-y-aš-rā tiz kard-and*] '(the goat) went and had her horns sharpened' lit. 'she gave, they sharpened'.

Participial formations are already found in the early prose texts, most of which originate in the east. For example, continuity was expressed by *dāšt-*

an 'to keep, hold, behold' with transitives and by *mānd-an* 'to remain, stay' with intransitives, as in [*girift-a*] *dār-ad* 'he keeps [holding]' and [*halāk šud-a*] *bi-mān-and* 'they will keep [perishing]'. Again, in Classical Persian these eastern features were eliminated.

However, the 'passive' in contemporary Persian does originate in such a formation. In Early New Persian there existed a participial formation based on either *āmad-an* 'to come' or *šud-an* 'to become', earlier 'to go', which occurred with both transitives and intransitives, e.g. [(*ān-rā*) *yād kard-a*] *āmad-a*/*šud-a ast* 'it has been recalled', and [*būd-a*] *šud*/*āmad* 'it came into [being]'. In Classical Persian, the use with intransitives and 'come' is lost, and the active participle eliminated: (*ān*) *yād šod-a ast*.

Bibliography

Windfuhr (1979) is the 'state-of-the-art' concise survey of the study of Persian grammar, theoretical approaches and analyses, including new insights into syntax-semantics and phonology with extensive references, together with the most comprehensive alphabetical and topical bibliographies to date. Lazard (1957) is an excellent detailed descriptive-structuralist grammar of contemporary Persian. Phillott (1919) is the most extensively documented grammar of Persian to date, with notes on dialectal variations and many illuminating insights into the pragmatic use of the language. Lumsden (1810) is still the only grammar to make thorough use of the indigenous Muslim grammatical theory and insights, many of which were only rediscovered more recently. Jensen (1931) is a comprehensive descriptive and comparative grammar of Classical Persian with notes on contemporary Persian. For the earlier history, Lazard (1963) provides an abundantly documented analytic description of the Persian of prose texts of the eleventh and twelfth centuries, with historical and dialectal annotation.

Acknowledgement

Work on this chapter was supported by a generous grant from the National Endowment for the Humanities for the comprehensive study of the languages and dialects of Iran.

References

Jensen, H. 1931. *Neupersische Grammatik, mit Berücksichtigung der historischen Entwicklung* (Carl Winter Universitätsverlag, Heidelberg)

Lazard, G. 1957. *Grammaire du persan contemporain* (Klincksieck, Paris)

—— 1963. *La langue des plus anciens monuments de la prose persane* (Klincksieck, Paris)

Lumsden, M. 1810. *A Grammar of the Persian Language; Comprising a Portion of the Elements of Arabic Inflection, Together with Some Observations on the Structure of Either Language Considered with Reference to the Principles of General Grammar*, 2 vols. (Calcutta)

Phillott, D.C. 1919. *Higher Persian Grammar for the Use of the Calcutta University, Showing Differences Between Afghan and Modern Persian with Notes on Rhetoric* (The University Press, Calcutta)
Windfuhr, G.L. 1979. *Persian Grammar. History and State of its Study* (Mouton, The Hague, Paris and New York)

7 Pashto

D.N. MacKenzie

1 Introduction

Long recognised as the most important language of the North-West Frontier Province of British India, now Pakistan, where it is spoken by 90 per cent of the population, Pashto was by royal decree of 1936 also declared to be the national language of Afghanistan in place of 'Dari' Persian. This official preeminence was artificial, however, and it now shares the honour with Persian. The areas of Afghanistan to which Pashto is native are those in the east, south and south-west, bordering on Pakistan, but in recent years Pashto speakers have also settled in parts of the northern and eastern provinces of the country. Reliable census figures of the number of speakers are only available from Pakistan. There, in the fifties, the total number of Pashto speakers was stated to be nearly 5.35 million, of whom 4.84 million (4.47 million of them in the North-West Frontier Province and 270,000 in Baluchistan) claimed it as their mother tongue. In Afghanistan in the same period semi-official estimates gave the number of speakers (presumably including those for whom it was a second language) as between 50 and 60 per cent of the total population of 13 million, i.e. between 6.5 and 7.8 million. Even allowing for some nationalistically inspired exaggeration in these figures, it seems permissible to assume that today at the very least 10 million people in Afghanistan and Pakistan are native speakers of Pashto. In terms of numbers it is, therefore, the second most important of modern Iranian languages.

The name of the language, properly *Pašto*, also denotes the strong code of customs, morals and manners of the Pashtun (*Paštun*, Indianised as *Paṭhān*) nation, also called *Paštunwālay* — whence the saying *Paštun haγa nə day če Pašto wāyi lekin haγa če Pašto lari* 'A Pashtun is not he who speaks Pashto, but he who **has** Pashto.'

2 History

Pashto belongs to the North-Eastern group within the Iranian branch of Indo-European. The relationship can best be demonstrated by two phonological features characteristic of most members of this branch, viz. the development of the Old Iranian initial voiced plosives *b*, *d*, *g* and of the dental groups *-ft-*, *-xt-*. Initial *b*, *d*, *g*, preserved in Western Iranian, regularly became the voiced fricatives *β*, *γ*, *δ* in Khwarezmian and Sogdian. For example, Old Iranian *brātar-* 'brother', **buza-* 'goat', **duγdar-* 'daughter', *dasa-* 'ten', *gauša-* 'ear', **gari-* 'mountain' yield Sogdian *βr't*, *'βz-*, *δwγt'*, *δs'*, *γwš*, *γr-*, Khwarezmian *βr'd*, *'βz*, *δγd*, *δs*, *γwx*, *γryck*. Pashto shows the same development of *g-*, in *γwaǧ* 'ear', *γar* 'mountain'; *b-*, however, has passed through *β-* to the labial continuant *w-*, *wror* 'brother', *wəz* 'goat', and *d-* through *δ-* to *l-*, *lur* 'daughter', *las* 'ten'.

The dental group *-ft-*, also preserved in Western Iranian, becomes voiced in Eastern Iranian to [-βd-]: e.g. Old Iranian **hafta-* 'seven', **tafta-* 'heated', **xšwifta-* 'milk' give Sogdian *'βt*, *tβt*, *xšyβt*, Khwarezmian *'βd*, —, *xwβcy* [*xuβji]. In Pashto the group has been simplified either to *-(w)d-* (cf. Khotanese Saka: *hauda*, *ttauda*, *svīda*), as in *tod*, feminine *tawda* 'hot', *šodə/e* 'milk', or to *-w-*, as in *owə́* 'seven'. *-xt-* coincides with *-γd-* in Eastern Iranian, e.g. *suxta-* 'burnt', *baxta-* 'shared', *duγdar-* 'daughter' give Sogdian *swγt*, *βγt-*, *δwγt'*, Khwarezmian —, *βγd*, *δγd*. Just as *-γd-* was reduced in Khotanese, via [-d-], to a hiatus-filling [-w-] (*sūta* [*sūda-] > *-suva*, *būta* [*būda] > *būva*, *dūta* [*dūda] > *dūva*), so in Pashto it has either become *w* or, finally, dropped without trace: *sə́way* 'burnt', *su*, feminine *swa* 'it burnt', *tə* 'went' < **taxta-*, *tar-lə́* 'father's brother's daughter' < **-duγda-*.

The change of *d* to *l*, already mentioned, is found in other neighbouring languages: there is evidence for it having occurred in at least some Sogdian dialects and in Bactrian (e.g. *Βαγολαγγο* < **bagadānaka-*, the modern Baghlan), and it is normal in modern Munji (where *luγda* 'daughter', *pāla* 'foot' < **pādā-*). Pashto goes further, however, in that all dentals, *t*, *θ*, *d*, become *-l-* post- or intervocalically; e.g. OIran. *pitar-* 'father', *sata-* 'hundred', *paθana-* 'broad', **čaθwar-* 'four', **gada-* 'robber', **wadi-* 'stream', yield Pashto *plār*, *səl*, *plən*, *calor*, *γal*, *wāla*. In other contexts though the dentals were often preserved, e.g. *tə* 'thou' < *tú*, *dre* 'three' < **θrayah*, *atə́* 'eight' < *ašta*, (*yaw-*, etc.)*wišt* 'twenty(-one, etc.)' < **wī́sati* (contrast *šəl* 'twenty' alone < **wīsáti*).

Only a few other sound changes can be mentioned. Perhaps the most striking in Pashto, as in the Pamir languages, are those undergone by some *r*-groups. Both *-rt-* and *-rd-* changed into the retroflex *-r̂-*, and *-rn-* into its nasalised counterpart *-n̂-*: e.g. **ārta-* 'milled' > *or̂ə́* 'flour', *mr̥ta-* 'dead' > *mər̂*, **zr̥dya-* 'heart' > *zr̂ə*, **amarnā-* > *man̂ā́* 'apple', **karna-* 'deaf' > *kun̂*. The presence of a sibilant complicated matters. *sr* and *rš* became *x̌* and *ǧ* respectively (on the phonemes written *x̌*, *ǧ*, see below), e.g. **hwasrū-* 'mother-in-law' > *xwā́x̌e*, **r̥ša-* 'bear' > *yaǧ*, and in *-str-*, *-štr-*, *-ršt-* the *-t-* was lost, leaving *-x̌-*, e.g. *uštra-* 'camel' > *ux̌*, *wāstra-* 'grass' > *wāx̌ə́*, **hr̥štaka-* 'left' > *íx̌ay*. *-rs-*, on the other hand, coincided with *-rst-* to yield *-x̌t-*, and *-rz-* similarly gave *-ǧd-*, e.g. **uz-kr̥staka-* 'cut out' > *skə́x̌tay*, *pr̥sa-* 'ask' > *pux̌t-*, **warsya-* 'hair' > *wex̌tə́*, **br̥z-* > *uǧd* 'long', **arzana-* 'millet' > *ǧdən*. It is an example of this development of *-rs-* that has given *Paxto* its name, from an original **Parsawā-* closely akin to the old names of the Persians and Parthians, respectively *Pársa-* (< **Parswa-* ?) and *Parθawa-*. *Paxtun* probably continues an old **Parswāna-*.

The Pashto lexicon is as fascinating as an archaeological museum. It contains side-by-side words going back to the dawn of Iranian, neologisms of all ages and loanwords from half a dozen languages acquired over a couple of millennia. The oldest of these loans date from the Greek occupation of Bactria in the third century BC, e.g. *mečə́n* (feminine) 'hand-mill, quern' taken over from *mēkhanḗ* at a time when *kh* was still an aspirated *k*, or *mačóγna*, *mačnóγza*, *mačlóγza* 'sling', which may be evidence for a weapon called *manganiká* (cf. Arabic *manǰanīq* 'mangonel') already at the same period. No special trace of a Zoroastrian or a Buddhist past remains, but the Islamic period has brought a great number of Arabic and Persian cultural words. Throughout the centuries everyday words also have been borrowed from Persian in the west and from Indo-Aryan neighbours in the east. Usually it is difficult to establish when: *marγalára* 'pearl', for example, could be from Greek *margarítēs*, or like it from an Old Persian **margāritā-*, or later from a Parthian or Sogdian form. Irregular assimilation makes it hard to decide when, say, *blā́rba* 'pregnant', *cerá* 'face, picture', *ǰalā́* 'separate', *pex̌* 'happening' were acquired from Persian *bārbar*, *čihra*, *ǰudā*, *peš*, but it was long ago. The different stages of assimilation show that *žranda* 'water-mill' and *ǰandra* 'padlock' have been borrowed at different times from Lahnda (Western Panjabi) *ǰandar* 'mill' and *ǰandrā* 'padlock'. The sources of the many such Indian loanwords are particularly hard to distinguish. It is only when we come to *ǰarnáyl* 'general', *lāt̂* 'lord', *palt̂ə́n* 'platoon, regiment', *t̂ikə́s* 'ticket, stamp' and *t̂wal* 'towel' that we are on firm ground again. The greater part of the basic vocabulary is nevertheless inherited Eastern Iranian. Still it is noteworthy how many original words have given way to neologisms. Most striking among these are some words for parts of the body: *γāx̌* 'tooth' (< **gaštra-* *'biter'), *stə́rga* 'eye' (< **stṛkā-* *'little star'), *tənday* or *wəčwúlay* 'forehead' (the *tə́nda* 'thirsty' or *wəč* 'dry' part), *tóray* 'spleen' (the *tor* 'dark, black' organ), and several of unknown origin, such as *šā* 'back', *xwla* 'mouth'.

3 Phonology

The maximum inventory of segmental phonemes in Pashto is set out in table 7.1. Besides the common consonant stock of most modern Iranian languages, it comprises the dental affricates *c*, *j* [ts dz] and, thanks to its neighbourhood to Indo-Aryan languages, a set of retroflex, or cerebral, sounds. While the retroflex stops *t̂*, *d̂* occur only in loanwords, the *r̂* has, as we have seen, also developed within Pashto. In distinction from the alveolar trill *r* and from the dental (or alveolar) lateral *l*, it is basically a retroflexed lateral flap. Its nasal counterpart *n̂*, which does not occur word-initially, is a nasalised *r̂* — the nasalisation often extending to the preceding vowel — and not simply a retroflex nasal (which latter only occurs as an allophone of dental *n* before *t̂*, *d̂*).

Table 7.1: The Segmental Phonemes of Pashto

Vowels

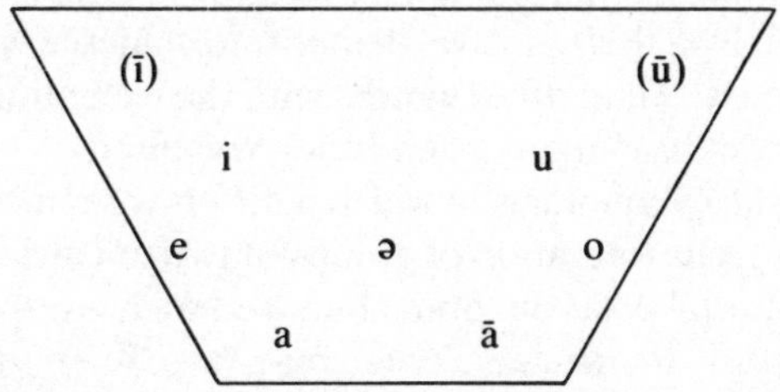

(ī) (ū)

i u

e ə o

a ā

Consonants

	Plosive	Affricate	Fricative	Nasal	Lateral	Trill	Semi-vowel
Bilabial	p b			m			w
Labio-dental			(f)				
Dental	t d	c j		n	l		
Alveolar			s z			r	
Retroflex	t̂ d̂		(x̌ ǧ)		n̂ r̂		
Post-alveolar		č ǰ	š ž				y
Velar	k g		x γ				
Uvular	(q)						
Glottal	(ʼ)		h				

The bracketed *f*, *q* and ʼ occur only in the elegant pronunciation of unassimilated loanwords from Persian and Arabic. Generally *f* is replaced by *p* (occasionally by *w*) and *q* by *k*, e.g. *fatīla* > *palitá* 'wick', *tafaḥḥuṣ* > *tapós* 'enquiry', *lafz* > *lawz* 'word, promise', *qiṣṣa* > *kisá* 'story', *qawm* > *kām* 'tribe'. The glottal stop (representing both Arabic *hamza* ʼ and ʿ*ayn* ʿ) is usually dropped, either without trace, e.g. *masʼala* > *masalá* 'question, matter', or having widened the adjacent vowel, as in *šarʿ* > *šára* 'holy law', *maʼmūr* > *māmúr* 'official', *šurūʿ* > *šuró* 'beginning', *mawẓiʿ* > *mawzé* 'place'. This resembles the treatment of word- and syllable-final *h*, *ḥ* in loanwords, e.g. *ṣaḥīḥ* > *sahí* 'correct', *fatḥ* > *fáta* 'victory', *iḥtirām* > *etərấm* 'respect', *makrūh* > *makró* 'abominable'.

Characteristic of Pashto are the two phonemes written *x̌*, *ǧ*. These developed originally as retroflex spirants [ŝ ẑ] and continue generally as such in the southwestern dialects, particularly the prestigious one of Qandahar, where they contrast with the post-alveolar *š*, *ž*. In the southeastern dialects this contrast has been lost. In most central dialects these phonemes are still realised distinctly, but as palatal spirants [x̌ γ̌]. In the north-east, however, they have coincided entirely with velar *x* and *g* (not *γ*!). The non-phonetic symbols *x̌*, *ǧ* thus represent a compromise between [ŝ/š/x̌/x] and [ẑ/ž/γ̌/g] respectively. This wide and striking variation between southwestern [paŝto] and north eastern [paxto] accounts for the description of the different dialects as 'soft' and 'hard' Pashto. It is noteworthy that the hard dialects, most directly exposed to Indo-Aryan influence, have also abandoned the dental affricates *c*, *j* (which lose their plosive element, to coalesce with *s*, *z*) and *ž* (which joins the affricate *ǰ*): in other words, with the exception of *x*, *γ* and *z*, their phonemic system has largely been Indo-Aryanised.

A notable feature of Pashto phonology, in which it differs from most other modern Iranian languages, is its toleration of groups of two or (including *w*) three consonants in word-initial position. Some hundred such groups occur, e.g. eleven with *š*- alone: *šp*-, *št*-, *šk*-, *šx*-, *šxw*-, *šm*-, *šn*-, *šl*-, *šr*-, *šr̂*-, *šw*-. Such initial groups are particularly unstable, being subject to various metatheses, assimilations and dissimilations. Thus *px̌a* 'foot', *kx̌əl* 'pull' and *psarláy* 'spring' become hard *xpa*, *xkəl*, and *sparláy* respectively; *nwar* 'sun' occurs in different dialects as *nmar* and *lmar*, *rwaj* 'day' as *wraj*, *ǧmənj* 'comb' as *g(u)manj*, *mangáz*, and so on.

The vowel phonemes in table 26.1 are the stressed ones of standard Pashto, stress also being phonemic. The following diphthongs also occur: *ay*, *əy*, *āy*, *oy*, *uy*; *aw*, *āw*. The phonemic status of the historically long vowels *ī*, *ū* is questionable. In most dialects they have been reduced to coincide with *i*, *u*; i.e. length is here, as in the case of *e*, *o*, no longer significant but depends on position and stress. Stressed *a*, *ə*, are entirely distinct, e.g. *bal* 'alight': *bəl* 'other', *γla* 'female thief': *γlə* 'male thieves'. In unstressed position, however, they are usually in free variation. It is convenient to regard unstressed [a ə] both as allophones of *a*, i.e. to regard *ə* only as a strong- or weak-stressed phoneme. Otherwise (as is unfortunately the case in some modern works on Pashto, both Afghan and foreign) there are some dangers of confusion, for example in writing the diphthongs unstressed *ay* [~ əy] and stressed *ə́y*. In fact there is an important morphophonemic distinction between final *-áy*, *´-ay* and *-ə́y*. In the hard dialects *-ay* is generally monophthongised to an open [ɛ(:)], allowing *-əy* to shift and take its place at [ɛ̯i]. In all dialects, but especially those of the south-west, there is a tendency towards regressive vowel harmony, in that the middle vowels *e*, *o* in syllables preceding high vowels *i*, *u* are themselves raised. Also in the south-west unstressed final *e*, *o* often coalesce with *i*, *u*, but not to the extent that morphological distinctions are lost. Thus *óse* 'you dwell' remains, in contrast to *ósi* 'he dwells'. *mor*, oblique *móre* 'mother', however, becomes *móri* [mu:ri], though still without rhyming with *lur*, obl. *lúre* 'daughter' > *lúri*. In some non-standard mountain dialects of the Afghan-Pakistan borderland, particularly of the Afridi and Wazir tribes, there is a vowel shift of *ā* to [ɔ:], *o* to [œ: > ɛ:], and *ū* to [i:] (but not *u* > *i*); e.g. Waziri [plɔ:r] 'father', [mɛ:r] 'mother', [li:r] 'daughter'.

Three degrees of stress can be recognised: strong, medium and weak. Strong stress is comparatively free, in that it can occur on any syllable of a word, but it is mainly restricted to the first, last or penultimate syllables. It can also, particularly in verbal inflection, be mobile, though the shifts involved follow regular patterns, e.g. from *prewatə́l* 'to fall', also 'they (masculine) were falling', *préwatəl* 'they fell' and *prewátay* 'fallen (masculine singular)'. Occasionally lexical items may be distinguished solely by stress, e.g. *áspa* 'mare' : *aspá* 'spotted fever', *gorá* 'fair-skinned, European' : *góra* 'look!', *palitá* 'wick' : *palíta* 'indecent woman', *wār̂ə́* 'small (masculine plural)' : *wā́r̂a* [-ə] 'all'.

4 Script

The earliest authenticated records of Pashto as a literary language date from the late sixteenth century, at a time when the whole area was, if turbulently, a part of the Mogul empire. The language has always been written in the

Table 7.2: Pashto Alphabet, with Transliteration

*	ا		ā medial		س	سـ	s
	آ		ā initial		ش	شـ	š
	ب	بـ	b		ښ	ښـ	x̌
	پ	پـ	p	[	ص	صـ	ṣ]
	ت	تـ	t	[	ض	ضـ	ẓ]
	ټ	ټـ	t̂ (P also Urdu ٹ)	[		ط	ṭ, occasionally for t̂]
[	ث	ثـ	s̱]	[		ظ	ẓ̄]
	ج	جـ	ǰ	[	ع	عـ	ʿ]
	چ	چـ	č		غ	غـ	γ
	ځ څ	ځـ څـ	j (A ځ) / c		ف	فـ	f
[	ح	حـ	ḥ]	[	ق	قـ	q]
	خ	خـ	x		ک	کـ	k
		د	d		ګ	ګـ	g
		ډ	d̂ (P also Urdu ڈ)		ل	لـ	l
[		ذ	ẕ		م	مـ	m
		ر	r		ن	نـ	n
		ړ	r̂ (P also Urdu ڑ)			ڼـ	n̂ (A ڼ ڼ)
		ز	z	*		و	w
		ژ	ž	*	ه	هـ	h
		ږ	ǧ	*	ی	یـ	y

Note: *On the function as vowel carrier of ا and ه in word-initial and final position respectively, and of و and ی medially and finally, see the discussion in the chapters on Arabic and Persian and table 7.3.

Perso-Arabic script (see the discussion of script in the chapters on Arabic and Persian), with the addition of certain modified letters to represent the peculiar consonant phonemes of Pashto. In the earliest manuscripts, from the late seventeenth to early eighteenth century, there is considerable variety in the representation of these consonants, but later a standard system emerged which persisted until recently. Since the adoption of Pashto as a national language in Afghanistan a number of innovations have been introduced into the script, which in the main make for more clarity. In Pakistan, on the other hand, there have been some tendencies, e.g. the occasional use of Urdu forms of letters and the phonetic representation of hard dialect forms (*ǧ* as *g*, *x̌* as *x*, *j* as *z* etc.), causing a departure from the classical standard. In table 7.2 the standard alphabet is given, with the modern Afghan (A) and Pakistani (P) forms as variants. The letters in square brackets occur only in unassimilated Arabic loanwords and the diacritics used in the transliteration are merely for mnemonic purposes, and have no phonetic significance. Thus ذ *z̲*, ض *ẓ*, ظ *z̤* are all pronounced [z], i.e. are all allographs of the phoneme *z*, usually written ز .

The Perso-Arabic script is by nature a consonantal one. The means by which the relatively simple vowel systems of Arabic and Persian are represented in it are inadequate for Pashto, where vowel representation is thus somewhat complicated: see table 7.3. The short vowels *a*,
but are represented notionally by the superscript signs ´ *zwar* for *a*, ˉ *zwar-akay* for *ə*. In standard script the latter is sometimes represented by the sign *hamza*, e.g. زهٔ *zə* 'I'. The signs ˏ *zer* and ˒ *pex̌* can represent *i* or *e* and *u* respectively, though all these vowels may also (particularly in Afghan practice) be written *plene* with the appropriate semi-vowel letters ی and و respectively; e.g. *injə́r* انځر or اينځر 'fig', *kisá* قصه or کيسه 'story', *de* دِ or دې 'your', *gul* گل or کول 'flower'.

Table 7.3: Vowel Representation

	Initially	*Medially*	*Finally*
a	أ	ـَ	ـه
ā	آ	ا	ا
ə	-	ـٓ	ـه (P ـهٔ)
e	ايـ	ـېـ	ې (P ے) (P ـِ in particles)
ay	أيـ	ـيـ	ي (P ے)
əy	-	-	ئ (A ی nominal, ۍ verbal)
			-
i	اِ	ـِ (A ـيـ)	-
ī	ايـ	ـيـ	ي
o	او	و	و
aw	او	و	و
u	أ	ـُ (A و)	و (P ۇ)
ū	او	و	و

5 Morphology

Although it has departed considerably from the morphological patterns of Old and even Eastern Middle Iranian (as evidenced, for example, by Sogdian and Khotanese Saka) Pashto has nevertheless a remarkably complex nominal and verbal morphology. Two grammatical genders (masculine and feminine) and two numbers (singular and plural) are distinguished in both noun and, in part, verb. Although the nominal case system has essentially been reduced to a contrast between direct and oblique, there is in the singular also a vocative and a second oblique case used in conjunction with certain prepositions. Moreover the formatives used are not, as in practically all other still inflectional Iranian languages, restricted to suffixes. Alterations of stem vowels and stress and the substitution of endings also come into play.

Old Iranian masculine stems in *-a*, *-i*, (*-u*) have generally lost their final vowel, to appear in Pashto as consonant stems: *kāra-* > *kor* 'house, family', *gauša-* > *γwağ* 'ear', **gari-* > *γar* 'mountain'. The old feminine stems in *-ā* alone have survived practically unscathed as *-a* stems: *aspā-* > *áspa* 'mare', *uštrā-* > *úx̌a* 'she-camel', *wanā-* > *wə́na* 'tree', *xšapā-* > *špa* 'night'. Old *-an-* stems similarly preserved their nominative singular *-ā* to emerge as masculine nouns in *-a*: **maiθman-* > *melmá* 'guest'. Feminine stems in *-ī*, (*-ū*) also lost their final vowel, e.g. *hapaθnī-* > *bən* 'co-wife', **raθī-* > *lār* 'way, road', **witasti-* > *wlešt* 'span', but generally they adopt an *-a* from the general feminine form: **sraunī-* > *x̌n-a* 'buttock, leg', **strī-čī-* > *x̌ə́j-a* 'woman', **wahunī-* > **wēn* > *wín-a* 'blood', **zanu-* > *zə́n-a* 'chin'. Neuter stems joined either masculine or feminine, in the latter case also generally adopting a final *-a*: *raučah-* > *rwaj* f. 'day', **asru-* > *óx̌-a* 'tear', **gauna-* > *γún-a* 'colour', **parna-* > *pāṅ-a* 'leaf'. Only rarely do old masculines become feminine, e.g. *angušta-* > *gút-a* 'finger', *safa-* > *sw-a* 'hoof'. Several forms in *-ya-*, nominal or adjectival (including the comparative in *-yah-*) yield Pashto *-ə*: **(p)tr̥wya-* > *trə* 'paternal uncle', **t(a)igriya-* > *terə́* 'sharp', *srayah-* 'better' > *x̌ə* 'good', **abrya-* > *orə́* 'cloud'. A more common formative, however, as in Sogdian and Khotanese Saka, was the suffix *-ka-*. The resulting stems in *-aka-*, *-ika-*, *-uka-* became, via nominative or genitive **-ai* (as in Khotanese), either stressed or unstressed *-ay*. The feminine equivalent, originally **-akī-*, became *-ə́y* when stressed but *-e* when not: **daru-ka-ka-* > *largáy* 'wood', **sarda-ka-* > *saṙáy* 'man', **spaka-* > *spay* 'dog' : **spakī-* > *spəy* 'bitch', **āsu-kī-* > *(h)osə́y* 'deer', **náwa-ka-* > *nə́way* m. 'new' : **náwa-kī-* > *nə́we* f. 'new'. The result of these far-reaching changes was three main masculine stem-types, ending in a consonant, stressed *-áy* or unstressed *-ay* respectively, and three corresponding feminine stem-types, ending in (generally unstressed) *-a*, stressed *-ə́y* or unstressed *-e*. There are also several exceptions which fit into this scheme as best they can, e.g. masculines ending in *-ə*, *-ā*, *-ū* and feminines in a consonant, *-ā*, *-e*, *-o*, all unchanged in the singular but approximating to the masculine consonant or feminine *-a* declension in the plural, or again masculines (professions) and feminines (abstracts) in *-i* joining the *-áy* and *-ə́y* stems respectively. The stem-types pair up in the case of adjectives to form the three declensions numbered 1, 4, 5 in the chart of adjectival declension. In all adjectival declensions the oblique singular forms are identical with the direct plural. Only nouns generally distinguish plural forms by plural markers, of bewildering variety. The 'prepositional' case is marked in the masculine by an unstressed *-a*, which probably represents an old ablative ending *-āt*, added to the direct case stem. In the feminine it coincides with the direct case. The vocative coincides in most, but not all, masculine singulars with the prepositional form and in most feminines with the oblique. The oblique, and also vocative and prepositional, plural marker *-o* (in soft dialects, stressed *-ó*, unstressed *-u*) is common to all declensions.

Adjectival Declension

	1 'other'	*2* 'ripe, cooked'	*3* 'bitter'	*4* 'thin, narrow'	*5* 'new'
Masculine					
Singular					
Direct	bəl	pox	trix	naráy	nə́way
Vocative	bə́la	póxa	tríxa	naráya	nə́we
Prepositional	bə́la	póxa	tríxa	naráya	nə́wi
Oblique	bəl	pāxə́	tarxə́	narí	nə́wi
Plural					
Direct	bəl	pāxə́	tarxə́	narí	nə́wi
Oblique (Voc., Prepl.)	bə́lo[2]	paxó	tarxó	narío[2]/naró	nə́wyo[2]/nə́wo[2]
Feminine					
Singular					
Direct	bə́la	paxá	tarxá	narə́y	nə́we
Vocative	bə́le[1]	paxé	tarxé	narə́y	nə́we[1]
Prepositional	bə́la	paxá	tarxá	narə́y	nə́we[1]
Oblique	bə́le[1]	paxé	tarxé	narə́y	nə́we[1]
Plural					
Direct	bə́le[1]	paxé	tarxé	narə́y	nə́we[1]
Oblique (Voc., Prepl.)	bə́lo[2]	paxó	tarxó	narə́yo[2]/naró	nə́wyo[2]/nə́wo[2]

Note: Qandahari: [1]bə́li, nə́wi. [2]bə́lu, naríu, nə́w(y)u.

There are also two further types of consonant stem (declensions 2, 3), represented among both nouns and adjectives, in which stress and vowel changes occur which may go back to a very early stage of the language. In the first type, comprising some (but not all) monosyllabic nouns and adjectives with the stem vowel *o* or *u* and some nouns with final *-un*, the oblique singular and direct plural masculine substitute the vowel *-ā-*, and the oblique plural and entire feminine the vowel *-a-*, all with additional stressed endings. In the other type the same stressed endings occur with a stem either unchanged or with the stem vowel reduced to an *-a-* or nil. Thus *kuṅ* 'deaf' has the plural *kāṅə́* and feminine *kaṅá*, but *ruṅ* 'light' plural *ruṅə́*, feminine *ruṅá*; *soṙ* 'cold', plural *sāṙə́*, but *sur* 'red' plural *srə*. Similarly declined are a few words ending in stressed *-ə*: *x̌ə* 'good', singular and plural masculine, *x̌a* feminine singular, *x̌e* plural. A last set of adjectives comprises all those which end in any other vowel — *a, ā, e, i, o, u*. These are indeclinable for number, gender or case, except that they may take the universal oblique plural *-o*.

The plural of masculine nouns of the first declension, which also includes those ending in *-ə, -a, -u*, is generally *-úna*, oblique *-úno*, e.g. *lās* 'hand', *lāsúna*, *zṙə* 'heart', *zṙúna*. Animate nouns take the suffix *-ā́n*, borrowed from Persian, oblique *-ā́no*, e.g. *ux̌* 'camel', *ux̌ā́n*, *lewə́* 'wolf', *lewā́n*; before this suffix a *-y-* is inserted after *-ā*, e.g. *mullāyā́n* 'mullahs', or a *-g-* after other vowels, e.g. *nikəgā́n* 'ancestors'. Inanimate nouns in *-u* take the same ending: *bāṅugā́n* 'eye-lashes'. Feminine nouns of this declension ending in a consonant or *-a* behave like adjectives even in the plural, e.g. *lār* 'road', plural *lā́re*, *xwla* 'mouth', *xwle*. Animate ones ending in *-o*, however, take the mixed Persian and Pashto suffix *-gā́ne*, e.g. *pišogā́ne* 'cats', and those in *-e* change this to *-yā́ne*, e.g. *xwā́x̌e* 'mother-in-law', *xwāx̌yā́ne*. Inanimate feminine nouns in *-ā, -o* on the other hand take an unstressed plural ending *-we*, e.g. *mlā́we* 'waists'. Nouns of declension 2 generally follow the adjectival pattern, e.g. *sor* 'rider', direct plural *swārə́*, oblique *swaró*, *pax̌tún* 'Pashtun', plural *pax̌tānə́*, feminine *pax̌taná* 'Pashtun woman', etc. Some such nouns, however, follow declension 1 in the plural, e.g. *žwandún* 'life, livelihood', oblique singular *žwandānə́*, plural *zwandunúna*. This is also the case with declension 3: *γar* 'mountain', plural *γrə* or *γrúna*, *trə* 'paternal uncle', *trə* or *trúna*. A number of nouns which only modify the vowel of their final syllable can also be classed here: *melmá* 'guest', plural *melmə́* (or *melmānə́*), *dux̌mán* 'enemy', *dux̌mən*. A few nouns ending in *-ba* (sometimes alternating with *-bun*) follow declension 3 in the singular and 2 in the plural, e.g. *γobá* (or *γobún*) 'cowherd', oblique singular *γobə́* (*γobānə́*), plural *γobānə́*, *γobanó*. Nouns of declensions 4 and 5 also follow the adjectival pattern, except that animates may also take the appropriate *-ān* ending, e.g. *spay* 'dog', plural *spi* or *spiā́n*, *spəy* 'bitch', *spəy* or *spiā́ne*, *buḍ̂əy* 'old woman', *buḍ̂əygā́ne* or *buḍ̂yā́ne*. Even this catalogue does not exhaust the full variety of plural forms. The class of nouns of relationship is particularly rich in irregularities, as the following list will show: *plār* 'father', plural *plărúna*; *mor* 'mother', *máynde* (*mándi*); *xor* 'sister', *xwáynde* (*xwándi*); *tror* 'aunt', *tráynde* (*trándi*), *troryā́ne*; *yor* 'husband's brother's wife', *yúṅe*; *lur* 'daughter', *lúṅe*; *wror* 'brother', *wrúṅa*; *wrārə* 'brother's son', *wrerúna*; *zoy* (*zuy*) 'son', *zāmə́n*.

Several nouns, particularly those denoting substances, occur only in the plural, whether masculine, e.g. *čars* 'hashish', *γanə́m* 'wheat', *γwaṙí* 'cooking oil', *māγzə́* 'brain', *oṙə́* 'flour', *tambākú* 'tobacco', *wāx̌ə́* 'grass', or feminine, e.g. *čāy* 'tea', *obə́* 'water', *orbə́še* 'barley', *šomlé* 'buttermilk'. To these may be added words with a collective meaning, such as *xalk* 'people', onomatopoeics ending in *-ahā́r* denoting noises, e.g. *šrapahā́r* 'splashing' and all verbal infinitives used as nouns. A last quirk of nominal declension concerns masculine consonant stems, mostly inanimate, when qualified by and directly following a cardinal number higher than 'one', or a similar adjective such as *co* 'several, how many?'. Instead of appearing in the plural, as all other nouns then do, they take a 'numerative' ending *-a* in the direct case. This also affects the higher numbers (*šəl* 'score', *səl* 'hundred', which then takes the form *saw*, *zər* 'thousand') and the enumerative words which frequently appear between number and noun: *co jə́la* 'how many times?', *dre kā́la* 'three years', *calór sáwa saṙí* 'four hundred men', *pinjə́ zə́ra míla* 'five thousand miles', *atə́ kitā́ba* or *atə ṫuka kitābúna* 'eight (volumes) books'. This numerative ending may well be a last relic of the ancient dual.

The direct case of nouns serves both for the grammatical subject and direct object of verbs. Case relationships are all expressed by pre- and postpositions or a combination of both, used with one of the oblique cases: an oblique form alone may have adverbial sense, e.g. *yáwa wráje* 'one day'. The simple prepositions are *da* 'of', which provides the only means of expressing a genitive or possessive relationship, *la* 'from', *pa* 'in, at etc.', *tar* 'to, from': postpositions, appearing independently or in combination with prepositions, are *na* 'from', *ta* 'to', *bā́nde* 'on', *cə́xa* and *jə́ne* 'from', *kx̌e* (generally reduced to *ke*, *ki*) 'in', *lā́nde* 'under', *lará* 'for', *pās* 'above', *pasé* 'after', *póre* (*púri*) 'up to', *sará* 'with'. Combinations of pre- and postpositions vary somewhat from dialect to dialect: common examples are *da... na* 'from', *la... sará* 'with', *pa... kx̌e* 'in', *pa... bā́nde* 'on', *tar... póre* 'up to, till'. Most pre- and all postpositions take the main oblique case. The second oblique case, which as it serves no other function can for convenience be called the 'prepositional' case, is as a rule taken only by the simple prepositions *be* 'without', *la* and *tar* and by *pa* (*...kx̌e*), but this last, remarkably, with feminine nouns only.

With pronouns things are somewhat different. Pashto has, in fact, comparatively few independent pronouns. Besides those for the first and second persons, singular and plural, there are proximate and remote demonstrative pronouns, which double for the third persons, and a few indefinite and interrogative forms. For the rest paraphrase is used, much as in English. e.g. *jan* 'body, self' for 'my-, your-, himself etc.', *yaw... bəl* 'one... other' for 'each other'. The place of a relative pronoun is taken by the conjunctive particle *če* 'that', '(the man) who came' being expressed as 'that he came', and 'whose house...' as 'that his house...' and so on.

Pronouns

	Singular		*Plural*			*'who?,*	*'what?,*
	1	2	1	2		*somebody'*	*something'*
Direct	zə	tə	muǧ[1]	tā́so	(tā́si)	cok	cə
Oblique	mā	tā	muǧ	tā́so	(tā́si)	čā	cə
Possessive	jmā	stā	jmuǧ[1]	stā́so	(stā́si)	da čā	

		'this'		*'that'*
Masculine				
Direct	day		dáγa	háγa
Oblique	də		dáγə	háγə
Feminine				
Direct	dā		dáγa	háγa
Oblique	de		dáγe	háγe
Plural				
Direct	duy		dáγa	háγa
(Personal)			dáγuy	háγuy
Oblique	duy, dío		dáγo	háγo

Note: [1] Hard dialects, mung, zmung.

Of those pronouns which show a difference, the first and second person singular ones are unique in that the direct forms act only as subject, the oblique case forms (distinct only in the singular) being used both for the direct and a prepositional object. The personal pronouns also have distinct possessive forms, combining the old preposition *hača* 'from' in the form *j*-, (*z*-), *s*-, which may also occur with postpositions usually combined with *da*, e.g. *jmā na* 'from me'. There are also two kinds of pronominal particle, one independent and one enclitic. The enclitics are only incompletely distinguished for person and number: 1st singular *me*, 2nd singular *de*, 3rd singular and plural *(y)e*, 1st and 2nd plural *mo*. They fulfil all the oblique functions of the pronouns except that of prepositional object, though even in this case there are traces of the third person form to be seen in combinations of the sort of English 'therefrom, -on, -in', Pashto *tre* < **tar-e*, *pre* < **par-e*, *pakx̌e* < **pa kx̌é-ye*. The independent forms, *rā*, *dar*, *war*, are by origin local adverbs 'hither, thither' and 'yonder' and still act as such when no person is involved. They come to act as pseudo-pronouns, however, distinguishing only person, neither number nor gender. Thus they may be governed by post- but not prepositions, e.g. *dar sara* 'with you', or serve as a prepositional object with certain verbs: *war ba nənawə́zəm* 'I shall enter therein' or 'go in to him', according to context.

The verbal morphology of Pashto, as with all other modern Iranian languages, is based on the opposition between two stems, one present and one past. Present stems are either simple (inherited or borrowed ones) or secondary (made with the formatives *-eǧ-* intransitive or *-aw-* transitive and causative). These latter both generally form denominatives (*num-eǧ-* 'be named') or serve to assimilate loan-words (*bah-eǧ-* 'flow', from Hindi *bahnā*), but in some cases *-eǧ-* also distinguishes a continuous sense from a timeless or habitual one: *dəlta d̂era wāwra óri* 'here much snow falls (lit. rains)' : *oréǧi* 'it is raining'. The past stems are essentially old perfect passive participles in *-ta-*, though more often than in any other Iranian language phonetic developments have disguised the characteristic dental ending. In contrast, for example, to Persian *sūz-ad*, *sūxt* 'it burns, burnt', Pashto has *swaj-i*, *su*. A dental may even arise in the present and disappear from the past, e.g. *təx̌t-* 'flee' < **tṛsa-*, against *təx̌* 'fled' < **tṛšta-*, or the two stems may coincide, as in *ačaw-* 'throw' < **ā-škaba-* and *-škafta-*. As a result a new past marker has emerged, a stressed *-ə́l-*, identical with the infinitive ending *-ə́l* (<**-ati-*), which is added to the past stem whenever the need is felt to arise. Corresponding to the intransitive present formative *-eǧ-*, and generally but not always paired with it, there is a past formative *-ed-*.

On the basis of these two stems simple tenses are formed by the addition of personal endings, stressed or not according to the stem, which distinguish first and second persons singular and plural, but third person only, without difference of number. Thus, from *lwedə́l* 'fall' and *ačawə́l* 'throw' are formed the present and past paradigms shown here.

		Present		*Past*	
Singular	1	lwéǧ-əm	acaw-ə́m	lwéd-əm	ačaw-ə́l-əm
	2	lwéǧ-e	acaw-é	lwéd-e	ačaw-ə́l-e
	3 m.	lwéǧ-i	acaw-í	lwéd(-ə́)	ačāwə́
	3 f.			lwed-ə́la	ačaw-ə́la
Plural	1	lwéǧ-u	acaw-ú	lwéd-u	ačaw-ə́l-u
	2	lwéǧ-əy[1]	acaw-ə́y[1]	lwéd-əy[1]	ačaw-ə́l-əy[1]
	3 m.	lwéǧ-i	acaw-í	lwed-ə́l	ačaw-ə́l
	3 f.			lwed-ə́le	ačaw-ə́le

Note: [1] Qandahari, 2nd plural *-āst*, thus *lwéǧ-āst* etc.

The original composition of the past tense, from a passive participle and the copula, is still clear in the third person, where the copula is lacking and the forms are declined like adjectives, though frequently with an irregular masculine singular form in which a stem vowel *-a-* is lengthened to *-ā-* or changed to *-o-* (*xatə́l* 'rise', *xot* 'rose'). Moreover the old participle of transitive verbs, as past stem, retains its passive meaning throughout: *ačawə́m* 'I throw', but *ačawə́ləm* 'I was being thrown'. This is also true of the modern past participle, a regular adjective of declension 5, e.g. *lwedə́lay* 'fallen', *ačawə́lay* '(having been) thrown', which with the auxiliary verb 'be' forms periphrastic tenses. The modern copula similarly betrays the probable pronominal origin of its third person forms. The simple perfect, for example, is formed as in the chart given here.

	Masculine	Feminine	M./F.
Singular 1	lwedə́lay yəm	lwedə́le yəm	ačawəlay/e yəm
2	lwedə́lay ye	lwedə́le ye	ačawəlay/e ye
3	lwedə́lay day	lwedə́le da	ačawəlay/e day/da
Plural 1	lwedə́li yu	lwedə́le yu	ačawəli/e yu
2	lwedə́li yəy	lwedə́le yəy	ačawəli/e yəy
3	lwedə́li di	lwedə́le di	ačawəli/e di

'I have fallen' etc., but 'I have been thrown', etc. In contrast to the present tenses, 'I throw it' etc., there is thus no means of expressing the active non-present tenses of the transitive verbs by forms in concord with a logical subject or agent in the direct case. Instead of 'I threw it', therefore, an ergative construction is obligatory, which — to avoid the passive 'it was thrown by me' — can only be expressed in English as 'me thrown it'. In Pashto the logical object but grammatical subject, inherent in the verb, may of course be expressed by an independent form, but if it is pronominal it need not be. The agent, however, must appear, in the oblique case. A personal pronoun may then be represented either by an independent form (*mā* etc.), which then generally precedes the grammatical subject, or by an enclitic (*me*, etc.). Various different possible paradigms thus arise (a matter to which we shall return), e.g.:

mā kāñay...	or *kāñay me ačawə́lay day*	'I have thrown a stone',
tā zə...	or *zə de ačawə́lay yəm*	'you have thrown me',
haγə ačawə́lay day	or *ačawə́lay ye day*	'he has thrown it'.

In contrast to this a real passive usually only occurs when the agent is unknown or at least not expressed. Such a passive is formed by the past participle, or in soft dialects the 'old past participle', i.e. the third person past forms, with the auxiliary verb *kedəl/šwəl* 'become': *ačāwə́/ačawə́lay keğəm* 'I am being thrown', *ačawə́la/ačawə́le šwa* 'she was thrown', *ačawə́l/ačawəli šə́wi di* 'they have been thrown'. A full passive, with the agent expressed by a prepositional phrase like 'by means of', as in *kāle če da nāwe la xwā roγ šəwe wi* 'clothes which will have been made by (lit. from the side of) the bride', is a rarity.

Pashto employs two further means, besides the different temporal stems, for distinguishing a series of forms which intricately mark differences of mood and aspect. The one means is to provide each verb with secondary stems, present and past II. This is mostly done by means of a stressed separable prefix *wə́* (eastern *(w)u*), e.g. *wə́lweğ-*, *wə́lwed-*. With an initial *a-* the prefix forms *wā-*, which then makes itself independent of the verb as a pseudo-preverb, e.g. *wā́čaw-*, *wā́čawəl-*. True preverbs, like *kx̌e* and *nə́na* 'in', *póre* 'to, across', *pre* 'off, from', exclude the prefix *wə́*. Instead they attract the stress to themselves, e.g. from *kx̌ewatə́l* 'enter', present stem I *kx̌ewə́z-*, II *kx̌éwəz-*, past II *kx̌éwat-*. Half a dozen of the commonest verbs combine stems of widely different origins, so that the I and II stems are sufficiently distinct to dispense with the help of *wə*. Among these are *kedə́l* 'become', present I *kéğ*-, II *š́*-, past II *šw*-; *kawə́l* 'do, make', present I *kaw-´*, II *k(r̂)-´*, past II *kr̂*-; and the particularly complicated *tləl* 'go', present I *j*-, II *wlār̂ š́*-, past II *wlār̂*-, but *rā-tlə́l* 'come (hither)', present I *rā-j-´*, II *rā́-š́*-, past II *rā́-γl*-, which follows the same pattern with alternative prefixes in *dar-tlə́l* 'come, go to you', *war-tlə́l* 'go to him'. Denominative verbs distinguish their I and II stems in yet another way. Here the composite primary stems are opposed to secondary stems in which the independent inflected nominal form is compounded with the secondary stems of *kedəl* or *kawəl*: thus from *ǰor̂* 'well, ready, agreeable', *ǰor̂edə́l* 'get well, be made, made ready, agree', present I *ǰor̂éğ*-, II *ǰór̂ š́*-, past II *ǰór̂ šw*-. The contrast is even more marked with words of declension 2 or 3, since they form denominatives from the 'weak' feminine stem, e.g. from *pox* 'cooked, ripe', *paxawə́l* 'cook', present I *paxaw-´*, II *póx k(r̂)*-, past II *póx kr̂*-.

The other means is a movable enclitic particle *ba*. Its movements call to be described below, but for the moment we shall consider it in relation to the finite verb alone. It remains only to mention the distinctive endings of the imperative (singular *-a*, plural *-əy*) and of the conditional mood (*-āy*, eastern *-ay*, for all persons) and we have all the ingredients for the first part of the verbal system sketched in table 7.4. The lower part comprises both the periphrastic tenses, formed from the past participle, and the forms expressing the potential mood, which are compounded of the simple conditional form and the auxiliary verb *šwəl* (Qandahari *swəl*) 'be able', the forms of which chance to be identical with the secondary ones of *kedəl* 'become'. Here the prefix *wə* seems to have lost its significance, to become facultative.

Between the present I and II there is a difference of mood, I being indicative, 'falls, is falling', II subjunctive, '(that, if) it fall'. In the corresponding future forms, however, with the addition of the particle *ba*, there is a distinction of aspect, I being durative, 'will be falling', II perfective, 'will fall'. This holds good also in part for the imperative, I 'keep on falling', II 'fall'. But the prohibitive, with the particle *ma* 'not', cuts across this. It is normally only formed from stem I, regardless of aspect: *má lweğa* 'do not fall'. The past II is again perfective, 'fell', in contrast to the past I with durative sense, 'was falling', or occasionally inchoative, 'was about to fall'. The addition of *ba* in this case, although giving a sense of customariness, does not entirely remove the aspectual distinction: III 'used to fall, be falling, continuously' : IV 'used to fall repeatedly'. With the conditional forms I and II no aspectual difference can be seen: both can express present or future conditions, '(if) it were falling' or 'were to fall', the possible consequences '(then) it would fall' being expressed either by the past III or IV, or the conditional III (IV being unusual). The periphrastic tenses are by nature all perfective. With the perfect forms the sense follows that of the

Table 7.4: The Verbal System

Present I lwéği	Present II wə́lweği	Future I lwéği ba	Future II wə́-ba-lweği
Imperative I lwéğa	Imperative II wə́lweğa		
Past I lwedə́	Past II wə́lwed	Past III lwedə́ ba	Past IV wə́-ba-lwed
Conditional I lwedắy	Conditional II wə́lwedăy	Conditional III lwedắy ba	
Perfect I lwedə́lay day	Perfect II lwedə́lay wi		Future Perfect lwedə́lay ba wi
Past Perfect I lwedə́lay wə		Past Perfect III lwedə́lay ba wə	
Perfect Conditional I lwedə́lay wăy		Perfect Conditional III lwedə́lay ba wăy	
Potential Present (wə́)lwedắy ši		Future (wə́)lwedắy ba ši	
Past (wə́)lwedắy šu		Past III (wə́)lwedắy ba šu	
Conditional (wə́)lwedắy šwăy			

auxiliary verb, i.e. between perfect I and II there is a difference of indicative, 'has fallen', and subjunctive, '(if) it (should) have fallen', in the third person only, as the other persons of the copula have common forms for both I and II. The future perfect only occurs in the II form, there being no durative future form of the copula. It has both senses of the corresponding English tense, 'it will (i.e. must) have fallen (by now, or some past time'), or 'it will have fallen (by some future time)'. The perfect conditional I expresses no longer possible conditions, '(if) it had fallen', and the past perfect III or the perfect conditional III the consequence, '(then) it would have fallen'.

6 Syntax

The first important syntactic feature to be considered is word order, which, starting from the noun phrase, is fairly inflexible in Pashto. All qualifiers precede the head of a noun phrase. The English freedom to say 'that man's hand' or 'the hand of that man' is denied a Pashto-speaker, who has only *da hayə saȓi lās* 'of that man hand'. Missing is an article in Pashto, though this lack may occasionally be made up by the use of a demonstrative or the word *yaw* 'one'. Combining *yaw zoȓ kə́lay* 'an old village' and *tange kucé* 'narrow streets' yields *da yawə zāȓə kə́li tange kucé* 'an old village's narrow streets'. Only the personal possessive forms can precede the *da* group: *stā́so da kə́lo kucé* 'your villages' streets'. The apparent parallelism breaks down, however, when the noun phrase is governed by a pre- or postposition. The postposition appears at the end of the entire phrase, but a lone or accompanying preposition must be placed immediately before the head and its attributes. Thus 'from the very narrow streets of your old villages' can only be *stā́so da zaȓo kə́lo la d̂ero tango kucó na* 'your of-old-villages from very-narrow-streets-from'.

Since both subject and direct object of a non-past transitive verb appear in the direct case, only a fixed word order can disambiguate them. Pashto has therefore become an inflexible subject–object–verb language: *saȓáy x̌ə́ja wíni* 'man woman sees' can only mean 'the (a) man sees the (a) woman'. The positioning of adverbial phrases is freer. The order of the following sentence seems to be the most natural one: *(A:hara wraj) (B:pa kum waxt če kəli ta ji) yaw saȓay (C: pa d̂er tāǰub) yawa barband̂a x̌əja (D: pa lāra kx̌e) wini* '(every day) (at what time he goes to the village) a certain man (to his great surprise) sees a naked woman (on the road)'. But an alternative arrangement *(A) (C) yaw saȓay (B) (D) yawa barband̂a x̌əja wini* is just as thinkable as the English '(A), (C), a certain man, (B), sees (D) a naked woman'. Given the inflexibility of the SOV order in the non-past, it is not surprising that the ergative construction of the past parallels it. With independent forms the necessary word order is agent–patient–verb or, translated into terms of grammatical concord, agent (oblique)–subject (direct)–verb (concord): *mā saȓáy wə́lid* 'I saw the man', *saȓí x̌ə́ja wə́lidəla* 'the man saw the woman', *zaȓo kə́lo ba tange kucé larə́le* 'old villages used to have narrow streets'. This simple rule is disturbed, however, by the fact already noted that a pronominal agent may be expressed by an enclitic form, and enclitics are a law unto themselves in Pashto.

Besides those already met, pronominal *me*, *de*, *(y)e*, *mo* and verbal *ba*, Pashto has a few more enclitics. *de (di)* may lose its original pronominal force and, as an ethic dative, simply give the present II (subjunctive) form a jussive sense: *kitābúna de rā́wȓi* 'let him bring the books'. Then there are the conjunction *xo* 'but' and the adverb *no* 'so, then, still, yet', which can be used enclitically. Two or three of these may occur together, when they have the following fixed pecking order:

xo / ba / me, de, ye, mo / no

pré-xo-ba-ye-nə́-ğdəm 'but I shall not leave it', *dā́-xo-ba-me nə́ kāwə* 'but this I used not to do'. As a group they always seek the earliest possible support in a clause, namely the first syntagm, be it word, phrase or more, bearing at least one main stress. In short, when the agent is expressed by an enclitic pronoun its position is not relative to the grammatical subject at all, but is governed by the word order of the clause as a whole: *šikāyát-ye wə́kəf̂* 'complaint him made', i.e. 'he complained', *(da xéṭe la xwə́ǧ cəxa)-ye šikāyát wə́kəf̂* '(of stomach from pain-from) him complaint made', i.e. 'he complained of stomach ache', *hálta-ye (da... cəxa) šikāyát wə́kəf̂* 'there he complained (of stomach-ache)'. Conversely as the content of a sentence is reduced an enclitic agent is forced back until it may be supported by parts of the verb, including a preverb, alone: *paroskā́l-ba-mo xar rā́wost/xár-ba-mo rā́wost/rā́-ba-mo-wost* '(last year) we used to bring (the donkey) it'. All this is equally true of the enclitic pronouns in their other functions, as direct object or possessive: *nə́-ye wažni* 'he does not kill it', *magar wažnə́y-ba-ye nə́* 'but kill them you shall not'; *(stā da xeṭe ilā́j kawa* or) *da xeṭe ilā́j-de kawa* 'have your stomach treated', *xayrāt pradáy wə, no xéṭa-xo-de xpə́la wa* 'the free food was provided by somebody else, but the stomach was your own'. Even poetic licence and transpositions *metri causa* cannot affect the rule. Instead of prosaic **mine-ba-me laryun da tan kor səway wə, ka-me žaf̂ā pa himāyat nə rātlay* 'love would long since have burnt the house of my body, if weeping had not come to my support (in dousing it)', the poet ʿAbdul Hamid Mohmand has:

> da tan kór-ba-me laryún wə mine sə́way
> ka-me nə́ rātlay žaf̂ā́ pa himāyát.

The only constituent that can hold an enclitic back from its natural support is a relative clause immediately following it. A clause is clearly felt to be too diffuse to support enclitics, which are forced to attach themselves to the next best, i.e. following, syntagm: *haya nǰələ́y-me māxā́m sinemā́ ta byāyi* 'that girl is taking me to the cinema this evening', *haya nǰələ́y, če os-mo wə́lidəla, māxā́m-me sinemā́ ta byāyi* 'that girl we just saw is taking me to the cinema this evening'. Sometimes, however, an enclitic may burst the bounds of its own subordinate clause to move to the front of the main clause, e.g. instead of *har sabā če γrə-ta-ba tə*, 'every morning, when he would go to the mountain', we find *har sabā-ba če γrə-ta tə*; instead of *pa har jāy-kxe če mumí-ye*, 'in whatever place he finds it' — *pa har jāy-kxe-ye če mumi*.

Of agreement in Pashto there is little to be said except that, where the forms permit it, it is all-pervading. Adjectives, whether attributive or predicative, agree in number, gender and case with their head nouns or subjects respectively: *zmā grā́na aw mehrabā́na plā́ra* 'my dear and kind father!' (masculine singular vocative), *kláka zmə́ka* 'firm earth', *zmə́ka kláka da* 'the earth is hard' (feminine singular direct), *če stā mlā sáma ši yā da nóro xálko mlāgā́ne kubə́y ši* (they asked a hunchback whether he wanted) 'that your back should become straight (feminine singular direct) or other people's (masculine plural oblique) backs should become hunched (feminine plural direct)'. This agreement extends to adjectives used adverbially, e.g. *d̂er* 'much, many' but also 'very', *hawā́ d̂éra tawdá wi* 'the climate is (always) very hot' (feminine singular direct), *kiх̌tə́y-e kláka wə́niwəla* 'he siezed hold of the boat firmly' (feminine singular direct). While the agreement of subject and verb is normally restricted to person and number (note *Tor zə aw tə botlu* 'Tor took (1st plural) me and you'), with the third person singular copula gender also comes into play: *ā́s day* 'it is a horse', *áspa da* 'it is a mare'. In the ergative construction, with all third person forms both gender and number are marked throughout: *х̌ə́je ās wə́wāhə* 'the woman struck the horse', *áspa-ye wə́wahəla* 'he/she/they struck the mare', *āsúna-ye wə́wahəl* '...struck the horses', *áspe-ye wə́wahəle* '...struck the mares'. In the perfective forms of denominative verbs, in which the nominal element is free, agreement is naturally to be expected: *zə bāyad γwáх̌e paх̌é kəm* 'I must cook some meat (feminine plural direct of *pox*)'. More unexpectedly, even nouns forming denominatives become adjectivised in this context: thus from the Persian loanword *yād* 'memory', forming *yādedə́l* 'be remembered', we find *haγa х̌ə́ja-me yā́da šwa* 'I remembered that woman'.

If we compare the archaic structure of Pashto with the much simplified morphology of Persian, the leading modern Iranian language, we see that it stands to its 'second cousin' and neighbour in something like the same relationship as Icelandic does to English.

Bibliography

The best modern study in English is Penzl (1955), despite minor errors; it is based on the work of Afghan grammarians. Trumpp (1873) remains, despite its age, the best grammar based on classical Pashto literature. For syntax, Lorimer (1915) is an amateur study, but a mine of information. Morgenstierne (1942) is a unique historical study, by the leading specialist.

References

Grjunberg, A.L. 1987. *Očerk grammatiki afganskogo jazyka (Pašto)* (Nauka, Leningrad)

Lorimer, D.L.R. 1915. *(A) Syntax of Colloquial Pashtu* (Oxford University Press, Oxford)

Morgenstierne, G. 1942. 'Archaisms and Innovations in Pashto Morphology', *Norsk Tidskrift for Sprogvidenskap*, vol. XII, p. 87–114

Penzl, H. 1955. *A Grammar of Pashto* (American Council of Learned Societies, Washington, DC)

Trumpp, Ernest. 1873. *Grammar of the Paṣ̌tō or Language of the Afghans* (Trübner, London)

8 AFROASIATIC LANGUAGES

Robert Hetzron

1 Introduction

The approximately 250 Afroasiatic languages, spoken by about 175 million ethnically and racially different people, occupy today the major part of the Middle East, all of North Africa, much of North-East Africa and a considerable area in what may roughly be defined as the northwestern corner of Central Africa. Though the distribution and spread of the specific languages was substantially different, about the same area was covered by Afroasiatic languages in antiquity. In the Middle Ages, the southern half of Spain and Sicily were also conquered by those who were to become the largest Afroasiatic-speaking people, the Arabs. Today, only Maltese represents this family as a native language in Europe.

The term 'Semitic' was proposed in 1781 for a group of related tongues, taken from the Bible (Genesis 10–11) where Noah's son Shem is said to be the ancestor of the speakers of these languages — showing, incidentally, awareness of linguistic relationships at this time. When it was realised that some other languages were further related to this group, the term 'Hamitic', based on the name of Shem's younger brother Ham (Cham), the biblical ancestor of Egypt and Kush, was coined for the entire family. Later the composite term Hamito-Semitic (sometimes Semito-Hamitic) was introduced. However, this created the wrong impression that there exists a 'Hamitic' branch opposed to Semitic. Of all the other terms proposed (Erythraic, Lisramic, Lamekhite), 'Afroasiatic' has been gaining ground. Even this name has the inconvenience of being misinterpreted as a group including all the languages of Africa and Asia. To dispel this, a further contraction, Afrasian, has also been used.

2 Division

Afroasiatic is composed of several branches. Various proposals have been made concerning the internal relationship between the branches, but none of these subdivisions are convincing enough to be adopted. The main branches are the following.

(a) **Egyptian** is the extinct language of one of the major civilisations of antiquity, that of Pharaonic Egypt (in today's Egypt, Arabic is spoken). This language can boast the longest continuous history. Its earliest documentations are from 3000 BC. From AD 300 on, the term 'Coptic' is used for the Egyptian idiom of monophysite Christians. It was spoken till the sixteenth century, perhaps even later; it is still used as a liturgical language.

(b) **Semitic** (see separate chapter).

(c) **Cushitic** consists of about 40 languages, spoken by 15 million people in Ethiopia, Somalia, northwestern Kenya and adjacent areas. Beja (of eastern Sudan and northern Ethiopia), with about 200,000 Muslim speakers, has been classified as North Cushitic, but there is some likelihood that it constitutes a separate branch of Afroasiatic. Central Cushitic or Agaw used to be the major language of Ethiopia before the Semitic conquest. It has split into a number of languages and is still spoken, by few, in scattered enclaves. Rift Valley (or Highland East) Cushitic is spoken by nearly two million people around the Ethiopian Great Rift Valley. Its best known representative is Sidamo. Lowland (East) Cushitic is numerically the most important group. Among others, it comprises Afar-Saho (Dankali) along the Red Sea, Oromo (formerly Galla), spoken by 8–10 million people, Somali, the official language of the Republic of Somalia and the vehicle of about 4 million Muslims, the Dullay languages etc. The status of South Cushitic is debated; many consider it a separate main branch, but it may also be a southern offshoot of Lowland Cushitic.

The oldest Cushitic texts are from the eighteenth century. Note that the term 'Cush' was originally applied to an unrelated country and civilisation: Meroë.

(d) **Omotic** is the name of a group of about 40 languages in the Omo Valley of southern Ethiopia, with about 1,300,000 speakers. It used to be classified as West Cushitic. Yet the great divergences led scholars to list it as a separate branch. On the other hand, since the divergences mainly consist of absence of some typical Cushitic features, Omotic may also be a simplified, pidginised offshoot of some branch of Cushitic.

(e) **Berber** is a cluster of closely related yet not always mutually intelligible dialects. Once the major language of all of North Africa west of Egypt, it still has some 10 million speakers, with the heaviest concentration in Morocco. The earliest documentation is provided by the Lybian inscriptions (the only one dated is from 139 BC). The major dialects are Tuareg, Tamazight, Tshalhit, Tirifie, Kabyle, Chawiya and Zenaga. An old consonantal alphabet, the *tifinagh*, has survived among the Tuareg. The extinct language of the Canary Islands, Guanche, may have also been a Berber tongue.

(f) **Chadic** (see separate chapter).

3 Problems of Relationship

The assertion that certain languages are related means that it is assumed that they are descended from a single common ancestor. Naturally, this is not necessarily true of the speakers themselves. It often happens that the same sedentary population switches language, adopting, with a certain degree of modification, the type of speech that has been imported by a relatively small, yet dominant group of newcomers. Thus, it could be just the language that wanders, whereas the people remain stationary and only change linguistic allegiance. This explains why so many anthropological types are found in this family: the brown-skinned Mediterranean Semites, the white-skinned Berber, the black-skinned, yet in many ways still different, Cushites and Chadic speakers.

Since Semitic, a linguistically fairly homogeneous group, seems to have had its major branches already established at least 5,000 years ago, and further, taking into consideration the great internal heterogeneity of Cushitic and Chadic, the period when the putative ancestral common Afroasiatic language was spoken must be placed at a much earlier period than the usually assumed sixth millennium BC. The location of this hypothetical tongue has been assumed to have been in North Africa, perhaps in the area which is now the Sahara desert, and the various branches must have diffused from there.

Theories have been advanced about further relationships of Afroasiatic with other languages, especially with Indo-European within a wide superfamily, Nostratic, also including Uralic, Altaic, Kartvelian, Dravidian etc. In view of the enormous time-depth that has to be accounted for, it is extremely hard to form any critical opinion of the reconstructions proposed to support this or other such proposals.

4 On Afroasiatic Comparison

In view of the great diversity among the branches of Afroasiatic, one should not expect many features in common that are to be found everywhere. Some such features do exist, such as gender distinction with *t* as a mark of the feminine, an element *k* as a mark of the second person, some vocabulary items such as the root **mut* 'die'. Otherwise, we have to content ourselves with features that are found in several, but not all, branches, yielding an intertwined system that ultimately makes the unity of the family quite obvious. Thus, the root **šim* 'name' is found everywhere but in Egyptian, the prefix conjugation is attested in Semitic, Cushitic and Berber, the stative suffix conjugation in Semitic, Egyptian, Berber and possibly Cushitic, etc. Naturally, for comparative purposes, it is sufficient for an item to be attested in at least one language of a branch to be used as an isogloss, e.g. the suffix conjugation only in Kabyle within Berber, the root **mut* clearly only in Rendille within Cushitic.

Because of the fact that Semitic exhibits such a great deal of regularity and also because of its being the best known branch, some of the reconstructions have been strongly inspired by phenomena of Semitic. The opposite attitude, rejecting Semitic phenomena in reconstruction in order to avoid bias, has also been seen. Other disturbing factors are: lack of knowledge of Egyptian vowels (only Coptic provides clues about them), quite recent attestation and no ancient documents of most Cushitic, Omotic and Chadic languages, contrasting with millennia-old Semitic and Egyptian data. Nevertheless, one should not dogmatically believe that older data necessarily reflect a more archaic situation. Some phenomena found in recently discovered languages may be direct survivals from the oldest times.

5 Some Afroasiatic Features

The following is a brief listing of linguistic features that may be original Afroasiatic.

5.1 Phonetics

All branches except Egyptian exhibit a special set of consonants, besides voiced and voiceless pairs, the 'emphatic' series, realised as pharyngealised (velarised) in Arabic and Berber, glottalised (ejective, explosive) in South Arabian, Ethiopian and Cushitic and glottalised (explosive or implosive) in Chadic; Egyptian, incidentally, also lacked voiced consonants (*d* stands for /t/, *t* for /tʰ/, in the standard transliteration). There is evidence for several lateral consonants in Proto-Semitic; they are still used in modern South Arabian, South Cushitic and some Chadic languages (e.g. *balsam* ultimately comes from the Semitic root *bśm* where *ś* must have been a lateral fricative). Laryngeal sounds ʿ, *ḥ* and *x* are found in Egyptian, Cushitic, Berber and Semitic. A prenasalised phoneme $*^{m}b$ has also been reconstructed.

The original vowel system is assumed to be long and short *a*, *i*, *u*, as still in Classical Semitic. Cushitic, Omotic and Chadic have tonal systems, e.g. Awngi (Cushitic, Agaw) *aqá* '(turn) into a man', *aqâ* 'I have been' and *áqâ* 'I have known'; *a* represents mid tone, *á* high tone, *à* low tone and *â* falling tone.

5.2 Morphology

In the pronominal system, **an* for 'I' in Semitic and Cushitic vs. **ana:ku* 'I' with a further velar in Egyptian and marginally in Semitic (perhaps also in the Berber suffix -*γ*), or *ka* for masculine 'thee, thy' in Semitic and Chadic vs. *ku* in Cushitic and marginally in Semitic (unclear for Egyptian) with different vowels, may represent original dialectal variations in Afroasiatic. The opposition *u*/*i* for masculine/feminine, especially in third person singular pronouns, seems to be original as well: Akkadian (Semitic) *šu:*/*ši:*, Somali (Cushitic) *-uu*/*-ay* 'he/she', Omotic: *-o*/*-e* gender markers in Kafa, parts of the third person singular masculine/feminine verb endings in Dizi, noun gender markers in Mubi (Chadic) (e.g. *mùndúrò/mìndíré* 'boy/girl') and perhaps Egyptian *-f/-s* 'his/her' (from *h^w/h^y?).

In the demonstrative system the following gender-and-number markers are found: m. sg./f. sg./pl. *n/t/n* (Semitic, Chadic, traces in Berber), *ku/ti/hu* (Cushitic, also Chadic: Mubi *g-/d-/h-*), *p/t/n* (Egyptian) and for m./f. *w/θ* (in Berber). It is possible that both *p* and *w* come from **ku*.

Two verbal conjugation systems are found in more than one branch. One, found in Semitic, Cushitic and Berber, operates with the prefixes: *ʔ-* or *a-* for first person singular, *n-* for first person plural, *t-* for second person and for third person singular feminine and *y-* for the other third persons. Further suffixes added to the second and third person plurals and, in Semitic and Beja, to the second person singular feminine make up the full conjugations. Note the homonymy of second person singular masculine and third person singular feminine. The Cushitic languages have all switched to suffix conjugations by means of prefix-conjugated postposed auxiliaries, though a few of them have maintained the original conjugation for a limited number of verbs. This suffix conjugation is not to be confused with the original Afroasiatic suffix conjugation which can be reconstructed for predicates expressing a state, rather than an action, and is attested in Semitic (with the original value in Akkadian), Egyptian, Kabyle (Berber, for predicative adjectives) and probably in Cushitic.

In spite of its absence from Egyptian, Omotic and Chadic, it is likely that the prefix conjugation harks back to Proto-Afroasiatic.

Internal inflection, i.e. internal vocalic changes within a consonantal root to express tense, mood and other categories (the *root-and-pattern* system) is an operative principle in Semitic (Akkadian *i-prus* 'he divided', *i-parras* 'he divides', root *p-r-s*), less systematically in Berber (*-θ-lal* 'she (will) be born', *θ-lula* 'she was born'), in traces in Cushitic (Beja *ʔadanbíil* 'I collect', *ʔadbìl* 'I collected', root *d-b-l*). In Chadic, where the person of the subject is expressed by means of preposed particles which are very similar in shape to the oblique pronouns of other branches and where other categories like tense, mood etc. are either expressed by elements attached to these particles or, in part at least, by the stem form of the verb, alternations like Mubi *ní-túwà* 'I (will) eat'/*nə́-tì̀* 'I ate' have been considered traces of the Afroasiatic internal inflection by some scholars, while others have attributed them to independent developments. It is likely that an internal *a* is to be posited to mark the non-past in Afroasiatic. Internal *a/u* for non-past/past is attested in Semitic, Berber and Cushitic.

The verbal derivation system plays an important part in Afroasiatic vocabulary. Verbal roots are subject to modification; new verbs are created by the addition of derivative affixes. The element *s* produces a causative, the addition of *t* or *n* makes the verb intransitive (passive or reflexive). Repetition of the root or part of it or mere consonantal gemination expresses repeated action. Berber: *ayəm* 'to get water', *ss-iyəm* 'cause to get water', *ttuy-uyəm* '(water) be drawn'; Beja *tam* 'eat', *tamtam* 'gobble'.

Classical Semitic and Egyptian used to have a dual in their nominal system, e.g. Egyptian *sn* 'brother', *sn.wy* 'two brothers', *sn.w* 'brothers'. For plural marking, several devices are found. The endings *-u:/-w* and *-n* seem to be attested all over. Repetition of the last consonant is found in Cushitic (Somali *miis/miisas* 'table/tables') and Chadic (Mubi *lísí/lésas* 'tongue'). In Cushitic and Chadic, one finds singulative systems where the basic form is a collective and the addition of a suffix makes it singular, e.g. Mubi (Chadic) *mándàr* 'boy(s) (in general)'/*mùndúrò* 'boy'. Yet the most interesting plural formation is what has been called the broken plural, based on internal inflection, *sinn-/asna:n-* in Arabic (Semitic), *sini/san* in Logone (Chadic) for 'tooth/teeth', Xamta (Agaw, Cushitic) *gezéŋ/agzéŋ* 'dog/dogs', Berber *ikərri/akrarən* (with a further *-n*) 'ram/rams'. Though the basic principle seems to be the infixation of an *a*, the broken plural forms cannot be predicted automatically from the singular. This is also an argument in favour of their archaic character. Thus, some form of internal inflection *must* have existed indeed in Afroasiatic. The Afroasiatic noun also distinguished between the genders masculine and feminine. The latter is used not only for female animates, but often also for derivatives such as diminutives, e.g. Berber *axam* 'tent' – *θaxamθ* 'small tent'. Furthermore, Semitic and Cushitic have traces of polarity whereby a noun changing number may also change its gender, e.g. Sidamo (Cushitic) *ko beetti* 'this boy'/*te ooso* 'these boys' vs. *te seemo* 'this girl'/*ko seenne* 'these girls' (m. *ko*, f. *te*).

In nominal derivation, the prefix *ma-* plays an important role to form agent, locative or instrumental nouns.

5.3 Word Order

Classical Semitic, Egyptian and Berber are VSO languages, Cushitic is almost all SOV, while Chadic is mainly SVO. The reconstruction of Proto-Afroasiatic word order is open to speculation.

Bibliography

Diakonoff (1965) is a short yet highly informative comparative presentation, the best so far in the field. Hodge (1971) is a collection of chapters from the *Current Trends in Linguistics* series, somewhat uneven, partly inevitably obsolete, but still an important research tool. Cohen (1947) is a pioneering work in comparative Afroasiatic, but restricted to vocabulary and with only few references to Chadic. Bender (1976) provides concise yet comprehensive sketches of the structure of the major Cushitic languages, with state-of-the-art introductions, and is a ground-breaking publication. Valuable discussions of Afroasiatic are also included in two more general Africanist publications: Greenberg (1963) and Heine et al. (1981).

References

Bender, M.L. (ed.) 1976. *The Non-Semitic Languages of Ethiopia* (Michigan State University, East Lansing)
Cohen, M. 1947. *Essai comparatif sur le vocabulaire et la phonétique du chamito-sémitique* (Champion, Paris)
Diakonoff, I.M. 1965. *Semito-Hamitic Languages* (Nauka, Moscow)
Greenberg, J.H. 1963. *The Languages of Africa* (Indiana University, Bloomington and Mouton, The Hague)
Heine, B. et al. (eds.) 1981. *Die Sprachen Afrikas* (H. Buske, Hamburg)
Hodge, C.T. (ed.) 1971. *Afroasiatic: A Survey* (Mouton, The Hague)

9 Semitic Languages

Robert Hetzron

1 Introduction

Originally limited to the area east of the Mediterranean Sea, the Semitic languages and civilisations spread into North Africa, southern Europe and the Horn of Africa. In antiquity, the Assyrian and Babylonian Empires were major centres of civilisation. Phoenician traders were roaming and establishing colonies all over the Mediterranean basin. Hebrew culture, through its monotheistic religion, Judaism, has exerted an exceptional influence, directly or indirectly (through the two great religions inspired by it: Christianity and Islam), on all of mankind. Arabic, in addition to being the carrier of an important medieval civilisation, has become one of the major languages of the world today.

While the ancestor of Semitic, Proto-Afroasiatic, is assumed to have originated in Africa, the homeland of Semitic itself, i.e. the area where, having arrived from Africa, the different branches started to split off, may have been approximately the region where the Arabian peninsula reaches the continental bulk of the Near East.

2 Division

The following is a listing of the Semitic languages according to the latest classification, with summary information on the speakers.

(A) East Semitic: Akkadian was the language of ancient Mesopotamia (approximately today's Iraq), the carrier of a grandiose civilisation from c. 3000 BC to the beginnings of the Christian era. Akkadian gradually replaced the unrelated Sumerian which had greatly influenced it. It was soon divided into Assyrian (northern) and Babylonian (southern) branches, corresponding to a political division. The last written documents date from the first century AD. Afterwards, Akkadian was completely forgotten and had to be rediscovered, with its writing system deciphered, in the nineteenth century. The Akkadian script, usually written from left to right, is called cuneiform, i.e. 'wedge-shaped', because of the graphic components of the symbols.

(B) West Semitic, the other major branch of Semitic, is divided into two sub-branches.

(a) South Semitic is composed of three groups, the exact relationship of which has not yet been determined.

(i) Epigraphic South Arabian (attested from the ninth century BC to the sixth century AD) is known only from short inscriptions written in a consonantal script. Its dialects were Sabaean (of Sheba), Minean, Awsani, Qatabani and Hadramauti. Once spoken in the southern half of the Arabian peninsula, they were completely replaced by Arabic.

(ii) Modern South Arabian, a group of non-Arabic languages (that are apparently not the descendants of Epigraphic South Arabian), is still spoken by some 25,000 people in the Dhofar (Oman): Shahri, Mahri and Harsusi, and on the island of Socotra off the Arabian coast: Soqotri. Serious investigation of them has started only recently.

(iii) Ethiopian. Speakers of South Arabian crossed the Red Sea millennia ago — much earlier than the usually given date of the fourth century BC — into the highlands of Ethiopia and mixed with the local Cushitic population, who gradually adopted their language and modified it to a significant extent. The Ethiopian Semitic (Ethio-Semitic) languages are to be divided into two main branches.

(α) North Ethiopic comprises the following: the now extinct Ge'ez, attested between the fourth and ninth centuries AD, was the language of the Axumite Empire. It is still used as the liturgical language of the Ethiopian Coptic Church, occasionally also for literature. Almost all of the Ge'ez material comes from a period when it was no more in everyday use, which makes the data less reliable. Tigrinya has nearly four million speakers in Eritrea and in the Tigre Governorate-General. Tigré is spoken by about 350,000 Muslims.

(β) South Ethiopic has two branches: (I) Transversal South Ethiopic which comprises Amharic, the official language of modern Ethiopia, the native language of about eight million Coptic Christians and the secondary language of about as many more; the almost extinct Argobba; Harari (Adare), the language of the Muslim city of Harar, and East Gurage (Zway, the Selti-Wolane-Ulbarag cluster), a practically undescribed unit. (II) Within Outer South Ethiopic, the very recently extinct Gafat, Soddo (the language of about 100,000 Christians) and Goggot constitute the *n*-group; Muher and Western Gurage (Masqan, the 'Central' Ezha-Gumer-Chaha-

Gura cluster and the 'Peripheral' Gyeto-Ennemor-Endegeñ-Ener cluster) make up the *tt*-group. As can be deduced, Gurage is not a valid linguistic term, it designates a number of Semitic languages belonging to different branches, spoken in one specific area.

(b) Central Semitic has fared relatively the best in this family.

(i) Aramaic is the label for a group of related dialects, originally spoken in what is Syria today. It is attested since the beginning of the first millennium BC. It later spread to all of the Near East, replacing Akkadian, Hebrew and other languages, only to be replaced, in turn, by Arabic after the rise of Islam in the seventh century AD. Major parts of the biblical books of Ezra and Daniel are in Aramaic. Jesus' native tongue was Palestinian Aramaic. Nabatean was spoken by ethnic Arabs around the beginning of the Christian era. The Babylonian Talmud was written in Eastern Aramaic, a language close to Syriac, the language of the Christian city of Edessa (till the thirteenth century AD), still the liturgical language of the Nestorian and Jacobite Christian Churches. Classical and Modern Mandaic are associated with a Gnostic sect. Today, a variety of Western Aramaic is spoken in three villages near Damascus, Syria. Dialects of Eastern Neo-Aramaic (Modern Syriac) are still vigorous in Christian communities in north-western Iran and adjacent areas in Iraq, in Soviet Georgia and in scattered communities around the world. The speakers (at least 300,000) are sometimes inappropriately called Chaldean, (Neo-)Assyrian. Eastern Neo-Aramaic is further maintained by Jews coming from the same region in Israel and elsewhere. The consonantal Aramaic square script is used for Hebrew today (see the chapter on Hebrew).

(ii) South-Central Semitic

(α) Arabic (see separate chapter; the traditional assignment of Arabic to South Semitic is, incidentally, untenable).

(β) Canaanite. Ancient Canaanite inscriptions of Byblos are from the sixteenth and fifteenth centuries BC. Moabite (ninth century BC) is known from one inscription only. Three ancient, long-extinct languages may also be Canaanite, though further study is needed: Ugaritic, the language of the city-state of Ugarit (now Ras Shamra, Syria, on the Mediterranean) around the fourteenth/thirteenth centuries BC, with an impressive literature written in a cuneiform consonantal script; the poorly attested Amorite (the first half of the second millennium BC) and the recently discovered language of Ebla (the third millennium BC).

Phoenician was originally spoken on the coastal areas of today's Lebanon and is attested through inscriptions (from the twelfth century BC to AD 196). Phoenician merchants, however, established settlements all over the Mediterranean area: Cyprus, Greece, Malta, Sicily, Sardinia, southern France, southern Spain and, above all, North Africa. In the latter area, the city of *Qart Ḥadašt* 'New City', known in Europe as Carthage, founded in 814 BC, developed into a large empire after the fifth century BC. It was destroyed, under the rule of Hannibal, in 146 BC by the Romans. Their variety of late Phoenician is called Punic, attested till the fifth century AD.

The Phoenician consonantal script of 22 letters, written from right to left, practically identical with the old Hebrew script, is probably of Egyptian origin. It is the direct ancestor of the Greek and Latin alphabets. The Arabic, South Semitic (including Ethiopian) and Syriac scripts also come from the Canaanite writing system. Furthermore, the writing systems of Central Asia (e.g. Mongolian writing) and India (the Devanāgarī script) are also descended from the Syriac one.

For the historically most important Canaanite language, Hebrew, see the separate chapter.

3 The Structure of Semitic

3.1 Phonology

The original vowel system consisted of long and short *a*, *i* and *u*. Consonants occurred simple or doubled (geminated). A typical feature of the consonantal system is the existence of 'triads', groups of three consonants with the same point of articulation: voiced (e.g. *d*), voiceless (*t*) and 'emphatic' (*ṭ*). The latter are pronounced pharyngealised ('dark') in Arabic, as glottalised ejectives (where the glottal closure is maintained till high pressure is achieved, then the closure is released with an explosion) in Ethiopian and Modern South Arabian (though the two do not sound the same) and dropped in Modern Hebrew (where they are pronounced voiceless, except *ṣ* > *ts*). The nature of the articulation is unknown in the extinct languages. The original set of laryngeals, *ʔ*, *ʿ* (a voiced pharyngeal constriction), *ḥ* (voiceless pharyngeal constriction) and *x* (voiceless uvular constriction) has been maintained in full in Arabic only. Ethiopian script still marks them, but of all the living languages, only Tigrinya and Tigré kept all but *x* (but a *x* was secondarily developed). Akkadian had lost all of them (lost *ḥ* and *ʿ* left their trace in changing a neighbouring *a* into *e*).

In the causative prefix, in the third person independent pronouns, in the archaic dative endings and in some other cases, one finds an inter-lingual alternation *š* (e.g. Akkadian) ~ *h* (Hebrew), etc. This may go back to an old phoneme **ś* which merged with other phonemes in different ways, possibly an original voiceless lateral or palatal fricative. There is strong evidence for Arabic *ḍ* and Hebrew *ś* once having been lateral; Modern South Arabian still has the laterals *ś* and *ź*.

In Arabic and South Semitic, old *p* became *f*, and in most of Arabic, *g* became *ǰ*. In Aramaic, Hebrew and several Ethiopian languages, a morphophonemic process of spirantisation took place, leading to alternations in different forms of the same root. Post-vocalic non-geminate stops of Hebrew (see page 200): *p, t, k, b, d, g* became *f, θ, x, β, ð, γ* respectively. In modern North Ethiopic, only *k* and *q* were spirantised (the latter yielding a curious spirant ejective sound). In Outer South Ethiopic *tt*-languages, complicated spirantisation processes, also depending on position in the root, took place, *k*~*h* being the most basic. In some of these, all geminate consonants became voiceless and simple. Thus, there is Ezha *bäkkʸä-*, Chaha *bäkʸä-* 'he cried', but *yəβähʸ* 'he cries' for both (note the spirantisation *b*~*β* as well, root *b-k-y*). For 'he broke/breaks', Ezha has *säbbärä-/yəsäbər,* Chaha *säpärä-/yəsäβər* (root *s-b-r*).

3.2 Morphology

In the noun, there was a distinction between masculine and feminine genders (the latter marked by -*(a)t*), e.g. Ge'ez *nəgus* 'king'/*nəgəst* 'queen'; for number: a singular, a dual (for two units; alive in Arabic, Epigraphic and Modern South Arabian, only in traces in Akkadian and Hebrew, lost in Ethiopian; marked by *-a:/-ay*) and a plural. For plural marking, the suffixal (sound) plural had, as its markers: lengthening of the last vowel most often followed by *-n(a)* in the masculine and *-t* (i.e. *-a:t*) in the feminine, but most frequently internal vocalic changes formed it (the so-called 'broken plural'). Examples (sg./pl.): Akkadian *šarr-/šarr*+long vowel or *šarra:n-* 'king', Ge'ez *nəgəst/nəgəstat* 'queen' (sound), *ləbs/albas* 'clothing', *nəgus/nägäst* 'king' (broken). The *-t* of the latter is the trace of an interesting old phenomenon, polarity, whereby in changing number nouns also change gender. Hence the feminine ending after the plural of a masculine. For the opposite direction, much rarer, see Ge'ez *təʔmərt/təʔamər* 'miracle', where the plural loses its feminine ending. Polarity is never a truly consistent principle in any Semitic language, but it left traces in plural formation, in the Arabic agreement rules (see page 184) and in the numeral system (see below).

The type of vocalisation assumed by the broken plural form is predictable from the singular in a minority of cases only. Usually, it has to be memorised separately. One noun may have several broken plural forms, e.g. Ge'ez *kälb* 'dog', pl. *käläbat*, *akləbt* or *aklab* (cf. *kalb/kila:b* in Arabic), sometimes with differences of meaning. Broken plurals are widely used in Arabic, Modern South Arabian, North Ethiopic, with some traces in South Ethiopic and Hebrew (e.g. *kɛlɛƀ/klåƀīm* 'dog/dogs', with a further sound plural ending), no traces in Akkadian.

A further morphological category applying to nouns is 'state': the construct state (a phonetically shortened form in Hebrew, with an ending *-ä* in Ge'ez) is for the noun attached to a genitival noun; the pronominal state is used before possessive suffixes; the predicative state in Akkadian is the shape of a predicative noun, containing also subject endings; in Aramaic, the emphatic state (suffix *-å*) refers to a definite noun; otherwise the noun is in the absolute state (with an ending *-m* in the singular in Akkadian).

The basic case system consists of a nominative case and an oblique one. In the singular, the latter is subdivided into an accusative and a genitive. Construct state nouns have only a 'genitive/all the rest' opposition in Akkadian and no case in Ge'ez. In the singular, the endings are nom. *-u*, acc. *-a*, gen. *-i*; in the dual nom. *-a:*, obl. *-ay*; in the plural nom. *-u:*, obl. *-i:*. Prepositions combine with the genitive/oblique case. Proto-Semitic probably had a richer case system, as suggested by the evidence of some traces. The above system is found in Akkadian and Classical Arabic only, Ge'ez has acc. *-ä* vs. -Ø in the singular only (East Gurage has *-ä* for a definite accusative). The prepositional system that had been the mainstay of case marking since Proto-Semitic has completely taken over everywhere else (for dual and plural marking, the oblique forms were generalised), with further postpositions (forming circumpositions) developing in modern Ethiopian, and with postpositions only (some of them used to be prepositions) in Harari (e.g. Proto-Semitic **bi-bayt-i* 'in-house-gen.', Ge'ez *bä-bet*, East Gurage *bä-gar wəsṭ* (='inside'), Harari *gar-be* for 'in (a/the) house').

In the pronominal and verbal system, no distinction of gender is made in the first persons, but the second and third persons have both a masculine and a feminine, in the singular everywhere, but no more in the plural in modern East Aramaic, Transversal South Ethiopic and Gafat (and some modern Arabic dialects).

There are three basic sets of personal pronouns: independent ones for subject and predicate functions, possessive pronouns suffixed to nouns (Amharic *bet-e* 'house-my') or to prepositions (Hebrew *b-ī* 'in-my' for 'in me') and object pronouns attached to verbs.

Beside basic adjectives, nouns may be adjectivised by means of the suffix *-i:/-iyy* (the so-called *nisbe*), e.g. Arabic *bayt-iyy-* 'domestic, home-made'.

Numerals from 'three' to 'ten' (with some complications, from 'eleven' to 'nineteen' as well in South-Central Semitic) show clear traces of polarity. Numerals with a feminine ending precede masculine nouns and those without such an ending occur with feminine nouns. This harks back to the prehistoric period when the plural of a masculine was indeed a feminine and vice versa.

The centrality of the verb has always been pointed out in the description of Semitic. Verbal morphology is an essential part of grammar. Most nouns are derived from verbs and, conversely, most nouns that seem to be basic may be the sources of verbal roots (e.g. Arabic *ba:ta* 'spend the night' from *bayt-* 'house'). And it is here that the most important feature of Semitic morphology, the root-and-pattern system (see broken plurals above) ought to be properly introduced.

The Semitic root consists of a set of consonants, ideally three, but sometimes four, e.g. Akkadian *p-r-s* 'divide, decide, etc.'. There is strong evidence that pre-Semitic may have had also biconsonantal roots which were later made triconsonantal by the addition of another consonant; cf. the

Hebrew roots *p-r-d* 'divide', *p-r-m* 'open, seam', *p-r-s* 'break up, divide up', suggesting an old root **p-r*. Roots that behave regularly are called 'sound roots', as opposed to 'weak roots' which have a weak root consonant, such as a semi-vowel *y* or *w* which may be reduced to a vowel (*i/u* respectively) or disappear, for Akkadian and Hebrew also *n* which may assimilate to the subsequent consonant; or else, to be 'weak', the last two consonants may be identical, like *p-r-r* 'annul', which may be subject to contractions through the conjugation. Such roots are combined with patterns made up of vowels and often also consonants in a prefixal, suffixal or, more rarely, infixal position. Thus, in Akkadian, the pattern CC*u*C yields *-prus*, the past tense 'divided', whereas the present has C*a*C:*a*C, leading to *-parras* (where the gemination is part of the pattern); C*a:*C*i*C is the active participle: *pa:ris-* 'divider'; C*ta*C*a*C is the perfect theme *-ptaras* 'has divided'; *ša*CCVC is the causative stem, where the value of V depends on tense: *-šapras* for the present and *-šapris* for the past; with a further *mu-*, we obtain an active participle: *mušapris-* 'the one who makes divide'; some nominal patterns: C*i*C*i*C*t*- (*t* for feminine) *pirist-* 'decision', C*a*CC for *pars-* 'part' etc.

There are two sets of basic conjugations in Semitic, one called 'prefixal', in reality a combination of four prefixes and, in seven cases out of twelve, further suffixes, and one purely 'suffixal'. In table 9.1 are the forms that may be reconstructed for Proto-Semitic. (There are uncertainties about the first person dual. In the prefix conjugation, note the identity of second person singular masculine and third person singular feminine and, more puzzling, of the dual and the feminine plural. The first person plural typically has no suffix.)

Talbe 9.1: Person-markers of the Verb

	Prefix			*Suffix*		
	M.	Common	F.	M.	Common	F.
Singular						
1st		a-...			...-ku	
2nd	ta-...		ta-...-i:	...-ta		...-ti
3rd	ya-...		ta-...	...Ø		...-at
Dual						
2nd		ta-...-a:			...-tuma:	
3rd		ya-...-a:			...-a:	
Plural						
1st		ni-...			...-nu/-na:	
2nd	ta-...-u:		ta-...-a:	...-tumu:		...-tinna(:)
3rd	ya-...-u:		ya-...-a:	...-u:		...-a:

These affixes are attached to various stem forms to create verbal words. Stem forms (as the term is used here) consist of the verbal root and the pattern expressing tense, mood and type of derivation (see below). In the following, the root *p~f-r-s* (Akkadian 'divide', Arabic 'make a kill (of a predatory animal)', Ge'ez 'destroy') is used to illustrate the forms. For Proto-Semitic we reconstruct:

Non-past (= present or future) **-parrVs*	Prefix
Past **-prVs* ~ jussive (imperative-like) **-prVs*	Prefix
Stative (see below) **parVs-*	Suffix

The stative originally referred to the state in which the object, or sometimes the subject, finds itself as a lasting result of a previous action (e.g. Akkadian *parsa:ku* 'I have been cut away'). The past and the jussive were almost homophonous but, most probably, distinguished by the stress: on the prefix for the past and on the stem for the jussive (**y'iprus* 'he divided', **yipr'us* 'let him divide!'). 'V' above refers to the 'thematic vowel', *a*, *i* or *u*, specified for each verb in the lexicon, but not necessarily the same in the three basic forms of the same verb. It is most probably the remnant of an old semantic distinction between active and stative (transitive and intransitive?) verbs. *a* is still often associated with passive-intransitive.

The above system is more or less valid for Akkadian, which, however, had in addition a resultative-perfect (with an infix *-ta-* after the first root consonant: *-ptaras*). West Semitic dropped the old prefix-conjugated past (which, however, left some traces) and promoted the original stative into a past tense. Furthermore, South Semitic replaced the *-t-* of the second person suffixes by *-k-*, whereas Central Semitic changed the first person singular to *-tu*, Central Semitic underwent a radical change. It dropped the original non-past forms (*-parras*) and adopted the jussive forms followed by indicative endings as a new non-past. The vocalisation of the prefixes was also reorganised. Some examples of non-past/past (2 sg. f.): Akkadian *taparrasi:/taprusi:*, Ge'ez *təfärrəsi/färäski*, Arabic *tafrisi:-na/farasti*.

The verbal derivational system is of great importance in Semitic. The above samples represent the 'basic' form ('stem' in the traditional terminology). Derivation is made through root-internal and prefixal modification. A gemination of the middle radical throughout creates an 'intensive' form, mainly for repeated action. A long vowel after the first radical produces the 'conative' form, comparable to what is called 'applicative' in other language families (e.g. Bantu), i.e. with the function of making an indirect object into a direct one. This system of three units, basic-intensive-conative, is but one axis of the derivation. Prefixed *ni-* or *ta-* (the latter sometimes infixed) forms an intransitive — passive or reflexive. The prefix *ša-/ha-/ʔa-* produces a causative. A compound *a/ista-* is a causative or reciprocal or has other values. Originally, all of these prefixes (questionable for *ni-*, which may have been reserved to the basic form) could be combined with any of the root-internally distinguished forms (Ge'ez is still the closest to this), but now combinations are strictly limited according to the language.

Moreover, the meanings attributed to them above is actually true in part only. Only some of the derivations are free, only some of the meaning modifications may be predicted. The actual occurrences of a verb in various forms is defined by the lexicon. Thus, 'causative' is to be understood more as a morphological label than a semantic one, though many causative-prefixed verbs are indeed the causatives of the corresponding basic forms. Derived forms have no special thematic vowels and the internal and prefix vocalisation is also different.

In the South Central Semitic languages 'internal passives' are also found. The introduction of an *u* after the first consonant makes a form a passive: Arabic *tufrasi:-na/furisti* 'you (f. sg.) were killed (as prey by an animal)'. Modern South Arabian (Shahri) has *yə'rɔfəs/rə'fɔs* 'he kicks/kicked' and an internal passive *yər'fɔs/rə'fis* 'he is/was kicked', but the latter may be the remnant of the old thematic vowel change making a verb stative-intransitive.

3.3 Notes on Syntax

Proto-Semitic word order is assumed to have been VSO, still so in Classical Arabic, to a decreasing extent in Biblical Hebrew and, less clearly, in Ge'ez. Akkadian was SOV under the influence of the Sumerian substratum, as is modern Ethiopian, copying the Cushitic system. Later Hebrew and Arabic are basically SVO. The adjectives, however, always follow the noun, except in modern Ethiopian (and partly in Ge'ez). Numerals most often precede the noun. Demonstratives follow, except in Arabic and part of modern Ethiopian. Residual case endings aside, case marking is predominantly prepositional (see above). Subordinate clauses follow the head, except in modern Ethiopian.

Adjectives agree with the noun they qualify in gender and number and, when used attributively, also in suffixal case and definiteness/state (e.g. Akkadian *umm-a-m damiq-t-a-m* 'the good mother' lit. 'mother-acc.-abs. good-f.-acc.-abs.', Aramaic *yamm-å rabb-å* 'sea-the big-the'). For numeral agreement, see 'polarity' above. For Arabic subject-verb agreement, see page 189.

There are usually two genitive constructions, one using the construct state, one with a genitive particle, e.g. Ge'ez *betä nəguš* or *bet zä-nəguš* 'the king's house' (*bet* 'house', *zä-* 'of'). Except in modern Ethiopian, the order is always possessed-possessor (cf. Amharic *yä-nəgus bet* for the opposite order).

In Akkadian and Ethiopian (and originally in Aramaic), the 'of' particle also serves as a relative particle. The function of the head noun is marked by a pronoun next to the verb, as a suffix: Akkadian *awi:l-a-m ša šarr-u-m bi:t-a-m iddin-u-šu amur* 'man$_i$-acc.-abs. that king-nom.-abs. house-acc.-abs. he+gave-subordinate suffix him$_i$ I+saw', Amharic *nəgus bet-u-n yä-säṭṭu-t-ən säw ayyähu-t* 'king house-the-acc. that-he+gave-him$_i$-acc. man$_i$ I+saw-him' for 'I saw the man to whom the king gave the house'; with an independent prepositional pronoun: Akkadian *ša ittišu tuššabu*, Amharic *kəssu gar yämməttənor*, 'that with him you live', i.e. 'with whom you live' etc. As can be seen, the Akkadian verb has a special suffix for the subordinate verb (here *-u*).

Subordinating particles are clause-initial, except in modern Ethiopian where they are affixed to the clause-final verb. Another example of the latter in Tigré: *dərho ʔət bet kəm ʔatrafawo* 'chicken in house as they+left+him' for 'as they left the chicken at home'.

4 Closing Words

For the comparative linguist, the Semitic languages exhibit a great deal of similarity. The family is much more uniform than, say, Indo-European. Yet, from a practical point of view, these languages are very different, there being no mutual comprehensibility even between the close relatives. On the other hand, however compact the family, scholars do not always agree on matters of reconstruction. Semitic scholarship is a very active field, further enlivened by the recent involvement of other branches of Afroasiatic.

Bibliography

There is a serious need for an up-to-date manual on comparative Semitic. Brockelmann (1908–13) is the classical work in the field. Gray (1934) is a useful, but outdated, introduction. Moscati et al. (1964) is the result of the cooperation between specialists of the main branches; it is conservative in approach and to be used with caution. Bergsträsser (1983) is a collection of sample texts preceded by sketch grammars; while still valuable in many details, it is now altogether obsolete, in spite of attempts at updating by the translator.

References

Bergsträsser, G. 1983. *Introduction to the Semitic Languages* (Eisenbrauns, Winona Lake, Ind.; translated by P.T. Daniels from the German original, *Einführung in die semitischen Sprachen*, Max Hueber, Munich, 1928, 2nd ed. 1963)

Brockelmann, C. 1908–13. *Grundriß der vergleichenden Grammatik der semitischen Sprachen* (Reuther und Reichard, Berlin; reprinted G. Olms, Hildesheim, 1961)

Gray, L.H. 1934. *Introduction to Semitic Comparative Linguistics* (Columbia University, New York)

Moscati, S. et al. 1964. *An Introduction to the Comparative Grammar of the Semitic Languages, Phonology and Morphology* (O. Harrassowitz, Wiesbaden)

10 Arabic

Alan S. Kaye

1 Arabic and the Semitic Languages

Arabic is by far *the* Semitic (or indeed Afroasiatic) language with the greatest number of speakers, probably now in excess of 150 million, although a completely satisfying and accurate estimate is lacking. It is *the* major language throughout the Arab world, i.e. Egypt, Sudan, Libya, the North African countries usually referred to as the Maghrib (such as Tunisia, Morocco and Algeria), Saudi Arabia, Iraq, Jordan, the Gulf countries etc., and it is even the major language of non-Arab countries such as the Republic of Chad in central Africa (i.e. more Chadians speak Arabic as their mother tongue than any other language).

Arabic is also a minority language in other countries such as Nigeria, Iran and the Soviet Union (the speakers — some 4,000 — of Soviet Central Asian Arabic have probably all assimilated to another language). Furthermore, Arabic is in wide use throughout the Muslim world as a second language and as a learned, liturgical language (e.g. in Pakistan, India, Indonesia). Indeed among orthodox Muslims Arabic is *luɣat almalāʔikah* 'the language of the angels', and the language *par excellence* in the world since Allāh himself speaks Arabic and has revealed his Holy Book, the Qurʔān, in the Arabic language. One can also easily comprehend that the Arabs are very proud of their (most beautiful) language since there is even a verb *ʔaʕraba* 'to speak clearly and eloquently' from the root *ʕRB*, also occurring in the word *alʕarabiyyah* 'the Arabic language' or *lisān ʕarabī* 'the Arabic language' in the Qurʔān.

There is even a historical dialect of Arabic, Maltese, sometimes, although erroneously, called Maltese Arabic, which, due to its isolation from the rest of the so-called Arab world, developed into a new Semitic language in its own right (a similar, but weaker, argument could be made also for Cypriot Maronite Arabic). The two major reasons for my claiming that Maltese is not to be regarded synchronically as a dialect of Arabic are: (1) Maltese, if an Arabic dialect today, would be one without diglossia, i.e. it does not have Classical Arabic as a high level of language (more on this important topic later); and (2) it would be the *only* Arabic dialect normally written in the Latin script.

2 Arabic as Central Semitic

According to the new classification of the Semitic languages proposed by R. Hetzron (see the chapter on Semitic languages), there is evidence that Arabic shares traits of both South Semitic and North-West Semitic. Arabic preserves Proto-Semitic phonology almost perfectly (Epigraphic South Arabian is even more conservative), except for Proto-Semitic **p* > *f* and Proto-Semitic **ś* > *s*. But Arabic also shares features with Hebrew, Ugaritic and Aramaic such as the masculine plural suffix *-īna/īma* and the internal passive, e.g. Arabic *qatala* 'he killed' vs. *qutila* 'he was killed' and Hebrew *hilbīš* 'he dressed someone' vs. *hulbaš* 'he was dressed (by someone)'.

The morphology of the definite article in Hebrew (*ha-* + gemination of the following consonant if that consonant is capable of gemination) and Arabic (*ʔal-*, which assimilates before dentals or sibilants, producing a geminate) also points to a common origin and so on. The Hebrew *ha-*, in fact, also shows up in the Arabic demonstratives, *hāðā* 'this, m. sg.' *hāðihi* 'f.' and *hāʔulāʔi* 'pl.'. Even the broken plurals of Arabic may be compared with Hebrew *segholate* plurals such as *kəlāvīm* 'dogs' (cf. sg. *kɛlɛv* + *-īm* 'm. pl.'), where one can easily see the vocalic change in the stem (cf. Arabic *kilāb*).

There are some other very striking morphological affinities of Arabic with Hebrew such as the ancient dialectal Arabic relative particle *ðū*, cf. Biblical Hebrew *zū*, while the Western form *ðī* occurred in Arabic *ʔallaðī* 'who, m. sg.' and Aramaic *dī*. Some Eastern dialects also reflected Barth's Law, i.e. they had *i* as the imperfect preformative vowel with *a* of the imperfect system like the Canaanite dialects.

3 Some Characteristics of Arabic and the Designation 'Arabic'

Arabic sticks out like a sore thumb in comparative Semitic linguistics because of its almost (too perfect) algebraic-looking grammar, i.e. root and pattern morphology. It is so algebraic that some scholars have accused the medieval Arab grammarians of contriving some artificiality about it in its classical form. For instance, the root *KTB* has to do with 'writing'. In Form I (the simple form of the verb corresponding to the Hebrew *qal* stem), *kataba* means 'he wrote', imperfect *yaktubu* 'he writes', with three verbal nouns all translatable as 'writing' — *katb*, *kitāba* and *kitba*. In Form II (the exact nuances of the forms will be discussed in section 9), *kattaba*, imperfect *yukattibu* means 'to make write'; Form III *kātaba*, imperfect *yukātibu* means 'to correspond'; Form IV *ʔaktaba*, imperfect *yuktibu* 'to dictate'; Form VI *takātaba*, imperfect *yatakātabu* 'to keep up a correspondence'; Form VII *ʔinkataba*, imperfect *yankatibu* 'to subscribe'; Form VIII *ʔiktataba*, imperfect *yaktatibu* 'to copy'; Form X *ʔistaktaba*, imperfect *yastaktibu* 'to ask to write'. There are ten commonly used forms of the verb (five others occur but are very uncommon); the root *KTB* does not occur in Form V, which is often a passive of Form II ('to be made to write'?), or Form IX, which is a very special form reserved only for the semantic sphere of colours and defects (so we would not expect it to occur in this form). The linguists who have seen a much too regular *Systemzwang* in this particular case have doubted the authenticity of some of the forms with this root and have asked about an automatic plugging in of the root into the form to obtain a rather forced (artificially created) meaning.

There are also many other words derivable from this triconsonantal root by using different vocalic patterns. For instance, *kitāb* 'book' (vowel pattern = $C_1iC_2\bar{a}C_3$) with its pl. *kutub* ($C_1uC_2uC_3$), *kutubī* 'bookseller', *kuttāb* 'Koran school', *kutayyib* 'booklet', *kitābī* 'written', *katība* 'squadron', *maktab* 'office', *maktaba* 'library', *miktāb* 'typewriter', *mukātaba* 'correspondence', *ʔiktitāb* 'registration', *ʔistiktāb* 'dictation', *kātib* 'writer', *maktūb* 'letter, note' etc.

The Arabic dictionary lists words under their respective roots, thus all of the above are found under the root *KTB*. However, in most native but older dictionaries, a word is listed by what it ends with, so that all of the above words would be listed under /b/. The reason that this was done was to make life very easy for the poets (who were the real inventors of the classical language), since the usual state of a traditional Arabic poem was that it would have only one general rhyming pattern (Arabic poetry is also metrical).

It is very important to keep in mind that one must sharply distinguish what is meant by the term 'Arabic' language. Our preceding examples have all come from modern standard Arabic, sometimes called modern literary Arabic or modern written Arabic, which is essentially a modernised form of Classical Arabic. All of these three designations just mentioned are known as *ʔalʕarabiyya alfuṣħā* or *ʔalʕarabiyya alfaṣīħa* (the 'pure' or 'clear' language). On the other side of the coin is a language which many Arabs think is devoid of grammar, the colloquial language, *luɣat alʕāmma* or *ʔalluɣa alʕāmmiyya* or *addāriǰa* or *lahaǰāt* ('dialects').

ʔalʕarabiyya alfuṣħā originated from the ancient poetic language of the Arabs in pre-Islamic Arabia, which was a period of idol worship (known in Arabic as *ʔalǰāhiliyya* 'the period of ignorance'). The linguistic situation in ancient Arabia was such that every tribe had its own dialect, but there evolved a common koine used by the *rāwī*s (the ancient poets), which helped the preservation of the language and assisted in its conservatism. The Holy Qurʔān, written in this dialect (of course it was at first oral) but with linguistic features of Muħammad's speech (the Meccan dialect), eventually became *the* model for the classical language. Surprisingly enough, due principally to Islam, the classical language has changed in grammar very little since the seventh century AD. In fact, most students are amazed at the easy transition between reading a modern novel and a *sūra* of the Qurʔān (vocabulary and stylistics are other matters, however).

The colloquial dialects number in the thousands. The number reported on in an ever-growing literature runs in the hundreds. There are many remarkable parallels in the development of the modern Arabic dialects and the development of the Romance languages from a Latin prototype, the most notable of which is a general grammatical simplification in structure (i.e. fewer grammatical categories). Three such simplifications are: (1) loss of the dual in the verb, adjective and pronoun; (2) loss of case endings for nouns and adjectives; and (3) loss of mood distinctions in the verb. In addition to a demarcation of the colloquial dialects of various countries, cities, towns and villages, there are many sociolects which can be observed. Educated speech is, of course, quite distinct from that of the *fallāħīn* (peasants). In terms of comparative Arabic dialectology, more is known about urban dialects than rural (Bedouin) counterparts.

One should also keep in mind that the differences between many colloquials and the classical language are so great that a *fallāħ* who had never been to school could hardly understand more than a few scattered words and expressions in it without great difficulty. One could assemble dozens of so-called Arabs (*fallāħīn*) in a room, who have never been exposed to the classical language, so that not one could properly understand the other. One should also bear in mind that educated Arabs use their native dialect in daily living and have all learned their colloquial dialects first. Indeed all colloquial Arabic dialects are acquired systems but the classical language is always formally learned. This has probably held true from the beginning.

4 The Influence of Arabic on Other Languages

As Islam expanded from Arabia, the Arabic language exerted much influence on the native languages with which it came in contact. Persians and speakers of other Iranian languages such as Kurdish and Pashto, Turkic-speaking peoples, Indians, Pakistanis, Bangladeshians and many speakers of African languages such as Hausa and Swahili (this list is by no means exhaustive) used the Arabic script to write their own native languages and assimilated a tremendous number of Arabic loanwords. One did not have to become a Muslim to embrace Arabic as Judeo-Arabic proves (Jews in Arabic-speaking countries, who spoke Arabic natively, wrote it in Hebrew characters with a few diacritical innovations). Words of ultimate Arabic origin have penetrated internationally and interlingually. A recent study turned up 400 'common' Arabic loanwords in English based on the *Random House Dictionary of the English Language*, *Webster's Third New International Dictionary* and the *Shorter Oxford English Dictionary*. A few examples will illustrate: the *al-* definite article words such as *algebra*, *alkali*, *alcohol*, *alcove* and many other famous ones such as *Allah*, *artichoke*, *assassin*, *Bedouin*, *cadi*, *cipher*, *emir*, *gazelle*, *giraffe*, *harem*, *hashish*, *imam*, *Islam*, *lute*, *mosque*, *mullah*, *Muslim*, *nadir*, *saffron*, *sheikh*, *sherbert*, *syrup*, *talc* and *vizier*.

It is important to point out that some of the loanwords mentioned earlier have as many as five alternate spellings in English due to transliteration differences and preferences so that a word such as *cadi* (< Arabic *qāḍin* 'judge', *ʔalqāḍī* 'the judge' — there is no Classical Arab word **qāḍī*) can also be spelt *kadhi*, *kadi*, *qadi* and *qazi* (this latter pronunciation reflects a Perso-Indian influence since in those languages /ḍ/ > /z/); *emir* can also be spelt as *ameer*, *amir* or *emeer*.

5 Phonology

The consonantal segments of a fairly typical educated pronunciation of modern standard Arabic can be seen in table 10.1 (of course, there can always be a debate about the exact meaning of 'fairly typical').

Table 10.1: Arabic Consonant Phonemes

	Bilabial	*Labio-dental*	*Inter-dental*	*Dental*	*Emphatic*	*Palatal*	*Velar*	*Uvular*	*Pharyngeal*	*Laryngeal*
Stops	b			t d	ṭ ḍ		k	q		ʔ
Affricates						ǰ				
Fricatives		f	θ ð	s z	ṣ ð̣ (ẓ)	š		x ɣ	ħ ʕ	h
Nasals	m			n						
Liquids (lateral and trill)				l r	ḷ					
Approximants	w					y				

The symbols are IPA or quasi-IPA symbols (as used by linguists who specialise in Arabic and the other Semitic languages). The Arabic alphabet is a very accurate depiction of the phonological facts of the language, however it should be noted that there are some pronunciations different from the ones presented in table 10.1. For instance, /q/ is voiced in many dialects, both ancient and modern, i.e. [G], especially the Bedouin ones, which probably reflects its original pronunciation; the *ǰīm* (the name of the letter represented by the grapheme <ǰ>) corresponds to many pronunciations such as [d^y], [g^y], [g] or [ž], stemming from a Proto-Semitic */g/.

Every consonant may be geminated, in contradistinction to Hebrew, for example, which can not geminate the so-called 'gutturals' (*ʔ, ʕ, h, ħ* and *r*).

Classical Arabic does not have a /p/, but standard pronunciations tend to devoice a /b/ before a voiceless consonant, e.g. /ħabs/ → [ħaps] 'imprisonment' or /ħibs/ → [ħips] 'dam'. Some modern Arabic dialects, notably those in Iraq, have both /p/ and /p/ (emphatic); however, the great majority of Arabic speakers will produce English /p/s as /b/ due to interference modification (one Arab asks another, 'Which Bombay are you flying to? Bombay, India or Bombay (Pompei), Italy?'). Incidentally, Persian, Urdu and other languages which have /p/ have taken the grapheme for /b/ = ب and made پ by placing three dots underneath its basic configuration of ٮ = <p>. This grapheme, in turn, has been reborrowed by some Iraqi Arabs.

Classical Arabic does not have a /v/, but phonetically, due to regressive assimilation, a [v] might occur as in /ħifð̣/ → [ħivð̣] 'memory'. /n/ also assimilates regressively, i.e. *nb* → *mb*, and *nk* → *ŋk* as in /bank/ → [baŋk] 'bank'.

The 'emphatic' consonants, often misleadingly called velarised-pharyngealised, are depicted with a dot underneath the particular consonant. Perhaps nowhere else in Arabic linguistic literature is there more controversy and more debate than in this area of the emphatics and how they are to be described and how they function. The vowels around an emphatic consonant tend to become lower, retracted or more centralised than around corresponding non-emphatics (the very back consonants /x, ɣ, q, ħ, ʕ/ have a similar effect on vowels), which is why the vowel allophonics of Arabic are much more cumbersome and intricate than the consonantal allophonics.

In Old Arabic, the primary emphatics were, in all likelihood, voiced, i.e. /ḍ/ < [ẓ$^{\lambda}$] (ḷateralised), /ṭ/ < /ḍ/, /ð̣/ or /ẓ/ < /ð̣/ and /ṣ/ < /ẓ/.

W. Lehn reviewed much of the previous literature including Arab grammatical thought and concluded, at least for Cairo Arabic, that the minimum domain of emphasis is the syllable and the maximum domain is the utterance. Lehn has suggested that emphasis not be treated as a distinctive system of the consonant or vocalic system but as a redundant feature of both. In later works, Lehn underscores all emphatic syllables.

The /ḷ/, which occurs only in the name of God, /ʔaḷḷāh/ (but not after /i/ as in /bismillāh/ 'in the name of Allah') was shown to be a phoneme in Classical Arabic by C.A. Ferguson. Some modern Arabic dialects have many more examples of /ḷ/, especially those spoken in the Gulf countries.

Arabic is perhaps the best known of the world's languages to linguists for its vowel system. It has the classical triangular system, which preserves Proto-Semitic vocalism:

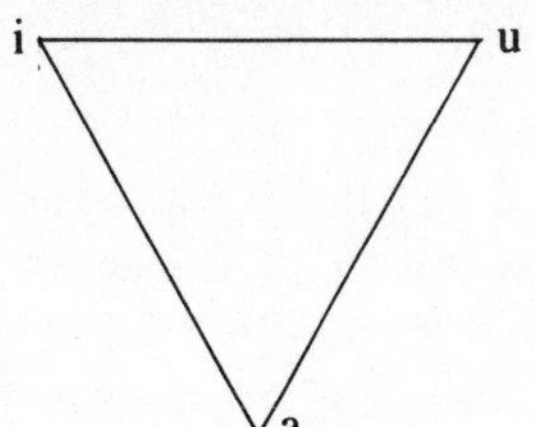

For Classical and modern standard Arabic, these may be short or long (geminated). Many modern Arabic dialects have, however, developed other vowels such as /ə/, /e/, /o/ etc., just as the other Semitic languages had done centuries earlier through the general process of 'drift' (i.e. parallel development).

The vowel allophonics are much richer than the consonantal allophonics chiefly because vowels take on the colouring of the adjacent emphatic and emphatic-like consonants (including /r/), while the non-emphatic consonants push the vowels to higher and less centralised qualities. What is important to keep in mind is that the pronunciation of the standard language or any oral interpretation of the classical language is all directly dependent on the nature of one's native colloquial dialect.

The vowel allophonics have been accurately described on the basis of detailed spectrographic analysis for the modern standard Arabic as used in Iraq. The rules may be stated as follows:

(1) /ī/ → [ɨ̄]/ – [+emphatic] – (except /ḷ/)
→ [Ī]/ – {ʕ, ɣ} –
→ [ī]/ ...

(2) /i/ → [ɨ]/ – [+emphatic] –
→ [I]/ – {ʕ, ɣ} –
→ [i]/ ...

(3) /ū/ → [Ū]/ – [+emphatic] – (except /ḷ/)
→ [ū]/ ...

(4) /u/ → [U]/ – [+emphatic] –
→ [u] ...

(5) /ā/ → [ā]/ [– {+emphatic, {q, r}} –]
→ [ʌ̄]/ [– {ʕ, ɣ} –]
→ [ǣ]/ ...

(6) /a/ → [ə]/ ——# (but not next to /q/, /ʕ/, /r/ and /ɣ/)
→ [a]/ [– {+ emphatic, {q, r}} –]
→ [ʌ]/ [– {ʕ, ɣ} –]
→ [æ]/ ...

What tends to happen in modern Arabic dialects is that the short vowels are more susceptible to change than the long ones. Thus Classical /i/ and /u/ in

Damascus Arabic, for instance, both merge into /ə/. Indeed /a/ can usually be regarded as the most stable and conservative of the three short vowels, yet it too is now becoming subject to change or deletion as in many dialects; /yā/ + /maħammad/ → /ya mħammad/ 'Oh Muhammad!'. Classical Arabic knows many doublets in its short vowel configuration such as /ħubs/ ~ /ħibs/ 'inalienable property, the yield of which is devoted to pious purposes' or /laṣṣ/ ~ /liṣṣ/ ~ /luṣṣ/ 'thief' (a triplet!).

Diphthongs are two in number: /aw/ and /ay/ as in /θawr/ 'bull' and /bayt/ 'house', respectively. In most of the colloquial dialects, diphthongs have monophthongised into /ē/ and /ō/, respectively (and /ī/ and /ū/ in Moroccan dialects, which occurred in Akkadian centuries before and is another good attestation of 'drift' in the Semitic languages).

There are two well-known phonological processes which deserve mention. The first is called *ʔimāla* (lit. 'inclination'), which refers to /ā/-raising, usually due to the umlauting influence of /i/, which means that words such as *ʕibād* 'slaves' could have had a dialectal (peculiar, at first, perhaps) pronunciation *ʕibēd* or *ʕibīd*. *ʔimāla* has produced the very distinctive high vowel pronunciations of /ā/ in many Syro-Lebanese dialects giving for /bāb/: [bēb] or [bīb] 'door' or phonetic qualities in between those or adjacent to them, which may be compared with Maltese *bieb* 'door' (Maltese has for Arabic *kalimāt* 'words' *kelmiet* and for Arabic *kitāb* 'book' *ktieb*).

The second process is known as *ʔišmām* ('delabialisation'), which explains /ū/ → /ī/ (through an intermediate stage of [ü]) as in *rūm* ~ *rīm* 'Rome' or some dialectal pronunciations of /rudda/ as /rüdda/ 'it was returned' or /qǖla/ for /qīla/ 'it was said', which derives from /quwila/, the passive form I of the root *QWL*. This phonological process may also explain why *ū* rhymes with *ī* in Koranic Arabic.

Stress is one of the most involved topics in Arabic phonology (even for the Nigerian dialect of Arabic I researched at first hand, stress was the most intricate part of the entire phonology). The Arab grammarians never mentioned it, and therefore the modern-day pronunciation of the standard (classical) language is directly dependent on the stress rules of the native colloquial dialect counterpart. Thus for the word 'both of them (f.) wrote', segmentally /katabatā/, graphemically <ktbtʔ>, which of the four possible syllables receives the main stress? Indeed some native Arabic speakers say: (1) /kátabatā/ (Iraqis); others (2), /katabátā/ (Egyptians); still others (3), /katabatā́/ (many Syrians and Lebanese); and others (4), may say /katábatā/. Thus it is possible to stress any of the four syllables and still be correct. This is one of the reasons why I consider modern standard Arabic an ill defined system of language, whereas I deem all colloquials well defined.

There are, however, rules of syllabicity which can be described with a greater degree of accuracy. Long vowels are shortened in closed syllables, which explains why one says /yákun/ 'let him be' (jussive of /yakūnu/ 'he will be') instead of the expected (apocopated imperfect) */yakūn/. The only exception is that /ā/ may occur in a closed syllable, but it is not necessary to enter into the details of this here. Also, syllable-initially and finally, only single consonants occur. Thus a borrowing like Latin *strāta* 'path' > /ṣirāṭ/ (the *str-* consonant cluster was, at first, simplified to *sr-* and then an anaptyctic vowel /i/ was inserted between the /ṣ/ and the /r/; further the emphatic /ṣ/ and /ṭ/ are typical of what Arabic does in its loanword phonology).

Rules for the assignment of lexical stress are:

(1) When a word is made up of CV syllables, the first syllable receives the primary stress, e.g. /kátaba/.

(2) When a word contains only one long syllable, the long syllable receives the primary stress, e.g. /kātib/.

(3) When a word contains two or more long syllables, the long syllable nearest to the end of the word receives the primary stress, e.g. /raʔīsuhúnna/ 'their (f. pl.) chief'.

The normal use of modern standard Arabic requires an understanding of pausal forms. When a pause occurs in speech (reflected in reading as well), speakers drop final short vowels (case and mood markers) and drop or shorten case endings. For example, Arabic marks indefiniteness by what is called nūnation (named after the Arabic letter *nūn*): *-un* for nominative, *-in* for genitive and *-an* for accusative (there are only three cases). At the end of an utterance (i.e. sentence, breath group), a word such as /mudarrisun/ 'a teacher' → /mudarris/, /mudarrisin/ → /mudarris/ but /mudarrisan/ → /mudarrisā/ (note that Arabic words are usually cited with nūnation, called in Arabic, *tanwīn*), and /mudarrisatun/ → /mudarrisah/ 'a teacher' (f. sg.).

6 Morphophonemic Changes

We shall not list all occurrences because that would require more space than allotted to us. We will rather present a few of the most common changes occurring in Classical Arabic.

(1) *awa* → *ā* — *qawama* → *qāma* 'he stood up'

(2) $C_1aC_2aC_2a \rightarrow C_1aC_2C_2a$ — *radada* → *radda* 'he returned'

(3) $\text{ʔ}\left\{\begin{matrix}\mathrm{a}\\ \mathrm{i}\\ \mathrm{u}\end{matrix}\right\}\text{ʔ} \rightarrow \text{ʔ}\left\{\begin{matrix}\bar{\mathrm{a}}\\ \bar{\imath}\\ \bar{\mathrm{u}}\end{matrix}\right\}$ – *ʔaʔlām* → *ʔālām* 'pains'

(4) *uw* → *ū* — *suwdun* → *sūdun* 'black' (m. pl.)

(5) *ūy* → *ī* — *būyḍun* → *bīḍun* 'white' (m. pl.); *mudarrisūya* → *mudarrisīya* 'my teachers' (m., all cases)

(6) *yw* → *yy* — *ʔaywāmun* → *ʔayyāmun* 'days'

(7) Haplology: *tataqātalūna* → *taqātalūna* 'you are fighting each other'

(8) Dissimilation: *madīnīyun* → *madanīyun* 'urban'
(9) *āw* → *āʔ* — *qāwilun* → *qāʔilun* 'speaker'

7 The Arabic Alphabet

The Latin script is used by more languages than any other script ever invented (and it is used for languages as diversified in structure as Polish, English and Vietnamese). After Latin, the Arabic alphabet is number two because it was or is used to write a vast number of different languages such as Persian, Urdu, Pashto (all Indo-Iranian), Hausa (the Chadic sub-branch of Afroasiatic), Swahili (Bantu), Turkish (Altaic), Malay (Austronesian) and over a hundred others. The reason for this diversity is undoubtedly due to the spread of Islam.

The earliest Arabic inscription is dated AD 512. According to an early Arab scholar, Ibn Khaldūn, the Arabic alphabet had evolved from the Epigraphic South Arabian script; however, we know that it was borrowed from the Nabatean alphabet (which was, in turn, borrowed from Aramaic), which consisted of twenty-two consonantal graphemes. The Nabateans added six more graphemes representing phonemes which did not occur in Aramaic (the oldest Nabatean inscription dates from AD 250, found at Umm al-Jimāl): ث, ذ, ض, ظ, خ, and غ. The oldest Arabic inscription written in the Nabatean script is the Namāra inscription, a grave inscription of seventy-one lines found in southeastern Syria, which dates from AD 328 (the inscription was discovered in 1902).

Like Phoenician, Hebrew, Ugaritic and other Semitic alphabets (or syllabaries), the adapted Nabatean system used by the pre-Islamic Arabs represents only consonants, which is appropriate to the root structure of Semitic.

The invention of diacritical marks to indicate vowels was borrowed from Syriac in the eighth century AD. In fact, the invention is attributed to Al-Khalil ibn Ahmad. Arabic's written development can be explained as follows. The Arabs grew tired with fifteen basic letter shapes for twenty-eight phonemes (the confusion must have been overwhelming), so dots were invented above and below the letters in groups of one to three to distinguish the underlying grapheme. The process of using the dots (inserting the diacritics) is called *ʔiʕǰām* and although it is used for Aramaic, the Arabs began to use it very systematically.

Arabic calligraphy is truly an art. There are many styles of the script, and table 10.2 presents the *nasxī* one, commonly used for print. Column 5 presents the final unconnected allograph of the grapheme. The script is written, like Hebrew, from right to left, and tends to be very cursive (although the Persians have gone even further), especially in handwritten forms. All the graphemes can be attached to preceding ones, but six never connect to what follows: *ʔalif*, *dāl*, *ðāl*, *rāʔ*, *zāy* and *wāw*. There are no

Table 10.2: The Arabic Alphabet

Transliteration	*Final*	*Medial*	*Initial*	*Alone*	*Name*	*Numerical value*
ā	ـا			ا	ʔalif	*1*
b	ـب	ـبـ	بـ	ب	bāʔ	*2*
t	ـت	ـتـ	تـ	ت	tāʔ	*400*
θ	ـث	ـثـ	ثـ	ث	θaʔ	*500*
ǰ	ـج	ـجـ	جـ	ج	ǰīm	*3*
ħ	ـح	ـحـ	حـ	ح	ħāʔ	*8*
x	ـخ	ـخـ	خـ	خ	xāʔ	*600*
d	ـد			د	dāl	*4*
ð	ـذ			ذ	ðāl	*700*
r	ـر			ر	rāʔ	*200*
z	ـز			ز	zāy	*7*
s	ـس	ـسـ	سـ	س	sīn	*60*
š	ـش	ـشـ	شـ	ش	šīn	*300*
ṣ	ـص	ـصـ	صـ	ص	ṣād	*90*
ḍ	ـض	ـضـ	ضـ	ض	ḍād	*800*
ṭ	ـط	ـطـ	طـ	ط	ṭāʔ	*9*
ð̣	ـظ	ـظـ	ظـ	ظ	ð̣aʔ	*900*
ʕ	ـع	ـعـ	عـ	ع	ʕayn	*70*
ɣ	ـغ	ـغـ	غـ	غ	ɣayn	*1000*
f	ـف	ـفـ	فـ	ف	fāʔ	*80*
q	ـق	ـقـ	قـ	ق	qāf	*100*
k	ـك	ـكـ	كـ	ك	kāf	*20*
l	ـل	ـلـ	لـ	ل	lām	*30*
m	ـم	ـمـ	مـ	م	mīm	*40*
n	ـن	ـنـ	نـ	ن	nūn	*50*
h	ـه	ـهـ	هـ	ه	hāʔ	*5*
w	ـو			و	wāw	*6*
y	ـى	ـيـ	يـ	ى	yāʔ	*10*

capital letters and table 10.2 presents the graphemes and their allographs as well as their older Semitic numerical values (the so-called *ʔabǰad*).

Handwriting generally shortens the strokes and replaces the three dots with ˆ and two dots with ˉ, allowing it to be written very quickly in comparison to the painstaking effort required for the printed forms.

The vowel diacritics are: *fatħa* ـَ /a/; *ḍamma* ـُ /u/; *kasra* ـِ /i/; and *sukūn* ـْ for zero (no vowel). Long vowels are represented thus: /ā/ by *ʔalif* or *ʔalif madda* (initially), آ; /ī/ by *yāʔ*; and /ū/ by *wāw*.

There are other details such as ligatures, nūnation, stylistic variations etc., for which the reader should refer to Mitchell (1953).

8 Diglossia

A very interesting and relatively rare linguistic phenomenon has developed in Arabic, called diglossia, which is often confused with bilingualism. There can be no doubt that it is an old phenomenon going back, in all likelihood, to the pre-Islamic period, although J. Blau states it arose as late as the first Islamic century in the towns of the Arab empire as a result of the great Arab conquests (I do not agree with Blau that there was no intermediary of the Arabic koine). Diglossia involves a situation in which two varieties of the same language live side by side, each performing a different function. It involves the use of two different variations of a single language whereas bilingualism definitely involves two different languages. The two variations are: (1) a 'high' one used in relatively formal situations; and (2) a 'low' one used colloquially and usually informally. Although the term was coined by the Arabist W. Marçais in 1930 (*diglossie*), it was C.A. Ferguson who brought it to the attention of general linguistics and ethnology.

'High' Arabic, which we have been calling modern standard Arabic, and 'Low' Arabic, a colloquial dialect which native speakers acquire as a mother tongue, have specialised functions in Arab culture. The former is learned through formal education in school like Latin, Sanskrit and Biblical Hebrew and would be used in a sermon, university lecture, news broadcast and for mass media purposes, letter, political speech (except, perhaps, after an informal greeting or the first few sentences, as was typical in the speeches of Gamal Abdul Nasser), while the latter is always an acquired system (no formal learning ever takes place to learn anyone's native tongue) and is the native language used at home conversing with family or friends or in a radio or television soap opera. It is important to realise that a small elite has developed in the Arab countries very proud of their linguistic skills in the standard language (Modern Classical Arabic). There have even been reports that certain individuals have adapted the standard language as their exclusive means of oral communication, yet I have reservations about this.

Many native speakers, regardless of the level of education, maintain a set of myths about the 'high' language: that it is far more beautiful than any dialect (colloquial), far more logical, more elegant and eloquent, has much more vocabulary available to it, especially for the expression of philosophical ideas, and is far better able to express all the complex nuances of one's thoughts. Arabs also believe (and other Muslims too) that Arabic is the most perfect of all languages since God speaks it and has revealed his message in the Holy Qurʔān in it. If asked which dialect is closest to the classical, many Arabs will respond that their own dialect is! Of course, this may be a relative answer depending upon who else is present and where the question is asked — another common answer is that the Bedouin on the desert speaks a dialect nearest to the classical. In fact, the Bedouin has often been called upon to settle linguistic arguments of all kinds.

Classical Arabic has always had situations where its use was required and it was never acquired by all members of the particular society in question. Modern standard Arabic continues the tradition and unifies the Arab world linguistically as it is the official language of Iraq, Jordan, Egypt, Sudan,

Tunisia, Algeria, Morocco, Kuwait, Saudi Arabia, Lebanon, Libya, both Yemens, Oman, the Gulf countries etc. It is the mark of *ʕurūba* or Arabism (pan-Arabism), since there can be a high degree of mutual unintelligibility among the various colloquial dialects, where a Syrian Arabic-speaking friend of mine once heard a tape of a Nigerian speaking Nigerian Arabic and confessed he understood almost nothing in it.

There is also a tremendous amount of sociological concern about language, dialect and variety in the Arab world. Let me illustrate what I mean by relating a true story. I once participated in a long conversation one entire afternoon in a Beirut coffee house with two other gentlemen. One fellow was Lebanese, but he did not want to appear uneducated, so he spoke French, a language he knew quite well and which he had studied for years formally. The other gentleman was French, but he did not want to come off as any sort of colonialist, so he was speaking colloquial Lebanese Arabic, which he knew beautifully, and I, an American-trained linguist who had studied a variety of modern dialects, spoke modern standard Arabic, since I knew that language better than the other two choices represented. And the conversation was delightful, each of us taking turns in this trialogue about all sorts of subjects.

It is important to realise that there are a few Arabic speech communities where diglossia is unknown. Cypriot Maronite Arabic spoken in Kormakiti, Cyprus, by about 1,200 (as of two decades ago) is one such example as are most dialects of Nigerian and Chadian Arabic.

Perhaps the most striking feature of diglossia is the existence of many paired vocabulary items (the examples are from C.A. Ferguson).

Classical Arabic	*Gloss*	*Egyptian colloquial Arabic*
raʔā	'he saw'	šāf
ħiðāʔun	'shoe'	gazma
ʔanfun	'nose'	manaxīr
ðahaba	'went'	rāħ
mā	'what'	ʔē(h)
ʔalʔāna	'now'	dilwaʔti

To demonstrate how different the modern dialects can be, consider 'now'. In addition to the words cited, Moroccan has *dába*, Algerian *delwóq* or *druk*, Tunisian *tawwa*, Saudi Arabian *daħħīn(a)*, Hassaniyya *dark*, Syrian *hallaʔ*, Nigerian *hatta* or *hassa* or *dātēn*; consider also 'good, well': Moroccan *mizyán* or *wáxxa*, Algerian *mlīeħ*, Syrian-Lebanese *mnīħ*, Libyan *bāhi*, Tunisian *ṭayyab*, Nigerian *zēn* or *ṭayyib*, Egyptian *kuwayyis*. Finally, consider 'nothing': Moroccan *wálu*, Algerian *ši*, Libyan *kān lbarka*, Tunisian *šay*, Saudi Arabian *walašay*, Nigerian *še*. Indeed sometimes it is in the basic everyday vocabulary that one can most easily spot such major distinctions.

To give the linguist somewhat of a feel for this, Ferguson cites the nearest English parallel such as *illumination* vs. *light*, *purchase* vs. *buy*, and *children* vs. *kids*. I should also mention the elegance one can immediately feel when one is invited to *dine* vs. plain 'ole *eat*. The verb *dine* certainly involves higher cost as well as getting dressed up and lovely and expensive surroundings (tablecloth, utensils, décor etc.). 'High' Arabic gives one the feeling of dining at a fine restaurant, whereas 'Low' Arabic is eating the same old thing day in and day out. In addition to the lexical distinctions, there are also different grammatical systems involved in diglossia.

In support of the hypothesis that modern standard Arabic is ill-defined is the so-called 'mixed' language or 'Inter-Arabic' being used in the speeches of, say, President Bourgiba of Tunisia, noting that very few native speakers of Arabic from any Arab country can really ever master the intricacies of Classical Arabic grammar in such a way as to extemporaneously give a formal speech in it. This may perhaps best be illustrated in the use of the Arabic numerals, in which the cardinal numbers from 'three' to 'ten' govern the indefinite genitive plural, but from 'eleven' to 'nineteen' govern the indefinite singular accusative (in addition to being indeclinable, with the exception of 'twelve'), whereas cardinal numbers such as 'one thousand', 'two thousand', 'three thousand', 'million' etc. take the indefinite genitive singular.

9 Nominal Morphology

Modern standard Arabic nouns are inflected for case, determination, gender and number. The function of the noun is usually indicated by short vowel suffixes — /u/ marking nominative, /i/ genitive and /a/ accusative (with added nūnation marking indefiniteness). Thus /kitābun/ 'a book' (nom.), gen. /kitābin/ and acc. /kitāban/ (this is an example of a triptote since it takes all three case endings). Determination is normally handled by the definite article which is /ʔal-/, but it assimilates before the so-called 'sun' letters (*t*, *d*, *θ*, *ð*, *s*, *z*, *ṭ*, *ḍ*, *ṣ*, *ð̣*, *n*, *l*, *r*, *š*) (they are called this because the word /šams/ 'sun' begins with one; all the others are called 'moon' letters because the word /qamar/ 'moon' begins with one). When /ʔal-/ prefixes a noun, there is no longer any reason to have the nūnation since it marks the indefinite, thus /ʔalkitābu/ 'the book' (nom.), with /ʔalkitābi/ (gen.) and /ʔalkitāba/ (acc.) (the /ʔ/ and initial vowel are subject to the rules of elision after vowels).

The diptote noun, which is in the minority when one compares to triptotes, does not take nūnation and merges the accusative *-a* with the genitive, e.g. /ʔaħmadu/ 'Ahmad' (nom.), with gen.-acc. /ʔaħmada/. Many broken (internal) plural patterns are diptotic, as are many proper names, elatives (i.e. comparatives and superlatives), colours and other forms.

Dual and so-called 'sound' (i.e. no morphophonemic alternation) plural suffixes also do not differentiate the genitive and accusative (called 'oblique'). 'Teachers' (m.) is /mudarrisūna/, obl. /mudarrisīna/, f. /mudarrisātun/, obl. /mudarrisātin/. The masculine forms remain the same with the article, but lose the nūnation with the feminine. The dual is marked by /-āni/, obl. /-ayni/; thus 'two teachers' (m.) is /mudarrisāni/, obl. /mudarrisayni/; feminine counterparts are /mudarrisatāni/ and /mudarrisatayni/, respectively.

Gender and number are obligatory grammatical categories. Feminine nouns take feminine concord and government and tend to be overtly marked with /-at/ followed by the case marker, e.g. /mudarrisatun/, pausal form /mudarrisah/ 'teacher'. Very few feminine-marked nouns are masculine, e.g. /xalīfatun/ 'caliph'. Many nouns which are not overtly marked feminine are so, e.g. body parts which occur in pairs (this is common Semitic) such as /riǰlun/ 'foot, leg' and the names of countries and cities; in addition, plurals of irrational beings are treated as feminine singulars.

Mention has already been made of the dual number and the 'sound' masculine and feminine endings. All lose nūnation in a construct state (*status constructus*), which is the normal means of expressing the possessive (genitive) relationship (/kitābu lmaliki/ 'the book of the king' or 'the king's book' — the first member of a construct (called in Arabic /ʔiḍāfa/) has neither the article nor nūnation), e.g. 'the teachers of the school' can be /mudarrisā lmadrasati/ (the second member of a construct state is always in the genitive), obl. /mudarrisay lmadrasati/, f. /mudarrisatā lmadrasati/, obl. /mudarrisatay lmadrasati/, m. pl. /mudarrisū lmadrasati/, obl. /mudarrisī lmadrasati/, f. /mudarrisātu lmadrasati/, obl. /mudarrisāti lmadrasati/.

Most Arabic nouns do not take the sound plurals but have a broken (ablaut) plural, which can involve the addition of prefixes and/or suffixes. There are several dozen possible patterns in common usage and very few are predictable. The three most common broken (sometimes also called 'inner') plural patterns, based on data in the Lane Lexicon, are: (1) $ʔaC_1C_2\bar{a}C_3$, e.g. /lawħun/ 'blackboard', pl. /ʔalwāħun/; (2) $C_1iC_2\bar{a}C_3$, e.g. /raǰulun/ 'man', pl. /riǰālun/; (3) $C_1uC_2\bar{u}C_3$, e.g. /baytun/ 'house', pl. /buyūtun/.

There are many prefixes and suffixes in derivational morphology such as the *nisba* (this is a well-known international linguistic term) /-īyun/, colloquial /-i/, which forms relative adjectives (which is well known since so many different languages have borrowed it, e.g. *Kuwait*, *Kuwaiti*), such as /lubnānīyun/ '(a) Lebanese', colloquial /lubnāni/, f. /lubnānīyatun/, m. pl. /lubnānīyūna/, obl. /lubnānīyīna/, f. pl. /lubnānīyātun/, obl. /lubnānīyātin/. Among the most common (and recognisable, due to loanwords such as 'Muslim') is /m-/, marking nouns of time or place, instruments, active and passive participles and verbal nouns (*maṣdar*), e.g. /maktabun/ 'office', /maktabatun/ 'library', related to /kataba/ 'he wrote', /maktūbun/ 'written', coming to mean 'anything written' or 'letter' (passive participle of Form I), /miftāħun/ 'key', related to /fataħa/ 'he opened'. (Incidentally, since a language like Persian, of the Indo-Iranian family, has borrowed so many Arabic loanwords and since a Persian dictionary is arranged alphabetically and not on the basis of a triconsonantal root, it is safe to say that, due to the statistically high occurrence of /m-/ from Arabic loanwords, /m-/-initial words make up the largest section in a Persian dictionary; thus in F. Steingass, *A Comprehensive Persian-English Dictionary* (Routledge and Kegan Paul Limited, London, 1863) the letter *mīm* (i.e. <m>) runs from pp. 1136 to 1365 — the entire dictionary has 1539 pages.)

10 Verbal Morphology

Some preliminary information on the algebraically predictable verbal system has been mentioned in section 3. Person, mood and aspect are marked by prefixes and suffixes. There are nine derived themes (forms) or stems of the verb plus a basic one, i.e. Form I, yielding a total of ten verbal forms (and five more that are archaic or very rare), each with a 'normal' range of semantic value, e.g. intensivity, causativity, reflexivity etc. Each form has its own set of active and passive particles and verbal nouns (sometimes called 'verbal abstracts'). Further, there is an internal passive for each one of the forms, formed by vocalic change from its corresponding active, in form but often not in meaning (i.e. the forms are therefore hypothetical).

Form I verbs are of three types dependent on the second vowel of the perfect: /qatala/ 'he killed', /ʕalima/ 'he knew', and /ħasuna/ 'he was good'. /i/ in the perfect usually marks an intransitive verb, denoting often a temporary state; /u/ in the perfect usually marks an intransitive verb expressing a permanent state.

Form II is formed by geminating the second radical of the root so that the verb functions like a quadriradical (statistically these are in the very small minority of roots, e.g. /tarjama/ 'he translated'), e.g. /ʕallama/ 'he taught'. Among the meanings of Form II are: (1) intensiveness, /kasara/ 'he broke' vs. /kassara/ 'he smashed'; (2) iterative, /qaṭaʕa/ 'he cut' vs. /qaṭṭaʕa/ 'he cut up'; (3) causativity, /ʕallama/ 'he taught' is the causative of /ʕalima/ 'he knew', i.e. 'to cause to know'; (4) estimation, /kaðaba/ 'he lied' vs. /kaððaba/ 'he considered someone a liar'; (5) denominative function, /xaymatun/ 'a tent' yields /xayyama/ 'he pitched a tent'; and (6) transitivity, /nāma/ 'he slept' produces /nawwama/ 'he put to sleep'.

Form III is formed by lengthening the first /a/. The meanings are; (1) reciprocity (directing an action towards somebody), e.g. /kātaba/ 'he corresponded with', /qātala/ 'he fought with and tried to kill'; and (2) the attempt to do something, e.g. from /sabaqa/ 'he preceded' one forms /sābaqa/ 'he competed with' (i.e. 'he attempted to precede').

Form IV is formed by prefixing a glottal stop (= Hebrew /h-/ and Ancient Egyptian /s-/) followed by /a/ and making the first radical vowel-less, e.g. /ǰalasa/ 'he sat (down)' has /ʔaǰlasa/ 'he seated' as its causative. In addition to the (primary) causative meaning, one encounters: (1) a declaration, e.g. /ʔakðaba/ 'he called a liar', related to /kaðaba/ 'he lied'; and (2) a characteristic (used with /mā/ 'how; what' in the third person perfect only), e.g. /mā ʔaħsanahu/ 'how handsome he is!' There are often Form IV verbs with the meaning 'became', e.g. /ʔaṣbaħa/ 'he became' (also /ʔamsā/ and /ʔaḍħā/. Also one finds denominatives of place names, e.g. from /naǰdun/ 'Najd' (north-central Saudi Arabia) one obtains /ʔanǰada/ 'to go to Najd'.

Forms V and VI are passives and reflexives of Forms II and III, respectively, and are both formed by prefixing /ta-/ to those forms. From /ʕallama/ 'he taught' one obtains /taʕallama/ 'he taught himself', i.e. 'he learned' or 'he was taught' (one can understand the verb both ways in terms of English). From /qātala/ and /kātaba/ one obtains /taqātala/ 'to fight each other' and /takātaba/ 'to correspond with each other', respectively. Form VI also denotes a pretence, e.g. from /mariḍa/ 'he was sick' one obtains /tamāraḍa/ 'he pretended to be sick', or from /nāma/ 'he slept' one obtains /tanāwama/ 'he pretended to be asleep' (this is a good example of what is called a 'hollow' verb because a morphophonemic //w// occurs in the root, which manifests itself in Form VI but not in Form I).

Form VII is formed by prefixing a vowel-less /n-/ to Form I. As no morpheme can begin with a vowel-less consonant, an anaptyctic vowel /i/ is inserted and, initially, a prothetic /ʔ/ precedes the /i/ since no morpheme can begin with a vowel. (This is true of Hebrew too, with only one exception.) It is usually the passive or reflexive of Form I, e.g. Form I /kasara/ 'he broke' (transitive) forms Form VII as /ʔinkasara/ 'it broke' (intransitive).

Form VIII, the only infixing form, infixes /-ta-/ between the first and second radicals. As the first radical is vowel-less, it uses the anaptyctic /i/ rule and glottal stop insertion, as did Form VII (see above). It is usually the reflexive of Form I, but contrary to Form VII, it may take a direct object. As examples, one notes: /ʔiktataba/ 'he was registered' and /ʔiqtatala/ 'to fight with one another'. Occasionally, there is no difference in meaning between Forms I and VIII, e.g. /šarā/, imperfect /yašrī/ 'he bought' (Form I) = /ʔištarā/, imperfect /yaštarī/.

Form IX is very restricted semantically, i.e. the meaning revolves around a colour or a physical defect, e.g. /ʔiswadda/ 'he became black' or /ʔiʕwaǰǰa/ 'he became bent'. It is made by geminating the third radical of the root and deleting the vowel of the first radical with the appropriate anaptyctic /i/ and glottal stop insertion (see the remarks for Form VII).

Form X is formed by making the first radical of the root vowel-less and prefixing /sta-/. Like the preceding forms, there is anaptyxis and glottal stop insertion (see the remarks for Form VII). It is the reflexive of Form IV or has to do with asking someone for something (for oneself) in terms of the basic sememe of the root. Also, there is a meaning of consideration. From /ʔaʕlama/ 'he informed' one obtains /ʔistaʕlama/ 'he inquires' (i.e. 'he asks for information for himself'); from /kataba/ 'he wrote' one obtains /ʔistaktaba/ 'he asked someone to write'; from /ħasuna/ 'he was good' one obtains /ʔistaħsana/ 'he considered (as) good'.

The conjugation of a regular verb in the perfect and imperfect (Form I) is shown in the chart given here.

Perfect

1	qataltu 'I killed or have killed'	qatalnā 'we killed'
2	qatalta 'you (m.) killed'	qataltum 'you (m. pl.) killed'
2	qatalti 'you (f.) killed'	qataltunna 'you (f. pl.) killed'
2	qataltumā 'you (m. and f. du.) killed'	
3	qatala 'he killed'	qatalū 'they (m.) killed'
3	qatalat 'she killed'	qatalna 'they (f.) killed'
3	qatalā 'they (m. du.) killed'	qatalatā 'they (f. du.) killed'

Imperfect

1	ʔaqtulu 'I kill, am killing, shall kill'	naqtulu 'we kill'
2	taqtulu 'you (m.) kill'	taqtulūna 'you (m. pl.) kill'
2	taqtulīna 'you (f.) kill'	taqtulna 'you (f. pl.) kill'
2	taqtulāni 'you (du.) kill'	
3	yaqtulu 'he kills'	yaqtulūna 'they (m.) kill'
3	taqtulu 'she kills'	yaqtulna 'they (f.) kill'
3	yaqtulāni 'they (m. du.) kill'	taqtulāni 'they (f. du.) kill'

There are five forms of the imperative of the regular verb: *ʔuqtul* 'kill!'. *ʔuqtulī* 'f. sg.', *ʔuqtulū* 'm. pl.', *ʔuqtulna* 'f. pl.', and *ʔuqtulā* 'du.'.

There are three moods of the imperfect: the indicative (given in the chart of regular verb forms), the subjunctive and the jussive. To form the subjunctive, the basic change is from the *-u* ending to *-a*. Those persons which end with *-na/i* preceded by a long vowel lose that ending after the last radical of the root. The second and third person feminine plural forms are the same in all three moods.

The jussive is formed by apocopating the imperfect indicative, i.e. those persons which end with the last radical of the root lose their final vowel. The other persons are the same as the subjunctive.

Perfect

1	qultu 'I said'	qulnā 'we said'
2	qulta 'you (m.) said'	qultum 'you (m. pl.) said'
2	qulti 'you (f.) said'	qultunna 'you (f. pl.) said'
2	qultumā 'you (m. and f. du.) said'	
3	qāla 'he said'	qālū 'they (m.) said'
3	qālat 'she said'	qulnā 'they (f.) said'
3	qālā 'they (m. du.) said'	qālatā 'they (f. du.) said'

Imperfect

1	ʔaqūlu 'I say'	naqūlu 'we say'
2	taqūlu 'you (m.) say'	taqūlūna 'you (m. pl.) say'
2	taqūlīna 'you (f.) say'	taqulna 'you (f. pl.) say'
2	taqūlāni 'you (du.) say'	
3	yaqūlu 'he says'	yaqūlūna 'they (m.) say'
3	taqūlu 'she says'	yaqulna 'they (f.) say'
3	yaqūlāni 'they (m. du.) say'	taqūlāni 'they (f. du.) say'

The conjugation of a Hollow verb (i.e. one with *w* or *y* as middle radical) is as shown above in the perfect and imperfect (Form I). The forms of the imperative are: *qul*, *qūlī*, *qūlū*, *qulna* and *qūlā*.

11 Verbal Aspect

Many Semitists agree that the semantic system of the Arabic verb is very difficult to examine from an Indo-European perspective. Arabic has a *māḍī* ('past' or generally-called 'perfect' or 'perfective') or suffixed conjugation and a *muḍāriʕ* ('similar to the triptote noun in taking three case endings'; 'imperfect' or 'imperfective' or 'non-past') or prefixed conjugation. The imperfect can refer to present, future and past; the perfect can refer to pluperfect, future or present. The fact that the perfect can refer to the present is illustrated by the following. In a buying-selling transaction, once the event is regarded (in the mind of the speaker) as completed (or 'manifest', to use a Whorfian term), one may say *biʕtuka hāðā* lit. 'I sold (perfect) you this', which means 'I sell you this' or 'I am (now) selling you this'. No money has yet exchanged hands, though. That the imperfect can express a past action is illustrated by the following: *ǰāʔū ʔābāhum yabkūna* lit. 'they came to their father — they will cry', which means 'they came to their father crying' or *ʔatā lʕayna yašrabu* lit. 'he came to the well — he will drink', which means 'he came to the well to drink'.

Few Arabic verbs embody unambiguous time. The great majority of Arabic verbs are either static or dynamic. In English this will often be reflected in a different verb. From the verbal nouns *rukūbun*, the static value is 'ride' — dynamic 'mount'; *ʔiħmirārun*, static 'be red' — dynamic 'turn red'; *ʔiqāmatun* 'reside' and 'settle', respectively; *ħukmun* 'govern' and 'decree', respectively; *ʕilmun* 'know' and 'get to know', respectively.

The colloquial Arabic dialects have felt the need for finer tense distinctions, in addition to the opposition perfect/imperfect, and have developed overt tense markers such as /ħa-/ marking future in Egyptian and other colloquial dialects.

The problem of aspect and tense in Arabic (and in Semitic in general) is one on which much has already been written, but much more research needs to be accomplished before the final answer is in. It remains one of the most debated and hotly-contested aspects of Semitic linguistics. Surely both aspect and (relative) tense are involved.

12 Syntax

Arabic uses a non-verbal construction for some verbs in English, the most notable of which is 'have'. Arabic uses the preposition /li-/ 'to, for' or /ʕinda/ 'with (Fr. *chez*)' for 'have', e.g. /lī kitābun/ or /ʕindī kitābun/ 'I have a book'.

English is more analytical than is Arabic. Thus in English one needs three words to say 'I killed him'. In Arabic, one word renders this sentence, *qataltuhu*. English again needs three words to say 'he is sad'; Arabic /ħazina/, or 'he makes (someone) sad', /ħazana/.

The basic word order for Classical Arabic is VSO, e.g. 'Muħammad went to school' is rendered *ðahaba* ('he went') *muħammadun* ('Muħammad', nom. sg.) *ʔilā* ('to') *lmadrasati* ('the school', gen. sg.). It is possible to begin the sentence with the subject for stylistic reasons; however, if that is done, it is usual to precede the subject with *ʔinna* 'indeed', which then forces the subject to be in the accusative, i.e. *ʔinna muħammadan*. This has been described by what has been called a focus transformation.

Colloquial Arabic dialects are basically SVO (although I think most are, I refrain from saying 'all') and there is now convincing evidence that modern standard Arabic has become SVO as well. D.B. Parkinson has investigated this by examining newspapers such as *Al-Ahrām* and *Al-Akhbār* from 1970–8 and the conclusion is that this change is still in progress. There is evidence too that SVO is the more archaic word order since proverbs may still preserve this Proto-Arabic stage, e.g. *ʔalǰāhilu yaṭlubu lmāla walʕāqilu yaṭlubu lkamāla*, 'the fool seeks wealth, the wise man seeks perfection'.

If the verb precedes its subject, usually it is in the singular (Classical Arabic is more rigid than modern standard Arabic), but if it follows the subject there must be agreement in gender and number, e.g. 'the two men bought a book' *ʔištarā rraǰulāni kitāban* lit. 'he-bought the-two-men (nom. du.) book (acc. sg.)' but *ʔinna rraǰulayni štarayā kitāban* 'indeed the-two-men (obl. du.) they-bought (du. m.) book (acc. sg.)'.

Interrogatives are placed at the beginning of the sentence, e.g. 'where did the teacher study?' *ʔayna* ('where') *darasa* ('he studied') *lmuʕallimu* ('the teacher', nom. sg.).

Two types of clauses have been studied in detail and the first is a hallmark of Arabic. The *ħāl* or circumstantial clause is usually introduced by /wa-/ 'and', which translates into English as 'while' or 'when', e.g. 'he wrote a letter while he was sick' — *kataba* ('he wrote') *maktūban* ('a letter', acc. sg.) *wahuwa* ('and he') *marīḍun* ('sick', nom. sg.) or 'he killed him while/when she was pregnant' — *qatalahu* ('he killed him') *wahiya* ('and she') *ħāmilun* ('pregnant', fem. sg. (but m. in form)). The second is the relative clause, which contains a pronominal reference to the modified noun but no relative pronoun occurs if the modified noun is indefinite, e.g. 'he wrote a book which I read' — *kataba* ('he wrote') *kitāban* ('a book', acc. sg.) *qaraʔtuhu* ('I read it', m. sg.) vs. 'he wrote the book which I read' — *kataba* ('he wrote') *lkitāba* ('the book', acc. sg.) *llaðī* ('which', m. sg.) *qaraʔtuhu* ('I read it').

Arabic sentence structures may be divided into the nominal sentence (usually also referred to as the equational sentence or Ø copula or *ʔalǰumlatu lismiyya* in Arabic) and the verbal sentence. The equational sentence is a favourite sentence type of Arabic. It consists of two parts: a topic or subject

(Arabic *mubtadaʔ*) and a comment or predicate (Arabic *xabar*). The topic is usually a noun or pronoun (or a phrase derived thereof) and the comment is a nominal, pronominal, adjectival, adverbial or prepositional phrase. Consider 'the university library is a beautiful building' — *maktabatu* ('library' in the construct state, nom. indefinite) *lǰāmiʕati* ('the university', gen. sg. definite) *bināʔun* ('building', nom. sg. indefinite) *ǰamīlun* ('beautiful', m. sg. nom. indefinite). Negation of the equational sentence is formed by the irregular verb *laysa* 'not to be', which governs a predicate in the accusative (as any other verb does). The negative of the above illustrative sentence is *laysat maktabatu lǰāmiʕati bināʔan ǰadīdan*.

When the comment of an equational sentence is an adverb or a prepositional phrase and there is an indefinite subject, the normal word order is comment–topic, e.g. '(there is) a book on the table' = *ʕalā* ('on') *lmāʔidati* ('the table', definite gen.) *kitābun* ('a book', indefinite nom.).

With non-present time reference, one finds verbal sentences. The verb 'to be', *kāna* in the perfect, *yakūnu* in the imperfect, occurs in the past and future and governs, like any other verb, the accusative case. The Arab grammarians also put the verb *laysa* 'not to be' into this same verbal category (called 'the sisters' of *kāna*) along with *mā zāla* 'continue to be', *mā ʕāda* 'no longer to be', *kāda* 'be on the verge of'. The following verbs all mean 'to become': *ṣāra, ʔaṣbaħa, bāta, ʔamsā* and *ʔaḍħā* and verbs meaning 'remain' such as *baqiya* also belong to this verbal category.

To illustrate, consider that *kāna tāǰiran* 'he was a merchant' has *tāǰiran* in the indefinite accusative singular, the plural of which is *kānū tuǰǰāran* (*tuǰǰār* is the broken plural of *tāǰir*). *Kāna tāǰirun* means 'there was a merchant'.

A major characteristic of *kāna*-type verbs is that they can govern a following imperfect instead of a noun in the accusative. Thus one can say *lā ʔadrī* 'I do not know' or *lastu* (< *laysa*) *ʔadrī* (lit. 'I am not-I know').

Bibliography

For classical Arabic, Fleisch (1956) is a solid overview, while Wright (1955), though originally published more than a century ago, remains a superbly documented grammar. Bravmann (1953) is one of the best syntaxes available, while for phonetics, Gairdner (1925) is probably one of the finest works ever written on the subject, dealing primarily with Koranic Arabic. Fück (1955) is a most important treatise on the history and development of Classical Arabic.

Pellat (1956) is a very good learner's manual for modern standard Arabic, while Stetkevych (1970) is a solid and thorough investigation of lexical and stylistic developments.

For the modern vernaculars, there are three superb grammars in the same series: Cowell (1964) on Syrian Arabic, Erwin (1963) on Iraqi Arabic and Harrell (1962) on Moroccan Arabic. Mitchell (1956), on Egyptian Arabic, is one of the finest pedagogical grammars ever written. Qafisheh (1977), on Gulf Arabic, is a very fine grammar, based on fieldwork in the Gulf countries, and deals with the vernacular dialects of important emerging countries. For Nigerian Arabic, references may be made to Kaye (1982), a dictionary of 6,000 lexemes with illustrative sentences and a linguistic introduction.

Mitchell (1953) is a very fine treatise on the writing system.

References

Bravmann, M.M. 1953. *Studies in Arabic and General Syntax* (Imprimerie de l'Institut Françąis d'Archéologie Orientale, Cairo)

Cowell, M.W. 1964. *A Short Reference Grammar of Syrian Arabic* (Georgetown University Press, Washington, DC)

Erwin, W.M. 1963. *A Short Reference Grammar of Iraqi Arabic* (Georgetown University Press, Washington, DC)

Fleisch, H. 1956. *L'Arabe classique: esquisse d'une structure linguistique* (Imprimerie Catholique, Beirut)

Fück, J. 1955. *ʿArabīya: Recherches sur l'histoire de la langue et du style arabe* (Marcel Didier, Paris; translated by C. Denizeau, with an introduction by J. Cantineau, from the German original, *Arabīyya: Untersuchungen zur arabischen Sprach- und Stilgeschichte*, Akademie-Verlag, Berlin, 1950)

Gairdner, W.H.T. 1925. *The Phonetics of Arabic* (Oxford University Press, London)

Harrell, R.S. 1962. *A Short Reference Grammar of Moroccan Arabic* (Georgetown University Press, Washington, DC)

Kaye, A.S. 1982. *A Dictionary of Nigerian Arabic* (Undena, Malibu, Calif.)

Mitchell, T.F. 1953. *Writing Arabic: A Practical Introduction to the Ruqʿah Script* (Oxford University Press, London)

—— 1956. *An Introduction to Colloquial Egyptian Arabic* (Oxford University Press, London)

Pellat, C. 1956. *Introduction à l'arabe moderne* (Adrien-Maisonneuve, Paris)

Qafisheh, H.A. 1977. *A Short Reference Grammar of Gulf Arabic* (University of Arizona Press, Tucson)

Stetkevych, J. 1970. *The Modern Arabic Literary Language: Lexical and Stylistic Developments* (University of Chicago Press, Chicago)

Wright, W. 1955. *A Grammar of the Arabic Language*, 3rd ed., 2 vols. (Cambridge University Press, Cambridge)

11 Hebrew

Robert Hetzron

1 Introduction

The importance of the Hebrew language is not to be measured by the number of its speakers at any time of its history. It is the language of the Jewish Bible, the Old Testament of Christians. It also has a very long continuous history. Kept in constant use by Jews from antiquity to modern times, its reformed version, in an unprecedented process of revival, became the official language of a recently created state, the State of Israel.

It is futile to ask whether Modern Hebrew is the same language as the idiom of the Hebrew Bible. Clearly, the difference between them is great enough to make it impossible for the person who knows one to understand the other without effort. Biblical scholars have to study the modern language if they want to benefit from studies written in Hebrew today and Israelis cannot properly follow Biblical passages without having studied them at school. Yet a partial understanding is indeed possible and the similarities are so obvious that calling them separate languages or two versions of the same tongue would be an arbitrary, only terminological decision.

Impressive as the revival of Hebrew as a modern language may be, one ought not to have an exaggerated impression of its circumstances. Since Biblical times, Hebrew has never been a dead language. True, it ceased to be a spoken language used for the 'pass me the salt' type of everyday communication, but it has been cultivated — applied not only to liturgy and passive reading of old texts, but also to correspondence, creative writing and, occasionally, conversation. Actually, it was so extensively used for writing that the language, through this medium, underwent all the changes and developments which are characteristic of a living language. The revival in Israel made it again an everyday colloquial tongue, also for all lay purposes.

2 The Script

Hebrew is written from right to left. This is essentially a consonantal script.

(In the following, capital letters will be used for the transliteration of Hebrew letters). A word like *šibbōlɛŧ* (*shibboleth*) 'ear of corn' is written in four letters *ŠBLT*. Yet, long *ū* and *ī* (but not long *ā* > *ō*) are indicated by the letters otherwise marking semi-vowels: *W* and *Y* respectively. Moreover, the original diphthongs **aw* and **ay*, which were legitimately represented by *W* and *Y* in the consonantal transcription, were mostly reduced to *ō* and *ē*, yet they kept their *W* and *Y* symbols, making these trivalent symbols for semi-vowels and both closed and mid labial and palatal vowels respectively. Thus, the word which was originally **hawbi:lu:* 'they carried', Biblical *hō*^{w}*ƀī*^{y}*lū*^{w}, modern /hov'ilu/, is written *HWBYLW*. Two more facts need to be added. The *aleph*, originally a symbol for the glottal stop *ʔ*, has been maintained in the orthography even after the *ʔ* ceased to be pronounced. Word-final *-H* was pronounced in a few cases only, otherwise the letter stands as a dummy symbol after a final vowel *-ɛ/-ē* or, more frequently, after final *-ā̊*. This latter is most often a feminine ending. The use of *-H* here preserves the second stage of the phonetic development of this ending: **-at* → *-āh* → *ā̊*.

These originally consonantal letters used for partial vowel marking are traditionally called *mātrēs lectiōnis* 'mothers (= helping devices) of reading'. I transcribe them with raised letters.

The old Hebrew consonantal script, practically identical with the Phoenician one, was gradually replaced, beginning at the end of the sixth century BC, by an Aramaic script which, through the centuries to come, evolved into what is known today as the Jewish 'square' script, the standard print. From the second century BC on, graphically more or less different cursive systems further developed for casual handwriting. Two of these are still in use today: the modern cursive and a calligraphic development of the so-called Mashait cursive, the latter used today chiefly for printing the commentaries on the Bible and the Talmud of the eleventh-century Jewish scholar, Rashi (hence the name 'Rashi script').

Table 11.1 presents the consonantal letters of the major alternative scripts. Note that the letters *K*, *M*, *N*, *P* and *Ṣ* have special 'final' versions when they occur at the end of the word. These are parenthesised in the table. The names represent the Modern Hebrew pronunciation, as they are currently used. In the transcription column, the capital letter stands for the transliteration of the script, the letters after '~' show the Modern Hebrew pronunciation. These letters may serve as number symbols up to four hundred. They may be combined — thus *KZ* stands for 'twenty-seven', *RMḤ* for 'two hundred and forty-eight' etc.

Writing systems that transcribe words incompletely or inconsistently (English is an example of the latter) may be viewed as basically mnemonic devices rather than truly efficient scripts. With the decline of Hebrew as a spoken tongue, the introduction of vowel symbols and other diacritics became necessary. In order not to alter the original sacred, consonantal texts, this was done by means of added symbols, dots or other reduced-size

Table 11.1: The Consonantal Letters

Phoenician (=Old Hebrew)	*Jewish Square* (modern print)	*Rashi*	*Cursive* (modern)	*Name*	*Transcription*	*Numerical Value*
𐤀	א	א	א	alef	ʔ	1
𐤁	ב	ב	ב	bet	*B*; *b*, *ƀ*~*v*	2
𐤂	ג	ג	ג	g'imel	*G*; *g*, *ǥ*	3
𐤃	ד	ד	ד	d'alet	*D*; *d*, *đ*	4
𐤄	ה	ה	ה	he	*H*; *h*	5
𐤅	ו	ו	ו	vav	*W*; *w*~*v*, *u*, *o*	6
𐤆	ז	ז	ז	z'ayin	*Z*; *z*	7
𐤇	ח	ח	ח	xet	*Ḥ*; *ḥ*~*x*	8
𐤈	ט	ט	ט	tet	*Ṭ*; *ṭ*~*t*	9
𐤉	י	י	י	yod	*Y*; *y*, *i*, *e*	10
𐤊	כ(ך)	כ(ך)	כ(ך)	kaf	*K*; *k*, *ꝁ*~x	20
𐤋	ל	ל	ל	l'amed	*L*; *l*	30
𐤌	מ(ם)	מ(ם)	מ(ם)	mem	*M*; *m*	40
𐤍	נ(ן)	נ(ן)	נ(ן)	nun	*N*; *n*	50
𐤎	ס	ס	ס	s'amex	*S*; *s*	60
𐤏	ע	ע	ע	'ayin	ʿ	70
𐤐	פ(ף)	פ(ף)	פ(ף)	pe	*P*; *p*, *ᵽ*~*f*	80
𐤑	צ(ץ)	צ(ץ)	צ(ץ)	tsade	*Ṣ*; *ṣ*~*c*(=*ts*)	90
𐤒	ק	ק	ק	qof	*Q*; *q*~*k*	100
𐤓	ר	ר	ר	resh	*Ṛ*; *r*	200
𐤔	ש	ש	ש	shin	*Š*; *š*	300
𐤕	ת	ת	ת	tav	*T*; *t*, *ŧ*~*t*	400

designs placed under, above and in some cases in the centre of the consonantal letters. These were always considered optional supplements, omissible at will. There were several such systems, chiefly the Babylonian and the Tiberian vocalisations; the latter alone is now used. The introducers of these systems are called Masoretes, the 'carriers of tradition', who carried out their work between AD 600 and 1000.

In the Tiberian Masoretic system, for example, a dot over the top left corner of a letter indicates *ō*, and if a *W* had traditionally been used for the same sound, the dot is placed over the *W*, to distinguish it from *ū*, which has the dot in the middle. Dots in the middle of consonantal letters other than those marking laryngeals and, with some exceptions, *r* may mark gemination, doubling of the consonant. Yet, in the beginning of syllables, a dot in *B*, *G*, *D*, *K*, *P*, *T* (this is the traditional order of listing) means that they are to be pronounced as stops; absence of dot points at the spirantised articulation, *β* or *v*, etc. (see below). A dot in a final *h* indicates that it is to be pronounced and is not a mere dummy symbol, a tradition that has usually not been observed.

One diacritic symbol is used for a true phonemic distinction. Hebrew has separate letters for *Š* and *S*, but in some cases, the former is read [s] as well.

To mark this, the *Š* symbol was supplemented with a dot in the right top corner for [š] and on the left for [s]. This latter is usually transcribed *ś* and represents an original separate phoneme, a lateral fricative.

The vocalic notation was brilliantly constructed, yet it is not always perfectly adequate for all traditional pronunciations. A small T-shaped symbol underneath a consonant usually stands for a long *å̄* but in some cases, in syllables that were originally closed, it may be a short *å* (< **u*), see the beginning of section 4.1. Two vertically aligned dots underneath a letter, called 'shwa', may indicate lack of vowel or, at the beginning of the word or after another shwa (and in some other cases), an ultrashort sound [ə]. After laryngeals, there are 'tainted shwas', ultrashort *ă*, *ĕ* and *å̆* (*ŏ*). At the end of the word, lack of vowel is indicated by lack of any vowel symbol, though final shwa is written in some grammatical endings under -*T* (with a dot in the middle) and always in a final -*K*.

The vowel symbol is supposed to be read after the consonantal letter to which it is attached, except in word-final *Ḥ*, ʿ and dotted *H* with an *A* underneath, where the vowel sounds first. This is called a 'furtive *a*', a euphonic development.

Table 11.2 illustrates the use of vowels and other diacritic symbols, traditionally called 'pointing'.

As we have seen, the Biblical Hebrew script was not exclusively

Table 11.2: The Pointing

A. The dot in the consonant (*dagesh*)

a. Spirantisation.

ŧ ת, *t* תּ ; *ᵽ* פ(ף), *p* פּ ; *ꝁ* כ(ך), *k* כּ(ךּ) ; *đ* ד, *d* דּ ; *ǥ* ג, *g* גּ ; *ƀ* ב, *b* בּ

b. Gemination.

...*qq* קּ ...*mm* מּ ...*ww* וּ ...*bb* בּ

B. The letter *Š*.

ś שׂ , *š* שׁ

C. The vowels (combined with various consonants).

Long		*Short*	*Ultrashort*
	ṭå̄ טָ	*ṭa* טַ	*ʿă* עֲ
lē^{y} לֵי	*lē* לֵ	*lɛ* לֶ	*ʔĕ* אֱ
mō^{w} מוֹ	*rō* רֹ	*ṣå* צָ	*ḥå̆* חֳ
tī^{y} תִי		*si* סִ	*zə*, *z* זְ
	nū^{w} נוּ	*nu* נֻ	

consonantal. The *mātrēs lectiōnis* indicated some of the vowels. The use of these was later extended. Already in Late Biblical Hebrew, we find *W* also for *ō* that does not come from **aw*. In Modern Hebrew, except for some very frequent words and common patterns (where a certain degree of convention has still been maintained), *W* may be used for any /u/ or /o/, and *Y* for any /i/.

In modern practice, consistent vowel marking is restricted to Biblical texts, poetry, dictionaries and children's books. Otherwise, only the consonantal script is used, with fuller application of *mātrēs lectiōnis* and with occasional strategically placed vowel symbols to avoid potential ambiguities. It should be noted that the duality of 'obligatory' *W*'s and *Y*'s sanctified by tradition and 'optional' ones which may appear in unvocalised texts only is very confusing to the student of Modern Hebrew. Another serious problem, for native Israelis too, is that no consistent system has been worked out for the transcription of foreign words and names. Some conventions do exist, such as *G* with an apostrophe marking [ǰ], non-final *P* in word-final positions for final *-p*; yet this is insufficient, and many such words are often mispronounced.

It should be added that the texts of the Old Testament print cantillation marks (some above, some beneath the word) which note the melodic pattern to be used in chanting the texts in the synagogue service. Their exact position provides a clue to stress in Biblical Hebrew.

Table 11.3 reproduces part of verse 24 in chapter 13 of the book of Nehemiah. First the consonantal text is presented, then the same with full pointing.

Table 11.3: Part of Nehemiah 13.24

ואינם מכירים לדבר יהודית

Transliteration: WʔYNM MKYRYM LDBR YHWDYT

וְאֵינָם מַכִּירִים לְדַבֵּר יְהוּדִית

Transliteration: wəʔē^{y}n'ā̊m makkī^{y}r'ī^{y}m ləđabb'er yəhū^{w}đ'ī^{y}ŧ

Translation: 'and-they-do-not know [how]-/to/speak Judean'

---

3 The Periods of Hebrew

Hebrew may be historically divided into distinct periods on the basis of grammar and vocabulary.

3.1 Pre-Biblical Hebrew

Hebrew is a Canaanite language, closely related to Phoenician. It is even likely that its northern dialect barely differed from Phoenician. There exist Canaanite documents from the mid-twentieth century to the twelfth century BC, transcribed in Akkadian and Egyptian documents. It is hard to assess their exact relationship to the contemporary ancestor of Hebrew, but the two may be assumed to be identical in essence. Case endings and other archaic elements in phonology and morphology are found here. The most important source of these data are fourteenth-century BC letters found in Tell el-Amarna, Egypt.

3.2 Biblical Hebrew

This is the most important period, documented through the Old Testament (note that substantial portions of the books of Daniel and Ezra are in Aramaic). This collection of texts spans over a millennium-long period (1200–200 BC). The literary dialect was based on southern (Judean) Hebrew, though the northern dialect of some authors does show through. It is wrong to think of Biblical Hebrew as a homogeneous dialect. It covers different places and periods.

This heterogeneity, in particular the coexistence of doublets (e.g. a dual tense system for the verb, see below), led some scholars to declare that Biblical Hebrew was a *Mischsprache*, a mixed language, representing the coalescence of the speech of Israelites arriving from Egypt and of the local Canaanites. Yet the doublets attested do not seem to be particularly exceptional in the history of standard dialects.

It is customary to speak of Early Biblical Hebrew (the Pentateuch, Joshua, Judges, Samuel, Kings, the prophetic books) and Late Biblical Hebrew (Chronicles, Song of Songs, Esther etc.) but this is a simplification. The Song of Deborah (Judges 5) is considered to be the oldest text. In several books one finds traces of their having been compiled from different sources. Poetic texts such as the Psalms, the Song of Songs and poetic inserts elsewhere have their own lexical and grammatical features.

It should also be remembered that no matter how rich the material contained in the Hebrew Bible may be, no document of even that length may represent the full riches of a living language. We shall never know the true dimensions of Biblical Hebrew as spoken at that time.

Biblical Hebrew ceased to be spoken at some unspecified time (the destruction of the First Temple of Jerusalem in 586 BC may have been a major factor), yielding to Mishnaic Hebrew (see below) and Aramaic. The very last period of written Late Biblical Hebrew extends, however, into the Christian era, as represented by texts found in Qumran, known as the Dead Sea Scrolls.

One should thus keep in mind that what is described under the label 'Biblical Hebrew' is basically hybrid material: text in a consonantal script from between 1200–200 BC, while the pointing (vowels, indication of stress, gemination, spirantisation) comes from a much later date (after AD 600), when even the next stage of Hebrew, Mishnaic, had long ceased to be spoken. True, the pointing is based on authentic tradition, but certain distortions through the centuries were unavoidable.

3.3 Mishnaic Hebrew

This dialect represents the promotion into a written idiom of what was probably the spoken language of Judea during the period of Late Biblical Hebrew (sixth century BC) and on. It ceased to be spoken around AD 200, but survived as a literary language till about the fifth century AD. It is the language of the Mishnah, the central book of the Talmud (an encyclopedic collection of religious, legal and other texts), of some of the older portions of other Talmudic books and of parts of the Midrashim (legal and literary commentaries on the Bible).

3.4 Medieval Hebrew

This was never a spoken language, yet it is the carrier of a rich literary tradition. It was used by Jews scattered by now around the Mediterranean world, for poetry (both religious and secular), religious discussions, philosophy, correspondence etc. The main spoken languages of Jews from that time on were varieties of Arabic, Spanish (later Judaeo-Spanish, Ladino) and Judaeo-German (Yiddish). The earliest layer of Medieval Hebrew is the language of the *Piyyuṭ*, poetry written for liturgical use from the fifth to sixth centuries. After a period of laxity, the great religious leader of Babylon, Saadiah Gaon (892–942), heralded a new epoch in the use of Hebrew. This reached its culmination in the Hebrew poetry in Spain (1085–1145). The eleventh to fifteenth centuries saw a richness of translations into Hebrew, mainly from Arabic. The style developed by Jews of eastern France and western Germany, who later moved to eastern Europe, is known as Ashkenazic Hebrew, the written vehicle of speakers of Yiddish. The origin of the Ashkenazic pronunciation as known today is unclear; the earliest Ashkenazim did not have it.

The Medieval Hebrew period ended along with the Middle Ages, with the cessation of writing Hebrew poetry in Italy. In the interim period that followed, Hebrew writing was confined to religious documents.

3.5 Modern Hebrew

Even though Spanish and Italian Hebrew poetry did treat non-religious topics, it was the period of Enlightenment (Hebrew *Haskalah*, from 1781 on) that restored the use of Hebrew as a secular language. This led to important changes in style and vocabulary. Words denoting objects, persons, happenings of modern life were developed. Hebrew was becoming a European language. This development was concentrated in eastern

Europe, with Warsaw and Odessa as the most important centres. The great writer Mendele Moikher Sforim (Sh. J. Abramowitz, 1835–1917) was perhaps the most important and most brilliant innovator. Hebrew began to be spoken regularly only with the establishment of Jewish settlements in Palestine, mainly from Russia. In this revolutionary development, Eliezer Ben-Yehuda (1858–1922) played the most important role as the initiator and leader of the movement. His first son, Itamar Ben-Avi, was the first native speaker of Modern Hebrew. Ben-Yehuda brought many innovations to the Hebrew language. The type of Hebrew developed for speech adopted the Sephardic pronunciation as uttered by an Ashkenazi. In 1922, Hebrew became one of the official languages of Palestine under the British Mandate. Hebrew literature, now transplanted to the Holy Land, experienced an impressive upsurge. With the creation of the State of Israel (1948), the status of Modern Hebrew as the national language was firmly established. Modern Hebrew has been to a great extent regulated by the Academy of the Hebrew Language. On the other hand, native speakers have become a majority in Israel, many of them children of native speakers themselves. In order to express themselves, they do not consult grammars and official decisions, but create their own style, their own language, based on the acquired material modified according to the universal laws of linguistic evolution. This dialect, Spoken Israeli Hebrew, itself a multi-layered complex entity, has not yet been systematically described, but its existence has been noted and its importance acknowledged. Israeli Hebrew has about four million speakers.

4 The Structure of Hebrew

In the following, emphasis will be placed on the culturally most important dialect, Biblical Hebrew. When warranted, indications will be given of parallel phenomena in later periods. Modern Hebrew data will be quoted below in phonemic transcription, between /oblique strokes/.

4.1 Phonology

There are many traditional schools of pronunciation for Hebrew. That of Biblical Hebrew is only a reconstruction. It is customary to divide the numerous traditions into two major trends: Sephardi(c) (Mediterranean), and Ashkenazi(c) (Central and Eastern European). The most striking differences between these are the pronunciation of *å̄* as Seph. *a* vs. Ashk. *o* (but short *å* is realised as *o* even in the Sephardic tradition) and *θ* as Seph. *t* vs. Ashk. *s*. To a declining extent *ḥ* and *ʿ* have been preserved in Sephardic only, vs. Ashk. *x* and zero respectively.

For consonants, in the laryngeal domain, the Semitic sounds *γ* and *ʿ* are represented by the single letter *ʿ*, and *x* and *ḥ* also by a single *Ḥ* in the Biblical Hebrew consonantal script. The emphatic consonants of Biblical Hebrew: *ṭ*, *ṣ*, *q* (or *ḳ*) may have been pronounced glottalised (though there is no explicit proof of this). Today, there is no feature 'emphasis' and the three consonants are realised respectively /t/, /c/ (=*ts*) and /k/. Thus, only the middle one remained a separate entity, the other two are pronounced the same way as original *t* and *k*.

Except for the laryngeals *ʔ*, *ʿ*, *h*, *ḥ* and *r* (this one may have been at some time a uvular, since it belongs to this class), all consonants may be single or double (geminate) in Biblical Hebrew. Gemination disappeared from Modern Hebrew. Moreover, in the Masoretic tradition, the stops *b*, *d*, *g*, *p*, *t*, *k* were spirantised respectively into *β*, *ð*, *γ*, *f*, *θ*, *x* in a post-vocalic, non-geminate position, e.g. *bayiθ* 'house', *bəβayiθ* 'in a house', vs. *babbayiθ* 'in the house', *bắttīʸm* 'houses'. As can be seen, alternations within the root have resulted from this conditioned spirantisation. Some incongruities in the system (such as 'houses' with a geminate after an apparently long vowel, *habbayθắh* '(to) home' with *θ* after a diphthong) make the phonemic status of both vocalic length and spirantisation rather unclear. Therefore, a non-committal transcription *ƀ*, *đ* etc., rather than the independent symbols *β*, *γ*, etc., will be used below. Modern Hebrew has only the alternations /b/~/v/, /p/~/f/ and /k/~/x/.

The vowel system, as noted by the Masoretes, does have its problems. As just mentioned, the phonemicity of vowel length is debatable. This is why it is advisable to use the macron and not the modern symbol 'ː' to mark this questionable length. Yet it is clear that vocalic length was once indeed present in the Biblical Hebrew system and played an important role in it.

It seems that at some point of its history, Hebrew equalised the length of all full-vowelled syllables (other than *ə*). Already in Proto-Semitic, long vowels could occur in open syllables only. Now, all vowels in an open syllable became either long: **a* > *å̄*, **i* > *ē*, **u* > *ō*, or *ə*. Short vowels were confined to closed syllables. However, word-final short vowels with grammatical functions survived for a while. The subsequent loss of these, which made a CV̄CV# sequence into CV̄C#, did not occasion the shortening of V̄, even though the syllable became closed. This produced minimal pairs such as *zắƙar* 'he remembered' (from **zakar*) vs. *zắƙår* 'male' (from **zakar* + case ending).

The ultrashort vowel *ə* caused spirantisation of a subsequent non-emphatic stop. After laryngeals, it has the allophones: ultrashort *ă*, *ĕ* and *ŏ*, selected according to the context, mainly on a harmony principle. The vowel [ə] is called *shwa mobile* in contrast with *shwa quiescens*, i.e. lack of vowel, which is marked by the same diacritic symbol. From the written sign's point of view, the shwa is supposed to be pronounced (mobile) after the first consonant of a word, after a consonant cluster or a geminate and, in principle, after a long vowel; the shwa symbol stands for zero (quiescent) elsewhere. However, in some cases, a traditionally quiescent shwa does spirantise the subsequent stop (as it comes from an original short vowel). This is called *shwa medium*.

Vocalic reductions producing shwas would occur when suffixes were added: *då̄ƀå̄r* 'thing, word', pl. *dəƀå̄rīʸm*; *dibbɛr* 'he spoke', pl. *dibbərūʷ*.

Modern Hebrew gave up all length distinction and simplified the system. Shwa is pronounced (as /e/) only when otherwise an unpronounceable cluster would result.

Because of the tightly regulated syllable structure (only aggravated by some loop-holes), it is impossible to decide which one(s) of the following features: spirantisation, vocalic length, gemination and shwa were phonemically relevant in Biblical Hebrew. By dropping length, Modern Hebrew unequivocally phonemicised spirantisation: BH *så̄ᵽar* 'he counted' and MH *sappå̄r* 'barber' respectively became Modern Hebrew /safar/ and /sapar/.

Biblical Hebrew stress fell on one of the last two syllables of the word. In many cases it can be shown that final stress occurs when a word-final short open vowel had disappeared. Hence it was assumed that Proto-Hebrew had uniform penultimate stress. Yet, in other cases of final stress no such development may be posited, e.g. *ʔatt'å̄ʰ* 'thou (m.)', *dibbər'ūʷ* 'they (m.) spoke'. It is then possible that originally the placement of the stress was not conditioned, but may have been functionally relevant (see the discussion of the tense system below). In transcription, only penultimate stress is traditionally marked, not the final one.

A remarkable feature of Biblical Hebrew is the existence of 'pausal' forms. At the end of sentences, many words have special shapes, e.g. contextual/pausal: (a) *šå̄mərūʷ/šå̄m'å̄rūʷ* 'they guarded'; (b) *k'ɛ̄lɛƀ/k'å̄lɛƀ* 'dog', *b'ɛ̄ǥɛđ/b'å̄ǥɛđ* 'clothing'; (c) *m'ayim/m'å̄yim* 'water', *bå̄ṭ'aḥtå̄/bå̄ṭ'å̄ḥtå̄* 'you (m. sg.) trusted'; (d) *yiŧhall'ēꝁ/yiŧhall'å̄ꝁ* 'he walks about'; (e) *wa-y-y'å̄måŧ/wa-y-yå̄m'ōŧ* 'he died'. Though the pausal form of (a) and (d) have archaic vowels, it would be wrong to view the pausal shapes as simple survivals, especially in the domain of stress. They contain melodic signals of terminality, an artistic-expressive procedure. The basic principle was that stress, or rather the melismatic tune, fell on the last vowel of the word that was followed by a consonant. This refers to the period when pausal chanting was adopted. Thus, the penultimate vowel of (a) was saved from later reduction. The penultimate stress in (e) was brought to the end. In 'water' in (c), the *i* was not syllabic (**maym*). In (b), an epenthetic *ɛ* was added. With few exceptions, the melismatic syllable had to be long, thus original short vowels were lengthened. The retention of the original vowel in (d) needs clarification. Example (b) shows that we do not have here mere archaisms: 'dog' used to be **kalb-* indeed, and the *å̄* may be viewed as a survival; yet 'clothing' was **bigd-*, and the pausal *å̄* is only the result of a secondary lengthening of the *ɛ*.

4.2 Grammar

The Semitic root-and-pattern system (see the chapter on Semitic languages, pages 165–6) was complicated in Hebrew by the alternations introduced by spirantisation as imposed on root consonants according to position. Thus, the root *K-P-R* has, among others, the following manifestations: *kå̄p̄ar* (MoH /kafar/) 'he denied', *yik̄pōr* (MoH /yixpor/) 'he will deny'; *kippɛr* (MoH /kiper/) 'he atoned', *yək̄appēr* (MoH /yexaper/) 'he will atone'.

Inspired by their Arab colleagues, Hebrew grammarians adopted the practice of marking patterns by means of the 'dummy' root *P-ʿ-L* ('do, act' in real usage), e.g. *puʿʿal* means a form where the first root consonant is followed by an *u*, the second one is doubled and is followed by an *a*.

In the verbal system, seven derivational classes (*binyanim* 'structures') are to be distinguished: (I) *på̄ʿal* or *qal*, the basic form (with a special subclass where the non-past has the thematic vowel *a* instead of the usual *ō*); (II) *nip̄ʿal* (marked by a prefix *n-*, assimilated to the first radical after a prefix), a passive of I if transitive, always an intransitive verb itself, occasionally inchoative; (III) *piʿʿēl* (with gemination of the middle radical), originally an iterative (for repeated actions), denominative and some other functions (often vaguely labelled 'intensive'); (IV) *puʿʿal*, the passive of III; (V) *hip̄ʿī̄l*, originally a causative; (VI) *håp̄ʿal*, later *hup̄ʿal*, the passive of V and (VII) *hit̄paʿʿēl*, a reflexive or reciprocal, from Medieval Hebrew on, also a passive of III and with some more functions. Note that the derivational 'meanings' are not always to be taken literally. From the transitive *binyanim* I, III and V, passive II, IV and VI may be freely formed, but a II verb does not necessarily come from I. V may be the causative of I only when sanctioned by attestation in the sources; it is thus not productive. IV and VI have only restricted, mainly participial uses from Medieval Hebrew on. Some other derivational forms are occasionally found as archaisms or innovations.

In Biblical Hebrew the passive may have the syntax of an impersonal: *lōʔ yēʔåk̄ēl ʔɛθ bəśårōʷ* (Exodus 21.28) 'not will-be-eaten acc. its-flesh' = 'its flesh will not be eaten', where an object prefix precedes what should be the subject of the passive (or the object of the corresponding active).

The weak-root classes are designated by means of two letters, first which radical is weak (using the *P-ʿ-L* system) and then specifying the weak consonant which might disappear or be transformed in the conjugation. Thus *P:y* means that the *first* radical is a *y*. The main classes, beside regular (strong) roots, are: *P:y* (with two subgroups), *P:n*, *P:ʔ*, *ʿ:w*, *ʿ:y*, *L:y* (often named *L:h* because the grapheme *H* is used here when there is no suffix), *L:ʔ*, and *ʿ:ʿ* (verbs where the last two radicals are identical). For all these roots, the conjugation presents some special features in the various tenses and *binyanim*. When *ʿ* or *ḥ* is one of the radicals, changes occur in the vocalisation.

The tense system is among the most controversial and the most variable through the periods of Hebrew. The heterogeneity of Biblical Hebrew manifests itself the most strikingly precisely here.

It seems that the archaic system may be reduced to a dual opposition of two tenses (the traditional label 'aspect' for these is unjustified and rests on indefensible arguments): past and non-past (present and future in one, though the beginnings of a separate present already show), appearing in different guises in two main contexts: sentence-initial and non-initial. The jussive (the volitive mood, order, imperative, subjunctive) is homonymous with the non-past in most, but not all verb classes.

Like Semitic in general, Hebrew has a prefix conjugation and a suffix conjugation. In non-initial contexts (when a noun, a conjunction or an adverb opens the clause, in negation etc.), the former is a non-past (present-future) and a jussive (imperative) and the latter a past. Note that occasionally, and almost always cooccurring with a coordinated suffix form, the prefix form may stand for repeated, habitual actions in the past. This is a deviation from a straightforward pattern, yet it does not qualify for analysis as aspect. Sentence-initially, on the other hand, a prefix form preceded by *wa* + gemination of the next consonant (except when there is *yə-*) expresses the past and the suffix form preceded by *wə-*, with final stress in the first person singular and second person singular masculine (instead of a penultimate one) is non-past, actually very often a jussive because of the nature of the text. The following is a tabular representation of the four basic tense forms and the jussive, using two roots: *Q-W-M*, a *ʿ:w* root used here in the *paʿal* for 'get up', and *D-B-R* in the *piʿʿēl* 'speak, talk', in the second person singular masculine, with the prefix *t-* or suffix *-tå̄*.

<table>
<tr><th></th><th>Sentence-initial</th><th>Non-initial</th></tr>
<tr><td>Past</td><td>wa-t-t'å̄qåm, wa-t-tədabb'ēr</td><td>q̱'amtå̄, dibb'artå̄</td></tr>
<tr><td>Non-past</td><td>wə-qamt'å̄, wə-dibbart'å̄</td><td>tåq'ūʷm, tədabb'ēr</td></tr>
<tr><td>Jussive</td><td colspan="2">tå̄q'ōm, tədabb'ēr</td></tr>
</table>

For *D-B-R* there is syncretism, only one type of prefix form, but the stress difference is found in the suffix forms. For *Q-W-M*, the non-initial non-past has a long *ūʷ* (from an older **taqu:m-u* with an indicative ending), whereas the initial past and the jussive have a vowel with no *māter lectiōnis* in the same position (the differentiation *å/ō* is secondary). It is important to notice that this verb class exhibits a stress difference between the otherwise homonymous prefix past and the jussive. This suggests that the position of the stress must have been relevant in Proto-Hebrew (and in Proto-Semitic): **y'aqum* 'he got up'/**yaq'um* 'let him get up' (cf. **yaq'u:m-u* 'he gets up'), a distinction that must have disappeared in the other verb classes.

This dual system may be explained by the assumption that in the literary dialect an archaic system became amalgamated with an innovative one. Then, the latter 'non-initial' system prevailed and became the only one in later periods of Hebrew (complemented by a new present tense). The 'initial' system had preserved the original decadent prefix-conjugated past, reinforcing it with an auxiliary of the new type: **haway(a)* 'was', later reduced to *wa-:-*, to avoid confusion with the new non-past that had become completely homophonous with it in most verb classes. As for the *wə-*+suffix form for non-past and jussive, this may have been more or less artificially created to make the system symmetrical. The fact that the two systems were distributed according to position in the sentence is not hard to explain. Proto-Hebrew must have had a stricter VSO order, whereas Biblical Hebrew shows gradual relaxation of this and the slow emergence of SVO. Thus, the old morphology was associated with the old word order and the new morphology with the new word order.

The opposite roles of prefix and suffix conjugations in the two contexts inspired the term 'converted tenses' for those preceded by *w-*, itself called 'waw conversive'. The term 'waw consecutive' is still very common, based on the contestable assumption that for its origin it is to be identified with the conjunction *wə* 'and' used as a link with what precedes, in a system where the verb is claimed to express aspect with relation to the preceding sentence, rather than tense. This is untenable. Secondarily, however, and independently of tense use, the conversive *waw* came indeed to be identified by the speakers of Biblical Hebrew as a conjunction, an understandable case of popular etymology, hence the creation of the *wə-*+suffix forms, and, more importantly, the use of the true conjunction *wə-* 'and' in the beginning of sentences, even texts (e.g. the beginning of Exodus vs. the beginning of Deuteronomy), as a stylistic convention, before nouns, demonstratives etc. as well.

After late Biblical Hebrew, the converted (*w*-marked) forms disappeared. Beginning already in Biblical Hebrew, the active participle gradually took over the expression of the present. The prefix forms were restricted to the function of jussive in Medieval Hebrew (which used a periphrastic expression for the future), but were revived also as a future in subsequent periods. 'Was' plus the active participle has been used as a habitual past from Medieval Hebrew on.

Since conjugation fully specifies the subject in the prefix and suffix conjugations, no subject pronoun is required in the first and second persons. On the other hand, the active participle as a present form expresses in itself gender and number only, so that the cooccurrence of an explicit subject, noun or pronoun, is necessary. In Modern Hebrew, a third person pronoun is required in all tenses in the absence of a nominal subject. A third person plural masculine form without any pronoun or nominal subject is used as an impersonal: /hem amru/ 'they said', but /amru/ 'one said, it was said'. The first person distinguishes no gender.

Shown in the chart is the conjugation of the root *K-T-B* 'write' (*pa'al*) in Modern Hebrew. Note the alternation due to spirantisation /k/ ~ /x/. In verb-final position, only /v/ may represent *B*. In literary usage, past pl. 2 m./f. /ktavt'em/ktavt'en/ and pl. 2 = 3 f. /tixt'ovna/ are also attested. These continue the classical forms.

	Past		*Future*	
	Masculine	Feminine	Masculine	Feminine
Sg. 1.	kat'avti		ext'ov	
2.	kat'avta	kat'avt	tixt'ov	tixtev'i
3.	kat'av	katv'a	yixt'ov	tixt'ov
Pl. 1.	kat'avnu		nixt'ov	
2.	kat'avtem	kat'avten	tixtev'u	
3.	katv'u		yixtev'u	

	Present = Active Participle		*Passive Participle* ('written')	
	Masculine	Feminine	Masculine	Feminine
Sg.	kot'ev	kot'evet	kat'uv	ktuv'a
Pl.	kotv'im	kotv'ot	ktuv'im	ktuv'ot

Infinitive lixt'ov   Verbal Noun ktiv'a ('(the) writing')

In the nominal system, a distinction is made between a masculine and a feminine gender. The gender of objects is arbitrarily assigned. In the singular, feminine is most frequently marked by the ending *-å̄*^{h} (<*-*at*), but also by -V*t*. Some nouns are feminine without an external mark: most paired parts of the body (e.g. *ʿayin* 'eye') and a few more (*kikkå̄r* 'loaf'). Some nouns may have either gender (e.g. *š'ɛmɛš* 'sun', only feminine in Modern Hebrew). Beside the singular, there is a restricted dual and a plural. The dual ending -'*ayim* is used to express two units in a few nouns, mainly relating to time units (*šənå̄ŧ'ayim* 'two years'); it marks the plural for paired elements, such as some body parts (*ʿē*^{y}*n'ayim* 'two eyes' = 'eyes') and others (e.g. *mɛlqå̄ḥ'ayim* 'tongs'). It cannot be freely used, most nouns accept the numeral 'two' only for the expression of double occurrence.

The masculine plural ending is *-ī*^{y}*m* and feminine plural is *-ō*$^{(w)}$*ŧ*. Yet a restricted number of feminine nouns may have the apparently masculine plural ending (e.g. *šå̄nå̄*^{h} 'year', pl. *šå̄nī*^{y}*m*) and, more frequently, some masculine nouns may have the feminine plural ending (e.g. *lū*^{wa}*ḥ* 'tablet', pl. *lū*^{w}*ḥōŧ*). Syntactically, however, the gender of a plural noun is always the same as in the singular (e.g. *šå̄nī*^{y}*m rabbō*^{w}*ŧ* 'many years', where the quantifying adjective does carry the feminine plural ending). This morphologically incongruent plural marking may be a remnant of the old polarity system (see numerals below).

Nouns may change their internal vocalisation when they adopt the plural ending. An extreme and mysterious case is *b'ayiŧ/bå̄ttī*^{y}*m* 'house/houses'. The most systematic such change takes place in the case of the bisyllabic so-called 'segholate' nouns. These are characterised by a penultimate stress and a vowel ɛ (a *seghol*) in their last syllable, e.g. *m'ɛ̄lɛꝁ* 'king', *s'ēꝑɛr* 'book'. These originate in an old CVCC pattern **malk-* and **sipr-*, cf. still *malkå̄*^{h} for 'queen', *sifr'å̄*^{h} 'book(?)' in the feminine. The plural pattern of the segholates is CəCå̄C- — *məlå̄ꝁī*^{y}*m* 'kings', *məlå̄ꝁō*^{w}*ŧ* 'queens', *səꝑå̄rī*^{y}*m* 'books'. Though many scholars prefer to explain it as a phonetic reduction, this could very well be the survival of the old broken plural (see the chapter on Semitic languages, page 164).

Nouns may also appear in the construct state, which means that they precede a genitival noun. Here the feminine ending *-å̄^{h}* becomes *-aŧ*, penultimate *å̄* becomes *ə*, *-ayi-* is reduced to *-ē^{y}-*, the masculine plural has the ending *-ē^{y}* (borrowed from the dual) and some nouns do not change at all. Examples: *šənaŧ* 'year of', *šənō^{w}ŧ* 'years of', *ʿē^{y}n* 'eye of', *ʿē^{y}nē^{y}* 'eyes of', *bē^{y}ŧ* 'house of'; plurals of segholates: *mal(ə)ꝁē^{y}* 'kings of', *siᵽrē^{y}* 'books of', with the archaic singular vocalisation.

Hebrew has altogether three genitival constructions. The only one occurring in Biblical Hebrew consists of a possessum in the construct state followed by the possessor: *bē^{y}ŧ hå̄-ʔī^{y}š* 'house+of the-man' ('the man's house'). Here the possessum is always understood to be definite and never takes a definite article, but adjectives referring to it do. Moreover, this construction is not to be broken up by qualifiers. Adjectives follow the whole group, no matter which noun they refer to (only one of the nouns may be so qualified). Thus, *bē^{y}ŧ hå̄-ʔī^{y}š ha-g-gå̄đō^{w}l* 'house+of the-man the-big (m. sg.)' is ambiguously 'the great man's house' or 'the man's big house'. When the two nouns govern different agreements, ambiguity is dispelled: *mišp'aḥaŧ hå̄-ʔī^{y}š ha-g-gəđō^{w}lå̄^{h}* is only 'the man's big family', for feminine 'big' agrees with the feminine 'family', whereas *mišp'aḥaŧ hå̄-ʔī^{y}š ha-g-gå̄dō^{w}l* is clearly 'the great man's family'. There is no simple expression for 'the great man's big family' in Biblical Hebrew.

In the later stages of Hebrew the role of the above construction was reduced. In Modern Hebrew, it is basically a compounding device only, e.g. /bet xolim/ 'house+of sick+pl.' for 'hospital'. Here an article before the second noun definitises the whole expression: /bet ha-xolim/ 'the hospital'. Plurality is expressed on the first noun: /bate xolim/ 'hospitals' and /bate ha-xolim/ 'the hospitals'.

The other genitival constructions, introduced in Medieval Hebrew, use the genitive particle *šɛl* 'of', still in a possessum-possessor order, and no construct state: MoH /ha-b'ayit šel ha-iš/ 'the-house of the-man'. Here, an indefinite possessum may also occur. Alternatively, one may say /bet-o šel ha-iš/ 'house-his of the-man', where the possessum is always definite and its third person possessive pronominal ending agrees in number and gender with the possessor.

In Biblical Hebrew, pronominal possession is expressed by possessive endings. These are attached to a construct state-like form of the nouns, with archaic vocalisation for the segholates: *malk-ī^{y}* 'my king', *siᵽr-ī^{y}* 'my book', *bē^{y}ŧ-ī^{y}* 'my house', *šənå̄ŧ-ī^{y}* 'my year' etc. The plurality of the noun is expressed by a palatal element between the noun and the ending (which may be somewhat modified thereby): *ʿē^{y}n-ī^{y}* 'my eye', but *ʿē^{y}n-ay* 'my eyes'; *ʿē^{y}n-ēꝁ/ʿē^{y}n-'ayiꝁ* 'your (f. sg.) eye-eyes'; *ʿēn-ō^{w}/ʿē^{y}n-å̄^{y}w* 'his eye/eyes' (the last ^{y} is traditionally silent) etc. In the feminine plural, the ending *-ō^{w}ŧ* is retained:

šən-ōʷɫ-ay 'my years'. In Modern Hebrew, a periphrastic construction is used for this with a conjugated form of *šɛl* /šel/ 'of', e.g. /ha-s'efer šeli/ 'my book' ('the-book of+me'). Possessive endings are regularly used in a third kind of genitival construction (see above), occasionally in some kinship terms and other inalienable possessions (/šmi/ beside /ha-šem šeli/ for 'my name') and regularly, again, in idioms (/ma šlomxa/ 'how are you (m. sg.)?' lit. 'what (is) your+peace?'). Contrast /be-libi/ 'in my heart' used for 'inside me', 'in my thought' and /ba-lev šeli/ 'in my heart' in a physical sense.

Qualifying adjectives follow the noun and agree with it in gender, number and definiteness: *ha-m-məlā̊ƙ-ōʷɫ ha-ṭ-ṭōʷƀ-ōʷɫ* 'the good queens' ('the-king-f.pl. the-good-f.pl.'), in contradistinction to the predicative construction where no definiteness agreement is enforced: *ha-m-məlā̊ƙ-ōʷɫ ṭōʷƀ-ōʷɫ* 'the queens (are) good'.

Adjectives may be derived from nouns by means of the ending *-īʸ*, a device very productive in Modern Hebrew: /sifruti/ 'literary' from /sifrut/ 'literature'. Adjectives may act as nouns as well.

Demonstratives follow the noun-adjective group: *ha-m-malk-ā̊ʰ ha-ṭ-ṭōʷƀ-ā̊ʰ ha-z-zōˀɫ* 'this good queen'. Note the definite articles before all three words, omissible en bloc for stylistic variation. In predicative constructions the demonstrative is initial: *zōˀɫ malkā̊ʰ ṭōʷƀ-ā̊ʰ* 'this (is a) good queen'.

As examples have already shown, the definite article is a prefix *ha*+ gemination of the next consonant.

The numeral 'one' is a regular adjective. From 'two' up, cardinal numerals precede the noun (in Biblical Hebrew they may occasionally follow as well). 'Two' appears in the construct state. From 'three' to 'ten' (and with some complications from 'eleven' to 'nineteen') the external gender mark of the numerals (the 'teen' part for the latter group) is the opposite of what one would expect: *ʔarbā̊ʿ-ā̊ʰ bā̊n-īʸm* 'four sons', where the numeral has the ending *-ā̊ʰ*, elsewhere a feminine, before a masculine noun, vs. *ʔarbaʿ bā̊n-ōʷɫ* 'four daughters', where the feminine numeral carries no ending. Traditional grammars sometimes adopt the misleading practice of labelling numerals with *-ā̊ʰ* 'feminine' and stating that they cooccur with masculine nouns. This 'incongruence' is a residue of the old polarity system (see the chapter on Afroasiatic languages, page 158). Nouns appear in the plural after numerals, with few exceptions: 'year', 'day' and a few more have the singular after the round numerals 'twenty'... *ʔarbā̊ʿīʸm šā̊nā̊ʰ* 'forty years'.

Ordinal numerals, formed by means of the *-īʸ* ending for 'second' to 'tenth', are adjectives: *ha-y-yōʷm hā̊-rəƀīʸʿīʸ* 'the fourth day'. From 'eleven' they are homonymous with the cardinal numbers, but exhibit the syntax of adjectives: *ha-y-yōʷm hā̊-ʿarbā̊ʿīʸm* 'the fortieth day'.

The syntactic function of nouns in the sentence is expressed by means of prepositions. The subject carries no mark. The direct object has the preposition *ʔɛɫ* when the object is definite. Contrast: *rā̊ʔ'īʸɫīʸ ʔīʸš* 'I+saw (a) man/someone' and *rā̊ʔ'īʸɫīʸ ʔɛɫ hā̊ʔīʸš* 'I+saw acc. the+man'. Proper names as objects have *ʔɛŧ* even without the article. On the other hand, nouns with possessive endings, though otherwise definite, receive no *ʔɛŧ* in most cases in Biblical Hebrew. Three prepositions are written joined to the subsequent word: *lə-* 'to', *bə-* 'in, with (instrumental)' and *mi*C- (with gemination of the next consonant, an alternative to *min*) 'from'. The rest (*ʿal* 'on' etc.) are separate words. They are conjugated by means of possessive endings of the singular type *l-ī*^{y} 'to-me' or the plural type *ʿå̄l-ay* 'on-me'. For pronominal object (accusative), the separate word *ʔō*$^{(w)}$*ŧ-ī*^{y} etc. for 'me' and so on had been available since the beginnings of Biblical Hebrew, but alternatively in Biblical Hebrew and in archaising style later, object suffix pronouns attached to the verb were also used e.g. *rå̄ʔ'ī*^{y}*ŧī*^{y} *ʔō*^{w}*ŧō*^{w} 'I+saw him' or *rəʔī*^{y}*ŧī*^{y}*w* with the suffix.

In the pronominal domain, three sets of pronouns are to be listed: Independent subject or predicate pronouns, object pronoun suffixes and possessive pronoun suffixes. The latter are subdivided according to whether the preceding noun is a singular or a plural (see above). The object pronoun suffixes are homonymous with the singular possessive set, except in the first person singular, not considering the connective vowels (which are not specified in table 11.4). No gender distinction exists for the first person.

Table 11.4: Personal Pronouns

	Independent		*Object ~ Sg. Poss.*		*Pl. Poss.*	
	Masculine	Feminine	Masculine	Feminine	Masculine	Feminine
Sg. 1.	ʔănī^{y}=ʔå̄nōꝁī^{y}		-nī^{y} (obj.)/-ī^{y}(poss.)		-ay	
2.	ʔattå^{h}	ʔatt^{ə}	-ꝁå̄	-ēꝁ	-'ɛ̄^{y}ꝁå̄	-'ayiꝁ
3.	hū^{wʔ}	hī^{yʔ}	-ō^{w}/-w/-hū^{w}	-å̄h/-hå̄	-å̄^{y}w	-'ɛ̄^{y}hå̄
Pl. 1.	ʔăn'aḥnū^{w}		'-nū^{w} (unstressed)		-'ē^{y}nū^{w}	
2.	ʔattɛm	ʔatt'en(å̄^{h})	-ꝁɛm	-ꝁɛn	-ē^{y}ꝁɛm	-ē^{y}ꝁɛn
3.	h'em(må̄^{h})	h'ennå̄^{h}	-m	-n	-ē^{y}hɛm	-ē^{y}hɛn

For the indicative prefix-conjugated non-past, in those persons where no further suffix is used, the third person singular masculine/feminine object suffixes are *-nnū*^{w}*/-nnå̄*^{h}. Thus, *yišmōr* 'he guards/will guard' (indic.) or 'let him guard' (jussive) is disambiguated: *yišmər'ɛnnū*^{w} 'he will guard/guards him' vs. *yišmər'ehū*^{w} 'let him guard him'. These *-nn-*marked suffixes are not to be confused with the distributionally unlimited use of *-n-* between prefix-conjugated verbs and object suffixes, which are traces of the old 'energic' mood of the verb (for 'he *did* do; he did indeed'), the type *yišmər'ɛnhū*^{w} 'he will indeed guard/guardeth him'.

The basic Biblical Hebrew word order is VSO with the converted forms of the verb and 'verb-second' with a simple tense verb, where the first word is a topic. Medieval Hebrew is still basically VSO, but no more converted tenses are used. Yet, from late Biblical Hebrew on, SVO has been becoming more and more common, and it is the basic order in Modern Hebrew. Especially the adoption of the original active participle as a present tense encouraged the adoption of SVO.

Interrogative pronouns and the yes-no interrogative particle (Biblical Hebrew *hă-*, later *haʔim*) or the introduction of a question with an obvious answer ('isn't it the case that...?') *hălō*^{ʔ} or *hărē*^{y} are always sentence-initial. The negative particle *lō*^{ʔ} 'not' precedes the predicate. The rule that required that negation in the present tense should be effected by a pre-subject *ʔē*^{y}*n* (originally the negation of *yeš* 'there is') is widely disregarded in spoken Modern Hebrew. Contrast normative /eyn-i/ or /eyn'eni roce/ 'not-I want' and colloquial /ani lo roce/ 'I not want' for 'I don't want'.

Biblical Hebrew has no copula in the present. In later stages, a third person pronoun in agreement with the subject may stand for a present tense copula, obligatorily in Modern Hebrew if the predication is of some complexity: /g'ila hi ha-mora/ 'Gila is (=she) the-teacher' (definite predicate). Hebrew has no verb 'to have'. Possessive predication is expressed by means of constructions like 'there is to': *yeš l-*. An interesting development of colloquial Modern Hebrew is that when the element possessed (the grammatical subject) is definite, it receives the accusative preposition *et*, as if it were the object of a transitive verb 'have': /yeš li et ha-b'ayit/ 'I have the house'.

Relative constructions follow the Semitic pattern (see pages 168–9): *ha-m-måqō*^{w}*m ʔăšɛr ʔattå̄*^{h} *ʿō*^{w}*mēḏ ʿålå̄*^{y}*w* 'the-place that you (m. sg.) standing on+it' for 'the spot on which you are standing'. The invariable relative particle is *ʔăšɛr* in Biblical Hebrew, originally a noun meaning 'place' with a functional change 'where' → 'that'. Medieval Hebrew uses the archaic particle *šɛ-*, with the function also extended to many other subordinating functions. In Modern Hebrew /še-/ is the relative particle and the complementiser (Biblical Hebrew *kī*^{y}, cf. Biblical Hebrew *ʔåm'artī*^{y} *kī*^{y}..., Modern Hebrew /am'arti še-... / 'I said that...'). In Modern Hebrew there is a tendency to bring forward the referential pronoun of the relative construction right after the relative pronoun: /ha-makom še-alav ata omed/ (see above).

Bibliography

Chomsky (1957) is a vividly written, scholarly, but no longer up-to-date history of the Hebrew language, with special emphasis on its role among the Jews. Kutscher (1982), a posthumous publication, shows some unfortunate traces of being unfinished, yet is extremely rich in information on the history of the language and is characterised by depth of scholarship.

For Biblical Hebrew, Gesenius (1910) is an indispensable classic; Blau (1976) is a rigorously scientific descriptive grammar, recommended to the student; Lambert (1972) is perhaps the linguistically most solid grammar. Segal (1927) is a clear descriptive grammar for all students of post-Biblical Hebrew. For Modern Hebrew, Berman (1978) is a generative account, also useful as a descriptive grammar.

Further recommended are the articles on 'Hebrew Language' and 'Pronunciations of Hebrew' in the *Encyclopaedia Judaica* (1972, vol. 13, pp. 1120–45 and vol. 16, pp. 1560–1662); these are up-to-date presentations by C. Brovender, J. Blau, E. Y. Kutscher, E. Goldenberg, E. Eytan and S. Morag.

References

Berman, R. 1978. *Modern Hebrew Structure* (University Publishing Projects, Tel-Aviv)

Blau, J. 1976. *A Grammar of Biblical Hebrew* (Otto Harrassowitz, Wiesbaden)

Chomsky, W. 1957. *Hebrew, The Eternal Language* (The Jewish Publication Society of America, Philadelphia)

Gesenius, W. 1910. *Gesenius' Hebrew Grammar*, as edited and enlarged by the late E. Kautzsch, 2nd English ed. by A.E. Cowley (Clarendon Press, Oxford)

Encyclopaedia Judaica. 1972 (Keter, Jerusalem)

Kutscher, E.Y. 1982. *A History of the Hebrew Language* (The Magnes Press, Jerusalem and E.J. Brill, Leiden)

Lambert, M. 1972. *Traité de grammaire hébraïque*, reprinted with additions (Gerstenberg, Hildesheim)

Segal, M.H. 1927. *A Grammar of Mishnaic Hebrew* (Clarendon Press, Oxford)

12 Hausa and the Chadic Languages

Paul Newman

1 Chadic

The Chadic language family, which is a constituent part of the Afroasiatic phylum, contains some 135 languages spoken in the sub-Saharan region west, south and east of Lake Chad. The exact number of languages is not known since new languages continue to be discovered while other supposedly independent languages turn out to be mere dialects or terminological variants. The most important Chadic language is Hausa, with some 25 million native speakers and perhaps half again that number using it as a second language. Other Chadic languages range from close to half a million to less than a thousand speakers.

The family can be subclassified into three major branches plus a fourth independent branch. The West Chadic Branch, which includes Hausa, contains about 60 languages which fall into seven groups. All of the languages, with the exception of Hausa, which extends into Niger, are spoken in northern Nigeria. The Biu-Mandara Branch contains about 45 languages, assigned to eleven groups, extending from the Gongola and Benue River basins in Nigeria to the Mandara mountains in Cameroon. The smaller East Chadic Branch contains about 25 languages belonging to six groups. These are scattered across central Chad in a southwest-northeast direction from the Cameroon border to the Sudan border. The Masa Branch consists of a single group of five closely related languages spoken between the most southeasterly Biu-Mandara languages and the most southwesterly East Chadic languages. A comprehensive list of Chadic languages organised by branch and group is given in table 12.1. Within each group, the languages are listed alphabetically rather than according to closeness of relationship. Names in parentheses indicate alternative nomenclature or dialect variants.

Although the relationship of Chadic (specifically Hausa) to other Afroasiatic languages was proposed a century and a half ago, it has only recently gained general acceptance. The inclusion of Chadic within Afroasiatic is based on the presence of features such as the following: (a) a formative *t* indicating feminine/diminutive/singulative; (b) an *n*/*t*/*n* 'masculine/feminine/plural' agreement marking pattern in the deictic

Table 12.1: The Chadic Language Family (Inventory and Classification)

I. West Chadic Branch
   1. Hausa group: Gwandara, Hausa.
   2. Bole group: Bele, Bole (Bolanci), Deno (Kubi), Galambu, Gera, Geruma, Kanakuru (Dera), Karekare, Kirfi, Kupto, Maha, Ngamo, Pero, Piya (Wurkum), Tangale.
   3. Angas group: Angas, Chip, Gerka (Yiwom), Goemai (Ankwe), Koenoem, Kofyar (Mernyang), Mapun, Montol (Teel), Pyapun, Sura (Mwaghavul), Tal.
   4. Ron group: Fyer, Karfa, Kulere, Mundat, Ron (Bokkos, Daffo), Sha, Shagawu, Tambas.
   5. Bade group: Bade, Duwai, Ngizim.
   6. Warji group: Diri, Jimbin, Kariya, Mburku, Miya, Pa'a (Afa), Tsagu, Warji.
   7. Zaar group: Barawa, Boghom, Dass, Geji, Guruntum, Jimi, Ju, Mangas, Polchi, Zaar (Sayanci), Zari (Zakshi), Zeem.

II. Biu-Mandara Branch
   1. Tera group: Ga'anda (Gabin), Hona, Jara, Tera (Pidlimdi, Yamaltu).
   2. Bura group: Bura (Pabir), Chibak, Kilba, Margi, Putai (West Margi).
   3. Higi group: Bana, Higi (Kapsiki).
   4. Mandara group: Dghwede, Glavda, Guduf, Gvoko, Lamang (Hitkala), Mandara (Wandala), Podoko.
   5. Matakam group: Gisiga, Hurza-Vame, Mada, Matakam (Mafa), Mofu-Duvangar, Mofu-Gudur, Moloko, Muktele, Muyang, Uldeme, Zulgo.
   6. Sukur group: Sukur.
   7. Daba group: Daba (Kola, Musgoi), Gawar, Hina.
   8. Bata group: Bachama, Bata, Gude, Nzangi (Jeng).
   9. Kotoko group: Buduma (Yedina), Kotoko, Logone.
   10. Musgu group: Mbara, Musgu (Munjuk, Mulwi).
   11. Gidar group: Gidar.

III. East Chadic Branch
   1. Somrai group: Gadang, Miltu, Mod, Ndam, Somrai (Sibine), Tumak.
   2. Nancere group: Gabri (Tobanga), Kabalai, Lele, Nancere.
   3. Kera group: Kera, Kwang (Modgel).
   4. Dangla group: Bidiyo, Birgit, Dangla (Dangaléat), Jegu, Kujarke, Mawa, Migama (Jonkor of Abu Telfan), Mogum, Mubi, Toram.
   5. Mokulu group: Mokulu (Jonkor of Guera).
   6. Sokoro group: Barain, Saba, Sokoro.

IV. Masa Branch
   1. Masa group: Marba, Masa, Mesme, Musey, Zime (Lame, Peve).

system; (c) an *m-* prefix forming agential, instrumental and locational nouns; (d) formation of noun plurals *inter alia* by a suffix *-n* and an infix *-a-*; (e) a common pronominal paradigm; (f) a pattern of suppletive imperatives with the verbs 'come' and 'go'; (g) shared gender specification of individual words; and (h) cognate items for basic vocabulary including 'body', 'die', 'drink', 'fire', 'know', 'name', 'water' and 'what'. Some scholars have suggested that Chadic is the most distant Afroasiatic family member (apart from Omotic), while others have suggested a specially close tie with Berber; but so far, such proposals have been made essentially on impressionistic grounds.

In generalising about common Chadic characteristics, it should be understood that these features are neither present nor found identically in all Chadic languages, nor are they necessarily reconstructable for Proto-Chadic.

All Chadic languages, as far as we are aware, are tonal. One finds simple two-tone systems (e.g. Margi), two tones plus downstep (e.g. Kanakuru), three tones (e.g. Tera) and three tones plus downstep (e.g. Ga'anda). Vowel systems range from two vowels, /ə/ and /a/ (as in Mandara), to seven vowels, /i e ɛ a ɔ o u/ plus distinctive vowel length (as in Dangaléat). Vowel harmony of the common West African type is rare in Chadic but it does occur (e.g. Dangaléat and Tangale). A common Chadic feature is to have a different number of vowel contrasts depending on position. Thus, a language (such as Old Hausa) might have two vowels initially, three plus vowel length medially and five vowels without a length contrast finally. Most Chadic languages have a set of glottalised consonants (usually implosives) in addition to the voiced and voiceless ones. Goemai and some other languages in the Angas group have the unusual feature of contrasting ejective and implosive consonants at the same position of articulation, e.g. /p'/ vs. /ɓ/, /t'/ vs. /ɗ/. While the glottal stop /ʔ/ occurs as a phoneme in many languages, it invariably represents a secondary historical development: it is not reconstructable for Proto-Chadic. Finally one should note the widespread presence of lateral fricatives (/ɬ/ and /ɮ/) throughout the Chadic family. They have been lost in the East Chadic Branch and in the sub-branch of West Chadic to which Hausa belongs, but elsewhere they are extremely common.

In the realm of morphosyntax, Chadic languages typically have verb stems (inaccurately called 'intensives') that indicate the plurality of action: action done a number of times, by a number of subjects or affecting a number of objects. These 'pluractional' stems are formed by reduplication, gemination and/or by insertion of an internal *-a-*, e.g. Ga'anda *ɓəl-* 'kill', *ɓəɓal-* 'kill many'. In a few languages, the use of pluractional stems has become grammaticalised, resulting in ergative-type number agreement, i.e. obligatory use of pluractional stems with plural subjects of intransitive verbs and plural objects of transitive verbs, e.g. Kanakuru *nà ɗòpè gáḿínî* 'I tied the rams' (*ɗope* < **ɗoppe*); *gáḿínî wù ɗòpò-wú* 'the rams are tied'; cf. *wù ɗòwè gámî* 'they tied the ram'; *gámî à ɗòwè-ní* 'the ram is tied'. The Kanakuru examples illustrate another distinctive Chadic feature (but with a very scattered distribution), namely the so-called ICP ('Intransitive Copy Pronoun') construction. In various languages all or some intransitive verbs optionally or obligatorily suffix a pronoun that copies the person and number of the subject. In Ngizim, for example, the use of the ICP is optional and adds an extra meaning of completeness to the verb phrase. In

Kanakuru, on the other hand, the use of the ICP is obligatory with all intransitive verbs (but limited to certain tenses), whether simple intransitives or medio-passives, e.g. *kà pòrò-kó* 'you went out', not **ka poro; kílêì à tàɗè-ní* 'the pot broke', cf. *à tàɗè kílêì* 'he broke the pot'. Note that ICPs in Chadic do not have the same form as reflexive pronouns (usually made up of the noun 'head' or 'body' plus a possessive pronoun) which occur as direct objects of transitive verbs.

A common Chadic feature is for verbs to take derivational extensions generally indicating action in, towards, down, up, away or totally or partially done. Sometimes the extensions are more grammatical in nature, indicating benefactive, perfective or transitivisation or intransitivisation. In some languages, such as Tera, the extensions are separate particles; in some, such as Margi, they are semi-bound suffixes; in others, such as Hausa, they have become integrated into the verb stem. In a number of languages, former extensions have lost their meaning and have become frozen to individual verb stems, thus complicating the problem of identifying roots for comparative purposes. For example, Hausa *rúushèe* 'destroy, raze', which comes from **rib-* plus a frozen suffix *-sa*, and Ngizim *rə̀bgú* (same meaning), which comes from **rəb-* plus a frozen suffix *-gu*, are cognate although this is not evident on surface inspection.

Grammatical gender in Chadic is a fairly straightforward phenomenon that goes back to Proto-Chadic (and beyond). The many Chadic languages that do not now have gender have all lost it, this having happened independently a number of times at the level of language group, subgroup and cluster. Languages with gender distinguish two genders (masculine and feminine) in the singular only. Gender distinctions are absent in the plural. In the pronominal system, gender is typically marked in the second as well as the third person.

Finally, regarding word order, Chadic languages are generally prepositional and place the possessor following the thing possessed. The most common order for verbal sentences is S(ubject)–V(erb)–O(bject); but VSO does also occur, primarily in Biu-Mandara languages spoken in the Cameroon border area. SOV in Chadic is unattested. Although SVO is by far the most common order in Chadic, being found in all four branches of the family, there is evidence to suggest that the basic order in Proto-Chadic was VSO (also the most likely order for Proto-Afroasiatic).

2 Hausa

2.1 Introduction

The Hausa language is spoken as a mother tongue by the original Hausas as well as by people of Fulani ancestry who established political control over

Hausaland at the beginning of the nineteenth century and who have continued to settle among and assimilate with the Hausas. Hausa is the majority language of much of northern Nigeria and the neighbouring Republic of Niger and is spoken in small colonies of settlers and traders in many large towns in West Africa. In addition, there is a sizable Hausa-speaking community in Sudan, dating from the British take-over of northern Nigeria at the turn of this century.

Hausa is also widely spoken as a second (or third) language in northern Nigeria and Niger, functioning as a lingua franca for commercial, informational and governmental purposes. (Hausa is one of the three indigenous national languages recognised in the Nigerian constitution.) While higher education in northern Nigeria is generally in English, Hausa is commonly the language of instruction in the primary schools. Hausa is now offered as a major degree subject in a number of Nigerian universities. There are several Hausa language newspapers, a thriving literature and extensive use of the language in radio and television. Broadcasting in Hausa is done not only within Nigeria and Niger, but also by 'international' stations such as the BBC, Voice of America, Deutsche Welle and Radio Moscow. With upwards of 25 million speakers, Hausa ranks with Swahili as one of the most important languages in sub-Saharan Africa.

Within the Chadic family, Hausa constitutes a group by itself. (Gwandara, the only other member of the group, is a historically recent creolised offshoot of Hausa.) The groups most closely related to it, with which Hausa shares many features of phonology and grammar, are the Bole group and the Angas group. What sets Hausa apart from its sister (or cousin) languages is the richness of its vocabulary, due in large part to the enormous number of loanwords from other languages. Mande, Tuareg and Kanuri, for example, have all contributed to Hausa vocabulary; but the major influence by far has been from Arabic (sometimes by way of one of the just-mentioned languages). In certain semantic spheres, e.g. religion (particularly Islam), government, law, warfare, horsemanship, literature and mathematics, Hausa is literally swamped with words of Arabic origin. Interestingly, Hausa has had no difficulty in integrating these Arabic words into its own morphological system of noun plurals or verbal inflection. In this century, Hausa has had a new wave of loanwords from English (in Nigeria) and French (in Niger). This influence continues unabated. For a while it seemed that borrowings from Arabic had ceased; but recently there has been a move among Hausa intellectuals to turn to Arabic for the technical vocabulary required for modern scientific and educational purposes.

Compared with other African languages, Hausa exhibits remarkably little dialect variation. Nevertheless, on the basis of systematic differences in pronunciation and grammar, it is possible to distinguish a Western dialect (or dialects) (e.g. Sokoto and Gobir) from an Eastern dialect (Kano and Zaria). The dialect described here, which has become established as 'standard Hausa', is that of greater Kano, the largest and most important Hausa city.

2.2 Phonology

The phonemes of the standard dialect of Hausa are presented in table 12.2. There are thirty-two consonants twelve vowels (five basic vowels with corresponding long and short variants plus two diphthongs) and three tones (two basic tones plus a compound tone). The richness in the consonantal inventory is due to the presence of: (a) a set of glottalised consonants alongside the voiced and voiceless ones, e.g. /ɗ/ vs. /t/ and /d/; and (b) palatalised and labialised consonants alongside simple ones, e.g. /k^y/ and /k^w/ vs. /k/. In table 12.2 (and in all examples given), the symbols *c* and *j* represent the affricates [č] and [ǰ] respectively. The 'hooked' letters *ɓ*, *ɗ*, and *'y* represent laryngealised (sometimes implosive) stops and semi-vowel, while *ƙ*, *ƙy*, *ƙw* and *ts* are ejectives. The standard pronunciation for the consonant written with the digraph *ts* is [s'] (an ejective sibilant), but there is individual and dialectal variation, including [č'] and [ts']. The apostrophe /'/ is used in Hausa to represent the glottal stop phoneme /ʔ/. In standard orthography, it is not written in word-initial position.

Table 12.2: Phonemes of Hausa

Consonants								
	f	fy	t	c	k	ky	kw	
	b		d	j	g	gy	gw	
	ɓ		ɗ	'y	ƙ	ƙy	ƙw	ʔ
			s	sh				
			z					
			ts					
	m		n					
			l					
			r					
			ṛ					
				y			w	h
Vowels								
	Short					*Long*		
	i		u			ii		uu
	e		o			ee		oo
		a				ai	aa	au
Tones								
		High: á(a);		Low: à(a);		Fall (H + L):		âa

The Hausa /f/ phoneme is variably pronounced as [f], [ɸ] or [p]. It fills the *p*-slot in the consonantal inventory. Before back vowels it is pronounced (and written) as /h/, cf. *jèefí* 'throw' with *jéehóo* 'throw in this direction'. The nasals /n/ and /m/ are generally pronounced [ŋ] in final position, e.g. /nân/ 'here' [nâŋ]; /máalàm/ 'teacher' [máalàm] or [máalàŋ]. When immediately followed by a consonant, in the same word or across a word boundary, /n/ (always) and /m/ (usually) assimilate to the position of the abutting consonant, e.g. *sún bí* 'they followed' [súmbí]; *fàhímtàa* 'understand' [fàhíntàa]. Hausa has two distinct rhotics: a retroflex flap [ɽ] and an apical tap or roll [ɾ]. The two sounds are not distinguished in Hausa orthography. In linguistic works on the language, the tap/roll is commonly indicated /ṛ/ (as here) or /r̃/ to set it apart from the flap, which is written /r/, e.g. *ráanáa* 'sun', *fàrkáa* 'paramour', cf. *ṛíibàa* 'profit', *fáṛkàa* 'wake up'. All Hausa consonants can occur as geminates as well as singly, e.g. *címlàa* 'shoot far', cf. *cílàa* 'pigeon'; *díddígèe* 'heel' (< **dígdígèe*), cf. plural *dìgàadìgái*. Although from a technical perspective the geminates need to be analysed at some level as unitary segments, for most purposes they can be viewed simply as two identical abutting consonants, i.e. *cíllàa* = /C_1íC_2.C_3àa/.

The five long vowels in Hausa have typical IPA 'Italian' values. (Though written here with double letters, they are better thought of as single vowels with an attached phoneme of length.) In non-final position, short /i/, /a/ and /u/ are more lax and centralised. (Non-final short /e/ and /o/ have a questionable status in Hausa.) The contrast between long and short vowels is extremely important, both lexically and grammatically, e.g. *ɓáacèe* 'spoil', *ɓácèe* 'vanish'; *jíimàa* 'tanning', *jímàa* 'pass time'; *'ídòo* 'eye', *'ídó* 'in the eye'; *shàafée* 'wiping', *shàafé* 'wiped (past participle)'; *táa* 'she (perfective$_1$)', *tá* 'she (perfective$_2$)'. The two diphthongs /ai/ and /au/ are best treated as complex vocalic nuclei, although many Hausaists prefer to analyse them as /ay/ and /aw/. The former is generally pronounced [ei] or even [ee], tending to merge with /ee/; the latter varies in the [ao], [au], [ou] range, normally remaining distinct from /oo/.

Hausa has two basic tones: high, indicated *á(a)*, and low, indicated *à(a)*, e.g. *góoràa* 'bamboo', *gòoráa* 'large gourd', *màatáa* 'wife', *máatáa* 'wives', *kíráa* 'call', *kíràa* 'calling', *tá* 'she (perfective$_2$)', *tà* 'she (subjunctive)'. A sequence of high plus low on a single syllable is realised as a falling tone, e.g. *yâráa* 'children' (= /yáàráa/), *mântáa* 'forget' (= /máǹtáa/). In many cases falling tones are the result of the grounding of a low tone belonging to a following morpheme, e.g. *kóomôowáa* 'returning' (= /kóomóòwaa) comes from *kóomóo* 'return' plus *`-wáa* '-ing'. Falling tones, being tone sequences, only occur on heavy syllables, both CVC and CVV types. Hausa does not have a rising tone corresponding to the fall. A low-high sequence on a single syllable is simplified to high, e.g. *tàusái* 'pity' < **tàusàí* (= *tàusàyíi*); *ɗáukàa* 'take' < **ɗàúkàa*.

Hausa has only three syllable types: CV, CVV (where VV can be a long vowel or a diphthong) and CVC, e.g. *súu.nán.sà* 'his name', *kú.jèe.râṛ* 'the chair', *'à.kwàa.tì* 'box'. While consonants may abut across syllable boundaries, e.g. *kás.kàa* 'tick', there are no consonant clusters within a syllable. Syllable weight is an extremely important variable in Hausa. It is crucial for metrical and tonal rules and plays a major role in morphological processes. CV syllables are light; CVV and CVC syllables are heavy. Given the restriction on allowable syllable types, it follows that long vowels cannot occur in closed syllables. Such overheavy syllables, which are created in intermediate structure by morphological formations, are eliminated by automatic reduction of the nucleus, e.g. *'aíkìi-n-sà* → *'áikìnsà* 'his work' (lit. 'work-of-his'); *mâi-n gyàɗáa* → *mân gyàɗáa* 'groundnut oil'; **búuɗ-bùuɗée* → *búbbùuɗée* 'open many/often'; **fáaɗ mínì* → *fáṛ mínì* 'attacked me' (contracted form of *fáaɗàa mínì*).

2.2.1 Orthography

Hausa makes use of two writing systems, one, called *bóokòo*, based on the Roman alphabet, the other, called *'àjàmí*, based on the Arabic writing system. The Roman system was introduced by the British in Nigeria at the beginning of the twentieth century. The system as now established makes use of the symbols in table 12.2 with the following differences. Glottal stop (') is not written in word-initial position. For alphabetisation purposes, such words are treated as if they began with the following vowel. The phonemic distinction between the two *r*s is ignored. Vowel length is not marked, nor is tone. An earlier attempt in Niger to mark vowel length by double letters has been dropped, so that there is now a uniform Romanised orthography in the former French and former British countries. On the whole the writing system is phonemic (even subphonemic in places) although some assimilatory changes are not noted in order to preserve morphological regularity. Thus one writes *sun bi* 'they followed', not *súm bí*, and *ribar nan* 'this profit', not *ṛíibàn nán*. The standard Roman orthography is used in the schools, in the major Hausa newspapers and in most other modern books and magazines.

The writing of Hausa in Arabic script (*'àjàmí*) dates from the beginning of the nineteenth century, possibly a little earlier. Although government policy since the beginning of this century has been to replace *'àjàmí* by *bóokòo*, it is still widely known and used. The *'àjàmí* script is learned in Koranic schools and is preferred over *bóokòo* not only by religious writers but also by many of the more popular traditional poets. After a long period of purposeful neglect, *'àjàmí* has begun to be used again in newspapers in northern Nigeria.

2.2.2 Morphophonemic processes

Hausa exhibits a tremendous amount of morphophonemic alternation, sometimes due to active phonological rules, sometimes reflecting earlier historical changes. Depending on the phonological environment, the 'altered' segment may appear either in the basic form of a word or in a derived form. I shall here describe only some of the more general processes producing alternations. (a) When followed by a front vowel, *t*, *s* and *z* palatalise to *c*, *sh* and *j*, respectively, e.g. *sáatàa* 'stealing', *sàacé* 'stolen'; *dùkúshíi* 'colt', pl. *dùkùsái*; *míjìi* 'husband/male', pl. *mázáa* or *mázàajée*. The palatalisation rule does not apply automatically to recent loanwords, e.g. *tíitìi* 'street' (from English via Yoruba); *láfàzíi* 'pronunciation' (from Arabic). The voiced stop *d* also changes to *j* (with resulting neutralisation of the *d*/*z* contrast), but this change is not as regular as with the other alveolars, even in native words and constructions, e.g. *gídáa* 'house', pl. *gídàajée*; cf. *kádàa* 'crocodile', pl. *kádóodíi*; *kúdù* 'south', *bàkúdèe* 'southerner'. Palatalisation also affects velars, but it is not reflected in the orthography except in the case of the *w*/*y* alternation, e.g. *ɓàráawòo* 'thief', pl. *ɓàràayíi*. (b) As indicated above, long vowels are automatically shortened in closed syllables. At normal speech tempos, resultant short *e* and *o* merge with short *a*. The original quality of the vowel often shows up as palatalisation or labialisation of the preceding consonant, e.g. *dárée-n-nàn* → *dáránnàn* 'this night'; *dàshée-n-sù* → *dàshánsù* 'their seedlings' (cf. *dásàa* 'to transplant seedlings'); *gêeffáa* → *gyâffáa* 'sides' (pl. of *géefèe*); *kánóo-ncíi* → *kánáncíi* 'Kano dialect'; *ƙóon-ƙòonáa* → *ƙwánƙòonáa* 'keep on burning'. (c) Velar and bilabial stops (the latter in the Eastern dialects only) historically weakened to *u* in syllable-final position (with subsequent simplification of *iu* diphthongs to *uu*), e.g. *tálàkà* 'commoner', *táláucìi* 'poverty'; *búuzúu* 'Tuareg serf', pl. *búgàajée*; *júujíi* 'rubbish heap', pl. *jíbàajée*. (Note that some of these 'irregular' plurals are nowadays being replaced by more transparent forms such as *búuzàayée* and *júujàayée*.) The bilabial change also applied to *m*, but only when the abutting consonant was an alveolar sonorant, e.g. *'áurée* 'marriage', *'ámáryáa* 'bride'. (d) In syllable-final position, alveolar stops (and sometimes sibilants) change to the tap/roll *ṛ*, e.g. *mútù* 'die'; *múṛmútù* 'die one after the other'; *ɓátà* 'spoil', *ɓàṛnáa* 'destruction'; *kádà* = *kâṛ* 'negative subjunctive marker'; *fáaɗíi* 'breadth', *fàṛfáaɗáa* 'broad'; *mázámázá* = *máṛmázá* 'quickly'. When more than one process applies, related forms can differ considerably on the surface, e.g. *fáṛkée* 'trader', *fátáucìi* 'trading'. (e) Abutting sequences of C_a-C_b, where C_a is an obstruent, commonly simplify to a geminate $\widehat{CC}_b$. For alveolars, gemination is usually an alternative to rhotacisation, e.g. *káɗ-kàɗáa* → *kákkàɗáa* or *káṛkàɗáa* 'keep beating'; *rìigáa-t-sà* → *rìigássà* or *rìigáṛsà* 'his gown'; *zàaf-záafáa* → *zàzzáafáa* 'hot' (not **zàuzáafáa*).

2.3 Morphology

The Hausa pronominal system distinguishes five categories in the singular (1, 2-masculine, 2-feminine, 3-masculine, 3-feminine) and four in the plural (1-pl., 2-pl., 3-pl., and '4-pl', an impersonal subject). There is no gender distinction in the plural. Variant pronoun sets, differing primarily in tone and vowel length, are shown in the chart of independent, object and possessive pronouns. Their use is determined by surface syntactic position

Hausa Independent, Object and Possessive Pronouns

	a	*b*	*c*	*d*	*e*
1	níi	ní	-nì	-nì	-(w)á
2 m.	kái	ká	-kà	-kà	-kà
2 f.	kée	kí	-kì	-kì	-kì
3 m.	shíi	shí	-shì	-sà	-sà
3 f.	'ítá	tá	-tà	-tà	-tà
1 pl.	múu	mú	-mù	-nà	-mù
2 pl.	kúu	kú	-kù	-kù	-kù
3 pl.	súu	sú	-sù	-sù	-sù

Note: a = independent; b = object-pronoun; c = object-clitic; d = indirect object; e = possessive

and function. The independent pronouns (set (a)) are used as absolute pronouns, e.g. *níi nèe* 'it's me'; as subjects of equational sentences, e.g. *kái yáaròo née* 'you're a boy'; as objects of the particle *dà* 'and/with', e.g. *sún zóo dà 'ítá* 'they came with her', *níi dà kée mún yàṛdá* 'I and you (we) agree'; as direct objects when not immediately following the verb, e.g. *kàawóo mínì shíi* 'bring me it'; and as fronted, focused forms, e.g. *kée cèe múkà gáníi* 'you were the one we saw', *súu nèe súkà tàfí* 'they were the ones who went'. The object pronouns (set (b)) are used as direct objects of certain 'grades' of verbs (see pages 221–2), e.g. *náa káṛàntáa sú* 'I read them'. Pronouns of the same form are also used as subjects of the verboid *zâa* 'be going', e.g. *zâa tá kàasúwáa* 'she's going to market', and of the negative *bâa*, e.g. *bâa shí dà táawùl* 'he doesn't have a towel'. The object clitics (set (c)) are used as direct object of other 'grades' of verbs, e.g. *náa tàmbàyée sù* 'I asked them', and as object of the common word *'àkwái* 'there is/are', e.g. *'àkwái sù dà yáwàa* 'there are many of them' (lit. 'there-are them with many'). The forms in set (d) are bound to the indirect object marker *má-* (with an assimilatory vowel), e.g. *másà, mínì, múkù* 'to him, me, you-pl.'. The forms in set (e) are used with the gender-sensitive linkers **na* (masculine and plural),**ta* (feminine), e.g. *náakà* 'yours', *líttáafìnkà* 'your book', *táasù* 'theirs (feminine referent)', *móotàṛsù* 'their car' (*ṛ* < **t*). The first person is slightly irregular, e.g. *nàawá/tàawá* 'mine', *líttáafìináa* (*-náa* = *ná* + *á*) 'my book', *móotàatáa* (*-táa* = *tá* + *á*) 'my car'. In set (e) as well as (d), the third person singular masculine pronoun *-sà* is replaced in colloquial speech by *-shì*.

Hausa 'tenses' (which reflect tense, mood, aspect and aktionsart or a combination thereof) are indicated by a marker attached to a preverbal pronoun. Some of the markers are clearly segmentable while others consist only of tone or vowel length modifications of the basic pronoun. (In the case of the subjunctive, the marker is Ø.) Thus it has become the convention in Hausa studies to treat the pronoun plus marker as a fused tense/aspect pronoun, see the chart of tense/aspect pronouns. Negative tense/aspect pronouns which differ from the corresponding affirmative ones are listed separately. Apart from the continuous, which uses a single negative marker *báa*, and the subjunctive, which uses a negative particle *kádà*, verbal sentences are negated by means of a discontinuous morpheme *bà... bá*. The meanings of the tenses are roughly deducible from their labels and will not be discussed. The syntactic opposition between the two perfective and two continuous categories is described in section 2.4.

Hausa Tense/Aspect Pronouns

	a	*b*	*c*	*d*	*e*	*f*	*g*	*h*	*i*	*j*
1	náa	ná	bàn...bá	zân	nâa	nákạn	'ǹ	'ńnàa	nákè(e)	báanàa
2 m.	káa	ká	bàkà...bá	záakà	kâa	kákàn	kà	kánàa	kákè(e)	báakàa
2 f.	kín	kíkà	bàkì...bá	záakì	kyâa	kíkàn	kì	kínàa	kíkè(e)	báakyàa
3 m.	yáa	yá	bài...bá	zâi	yâa	yákàn	yà	yánàa	yákè(e)	báayàa
3 f.	táa	tá	bàtà...bá	záatà	tâa	tákàn	tà	tánàa	tákè(e)	báatàa
1 pl.	mún	múkà	bàmù...bá	záamù	mâa	múkàn	mù	múnàa	múkè(e)	báamàa
2 pl.	kún	kúkà	bàkù...bá	záakù	kwâa	kúkàn	kù	kúnàa	kúkè(e)	báakwàa
3 pl.	sún	súkà	bàsù...bá	záasù	sâa	súkàn	sù	súnàa	súkè(e)	báasàa
4 pl.	'án	'ákà	bà'à...bá	záa'à	'âa	'ákàn	'à	'ánàa	'ákè(e)	báa'àa

Note: a = perfective$_1$; b = perfective $_2$; c = neg-perfective; d = future; e = predictive; f = habitual; g = subjunctive; h = continuous$_1$; i = continuous$_2$; j = neg.-continuous.

Except for the imperative, which is marked by low-high tone (sometimes plus a final vowel change), the verb itself is not conjugated, tense, person and number being shown by the tense/aspect pronoun, e.g. *náa záunàa* 'I sat'; *bà nâa záunàa bá* 'I don't intend to sit'; *záamù záunàa* 'we will sit'; *mù záunàa* 'let's sit'; *tákàn káamàa sú* 'she catches them'; *tánàa káamàa sú* 'she is catching them'; cf. *zàunáa* 'sit!'; *kàamáa sú* 'catch them!'. Verbal morphology in Hausa reflects the verb's 'grade' and its syntactic environment. The morphological distinctiveness in each category is defined in terms of the verb's final vowel (or -VC) and overall tone. The pattern for each grade, indicated for di- and tri-syllabic verbs, is presented in table 35.3.

Grade 7 ('sustentative') indicates an agentless passive (or sometimes middle voice), action well done or potentiality of sustaining action, e.g. *náamàa yáa gàsú* 'the meat has been roasted'; *'àgóogó báayàa gyàarú-wáa* 'the watch is not repairable'. Grade 6 ('ventive') indicates movement in the direction of or for the benefit of the speaker, e.g. *kún sáyóo gíyàa?* 'did you buy (and bring) beer?'; *záatà fítóo* 'she will come out'. Grade 5 ('efferential'), traditionally termed 'causative', indicates action effected away from the speaker. It also serves to transitivise inherently intransitive verbs, e.g. *yáa 'áurár̹ dà 'yár̹sà* 'he married off his daughter'; *táa fítár̹* 'she took (it) out'; *dón mè kíkà sáishée tà* 'why did you sell it?'. Grade 4 ('totality') indicates an action totally done or affecting all the objects, e.g. *rúwáa yáa zúbèe* 'the water all spilled out';

Table 12.3: The Hausa Grade System

	Form A			Form B		Form C	
Grade 1	-aa		H L (H)	-aa	H L (H)	-a	H L (L)
Grade 2	-aa		L H (L)	-ee	(L) L H	-i	(L) L H
Grade 3	-a		L H (L)	———		———	
Grade 4	-ee		H L (H)	-ee	H L (H)	{-e -ee}	{H L (L) H L (H)}
Grade 5	-aṛ	(< *as)	H H (H)	-shee	H H (H)	———	
Grade 6	-oo		H H (H)	-oo	H H (H)	-oo	H H (H)
Grade 7	-u		(L) L H	———		———	

Note: grade 1 = basic-*a* and applicative; grade 2 = basic-*i* and partitive; grade 3 = basic-*a* intransitive; grade 4 = totality; grade 5 = efferential; grade 6 = ventive; grade 7 = sustentative.

záamù sáyè shìnkáafáa 'we will buy up the rice'. With many verbs, especially when used intransitively, Grade 4 is becoming a basic, semantically neutral form. Grade 3 is an exclusively intransitive grade containing verbs with lexically underlying final *-a*, e.g. *fitá* 'go out'; *cìká* 'be filled'. Grade 2 contains basic transitive verbs with underlying final *-i* as well as derived verbs with a partitive sense, e.g. *bàkà fàɗí gàskíyáa bá* 'you didn't tell the truth' (basic); *mù yànkí náamàa* 'let's cut off some meat' (partitive). Grade 1 contains basic transitive verbs with underlying final *-a* as well as derived 'applicatives' (often required with indirect objects). Like the efferential, grade 1 applicatives serve to transitivise intransitive verbs, e.g. *sún háƙà ráamìi* 'they dug a hole' (basic); *kà fáɗàa mánà gàskíyáa* 'you should tell us the truth' (applicative); *táa fásà tùulúu* 'she smashed the pot' (applicative). Hausa has a small number of high-frequency monosyllabic verbs, e.g. *cí* 'eat', *sháa* 'drink', *bí* 'follow', *jáa* 'pull'. These do not fit into grades 1, 2 or 3, but they do appear in the other grades (with slightly variant forms), e.g. *yáa shânyè rúwáa* 'he drank up the water' (gr. 4); *múkàn cíishée sù* 'we feed them' (gr. 5); *jàawóo nân* 'pull (it) here' (gr. 6); *hányàa tâa bìyú* 'the road will be followable' (gr.7).

Independent of grade, verbs have three syntactically determined forms (omitting the pre-indirect object position, which poses special problems). Form B is used when the verb is immediately followed by a direct object personal pronoun (Grades 1 and 4 take the high tone object pronouns; all other verbs take the low tone clitics.) Form C is used when the verb is followed by any other direct object. Form A is used elsewhere, e.g.

táa tàimàkí Múusáa	'she helped Musa'	(gr. 2, C)
táa tàimàkée shì	'she helped him'	(gr. 2, B)
Múusáa nèe tá tàimákàa	'it was Musa she helped'	(gr. 2, A)
mún káṛàntà jàṛíidàa	'we read the paper'	(gr. 1, C)
mún káṛàntáa tá	'we read it'	(gr. 1, B)
wàccée kúkà káṛàntáa?	'which did you read?'	(gr. 1, A)

Grade 5 ('efferential') verbs do not have a C form since the semantic objects are expressed as oblique objects introduced by the preposition *dà* 'with', e.g. *yánàa kóoyáṛ dà Háusá* 'he is teaching Hausa'. With pronominal objects, one may use either the B form or the A form with the oblique object, e.g. *yáa cíishée tà = yáa cíyáṛ dà 'ítá* 'he fed her/it'. Some verbs allow a short form (without the suffix *-aṛ*) before *dà*, e.g. *táa zúb dà rúwáa = táa zúbáṛ dà rúwáa* 'she poured out the water'. Historically it seems that the *-dà* in the short form was a verbal extension attached to the verb (as it still is in some Western dialects) which was reanalysed as the homophonous preposition.

2.3.1 Verbal nouns

While verbs as such are not inflected for tense, in the continuous tenses they are subject to replacement by verbal-nominal forms, of which there are three general classes. (1) *`-wáa* forms. When no object is expressed, verbs of grades 1, 4, 5 and 6 use a present participial-like stem formed with the suffix *`-wáa*, e.g. *báasàa kóomôowáa* 'they are not returning', cf. *bàsù kóomóo bá* 'they didn't return'; *tánàa rúfèewáa* 'she is closing (it)', cf. *tánàa rúfè táagàa* 'she is closing the window'. (2) Primary verbal nouns. Grades 2, 3 and 7 form verbal nouns with a suffix *-áa*. Monosyllabic verbs add *:`* (vowel length plus low tone). If the primary verbal noun is followed by an object, it takes a connecting linker (*-n* or *-ṛ*). The 'object' pronoun is represented by a possessive form, e.g. *tánàa tàmbáyàṛsà* 'she is asking him', cf. *táa tàmbàyée shì* 'she asked him'; *múnàa cîn* (< *cîi* + *n*) *náamàa* 'we are eating meat', cf. *mún cí náamàa* 'we ate meat'; *Múusáa nèe yákèe fìtáa* (< *fìtá* + *áa*) 'Musa is going out'; *báasàa gyàarúwáa* (< *gyàarú* + *áa*) 'they are not repairable'. (3) Secondary verbal nouns. Many verbs have lexically related verbal nouns that are used instead of or sometimes as an alternative to verbs or primary verbal nouns. Like primary verbal nouns, these forms require a linker before expressed objects. The shape of secondary verbal nouns is lexically specific and cannot be predicted from the form of the related verb. The following are the more common secondary verbal noun patterns:

(a) -ii H L: gínìi 'building'; ɗínkìi 'sewing'
(b) -ee L H: sàyée 'buying'; bìncìkée 'investigating'
(c) -aa H H: gyáaráa 'repairing'; néemáa 'seeking'
(d) -oo (variable): cíizòo 'biting'; kòoyóo 'learning'
(e) Ablaut H L: jíimàa 'tanning' (< jéemàa); súukàa 'piercing' (< sòokáa).

Finally, before leaving verbal morphology, two regular deverbal constructions should be mentioned. Adverbs of state are formed from verb stems by means of a suffix *-e* (with short vowel) and a L H tone pattern, e.g. *zàuné* 'seated', *dàfé* 'cooked', *wàṛwàatsé* 'scattered'. Past participial adjectives are formed from verbs by reduplicating the stem-final consonant in geminate form and adding a suffix *-ee* (masculine) or *-iyaa* (feminine) and L H H tone in the singular or a suffix *-uu* and L L H tone in the plural, e.g.

dàfáffée (m.), *dàfáffíyáa* (f.), *dàfàffúu* (pl.) 'cooked', *gàagàrárrée*, *gàagàrárríyáa*, *gàagàràrrúu* 'obstinate, rebellious'.

The major parameters in nominal morphology are gender and number. Hausa has two genders, masculine and feminine, morphologically and grammatically distinguished in the singular only. Masculine words are generally unmarked, exhibiting all possible phonological shapes. With a few exceptions, feminine words end in *-aa*, *-(i)yaa*, or *-(u)waa*, e.g. masculine: *kíifíi* 'fish', *zóobèe* 'ring', *bàkáa* 'bow', *nóonòo* 'breast', *tùulúu* 'pot'; feminine: *kúuráa* 'hyena', *múndúwáa* 'anklet', *kíbíyàa* 'arrow', *kàazáa* 'hen', *táɓáryáa* 'pestle'. Adjectives, which constitute a class of 'dependent nominals', are inflected for gender and number, the feminine being formed from the masculine by the addition of *-aa* (with automatic glide insertion where required), e.g. *fárii* (m.), *fáráa* (f.), *fáràarée* (pl.) 'white'; *shúuɗìi*, *shúuɗìyáa*, *shûɗɗáa* 'blue'; *dóogóo*, *dóogúwáa*, *dóogwàayée* 'tall'; *sàatáccée*, *sàatáccíyáa*, *sàatàttúu* 'stolen'.

At the derivational level, many feminine counterparts to masculine humans and animals make use of a suffix *-n(i)yaa*, e.g. *yáaròo*, *yáarínyàa* 'boy, girl'; *màkáahòo*, *màkáunìyáa* (< **màkáafnìyáa*) 'blind man, woman', *bírìi*, *bírínyàa* 'monkey m./f.'. Other male/female pairs use the inflectional *-aa* suffix, e.g. *jàakíi*, *jàakáa* 'donkey m./f.'; *kàrée*, *kàryáa* 'dog, bitch'.

Nominal plurals represent one of the most complex areas of Hausa morphology. On the surface there are some forty different plural formations making use of infixes, suffixes, reduplication etc. If, however, one focuses on tone and final vowel, the various plurals can be grouped into a manageable number of basic patterns, see table 12.4.

Although the plural of any given word is not totally predictable, there are correlations and restrictions that hold. For example, almost all singular words that have type (2) plurals have H H tone — but not all H H singulars have type (2) plurals — while type (3) plurals are limited to H L singulars. Within type (2), the variant manifestations of the plural are determined by canonical syllabic structure. If the singular has a light first syllable, it takes a reduplicated plural; if it has an initial open heavy syllable, it takes a glide suffixing plural; if it has an initial closed syllable, it takes an infixing plural. Since there is no one-to-one fit between singulars and plurals, it is not surprising that many words allow more than one plural, e.g. *léeɓèe* 'lip', pl. *lâɓɓáa* or *léeɓúnàa*; *ɓéeṛáa* 'rat', pl. *ɓéṛàayée* or *ɓeéṛàṛṛákíi*. An ongoing process in Hausa is the treatment of historically original plurals as singulars, with the subsequent formation of new plurals. In some cases the original singular form has to be postulated; in others, it still exists as a dialectal variant, e.g. *dúmáa* 'gourd' (orig. pl. of *dúmèe*), pl. *dúmàamée*; *háƙóoríi* 'tooth' (orig. pl. of **háƙrèe*, still found as *háurèe*), pl. *háƙòoráa*; *gídáa* 'home' (orig. pl. of *gíjìi*), pl. *gídàajée*.

Hausa has a number of productive and semi-productive nominal derivational constructions, in some cases using prefixes, in others suffixes.

Table 12.4: Hausa Common Plural Patterns

	Type	*Plural*	*(Singular)*	*'Gloss'*
(1)	-ooCii	gúnóoníi	(gúnàa)	'melon'
	All H	tsáróokíi	(tsárkìyáa)	'bowstring'
		túmáakíi	(túmkìyáa)	'sheep'
(2)	aa…ee	fágàagée	(fágée)	'field'
	H L H	zóomàayée	(zóomóo)	'hare'
		kásàakée	(káskóo)	'bowl'
(3)	aa…aa	síṛàadáa	(sírḍìi)	'saddle'
	H L H	sâssáa	(sáashèe)	'section'
		yâaráa	(yáaròo)	'boy'
(4)	-uKaa	ríigúnàa	(rìigáa)	'gown'
	H H L	cíkúnkúnàa	(cíkìi)	'belly'
	[K = *n*, *k*, *w*,	gáṛúkàa	(gàaṛúu)	'wall'
	or C_{final}]	yáazúuzúkàa	(yáajìi)	'spice'
		gárúurúwàa	(gàríi)	'town'
		cóokúlàa	(cóokàlíi)	'spoon'
(5)	-Kii/-Kuu	wàtànníi	(wátàa)	'moon, month'
	L L H	gòonàkíi	(góonáa)	'farm'
		ràanàikúu	(ráanáa)	'sun, day'
(6)	ee…aKii	gáṛèemáníi	(gàṛmáa)	'plough'
	H L H H	gáawàwwákíi	(gáawáa)	'corpse'
		márèemáríi	(mármáráa)	'laterite'
(7)	-ii/-uu	bàrèeyíi	(bàréewáa)	'gazelle'
	L L H	jèemàagúu	(jéemáagèe)	'bat'
		màgàngànúu	(màgánàa)	'speech'
(8)	-ai	kùnkùrái	(kùnkúrúu)	'tortoise'
	L L H	dùbbái	(dúbúu)	'thousand'
		fìkàafìkái	(fíffíkèe)	'wing'
(9)	Final vowel	yáatsúu	(yáatsàa)	'finger'
	change	máasúu	(máashìi)	'spear'
	…H	'áṛnáa	('áṛnèe)	'pagan'
		mázáa	(míjìi)	'husband, male'
		bíráì	(bírìi)	'monkey'
		cínái	(cínyàa)	'thigh'
		kàajíi	(kàazáa)	'hen'
		bàaƙíi	(bàaƙóo)	'stranger'

The following are some of the more common. (a) Ethnonymics, indicating a person's geographical or ethnic origin, social position or, less often, occupation are formed with a prefix *ba-* in the singular and a suppletive suffix *-aawaa* in the plural, e.g. *bàháushèe*, *bàháushìyáa*, *hàusàawáa* 'Hausa man, woman, people'. (b) Agentials are formed from verbs using a prefix *ma-*, a widespread Afroasiatic formative, e.g. *mánòomíi*, *mánóomìyáa*, *mánòomáa* 'farmer (m./f./pl.)'. (c) Instrumentals use the same *ma-* prefix as agentials, but with a different tone pattern and different plural formation, e.g. *mábúuɗíi*, *màbùuɗái* 'opener m./pl.'. (d) Locatives use the same *ma-* prefix, but are usually feminine and end in *-aa*, e.g. *má'áikátáa*, *mà'àikàtái* 'work-place f./pl.'. (e) Language names take a suffix *-(n)cii* and an all H tone pattern, e.g. *láṛábcíi* 'Arabic', *kánáncíi* 'Kano dialect' (but not **háusáncíi* — *háusá* being the language name). (f) Abstract nouns make use of an array of related *-(n)taa* and *-(n)cii* suffixes with varying tones, e.g. *bàu-táa* 'slavery', *gájár-tàa* 'shortness', *gùrgù-ntáa* 'lameness', *gwàní-ntàa* 'expertness', *fátáu-cìi* 'commerce', *súusá-ncìi* 'foolishness'. Another suffix *-(n)tákàa* is sometimes used instead of or in addition to the above, e.g. *shèegà-ntákàa* 'rascality', *jàaṛùn-tákàa* = *jáaṛúntàa* 'bravery', but *mùtùn-tákàa* 'human nature' ≠ *mútún-cìi* 'humaneness, decency'. (g) Mutuality or reciprocity is indicated by a suffix *-áyyàa* and/or *-éenìyáa*, e.g. *'àuràtáyyàa* 'intermarriage', *bùgáyyàa* = *bùgággéenìyáa* 'hitting one another', *yàṛjéejéenìyáa* 'mutual consent'.

2.4 Syntax

In this sketch of Hausa syntax we shall limit ourselves to a description of the internal structure of the simple noun phrase and of word order at the sentence level.

The key to the Hausa noun phrase is the 'noun phrase-of noun phrase' construction, e.g. *kàaká-n yáaròo* 'the boy's grandfather' (lit. 'grandfather-of boy'); *móotà-ṛ-kù* 'your car' (lit. 'car-of you (pl.)'); *móotóocí-n sárkíi* 'the chief's cars' (lit. 'cars-of chief'). The 'linker', as it is called by Hausaists, has two forms: *-n* (a contraction of *na*) and *ṛ* (a contraction of *ta*). The former is used if the first noun is masculine or plural, the latter if the first noun is feminine singular; the gender of the second nominal is irrelevant. Constructions with the linker have a wide variety of uses in Hausa, as can be seen from the following typical examples: *bángón ɗáakìi* 'wall of the room', *gàbán mákáṛántáa* 'in front of the school', *ɗáyáṛsù* 'one of them', *'yáa'yán 'ítàacée* 'fruit' (lit. 'offspring of tree'), *jírgín sámà* 'aeroplane' (lit. 'vehicle of sky'), *'úwáṛ rìigáa* 'body (lit. 'mother') of a gown'. The linker also serves to connect a noun and a following demonstrative, e.g. *jàakín nàn* 'this (here) donkey', *túnkìyâṛ nán* 'this (previously referred to) sheep', *dàwàakán càn* 'those horses'.

Hausa has a number of ways of expressing what in English are translated as adjectival modifiers. One means is to use 'true adjectives' (i.e. dependent nominals) before the modified noun in a linking construction, e.g. *fárí-n zánèe* 'white cloth', *fárá-ṛ rìigáa* 'white gown', *fàsàssú-n kwálàabée* 'broken bottles'. Alternatively (under poorly understood conditions) the adjective can occur to the right of the noun without the use of the linker, e.g. *zánèe fáríi*, *rìigáa fáráa*, *kwálàabée fàsàssúu*. Attributive cardinal numerals only occur in this post-nominal position, e.g. *jàakíi ɗáyá* 'one donkey', *máatáa 'úkù* 'three women', *máyàaƙáa dúbúu* 'a thousand warriors' (cf. *dúbú-n máyàaƙáa* 'thousands of warriors'). Ordinals also occur to the right of the noun, but make use of a linker (usually non-contracted), e.g. *ƙáṛnìi ná 'àshìṛín* 'twentieth century', *'àláamàa tá bíyú* 'the second sign'. Modifiers are also commonly expressed by use of *màilmàasú* 'owner, possessor of (sg./pl)' plus an abstract qualitative nominal, e.g. *ríijìyáa mài zúrfíi* 'a deep well' (cf. *zúrfíntà* 'its depth'), *léebúṛóoṛíi màasú ƙárfíi* 'strong labourers'. This construction has a negative counterpart using *máràṛlmáràsáa*, e.g. *ríijìyáa máràṛ zúrfíi* 'a not deep well', *léebúṛóoṛíi máràsáa ƙárfíi* 'not strong labourers'.

Hausa lacks an exact equivalent of the English definite and indefinite articles. The bare word *yáaròo* could mean 'a boy' or 'the boy' depending on the context. To specifically indicate that a word has been previously referred to or is the thing in question, there is a suffix identical in segmental shape to the linker but with inherent low tone: *-̀n* (m./pl.), *-̀ṛ* (f.), e.g. *yáaròn* 'the boy in question', *túnkìyâṛ* 'the sheep in question', *mútàanên* 'the men referred to'. To indicate particularised indefiniteness, Hausa uses the words *wání*, *wátá*, *wású* (= *wáɗánsú*) 'some (m./f./pl.)', e.g. *wání yáaròo yánàa kúukáa* 'a/some boy is crying'; *wású bàaƙíi súnàa jírànkà* 'some strangers are waiting for you'.

Hausa has four sentence types, which can be labelled existential, equational, verbal and statival. Existential sentences are formed with the word *'àkwái* 'there is' and the negative counterpart *bâa* (or *báabù*) 'there is not', e.g. *'àkwái 'àbíncí mài dáaɗíi* 'there is delicious food'; *bâa 'ìsásshén kúɗíi* 'there is not enough money'. Equational sentences have the structure (noun phrase) noun phrase *neelcee*, where *nee* has masculine and plural agreement and *cee* (< **tee*) has feminine agreement, e.g. *shíi sóojà née* 'he is a soldier', *móotàṛ nân sáabúwáa cèe* 'this car is new'. These sentences are negated by sandwiching the second noun phrase between *bàa* . . . *bá*, e.g. *shíi bàa sóojà bá nèe* 'he is not a soldier', *móotàṛ nân bàa sáabúwáa bá cèe* 'this car is not new'. If the first noun phrase is missing, one has an identificational sentence comparable to the English 'it's a . . .', e.g. *kàrée nèe* 'it's a dog'; *bàa tàawá bá cèe* 'it's not mine'. Equational sentences are not marked for tense; thus the preceding sentence could equally mean 'it wasn't mine'.

Verbal sentences have the core structure subject, tense/aspect pronoun, verb, indirect object, direct object or locative goal, instrumental, e.g. *yáròo yánàa gáyàa másà làabáaṛìi* 'the boy (he) is telling him the news'; *máháukácìyáa táa káshèe shí dà wúƙáa* 'the crazy woman (she) killed him with a knife', *wàkìilái záasù kóomàa ƙásáṛsù* 'the representatives will return to their countries'. Conditionals, temporals and other complement phrases and clauses occur both before and after the core, e.g. *'ín káa yàṛdá záamù záunàa nân sái táa zóo* 'if you agree we will sit here until she comes'. In sentences without overt subjects, the tense/aspect pronoun translates as the subject, but syntactically it should not be thought of as such. Thus the sentence *yáa húutàa* 'he rested' has the structure $\emptyset_{\text{subj.}}$ *yáa*$_{\text{tap}}$ *húutàa*$_{\text{verb}}$ parallel to the sentence *yáaròo yáa húutàa* 'the boy rested'. The tenses with the segmentally full markers *nàa, kèe* and *kàn* do not require the third person pronominal element if an overt subject is present, e.g. *mútàanée (sú)nàa bînsà* 'the men are following him', *dóm mèe yáarínyàa (tá)kèe kúukáa?* 'why is the girl crying?'.

The normal position for the indirect object is immediately following the verb and before the direct object. Indirect object pronouns are formed with *má-*; nouns make use of a prepositional element *wà* or *mà*, e.g. *kàakáa táa mácèe mánà* 'grandmother died on us', *kádà kà káawóo wà ɗáanáa bíndígàa* 'don't bring my son a gun'. A long and complex indirect object is likely to be expressed as a prepositional phrase occurring after the direct object. The preposition used in this case is *gà*, etymologically probably the same word as *wà*, e.g. *náa núunà tákàṛdáa gà mùtúmìn dà ná gàmú dà shíi 'à ƙóofàa* 'I showed the letter to the man I met (lit. 'man that I met with him') at the door'. Compare the normal *náa núunàa wà mùtúmìn tákàṛdáa* 'I showed the man the letter'.

Question words and focused elements are fronted. One consequence (shared with relativisation) is the obligatory substitution of perfective$_2$ and continuous$_2$ for the corresponding perfective$_1$ and continuous$_1$ tense forms, e.g. *mèe súkà sàyáa?* 'what did they buy?', cf. *sún sàyí kíifíi* 'they bought fish'; *wàa yákèe kíɗàa?* 'who is drumming?' cf. *Múusáa yánàa kíɗàa* 'Muusaa is drumming'; *'ítá cèe ná gáyàa wà* 'it was she I told', cf. *náa gáyàa mátà* 'I told her'. Another consequence is the use of resumptive pronouns to fill the place of fronted instrumentals and (optionally) indirect objects, e.g. *mèe záamù ɗáurè ɓàráawòo dà shíi?* 'what will we tie up the thief with (it)?'; *Hàdíizà múkèe kóoyàa mátà (= kóoyàa wà) túuṛáncíi* 'it's Hadiza we're teaching (to her) English'.

Stativał sentences make use of the continuous tense/aspect pronouns and a non-verbal predicate, of which there are three major types: locative, 'have' and stative, e.g. *múnàa nân* 'we're here'; *Wùdíl báatàa néesà dà Kánòo* 'Wudil is not far from Kano'; *súnàa dà móotàa mài kyâu* 'they have (are with) a good car', *kwáalín nàn yánàa dà náuyíi* 'this carton is heavy' (lit. 'is with heaviness'); *'àbíncí yánàa dàfé* 'the food is cooked' (< *dáfàa* 'to cook'); *tún jíyà súnàa zàuné 'à ƙóofàṛ gídánkà* 'since yesterday they have been sitting at the door of your house' (< *záunàa* 'to sit'); *múnàa sàné dà shíi* 'we are aware of it' (< *sánìi* 'to know'). As in the case of verbal sentences, fronting of a questioned or focused element triggers the use of continuous$_2$ tense/aspect pronouns. (The form differs slightly here in having a short final vowel.) For example, *'ìnáa súkè yànzú?* 'where are they now?'; *mèe kákè dà shíi?* 'what do you have?' (lit. 'what are you with it'); *tùulúu 'à cìké yákè* 'the pot is *filled*' (lit. 'the pot filled it is').

In summary, one can say that Hausa is a language with fairly fixed word order. Where changes from normal order occur, for example for questioned or focused objects, they are for specific grammatical or pragmatic purposes. Interestingly, Hausa does not deviate from normal word order for yes-no questions. These are indicated simply by a question tag (such as *kóo* 'or', or *fà* 'what about') or by question intonation (consisting in part of an old question morpheme, now reflected only as vowel length often with low tone), e.g. *Múusáa zâi yàṛdá kóo?* 'Muusaa will agree, right?'; *bàaƙíi sún fitâa?* 'did the guests go out?' (*fitâa* = *fitá* + *:̀*), cf. *bàaƙíi sún fitá* 'the guests went out'.

Bibliography

Newman (1977) is the standard work on Chadic classification and the reconstruction of Proto-Chadic. Jungraithmayr and Shimizu (1981) also treat Chadic vocabulary from a comparative perspective. Newman (1980) is an attempt to establish definitively the membership of Chadic within Afroasiatic. Abraham (1959), while terribly out of date — it dates from 1940 — is the only reliable reference grammar of Hausa available. Gouffé (1981) is the best concise sketch of Hausa available. Cowan and Schuh (1976) is a widely used pedagogical course, while Kraft and Kirk-Greene (1973) is an excellent introduction to the language in the familiar *Teach Yourself* format. Parsons (1981) is an invaluable collection of papers, lecture notes etc. by the leading Hausaist of our day. A comprehensive bibliography of works on Hausa language and literature is provided by Baldi (1977), supplemented by Adwe (1988).

References

Abraham, R.C. 1959. *The Language of the Hausa People* (University of London Press, London)

Adwe, Nicholas. 1988. 'A Hausa language and linguistics bibliography 1976–86 (including supplementary material for other years)', in G. Furniss and P.J. Jagger (eds.) *Studies in Hausa Language and Linguistics in Honour of F.W. Parsons* (Kegan Paul International, London), pp. 253–78

Baldi, S. 1977. *Systematic Hausa Bibliography* (Istituto Italo-Africano, Rome)

Cowan, J.R. and R.G. Schuh. 1976. *Spoken Hausa* (Spoken Language Services, Ithaca, NY)

Gouffé, C. 1981. 'La Langue haoussa', in G. Manessy (ed.) *Les Langues de l'Afrique Subsaharienne* (CNRS, Paris), pp. 415–28

Jungraithmayr, Hermann and Kiyoshi Shimizu. 1981. *Chadic Lexical Roots. II. Tentative Reconstruction, Grading and Distribution* (Marburger Studien zur Afrika- und Asienkunde, A-26, Dietrich Reimer, Berlin)

Kraft, C. H. and A.H.M. Kirk-Greene. 1973. *Hausa* (Teach Yourself Books, London)

Newman, P. 1977. *Chadic Classification and Reconstructions* (Undena, Malibu, Calif.)

—— 1980. *The Classification of Chadic Within Afroasiatic* (Universitaire Pers, Leiden)

Parsons, F.W. 1981. *Writings on Hausa Grammar*, ed. by G. Furniss, 2 vols. (School of Oriental and African Studies, London and University Microfilms International, Books on Demand, Ann Arbor)

13 TAMIL AND THE DRAVIDIAN LANGUAGES

Sanford B. Steever

1 The Dravidian Languages

The Dravidian language family, the world's fourth largest, consists of twenty-five languages spread over the South Asian subcontinent. It has four branches: South Dravidian with Tamil, Malayāḷam, Iruḷa, Koḍagu, Kota, Toda, Badaga, Kannaḍa and Tulu; South-Central Dravidian with Telugu, Savara, Goṇḍi, Koṇḍa, Pengo, Manḍa, Kūi and Kūvi; Central Dravidian with Kolami, Naiki, Parji, Ollari and Gadaba; and North Dravidian with Kūṛux, Malto and Brahui. Over the past fifteen years reports of other languages have appeared, but without adequate grammars we cannot determine whether these are new, independent languages or simply dialects of ones already known. Indu and Āwē have been reported in South-Central Dravidian; Kuruba, Yerava, Yerukula, Kaikuḍi, Korava, Koraga, Bellari and Burgundi in South Dravidian. Certain dialects of Goṇḍi and Kūṛux may prove under closer inspection to be independent languages. The Dravidian languages are spoken by approximately 175,000,000 people.

Though concentrated in South India (see map 13.1), the Dravidian languages are also found in Maharashtra, Madhya Pradesh, Orissa, West Bengal and Bihar; and, outside India, in Sri Lanka, Pakistan, Nepal and the Maldives. The Dravidian languages share the South Asian subcontinent with three other language families: the Indo-Aryan branch of Indo-European, the Munda branch of Austro-Asiatic and Sino-Tibetan. Commerce and colonisation have carried some Dravidian languages, par-

Map 13.1: The Dravidian Languages

1	Tamil	9	Irula	17	Ollari
2	Mal.	10	Kodagu	18	Gadaba
3	Telugu	11	Toda	19	Konda
4	Kan.	12	Kota	20	Kuyi
5	Gondi	13	Tulu	21	Manda
6	Kurux	14	Kolami	22	Pengo
7	Brahui	15	Naiki	23	Savara
8	Kui	16	Parji	24	Malto
				25	Badaga

Scale

0 250 500km

Map adapted from Bloch (1946)

ticularly Tamil, beyond South Asia to Burma, Indonesia, Malaysia, Fiji, Madagascar, Mauritius, Guyana, Martinique and Trinidad.

The Eighth Schedule of the Indian Constitution (1951) mandates the creation of states along linguistic lines, and accords official status to four Dravidian languages: Tamil in Tamil Nadu, Malayāḷam in Kerala, Kannaḍa in Karnataka and Telugu in Andhra Pradesh. These four have long histories, recorded in epigraphy and native literatures: Tamil dates from the second century BC; Kannaḍa from the fourth century AD; Telugu from the seventh century AD; and Malayāḷam from the tenth century AD.

Starting with Caldwell's (1875) *Comparative Grammar of the Dravidian Languages*, linguists have reconstructed a fragment of Proto-Dravidian. This fragment incorporates those features the Dravidian languages have in common and may be said to typify what is 'Dravidian' in a language. Proto-Dravidian has ten vowels, five short and five long: *a, ā, i, ī, u, ū, e, ē, o, ō*. It has sixteen consonants, including an unusual system of stops contrasting in six points of articulation: labial, dental, alveolar, retroflex, palatal and velar, viz. *p, t, R, ṭ, c, k*. Four nasals, *m, n, ṇ, ñ*; four resonants, *l, ḷ, r, ẓ*; and two glides, *v, y*, complete the inventory of consonants. Alveolars, retroflexes and resonants do not occur word-initially. Caldwell's Law describes the allophony of stops: they are voiceless when they occur initially or geminated, but voiced when they occur intervocalically or after nasals. Several metrical rules govern the composition of syllables, e.g. $(C_1)\bar{V}C_2$ alternates with $(C_1)\breve{V}C_2C_3$ as in the two stems of the verb 'see', **kāṇ-* vs. **kaṇṭ-*. Though bisyllabic roots are occasionally indicated, reconstructed lexical roots are by and large monosyllabic. While any of the five vowel qualities may appear in a root, only *a, i, u*, may appear in a derivative suffix.

Dravidian morphology is transparent, agglutinating and exclusively suffixal. The order of elements in a word is: lexical root, derivational suffix, inflectional suffix. Proto-Dravidian has two parts of speech: noun and verb, both of which appear in simple and compound forms. Nouns inflect for case, person, number and gender. Proto-Dravidian has eight cases: nominative, accusative, sociative, dative, genitive, instrumental, locative and ablative. These eight are supplemented by postpositions, derived from independent nouns or non-finite verbs. Predicate nominals can be inflected to agree with their subjects, e.g. in Ancient Tamil *-ōm* marks the first person plural in *nām nāṭṭ-ōm* 'we$_1$ (are) countrymen$_2$'. Proto-Dravidian has two numbers: singular and plural. Proto-Dravidian gender distinguishes animate and inanimate nouns on the basis of the natural gender of the referent, not 'grammatical' or conventional gender. Animate nouns may further be classified as honorific, masculine or feminine. A noun's animacy helps determine other of its grammatical features: animates take the locative case marker **-iṭam*, inanimates **-il*; most animates have the plural marker **-ir*, inanimates **-kaḷ*; the accusative case marker **-ay* is obligatory for animates, but optional for inanimates. The very extensive system of compound nouns can be illustrated by the set of deictic pronouns, which contrast in four degrees: **ivan* 'this man', **uvan* 'that man nearby', **avan* 'that man yonder', **evan* 'which, any man'. These are compound nouns, e.g. **avan* 'that man yonder' consists of the nouns **a-* 'that (one) yonder' and **-(v)an* 'man'. Complex compound nouns are often translated into English as a sequence of numeral, adjective and noun; but the internal structure of these Dravidian expressions is that of a compound noun.

Proto-Dravidian verbs are those forms that inflect for verbal categories such as tense and mood. There are two tenses, past and non-past, and two moods, modal and indicative. From a formal viewpoint verbs are finite or non-finite. Finite verbs inflect for tense and subject-verb agreement. These inflections are overt, or, in the imperative and optative, covert. Proto-Dravidian has a constraint that limits the number of finite verbs in a sentence to a maximum of one: that lone verb stands at the extreme end of the sentence and commands all other verbs within. In effect, it brings the sentence to a close. All remaining verbs in the sentence must be non-finite. The first major set of non-finite verbs is defined as those which combine with a following verb, with or without other grammatical material coming between the two. In this set we find the infinitive, conjunctive participle and conditional. The second major set comprises all those non-finite verbs that combine with a following noun to form relative clauses and similar structures. Dravidian languages rely on a rich system of compound verbs to extend the somewhat limited set of simple verb forms. Lexical compound verbs supplement the lexicon by providing a complex morphosyntactic vehicle for combinations of lexical meanings which are not encoded in any single lexeme of the language. For example, the Tamil lexical compound *koṇṭu vara* 'bring' consists of the conjunctive participle of *koḷḷa* 'hold' and an inflected form of *vara* 'come'. Auxiliary compound verbs, on the other hand, provide morphosyntactic vehicles for those verbal categories which are not encoded in any simple verb form of the language, e.g. perfect tense, benefactive voice. In this colloquial Kannaḍa example the auxiliary verb *iru* 'be' conveys the perfect tense: *nān band(u) iddīni* 'I_1 $have_3$ $come_2$'.

The basic word order in the Proto-Dravidian sentence is subject–object–verb (SOV). In Dravidian, as in other rigid SOV languages, genitives precede the nouns they modify, main verbs precede auxiliaries and complements precede their matrix clauses. Though explicit nominal morphology allows some freedom of variation in word order, verbs stay at the end of their clauses. Simple sentences consist of a subject and predicate. The subject is a noun phrase inflected for the nominative or, in certain predictable cases, the dative case; the predicate may be a verb or predicate nominal. Section 2.4 on Tamil syntax below addresses the issue of complex sentences in Dravidian, in particular how finite verbs and predicate nominals can be embedded.

Subsequent developments have naturally altered this picture. For example, metathesis in South-Central Dravidian permits alveolars, retroflexes and resonants to appear initially, e.g. Telugu *lē-* 'young (one)' from **iḷay* 'id.'. The influx of Indo-Aryan loanwords has introduced both initial voiced stops and the distinction between aspirated and non-aspirated stops in some languages, e.g. Malayāḷam, Kūṛux. The contrast between the dative and accusative cases has been neutralised in Pengo animate nouns in favour of what historically was the dative. When the joints of auxiliary compound verbs fuse, new conjugations arise, e.g. the Medieval Tamil present tense, the Kūi objective conjugation, the Pengo present perfect tense. The syntactic influence of neighbouring Indo-Aryan languages has reversed the order of complement and matrix in North Dravidian. Thus, Malto *ā loker ṭunḍnar tan laboh ote* 'those$_1$ people$_2$ saw$_3$ that$_4$ (it) was$_6$ heavy$_5$' contrasts with the common Dravidian order in Tamil *kaNamāka irukkiRatu eNRu avarkaḷ pārttārkaḷ* 'they$_4$ saw$_5$ that$_3$ (it) is$_2$ heavy$_1$'. Despite a certain measure of change in phonology and lexicon, Proto-Dravidian morphology and syntax has persisted remarkably well in South, South-Central and Central Dravidian.

2 Tamil

2.1 Historical Background

Tamil (*tamiẓ*) belongs to the South Dravidian branch of the Dravidian family: like other members of this branch it lost Proto-Dravidian **c*-, e.g. *il* 'not be' from **cil*-, *īy*- 'give' from **cīy*-, *āRu* 'six' from **cāRu*; and it replaced the Proto-Dravidian copula **maN* 'be located' with *iru* 'be located'. It has been spoken in southern India and northeastern Sri Lanka from prehistoric times. The earliest records of Tamil, lithic inscriptions in a variety of Aśōkan Brāhmī script, date from 200 BC. Alongside these inscriptions stands a vast and varied literature, preserved on palm-leaf manuscripts and by rote memory, covering two thousand years. Within this literary corpus is an indigenous grammatical tradition, separate from the Sanskrit grammarians: its two outstanding texts are *tolkāppiyam* (c. 200 BC) and *naNNūl* (c. AD 1000). There are three distinct stages of Tamil revealed in these records: Ancient Tamil, 200 BC to AD 700; Medieval Tamil, AD 700 to 1500; and Modern Tamil, AD 1500 to the present.

Ancient Tamil has just two tenses, past and non-past; Medieval and Modern Tamil have three, past, present and future. Ancient Tamil has many subject-verb agreement markers for each member of the paradigm, e.g. the first person singular is signalled by *-ēN*, *-eN*, *-aN*, *-al*, *-ku*, *-ṭu*, *-tu*. But Medieval Tamil retains only the first three, while Modern Tamil keeps only the first. In Ancient and Medieval Tamil, as opposed to their modern successor, predicate nominals can be inflected for subject-verb agreement, so that *-ai* marks the second person singular in *nī nāṭṭ-ai* 'you$_1$ (are a) countryman$_2$' while *-ēN* marks the first person singular in *nāN pāvi-(y)ēN* 'I$_1$ (am a) sinner$_2$'. In Medieval Tamil the set of verbal bases was open and accommodated many Sanskritic loanwords, e.g. Tamil *aNupavikka* 'to experience', derived from Sanskrit *anubhava* 'experience', but it is closed in Modern Tamil.

Between AD 800 and 1000 the western dialects of Tamil, geographically separated from the eastern by the Western Ghats, broke off and developed into Malayāḷam. Malayāḷam lost its rules of subject-verb agreement while Tamil maintained them, and it welcomed into its lexicon a great number of

Sanskrit loanwords. The Iruḷa language, spoken in the hilly spurs of the Nilgiris between Kerala and Tamil Nadu, is also closely related to Tamil.

During the past two thousand years, Tamil dialects have evolved along three dimensions: geography, caste-based society and diglossia. Today there are six regional dialects: (1) Sri Lanka; (2) Northern, spoken in the Chingleput, North Arcot and South Arcot districts; (3) Western, spoken in the Coimbatore, Salem and Dharmapuri districts; (4) Central, spoken in the Tirichirapalli, Tanjore and Madurai districts; (5) Eastern, spoken in the Putukottai and Ramanathapuram districts; and (6) Southern, spoken in the Nagercoil and Tirunelveli districts. Sri Lankan Tamil seems to be the most conservative: it preserves the four-way deictic contrast lost in the continental dialects during the Medieval period, e.g. *ivaN* 'this man', *uvaN* 'that man nearby', *avaN* 'that man yonder', *evaN* 'which, any man'. It still resists the use of initial voiced stops so that continental Tamil *dōcai* 'rice pancake' becomes *tōcai* 'id.' in Sri Lankan Tamil. Throughout its history, but most notably during the Chola Empire, AD 850 to 1250, Tamil travelled beyond South Asia to kingdoms in Burma, Cambodia, Sri Vijāya and Indonesia. During the British Raj of the nineteenth century, it was carried to South Africa, British Guiana and other parts of the British Empire.

The social dialects of Tamil particularly accentuate the distinction between brahmin and non-brahmin castes. Among brahmins the word for 'house' is *ām*, among non-brahmins *vīṭu*; among brahmins the polite imperative of *vara* 'come' is *vāṅkō*, among non-brahmins *vāṅka*. For 'drinking water' Vaisnavite brahmins say *tīrttam*, Saivite brahmins *jalam* and non-brahmins *taṇṇīr*. Even finer gradations of caste dialects can be found in kinship terminology and proper names.

Finally, Tamil dialects show diglossic variation in which a 'high' formal variety (*centamiẓ*) contrasts with a 'low' informal variety (*koṭuntamiẓ*). The difference between these two corresponds only roughly to the difference between written and spoken Tamil. The high variety is used in most writing, radio and television broadcasts, political oratory and public lectures. While the low variety is used in virtually all face-to-face communication, it also appears in the cinema, some political oratory and some modern fiction. In Akilan's novel *ciNēkiti* 'The Girl-Friend' (1951) both dialogue and narration are in the high variety; in Janakiraman's *ammā vantāḷ* 'Here Comes Mother' (1966) the former is in low, the latter in high Tamil; and in Jeyakantan's *cila nēraṅkaḷil cila maNitarkaḷ* 'Certain Men at Certain Moments' (1970) both are in low Tamil. In high Tamil the animate and inanimate locative case markers are *-iṭam* and *-il*, respectively; but in low Tamil they are *-kiṭṭa* and *-le*. The polite imperative of *vara* 'come' is *vāruṅkaḷ* in high Tamil, but *vāṅka* or *vāṅkō* in low. The word for 'much' or 'very' is *mika* in high Tamil, but *rompa* in low (both come from the infinitives of verbs that mean 'exceed' or 'fill'). Palatalisation of *-nt-* and *-tt-* following *i*, *ī*, or *ai* is common in low Tamil, but not in high, e.g. low *aṭiccu* 'beating' corresponds to high *aṭittu* 'id.'

All speakers of Tamil, even illiterates, have recourse to both varieties and, according to the situation, must navigate between the phonological, lexical and grammatical differences that distinguish them.

The Pure Tamil Movement (*taNit tamiẓ iyakkam*) of the 1900s, a cultural branch of the politically oriented Dravidian Movement, attempted to purge Tamil of its foreign elements, especially its Sanskritic vocabulary. The first part of the legacy of this movement is the intense loyalty that Tamils feel for their language; the second is that the scientific and bureaucratic gobbledygook is ultra-Tamil, not Sanskrit as in other Indic languages. At the turn of the century, the brahmin dialect of Madras City seemed destined to become the standard dialect of Modern Tamil. Today, however, it is the high non-brahmin dialect of the Central dialect, including the cities of Tanjore, Tirichirapalli and Madurai, that is emerging as the standard dialect. This chapter describes modern standard Tamil, which is based upon and shares features of both the written language and the standard spoken Central dialect.

Tamil is recognised as one of India's fourteen national languages in the Eighth Schedule of the Indian Constitution (1951). The Tamil Nadu Official Language Act of 1956 establishes Tamil as the first official language of Tamil Nadu and English as the second. In Sri Lanka, Tamil shares with Sinhalese the title of national language. Today, Tamil is spoken by approximately 45,000,000 in India, 2½ million in Sri Lanka, and one million elsewhere.

2.2 Phonology and Orthography

The lack of an adequate phonology of modern standard Tamil has led linguists to adopt the following strategy. A transcription of written Tamil is taken as the underlying phonological representation, which is simultaneously the output of the syntactic rules and the input to the phonological rules. The corresponding spoken form is taken as the surface representation, the output of the phonological rules. Hence, the rules that convert the one into the other are held to constitute the substance of Tamil phonology. In effect, these rules enable one to read a passage of written Tamil and pronounce it in spoken Tamil. While this strategy undoubtedly fails to address some facets of modern standard Tamil phonology, it does in the long run provide a good, general picture of the phonological structure. The reason for this success can be traced directly to the transparent, agglutinating morphology of modern standard Tamil, which inhibits the growth of complicated phonological alternations.

The inventory of systematic phonemes in modern standard Tamil has a 'low' native core and a 'high' borrowed periphery. Though both are used by educated speakers, the periphery is often assimilated to the core in informal settings and in rapid, unguarded speech. Both appear in table 13.1, where parentheses enclose the sounds of the periphery. The two nasals enclosed in square brackets are graphemically but not phonemically distinct from /n/.

Table 13.1: The Sounds of Modern Standard Tamil

	Stop vls.	vd.	*Fricative*	*Sibilant*	*Nasal*	*Lateral*	*Tap*	*Approximant*	*Glide*
Labial	p	(b)	(f)		m				v
Dental	t	(d)			n	l	r		
Alveolar	R				[N]				
Retroflex	ṭ	(ḍ)		(ṣ)	ṇ	ḷ		ẓ	
Palatal	c	(j)		(ś)	ñ				y
Velar	k	(g)			[ṅ]				(h)

		Front	*Central*	*Back*
High	long	ī		ū
	short	i		u
Mid	long	ē		ō
	short	e	(ə)	o
Low	long	(ǣ)	ā	(ɔ̄)
	short		a	
Diphthong		ai		au

Key: (X), X is part of the peripheral phonology of Tamil. [X], X is graphemically, but not phonemically distinct.

The core contains twelve vowels and sixteen consonants. It has five short vowels, *a*, *i*, *u*, *e*, *o*; five long vowels, *ā*, *ī*, *ū*, *ē*, *ō*; and two diphthongs, *ai*, *au*, each with the length of a short vowel. Included among the consonants are six stops, *p*, *t*, *R*, *ṭ*, *c*, *k*; four nasals, *m*, *n*, *ṇ*, *ñ*; two laterals, *l*, *ḷ*; two glides, *v*, *y*; one tap, *r*; and one approximant, *ẓ*. Subscript dots indicate retroflection, one of the more salient features of Tamil phonology. The sounds that appear word-initially are: all vowels, *p*, *t*, *ṭ*, *c*, *k*, *m*, *n*, *ṇ*, *ñ*, *l*, *r*, *y*, *v* (*ṭ* and *ṇ* occur in onomatopoeia, *l* and *r* often take a prosthetic *i*). The sounds that appear word-finally are all vowels except *e*, and *m*, *n*, *ṇ*, *l*, *ḷ*, *r*, *ẓ*, *y* (a half-short, high, back unrounded enunciative vowel often follows the consonants). In the following, words in italics represent a transliteration of the orthography; slashes enclose the phonemic analysis and square brackets the modern standard Tamil pronunciation.

Stops are voiced intervocalically and following nasals, e.g. /atu/ 'it' [aðu]; /aṅkē/ 'there' [aṅgē], but voiceless elsewhere, viz. initially, doubled or in other clusters. Intervocalic stops also undergo spirantisation so that /VkV/ becomes [VɣV], /VtV/ becomes [VðV] and /VcV/ becomes [VdʒV]. Moreover, the ɣ-allophone of /k/ becomes [h]; the dʒ-allophone of /c/, [s]. Initial /c/ is often pronounced as *s* in the speech of many educated speakers. Nasalisation converts a sequence of vowel and word-final nasal into a nasalised vowel, e.g. /maram/ 'tree' becomes [marã], but when the interrogative clitic is added to form *maram-ā* 'a tree?', nasalisation is blocked. Glide insertion transforms initial *ĕ-* and *ŏ-* into *yĕ-* and *vŏ-*, respectively. Palatalisation converts *-tt-* and *-nt-* into *-cc-* and *-ñc-*, respectively, when they follow *i*, *ī* or *ai*, e.g. /ciritteN/ 'I smiled' becomes [siriccẽ]. Cluster simplification eliminates triliteral consonant clusters either by the epenthesis of a vowel, e.g. Sanskrit *tattva* 'truth, reality' becomes Tamil *tattuvam*, or by the deletion of a consonant, e.g. /tīrtteN/ 'I finished' becomes [tīttẽ] (palatalisation precedes cluster simplification so [tīccẽ] does not occur).

Vowel lowering lowers the high vowels *i* and *u* to *e* and *o*, respectively, when followed by no more than one consonant and the vowel *ă* or *ai*, e.g. /vilai/ 'price' becomes [velai]; /utavi/ 'help', [oðavi]. The diphthongs *ai* and *au* undergo a number of changes. Non-initial *ai* becomes *e* so that /vilai/ 'price' becomes [velai], then [vele]; initial *ai* may be preserved, e.g. *vaikai* 'Vaigai River'; or become *a*, e.g. /aintu/ 'five' becomes [aiñcu] by palatalization, then [añcu]. *ai* and *au* are often reanalysed as *a+y* and *a+v*, respectively, so that /paiyaN/ 'boy' becomes [payyã], while English 'town' becomes [ṭavuṇ]. Occasionally, the front high and mid vowels, *ĭ* and *ĕ*, are transformed into their back counterparts, *ŭ* and *ŏ*, when they appear between a labial and a retroflex consonant, e.g. /vīṭu/ 'house' becomes [vūḍu]. While some brahmin dialects of Tanjore still pronounce *ẓ* as a voiced retroflex approximant, most dialects merge it with *ḷ*, e.g. /maẓai/ 'rain' becomes [maḷe]. *N* is pronounced as *n*; *R* as *r*, except in the Southern dialect where it is a trill as opposed to the flap *r*. The cluster *NR* is pronounced as *ndr* and, ultimately, *nn*, e.g., /eNRu/ 'saying' becomes [endru], then [ennu]; the cluster *RR* is pronounced as *ttr*, then *tt*, e.g., /viRRēN/ 'I sold' becomes [vittrẽ], then [vittẽ].

The peripheral sounds of modern standard Tamil include nine consonants, *b*, *d*, *ḍ*, *j*, *g*, *f*, *ṣ*, *s*, *h*, and three vowels, *ə*, *ǣ*, *ɔ̄*. In pronunciation, these sounds undergo rules that assimilate them to the nearest corresponding sounds of the phonological core. /f/ in /faiyal/ 'file' becomes *p* in *paiyal*. Voiced stops contrast with voiceless stops only in initial position because in non-initial position they are interpreted as the voiced allophones of the core's voiceless stop phonemes, so that Sanskrit *agrahāra* 'brahmin settlement' is phonemicised in modern standard Tamil as /akkirakāram/, where both Sanskrit *g* and *h* are treated as allophones of /k/. Initial voiced stops are usually devoiced in rapid speech so that both /bāvam/ 'facial expression' and /pāvam/ 'sin' are pronounced as [pāvã]. Sibilants tend to assimilate to /c/. The vowels *ə*, *ǣ* and *ɔ̄* assimilate to *a*, *ē* and *ā*, respectively. English loanwords have complicated the set of consonant clusters in modern standard Tamil: 'agent' is borrowed as *ēyjeṇṭu* with a cluster of nasal and voiceless stops, one which Tamil grammar traditionally prohibits.

Stress in modern standard Tamil is not distinctive and is fixed on the first syllable of every word. The syllabic structure of words is based on quantitative units known as *morae* (*acai* in traditional Tamil grammar). Handbooks of Tamil discuss other issues of segmental and suprasegmental phonology in greater detail.

Tamil is written in a syllabic script which historically derives from a version of Aśōkan Brāhmī script (see table 13.2). Each vowel has two forms in this syllabary: an independent symbol to represent it at the beginning of a word and an auxiliary symbol, which combines with consonant symbols, to represent it elsewhere. In initial position, *ā* is represented by ஆ ; but elsewhere by ா, as in கா *kā*, தா *tā*, and பா *pā*. In initial position, *i* is represented by இ ; but by ி elsewhere, as in கி *ki*, தி *ti*, and பி *pi*. Each consonant is represented by a basic symbol which has the inherent vowel *a* in the order C*a*, so that க is read as *ka*; த as *ta*; and ப as *pa*. When any auxiliary symbol is added to the consonant symbol, the inherent vowel *a* is suppressed, e.g. the symbols க *ka* and இ *i* combine to form the symbol கி, which is read as *ki*, not **kai*. The addition of a dot, called *puḷḷi*, above the consonant symbol removes the inherent vowel altogether, so that க் represents *k*; த், *t*; and ப் , *p*. The use of *puḷḷi* is instrumental in the correct representation of consonant clusters: இப்ப represents *ippa* 'now', not **ipapa*. The top row in table 13.2 presents the independent vowel symbols; the leftmost column, the basic consonant symbols modified by *puḷḷi*; and the column second from the left, the basic consonant symbol with the inherent vowel *a*. The remaining cells present the graphemic representation of the combination of basic consonant symbol and auxiliary vowel symbol.

Modern standard Tamil has a graphemic convention whereby initial stop consonants are doubled when preceded by certain forms such as the dative case marker, the accusative case marker and the demonstrative adjectives, e.g. /inta pāvam/ 'this sin' is written as *intap pāvam*. Doubling does not take place when the initial stop is voiced, e.g. /inta bāvam/ 'this facial expression' is written as *inta pāvam* (since *inta pāvam* is treated as a compound, *p* is treated as intervocalic and, therefore, voiced). The Tamil alphabetic order is *a, ā, i, ī, u, ū, e, ē, ai, o, ō, au, k, ṅ, c, ñ, ṭ, ṇ, t, n, p, m, y, r, l, v, ẓ, ḷ, R, N*. Six additional symbols may be used to represent letters in Sanskrit loans: *j, ś, ṣ, s, h, kṣ*. But these symbols may be replaced by others, e.g. *kṣ* by *ṭc*. The Tamil syllabary is adequate to represent the core phonology of modern standard Tamil.

2.3 Morphology and Parts of Speech

Although some grammars of Tamil list as many as ten parts of speech, all of them can be resolved into one of two formal categories: noun and verb. These two are distinguished by the grammatical categories for which they are inflected. (The so-called indeclinables, including interjections, seem to be variously nouns or verbs.) The morphology is agglutinating and exclusively suffixal: the inflections are marked by suffixes joined to the lexical base, which may or may not be extended by a derivational suffix.

Table 13.2: The Tamil Syllabary (Adapted from Pope 1979)

–	அ a	ஆ ā	இ i	ஈ ī	உ u	ஊ ū	எ e	ஏ ē	ஐ ai	ஒ o	ஓ ō	ஔ au
க் k	க ka	கா kā	கி ki	கீ kī	கு ku	கூ kū	கெ ke	கே kē	கை kai	கொ ko	கோ kō	கௌ kau
ங் ṅ	ங ṅa	ஙா ṅā	ஙி ṅi	ஙீ ṅī	ஙு ṅu	ஙூ ṅū	ஙெ ṅe	ஙே ṅē	ஙை ṅai	ஙொ ṅo	ஙோ ṅō	ஙௌ ṅau
ச் ç	ச ça	சா çā	சி çi	சீ çī	சு çu	சூ çū	செ çe	சே çē	சை çai	சொ ço	சோ çō	சௌ çau
ஞ் ñ	ஞ ña	ஞா ñā	ஞி ñi	ஞீ ñī	ஞு ñu	ஞூ ñū	ஞெ ñe	ஞே ñē	ஞை ñai	ஞொ ño	ஞோ ñō	ஞௌ ñau
ட் ḍ	ட ḍa	டா ḍā	டி ḍi	டீ ḍī	டு ḍu	டூ ḍū	டெ ḍe	டே ḍē	டை ḍai	டொ ḍo	டோ ḍō	டௌ ḍau
ண் ṇ	ண ṇa	ணா ṇā	ணி ṇi	ணீ ṇī	ணு ṇu	ணூ ṇū	ணெ ṇe	ணே ṇē	ணை ṇai	ணொ ṇo	ணோ ṇō	ணௌ ṇau
த் t	த ta	தா tā	தி ti	தீ tī	து tu	தூ tū	தெ te	தே tē	தை tai	தொ to	தோ tō	தௌ tau
ந் n	ந na	நா nā	நி ni	நீ nī	நு nu	நூ nū	நெ ne	நே nē	நை nai	நொ no	நோ nō	நௌ nau
ப் p	ப pa	பா pā	பி pi	பீ pī	பு pu	பூ pū	பெ pe	பே pē	பை pai	பொ po	போ pō	பௌ pau
ம் m	ம ma	மா mā	மி mi	மீ mī	மு mu	மூ mū	மெ me	மே mē	மை mai	மொ mo	மோ mō	மௌ mau
ய் y	ய ya	யா yā	யி yi	யீ yī	யு yu	யூ yū	யெ ye	யே yē	யை yai	யொ yo	யோ yō	யௌ yau
ர் r	ர ra	ரா rā	ரி ri	ரீ rī	ரு ru	ரூ rū	ரெ re	ரே rē	ரை rai	ரொ ro	ரோ rō	ரௌ rau
ல் l	ல la	லா lā	லி li	லீ lī	லு lu	லூ lū	லெ le	லே lē	லை lai	லொ lo	லோ lō	லௌ lau
வ் v	வ va	வா vā	வி vi	வீ vī	வு vu	வூ vū	வெ ve	வே vē	வை vai	வொ vo	வோ vō	வௌ vau
ழ் ẓ	ழ ẓa	ழா ẓā	ழி ẓi	ழீ ẓī	ழு ẓu	ழூ ẓū	ழெ ẓe	ழே ẓē	ழை ẓai	ழொ ẓo	ழோ ẓō	ழௌ ẓau
ள் ḷ	ள ḷa	ளா ḷā	ளி ḷi	ளீ ḷī	ளு ḷu	ளூ ḷū	ளெ ḷe	ளே ḷē	ளை ḷai	ளொ ḷo	ளோ ḷō	ளௌ ḷau
ற் R	ற Ra	றா Rā	றி Ri	றீ Rī	று Ru	றூ Rū	றெ Re	றே Rē	றை Rai	றொ Ro	றோ Rō	றௌ Rau
ன் N	ன Na	னா Nā	னி Ni	னீ Nī	னு Nu	னூ Nū	னெ Ne	னே Nē	னை Nai	னொ No	னோ Nō	னௌ Nau

Nouns and verbs both appear in simple and compound forms.

Nouns are inflected for person, case, number and gender. This class includes common nouns, proper names, numerals, pronouns and some so-called adjectives. There are two numbers: singular and plural. Tamil gender is based on the natural gender of a noun's referent, not on conventionally ascribed grammatical gender. There are two basic genders: 'rational' (*uyartiṇai*) and 'irrational' (*ahRiṇai*), corresponding roughly to human and non-human. Rational nouns are further classified as honorific, masculine and feminine. Nouns referring to deities and men are classified as rational; in some dialects women are classified as rational, in others as irrational. (Children and animals are normally classified as irrational.) In some cases, conventionally rational nouns are treated as irrational, e.g. when a proper name is given to an animal. By the same token, conventionally irrational nouns are treated as rational when used as epithets for men. In *ramu eṅkē? antak kaẓutai eṅkēyō pōy irukkiRāN* 'where$_2$ (is) Ramu$_1$? That$_3$ ass$_4$ has$_7$ gone$_6$ (off) somewhere$_5$' *kaẓutai* 'ass' is treated as a rational noun for the purposes of subject-verb agreement. A noun's gender determines other of its grammatical properties such as the choice between the animate locative case marker *-iṭam* and the inanimate *-il*.

Modern standard Tamil has eight cases: nominative, accusative, dative, sociative, genitive, instrumental, locative, ablative. There is just one declension: once the nominative singular, nominative plural and oblique stem are known, all the other forms can be predicted. Moreover, the nominative plural and oblique stem can generally be predicted from the gender and phonological shape of the nominative singular. The chart given here presents the declension of four nouns: *maNitaN* 'man', *maram* 'tree', *āRu* 'river' and *pū* 'flower'. In addition to eight cases, modern standard Tamil has postpositions, derived from independent nouns or non-finite verbs. The postposition *pārttu* 'towards', which governs the accusative case, e.g. *avaNaip pārttu* 'towards him', comes from the adverbial participle *pārttu* 'looking at'.

The Declension of Four Selected Tamil Nouns

Singular	maNitaN 'man'	maram 'tree'	āRu 'river'	pū 'flower'
Oblique Stem	maNitaN-	maratt-	āRR-	pū(v)-
Nominative	maNitaN	maram	āRu	pū
Accusative	maNitaN-ai	maratt-ai	āRR-ai	pūv-ai
Dative	maNitaN-ukku	maratt-ukku	āRR-ukku	pūv-ukku
Sociative	maNitaN-ōṭu	maratt-ōṭu	āRR-ōṭu	pūv-ōṭu
Genitive	maNitaN-uṭaiya	maratt-uṭaiya	āRR-uṭaiya	pūv-uṭaiya
Instrumental	maNitaN-āl	maratt-āl	aRR-āl	pūv-āl
Locative	maNitaN-iṭam	maratt-il	āRR-il	pūv-il
Ablative	maNitaN-iṭamiruntu	maratt-iliruntu	āRR-iliruntu	pūv-iliruntu

Plural	maNitarkaḷ	maraṅkaḷ	āRukaḷ	pūkkaḷ
Nominative	maNitarkaḷ	maraṅkaḷ	āRukaḷ	pūkkaḷ
Accusative	maNitarkaḷ-ai	maraṅkaḷ-ai	āRukaḷ-ai	pūkkaḷ-ai
Dative	maNitarkaḷ-ukku	maraṅkaḷ-ukku	āRukaḷ-ukku	pūkkaḷ-ukku
Sociative	maNitarkaḷ-ōṭu	maraṅkaḷ-ōṭu	āRukaḷ-ōṭu	pūkkaḷ-ōṭu
Genitive	maNitarkaḷ-uṭaiya	maraṅkaḷ-uṭaiya	āRukaḷ-uṭaiya	pūkkaḷ-uṭaiya
Instrumental	maNitarkaḷ-āl	maraṅkaḷ-āl	āRukaḷ-āl	pūkkaḷ-āl
Locative	maNitarkaḷ-iṭam	maraṅkaḷ-il	āRukaḷ-il	pūkkaḷ-il
Ablative	maNitarkaḷ-iṭamiruntu	maraṅkaḷ-iliruntu	āRukaḷ-iliruntu	pūkkaḷ-iliruntu

Modern standard Tamil has no formal class of articles: other grammatical devices assume their function. The numeral *oru* 'one' often functions as an indefinite article; so, by way of contrast, its absence with a rational noun conveys the meaning of a definite article, e.g. *oru maNitaN* 'a man' but Ø *maNitaN* 'the man'. Irrational direct objects are interpreted as indefinite when inflected for the nominative case, but definite when inflected for the accusative, e.g. *nāN maram pārttēN* 'I_1 saw_3 a $tree_2$', but *nāN marattaip pārttēN* 'I_1 saw_3 the $tree_2$'.

A small but significant subset is marked for first or second person. These are the personal pronouns: *nāN* 'I' (obl. *eN(N)-*); *nām* 'we and you' (obl. *nam-*); *nāṅkaḷ* 'we but not you' (obl. *eṅkaḷ-*); *nī* 'thou' (obl. *uN(N)-*); *nīṅkaḷ* 'you' (obl. *uṅkaḷ-*). There are two third person anaphoric pronouns, called reflexives, *tāN* 'self' (obl. *taN(N)-*); and *tāṅkaḷ* 'selves' (obl. *taṅkaḷ*); the antecedent must be a subject, either of the same or a superordinate clause. Modern standard Tamil has deictic pronouns which are formally compound nouns. *avaN* 'that man' consists of *a-* 'that (one)' and *-(v)aN* 'man'. Continental Tamil makes three deictic distinctions, e.g. *ivaN* 'this man', *avaN* 'that man', *evaN* 'which, any man', as opposed to Sri Lanka Tamil which preserves the older, Dravidian system with four. Distal pronouns, marked by *a-*, are less marked than the proximate, marked by *i-*: they appear in contexts of neutralisation and translate English, 'he', 'she', 'it', 'they' etc.

In Ancient and Medieval, but not modern standard Tamil, nouns, often predicate nominals, were inflected for person, e.g. *-ai* marks second person singular in *nī nāṭṭ-ai* 'you_1 (are a) $countryman_2$'. In Medieval Tamil such nouns could also be inflected for case: in *tēvar-īr-aip pukaẓntu* '$praising_2$ you (who are a) god_1' the accusative case marker *-ai* is suffixed to the second person marker *-īr* which in turn is suffixed to the noun *tēvar* 'god'.

Compound nouns are very common. The nouns *maram* 'tree' (obl. *maratt-*), *aṭi* 'base' and *niẓal* 'shadow' combine to form the compound *maratt-aṭi-niẓal* 'shadow at the base of the tree'. Coordinate compounds in which each part refers to a separate entity are also common, e.g. *vīratīracākacaṅkaḷ* 'courage, bravery and valour' consists of *vīram* 'courage', *tīram* 'bravery', *cākacam* 'valour' and the plural suffix *-kaḷ*. Such *dvandvā* compounds contrast with English compounds such as *secretary-treasurer* which refers to a single individual. Some of the so-called adjectives of modern standard Tamil are bound nouns which must occur in compound nouns, but not as their head, e.g. both *nalla nāḷ* 'good$_1$ day$_2$' and *nalla-(v)aN* 'good man' imply a noun *nal* 'goodness' which never occurs by itself. So pervasive are compound nouns that even the Sanskrit privative prefix *a-*, *ava-* 'not, without' has been reanalysed in Tamil as a noun in a compound. Tamil borrowed hundreds of pairs of Sanskrit nouns, one without the privative prefix and one with it, e.g. *mati* 'respect', *ava-mati* 'disrespect'. *ava-mati* is treated like the compound *maratt-aṭi* 'tree-base': the second element is identified with the independent noun *mati* 'respect', while the first element *ava-* is treated as the oblique form of an independent noun *avam* 'void, nothingness, absence'. This reanalysis preserves the strictly suffixal nature of modern standard Tamil morphology.

Verbs are inflected for verbal categories, participating notably in the oppositions of mood and tense. Formally, a verb consists of a verb base and grammatical formative. The base itself consists of a stem and, optionally, two suffixes, one for voice and one for causative. The stem lexically identifies the verb. Sixty per cent of modern standard Tamil verbs participate in the opposition of affective versus effective voice. An affective verb is one the subject of which undergoes the action named by the stem; an effective verb is one the subject of which directs the action named by the stem. The category of effectivity differs from both transitivity and causation. Affective *vilaka* 'separate' and effective *vilakka* 'separate' minimally contrast since both are transitive: *vaṇṭi pātai-(y)ai vilakiNatu* '(the) cart$_1$ left$_3$ (the) path$_2$' vs. *avaN vaṇṭi-(y)ai (pātai-(y)iliruntu) vilakkiNāN* 'he$_1$ drove$_4$ (lit. separated) the cart$_2$ (off the path)$_3$'. Though very productive in Medieval Tamil, the causative suffix *-vi*, *-ppi*, which conveys causation, is lexically restricted in modern standard Tamil, having given way to periphrastic causative constructions.

All modern standard Tamil verb forms are inflected for mood, the verbal category which characterises the ontological status of the narrated event either as unreal, possible, potential (modal) or as real, actual (indicative). Mood is implicitly marked in the grammatical formative following the verb base: the past tense, present tense and adverbial participle are indicative; the rest are modal. Modern standard Tamil has three simple tenses, past, present and future, as well as several periphrastic tenses like the perfect series. Some deverbal nouns, such as *pirivu* 'separation' derived from *piriya* 'separate', mark neither tense nor mood.

Modern standard Tamil verbs are finite or non-finite. Finite verbs are inflected for tense and subject-verb agreement, overtly or, in the imperative and optative, covertly. A verb's finiteness has a direct bearing on modern standard Tamil syntax: there can be only one finite verb per sentence. All remaining verbs must be non-finite and belong to one of three classes.

One class of non-finite verbs consists of relative participles, called *peyareccam* '(verbs) deficient in a noun', which are instrumental in the formation of relative clauses and similar structures. They are verb forms marked for tense which combine with a following noun: in the following examples the relative participle *vanta* 'which came' links the preceding clause to the following nouns, e.g. *nēRRu vanta oru mantiri* 'a$_3$ minister$_4$ (who) came$_2$ yesterday$_1$', *mantiri nēRRu vanta ceyti* '(the) news$_4$ (that) (the) minister$_1$ came$_3$ yesterday$_2$'. The second class of non-finite verbs, called *viNaiyeccam* '(verbs) deficient in a verb', includes the infinitive, adverbial participle, conditional, negative verbal participle and negative conditional. All are verb forms that combine with a following verb, with or without other lexical material coming between the two verbs. Given the restriction on finite verbs, these forms are crucial in the formation of complex sentences. The infinitive and adverbial participle are instrumental in the formation of compound verbs, as well. The third class of non-finite verbs includes all verbal nouns, called *viNaippeyar* 'verbal nouns', forms derived from verbs but capable of having nominal inflections. Some retain their verbal characteristics better than others: in the chart showing the conjugation of *piriya* 'separate', *piri-nt-atu* 'separation' takes a nominative subject while *pirivu* 'separation' takes a genitive. Consult the chart for the simple verb forms of Tamil, using *piriya* 'separate' as an example. Modern standard Tamil has seven morphophonemically distinct conjugations, details of which can be found in most grammars.

The conjugation of *piriya* 'separate'

Finite Verb Forms

	Past	*Present*	*Future*	*Future Negative*
1 sg.	piri-nt-ēN	piri-kiR-ēN	piri-v-ēN	piriya māṭṭ-ēN
2 sg.	piri-nt-āy	piri-kiR-āy	piri-v-āy	piriya māṭṭ-āy
3 sg. hon.	piri-nt-ār	piri-kiR-ār	piri-v-ār	piriya māṭṭ-ār
3 sg. m.	piri-nt-āN	piri-kiR-āN	piri-v-āN	piriya māṭṭ-āN
3 sg. f.	piri-nt-āḷ	piri-kiR-āḷ	piri-v-āḷ	piriya māṭṭ-āḷ
3 sg. irr.	piri-nt-atu	piri-kiR-atu	piri-(y)-um	piri-(y)ātu
1 pl.	piri-nt-ōm	piri-kiR-ōm	piri-v-ōm	piriya māṭṭ-ōm
2 pl.	piri-nt-īrkaḷ	piri-kiR-īrkaḷ	piri-v-īrkaḷ	piriya māṭṭ-īrkaḷ
3 pl. rat.	piri-nt-ārkaḷ	piri-kiR-ārkaḷ	piri-v-ārkaḷ	piriya māṭṭ-ārkaḷ
3 pl. irr.	piri-nt-aNa	piri-kiNR-aNa	piri-(y)um	piri-(y)ātu

Non-Future Negative: *piriya (v)illai* for all persons, numbers and genders.

	Imperative	*Negative Imperative*	*Optative*
Sg.	piri	piri-(y)ātē	
Pl., hon.	piri-(y)uṅkaḷ	piri-(y)ātīrkaḷ	piri-ka

Non-Finite Verb Forms

	Past	*Present*	*Future*	*Negative*
Rel. part.	piri-nt-a	piri-kiR-a	piri-(y)um	piri-(y)āta
V.n.	piri-nt-atu	piri-kiR-atu	piri-v-atu	piri-(y)ātatu
Adv. part.:	piri-ntu	infin.: piri-(y)a	neg. v. part.: piri-(y)āmal	
Cond.:	piri-ntāl	neg. cond.: piri-(y)āviṭṭāl		
De-v. n.:	piri-tal, piri-kai, piri-vu.			

Modern standard Tamil has two kinds of compound verb: lexical and auxiliary. Lexical compound verbs are complex morphosyntactic vehicles, made up of two or more simple verbs, that encode those lexical meanings which are not encoded in any single lexeme. *aruka vara* 'approach' consists of the infinitive *aruka* 'near' and an inflected form of *vara* 'come'; *kūrntu kavaNikka* 'peer' consists of the adverbial participle *kūrntu* 'sharpening (i.e. sharply)' and an inflected form of *kavaNikka* 'notice'. By contrast, auxiliary compound verbs are complex morphosyntactic vehicles, made up of two or more simple verbs, that encode those verbal categories which are not encoded in any simple verb form, such as the perfect tense or the causative. *varac ceyya* 'make$_2$ X come$_1$' consists of the modal auxiliary *ceyya* 'make, do' and the infinitive of the main verb *vara* 'come'; *vantu irukka* 'X has$_2$ come$_1$' consists of the indicative auxiliary *irukka* 'be' and the adverbial participle of the main verb *vara* 'come'. The two kinds of compound verbs have different grammatical properties: for example, additional lexical material can separate the components of a lexical compound, but not those of an auxiliary compound, e.g. *kūrntu avaḷaik kavaNikka* 'peer$_{1+3}$ (at) her$_2$', but **vantu vīṭṭukku irukka* 'X has$_3$ to the house$_2$ come$_1$'.

Modern standard Tamil has about fifty auxiliary verbs, half modal and half indicative. It lacks simple adverbs like English *not* and instead uses modal auxiliary verbs to express negation: in *vara māṭṭāN* '(he) won't$_2$ come$_1$' the auxiliary verb *māṭṭa* 'not' signals the future negative of *vara* 'come'. Ancient and Medieval Tamil had a synthetic negative conjugation, remnants of which survive in the third person irrational forms of the future tense.

Modern standard Tamil also compensates for the lack of basic adverbs by a very productive set of noun+verb compounds whose second member is the infinitive *āka* 'become' and which function adverbially. *cikkiramāka* 'quickly, urgently' consists of the noun *cikkiram* 'urgency' and *āka* 'become'.

2.4 A Skeleton Account of Simple and Complex Sentences in Modern Standard Tamil

Simple sentences in modern standard Tamil consist of a subject and a predicate. The subject is a nominal which is inflected for the nominative or, in certain cases, the dative case. The predicate is either a finite verb or a predicate nominal which appears without a copula. From the various combinations of subject and predicate, four basic sentence types emerge: (1) nominative subject and predicate nominal, e.g. *avaN oru maNitaN* 'he$_1$ (is) a$_2$ man$_3$'; (2) nominative subject and finite verb, e.g. *avaN vantāN* 'he$_1$ came$_2$'; (3) dative subject and predicate nominal, e.g. *avaNukku oru makaN* 'he$_1$ (has) a$_2$ son$_3$' (lit. 'to him (is) a son'); and (4) dative subject and finite verb, *avaNukkut tōcai piṭikkum* 'he$_1$ likes$_3$ dosais$_2$'.

While dative subjects do not trigger subject-verb agreement, unlike other datives they possess such subject-like properties as the ability to be the antecedent of a reflexive pronoun. Dative subjects typically combine with stative predicates, favouring particularly those that denote a mental or emotional state, e.g. *ataip paRRi avaNukku cantēkam* 'he$_3$ (has) doubts$_4$ about$_2$ that$_1$', *avaNukkuk kōpam vantatu* 'he$_1$ got$_3$ angry$_2$'. Nominative subjects do trigger subject-verb agreement. Verbs agree with their subjects in person, number and, in the third person, gender.

The four basic sentence types function as templates through which other syntactic structures are fitted. Modern standard Tamil has a rule of clefting, which postposes a nominal phrase to the right of the clause-final verb. Simultaneously, the verb becomes a verbal noun inflected for the nominative case and the oblique case marking on the postposed noun, if any, is optionally deleted. Clefting thus transforms *nāN maturai-(y)il piRantēN* 'I$_1$ was born$_3$ in Madurai$_2$' into *nāN piRantatu maturai* 'Madurai$_3$ (is where) I$_1$ was born$_2$', i.e. 'it is Madurai where I was born'. Observe how the output of clefting conforms to the first basic sentence type above, where a nominative subject, here the verbal noun *piRantatu*, and a predicate nominal, here *maturai*, combine to form a simple sentence.

The basic word order of modern standard Tamil is SOV. As in other rigid SOV languages, genitives precede the nouns they modify, main verbs precede their auxiliaries and complement clauses precede main clauses. Despite the use of cases and postpositions to mark the grammatical relations of noun phrases, modern standard Tamil word order is not entirely free. Although variations do exist, the verb in a simple sentence must remain at the extreme right end of the clause. The unmarked order of *avaN nēRRu avaḷaip pārttāN* 'he$_1$ saw$_4$ her$_3$ yesterday$_2$' can be varied as follows: *avaḷai avaN nēRRu pārttāN; nēRRu avaN avaḷaip pārttāN; avaN avaḷai nēRRu pārttāN*. No semantic difference accompanies these variations, but the verb remains fixed at the end of the clause. A subject may in rhetorically marked contexts be postposed rightwards over a finite verb, typically when its referent is the hero in a narrative whom the speaker wishes to make prominent, e.g. *cītaiyaip pārttāN rāmaN* 'Rama$_3$ saw$_2$ Sita$_1$'.

The structure of complex sentences is a particularly fascinating part of modern standard Tamil syntax. Recall that modern standard Tamil preserves the Proto-Dravidian constraint limiting the number of finite verbs in a sentence to a maximum of one. This necessitates the use of non-finite verbs such as the infinitive, adverbial participle or relative participle in the construction of complex sentences, be they coordinate or subordinate. In *maẓai peytu kuḷam niRaintatu* 'rain$_1$ fell$_2$, (and) the reservoir$_3$ filled$_4$', the adverbial participle *peytu* 'raining' joins two clauses to form a coordinate sentence. By contrast, in *avaḷ nāN colli kēṭka villai* 'she$_1$ didn't$_5$ listen$_4$ (to what) I$_2$ said$_3$', the adverbial participle *colli* 'saying' joins a subordinate clause to its main clause. In *makaN pōka makaḷ vantāḷ* '(as) the son$_1$ went$_2$, the daughter$_3$ came$_4$', the infinitive *pōka* 'go' conjoins two clauses in a coordinate sentence; but in *nāN avaNai varac coNNēN* 'I$_1$ told$_4$ him$_2$ to come$_3$', the infinitive *vara* 'come' joins the subordinate clause to the main clause. In *avaN vantāl avaN-iṭam nāN pēcuvēN* 'if$_2$ he$_1$ comes$_2$, I$_4$ will speak$_5$ with him$_3$', the conditional verb *vantāl* 'if X comes' simultaneously marks the protasis of a conditional sentence and joins it to the apodosis. In all these sentences the single finite verb appears at the extreme right end of the sentence, in the main clause. Non-finite verbs are still used in complex sentences even when the rightmost predicate is a predicate nominal, as in *kavalaippaṭṭu uṅkaḷukku eNNa payaN?* 'what$_3$ use$_4$ (is it) for you$_2$ to worry$_1$?'; the adverbial participle *kavalaippaṭṭu* 'worrying' links two clauses.

Relative participles also serve to build complex sentences. In *nēRRu vanta oru mantiri* 'a$_3$ minister$_4$ (who) came$_2$ yesterday$_1$' the relative participle *vanta* 'which came' joins a relative clause to the head noun *mantiri* 'minister'. Relative participles appear in factive complements, as well: in *mantiri nēRRu vanta ceyti* '(the) news$_4$ (that) the minister$_1$ came$_3$ yesterday$_2$', the relative participle *vanta* 'which came' joins the factive complement to the head noun *ceyti* 'news'.

Despite the ingenuity and dexterity with which non-finite verbs are used to create complex sentences, the restriction against more than one finite verb per sentence raises serious questions. First, how does one represent direct discourse, which requires the preservation of finite verbs in quoted material? Second, how does one embed sentences with predicate nominals? Neither task can be accomplished by recourse to non-finite verbs. Instead, modern standard Tamil employs two special verbs to solve these and other, related syntactic problems: *āka* 'become' and *eNa* 'say'. These verbs take as their direct objects expressions of any category and any complexity, without requiring any morphological change in those expressions (such as requiring the accusative case or a non-finite verb form). They can combine with single words, phrases or entire sentences without disturbing the form of these operands. As verbs, they may subsequently be inflected for non-finite verb morphology and, as described above, function in the construction of complex sentences, bringing their objects with them. The sentence *avaNukku oru makaN* 'he$_1$ (has) a$_2$ son$_3$' can be embedded under the verb of propositional attitude *niNaikka* 'think' using the adverbial participle *eNRu* 'saying' to link the two: *avaNukku oru makaN eNRu nāN niNaikkiRēN* 'I$_5$ think$_6$ that$_4$ (lit. saying) he$_1$ (has) a$_2$ son$_3$'. The conditional form *āNāl* 'if becomes' allows finite verbs to appear in the protasis of conditional sentences: *avaN varuvāN āNāl nāN avaNiṭam pēcuvēN* 'if$_3$ he$_1$ will come$_2$, I$_4$ will speak$_6$ with him$_5$'. These verbs also help to represent direct discourse: in *nāN varuvēN eNRu avaN coNNāN.* 'he$_4$ said$_5$, "I$_1$ will come$_2$"', the adverbial participle *eNRu* 'saying' embeds the direct quotation beneath the verb of quotation *colla* 'tell, say'. To make adverbial expressions, *āka* 'become' embeds individual nouns, while *eNa* 'say' embeds onomatopoeic expressions.

Modern standard Tamil uses the particles *-ē* 'even, and' and *-ō* 'or, whether' to subordinate finite verbs in complex sentences, as well. In *avaN* *vantāN-ō eNakku cantēkam* 'I_3 (have) $doubts_4$ whether (= *-ō*) he_1 $came_2$', the clitic *-ō* subordinates one clause to another. In *nēRRu vantān-ē nāN avaNaic cantittēN* 'I_3 met_5 him_4 (who) $came_2$ $yesterday_1$', the clitic *-ē* serves to join the two parts of a correlative relative clause, both of which have finite verbs, i.e. *vantāN* 'he came', *cantittēN* 'I met'.

The constraint against multiple finite verbs in a sentence must be revised in light of these other devices used to construct complex sentences. The number of finite verbs per sentence is limited to a maximum of $n+1$, where n equals the number of occurrences of *āka* 'become', *eNa* 'say', *-ē* 'even, and' and *-ō* 'or, whether' that function as complementisers.

This short sketch of Tamil syntax will show, I hope, how much modern standard Tamil syntax relies upon the morphological and lexical resources of the language. The cases of nouns, the distinction between finite and non-finite verbs and the lexemes *āka* 'become' and *eNa* 'say' are indispensable elements of the Tamil sentence.

2.5 The Grammar of Affective Language in Modern Standard Tamil

Like many languages of the world, modern standard Tamil provides its speakers with a variety of grammatical devices which are conventionally used to express the speaker's affective or emotional state. Three such stylistic devices are discussed to give the reader an idea of the rhetorical possibilities of the language.

Onomatopoeic words (*olikuRippu*) are so numerous in modern standard Tamil that they fill an entire dictionary. Such words generally represent a sound and are syntactically joined to a sentence by means of the verb *eNa* 'say', e.g. *kācu ṇaṅ eNRu kīḻē viḻuntatu* '(the) $coin_1$ $fell_5$ $down_4$ $with_3$ (lit. saying) a $clang_2$', *pustakam top(pu) eNRu kīḻē viḻuntatu* '(the) $book_1$ $fell_5$ $down_4$ $with_3$ (lit. saying) a $thud_2$'. Many occur reduplicated, e.g. *muṇumuṇu* 'murmur, mutter', *toṇutoṇu* 'sound of beating drums'. Often they acquire an extended meaning so that *toṇutoṇu* comes to mean 'bitching, complaining', while *kuRukuRu* 'scratching, throbbing pulse' comes to mean 'guilt', e.g. *avaN maNacu kuRukuRu eNRu mayaṅkiNatu* 'his_1 $mind_2$ was $confused_5$ $with_4$ (lit. saying) $guilt_3$'. Some onomatopoeic stems, but by no means all, can themselves be inflected as verbs, e.g. *avaN ōyāmal toṇutoṇukkiRāN* 'he_1 $bitches_3$ $ceaselessly_2$'. The phonological shapes of these words often depart from what the phonotactic rules of modern standard Tamil allow: *ṇaṅ* 'clang' has an initial retroflex and a final velar nasal. But despite that and despite the jaunty air they impart to a sentence, they are still an integral part of modern standard Tamil and cannot be dismissed as quaint and ephemeral slang. Such forms loosely correspond to English onomatopoeic expressions with the prefix *ka-* or *ker-*, e.g. *the bomb went ka-boom, the boy fell ker-splash into the lily pond*.

Like other Dravidian languages, modern standard Tamil has a verbal category called attitude, which characterises the speaker's subjective evaluation of the narrated event. It is grammatically encoded in a subset of the indicative auxiliary verbs. For the most part, these auxiliaries convey the speaker's pejorative opinion of the narrated event and its participants. The auxiliary *tolaiya* 'get lost', which combines with the adverbial participle of the main verb, expresses the speaker's antipathy towards the narrated event, e.g. *avaN vantu tolaintāN* 'he$_1$ came$_2$, damn it$_3$'. The auxiliary *oẓiya* 'purge' expresses the speaker's relief that an unpleasant event has ended, combining aspect and attitude, e.g. *tiruṭaN pōy oẓintāN* '(the) thief$_1$ left$_2$, whew$_3$ (am I glad)!' In *kaṇṇāṭi uṭaintu pōyiRRu* '(the) mirror$_1$ got$_3$ broken$_2$', the auxiliary *pōka* 'go' conveys the speaker's opinion that the event named by the main verb, *uṭaiya* 'break', culminated in an undesirable result. Modern standard Tamil has at least twelve such attitudinal auxiliaries which behave in all respects like other indicative auxiliary verbs, as opposed to modal auxiliaries and lexical compound verbs. Their stylistic impact on a sentence can be compared with the use of *up*, *get* and *go* in the following three English examples: *she upped and left him; he got himself beaten up; the thief went and charged a colour TV on my credit card*. Once again we see how compound verbs compensate for the lack of simple adverbs in modern standard Tamil, here ones that express the speaker's affective state of mind.

Modern standard Tamil has a series of compound words generated through reduplication, e.g. *avaN* 'that man' is reduplicated as *avaNavaN* 'each man, every man' while *vantu* 'coming' is reduplicated as *vantu vantu* 'coming time and again'. As these examples show, reduplicated compounds have a distributive and universal sense. However, modern standard Tamil has a special subset of reduplicated compounds in which the second member of the compound does not exactly duplicate the first. These are called echo-compounds: the second member, the echo-word, partially duplicates the first, the echoed word. The echo-word is the same as the echoed word except that it substitutes *ki-* or *kī-* for the first syllable of the echoed word, depending on whether it is short or long. Thus, from *viyāparam* 'business' we can form the echo compound *viyāparam-kiyāparam* 'business and such'; from *māṭu* 'cattle', *māṭu-kīṭu* 'cattle and such'. However, words which begin with *ki-* or *kī-* cannot themselves be echoed this way: from *kiNaRu* 'well' we cannot form the echo-compound **kiNaRu-kiNaRu* 'wells and such' even though vowel lowering would convert the echoed word, but not the echo-word, into *keNaRu* (echo-compounds can be formed from words whose initial syllable is underlying *ke-* or *kē-*). In such cases, an alternative echo-word with initial *hi-* or *hī-* may be formed, e.g. from *kiḷi* 'parrot' we can form *kiḷi-hiḷi* 'parrots and such'. But since initial *h-* belongs to the phonological periphery, many speakers prefer to form no echo-compound at all rather than to create an echo-word with initial *h-*. Verbs may be echoed as well as nouns (but not pronouns): in *pāttirattai uṭaittāy kiṭaittāy eNRāl uNNai cummāka viṭa māṭṭēN* 'if$_4$ (you) broke$_2$ (the) pots$_1$ or did-any-such-thing$_3$, (I) won't$_8$ let$_7$ you$_5$ alone$_6$', the echo-compound *uṭaittāy-kiṭaittāy* 'break or do some such thing' is based on the finite verb *uṭaittāy* 'you broke'.

Echo-compounds occur in rhetorically marked settings: in grammatical terms this includes modal verb forms such as the future tense and conditional, as well as negative and interrogative contexts, but not indicative forms, e.g. *māṭu kīṭu varum* 'Cows$_1$ and such$_2$ will come$_3$', but *?*māṭu kīṭu vantatu* 'Cows$_1$ and such$_2$ came$_3$'. Echo-compounds have two facets of meaning. First, like other reduplicated compounds, they have a distributive meaning so that the compound conveys the idea, 'entities or actions, of which the echoed word refers to a random example from a general range'. According to context, *māṭu-kīṭu* 'cows and such' could refer to a group of domestic animals, the components of a dowry etc. Second, echo-compounds conventionally carry a pejorative nuance to the effect that the speaker neither likes nor cares enough about the entity or action to specify it any further. And, in this respect, modern standard Tamil echo-compounds resemble those in Yiddish English where the echo-word is made with the prefix *shm-*, e.g. *fancy-shmancy*; *cordiality-shmordiality*; *Oedipus-Shmoedipus, at least he loves his mother!*

There are also echo-compounds in modern standard Tamil in which the shape of the echo-word is not predictable and is idiomatically associated with the echoed word, e.g. from *koñcam* 'little' comes the echo-compound *koñcam-nañcam* 'itsy-bitsy'. Most South, South-Central and Central Dravidian languages have both kinds of echo-compound, but as we pass from Central Dravidian into North Dravidian, the second kind comes to predominate.

These and similar grammatical devices, such as the affective lengthening of vowels, exist in other Dravidian languages. The fact that they conventionally encode the speaker's affective state is no reason to consider them anything less than an integral part of the language and its grammar. Since they can reveal as much about the phonological, morphological and syntactic structure of a language as other, more prosaic rules and constructions, they deserve greater recognition in grammatical theory than they have hitherto received.

Bibliography

For a general survey, reference may be made to Zvelebil (1983). Caldwell (1875) is the starting point of modern comparative Dravidian studies. Zvelebil (1970) is an excellent analysis and summary of phonological reconstruction in Dravidian. Bloch (1946) is the standard study of Dravidian comparative grammar, while Andronov (1970) is a good overview of Dravidian morphology. Emeneau (1967) shows, as does Bloch (1946), how much the non-literary languages can reveal about comparative Dravidian. Steever (1981) contains a number of essays concentrating on the analysis of some pressing morphological and syntactic problems in the Dravidian languages. Steever (1987) illustrates how closely Dravidian morphology and syntax are correlated in the property of finiteness.

For Tamil, Arden (1942) is a thorough grammar of modern literary Tamil, beginning with a helpful skeleton grammar, later amplified. Andronov (1969) is a comprehensive grammar, concentrating on morphology. Pope (1979) is a teaching grammar providing an introduction to modern literary Tamil. For the spoken variety of Tamil, Schiffman (1979) is a fine sketch, while Asher (1983) is a detailed grammar following the framework of the Lingua Descriptive Studies series (now Croom Helm Descriptive Grammars). Paramasivam (1983) is an excellent introduction to the linguistic structure of modern Tamil; an English translation is in preparation.

References

Andronov, M.S. 1969. *A Standard Grammar of Modern and Classical Tamil* (New Century Book House, Madras)

—— 1970. *Dravidian Languages* (Nauka, Moscow)

Arden, A.H. 1942. *A Progressive Grammar of the Tamil Language* (Christian Literature Society, Madras)

Asher, R. 1983. *Tamil* (North-Holland, Amsterdam; now distributed by Croom Helm, London)

Bloch, J. 1946. *Structure grammaticale des langues dravidiennes* (Adrien-Maisonneuve, Paris)

Caldwell, R. 1875. *A Comparative Grammar of the Dravidian or South-Indian Family of Languages*, 2nd ed. (University of Madras, Madras)

Emeneau, M.B. 1967. *Collected Papers: Dravidian Linguistics, Ethnology, and Folktales* (Annamalai University Press, Annamalainagar)

Paramasivam, K. 1983. *Ikkālat tamiẓ marapu* (Annam, Sivagangai)

Pope, G.U. 1979. *A Handbook of the Tamil Language* (Asian Educational Services, New Delhi)

Schiffman, H. 1979. *A Grammar of Spoken Tamil* (Christian Literature Society, Madras)

Steever, S.B. 1981. *Selected Papers on Tamil and Dravidian Linguistics* (Muttu Patippakam, Madurai)

—— 1987. *The Serial Verb Formation in the Dravidian Languages* (Motilal Banarsidas, New Delhi)

Zvelebil, K. 1970. *Comparative Dravidian Phonology* (Mouton, The Hague)

—— 1983. 'Dravidian Languages', in *The New Encyclopaedia Britannica, Macropaedia*, vol. 5 (Encyclopaedia Britannica, Chicago), pp. 989–92.

14 NIGER-KORDOFANIAN LANGUAGES

Douglas Pulleyblank

Niger-Kordofanian is the family to which the vast majority of the languages of sub-Saharan Africa belong. Hundreds of languages fall into this group and upwards of 100,000,000 people speak Niger-Kordofanian languages. Geographically, this group ranges from Senegal in the west to Kenya in the east and extends as far south as South Africa.

The proposal for the group 'Niger-Kordofanian' dates from Greenberg's (1963) classification of the languages of Africa into four families: Niger-Kordofanian, Nilo-Saharan, Afroasiatic and Khoisan. Greenberg's creation of Niger-Kordofanian differed from earlier work on the classification of the relevant languages with respect to both larger and smaller groupings, as well as in its assignment of certain languages to particular subgroups. For example, at the level of large groupings, he included 'Kordofanian' and 'Niger-Congo' within a single family; at the level of smaller groupings, he argued that Bantu was actually a sub-sub-subgroup of Niger-Congo — not an independent family of its own; with respect to particular languages, he argued (for example) that Fula properly belongs to the West Atlantic subgroup of Niger-Congo. The basic subdivisions for Niger-Kordofanian proposed by Greenberg are as follows: NIGER-CONGO: (1) West Atlantic, (2) Mande, (3) Gur (Voltaic), (4) Kwa, (5) Benue-Congo, (6) Adamawa-Eastern; KORDOFANIAN: (1) Koalib, (2) Tegali, (3) Talodi, (4) Tumtum, (5) Katla.

There are several problems encountered in the classification of the languages of this group. Apart from general problems involved in the classification of any group of languages, one finds a number of specific problems. There are very few historical records of these languages that go back more than a couple of hundred years and yet we are dealing with a very large, very diverse group of languages which has been splitting apart for thousands of years. Obviously the details of larger genetic groupings will ultimately depend on the reconstruction of smaller groups — a task that is a large one given the number of languages involved and the limited amount of knowledge about many of them. To illustrate this point, work by Elugbe and Williamson (1976) on the reconstruction of Proto-Ẹdo and Proto-Ịjọ (two subgroups of Kwa) calls into question the legitimacy of the distinction between Kwa and Benue-Congo. They show that properties considered to be identifying characteristics of Benue-Congo must also be reconstructed for 'Proto-Ẹdo-Ịjọ'. Their conclusion is that there is no evidence for separating Kwa from Benue-Congo, and that the two groups really constitute a single 'Benue-Kwa' subfamily of Niger-Congo. It is not within the scope of this short survey to review the work that has been done on the classification of African languages since Greenberg's influential work (although it is worth noting that studies such as that of Elugbe and Williamson serve to refine — not refute — Greenberg's work). Consequently, I will refer to languages and language groups according to their positions within Greenberg's (1963) classification. I stress that this is not intended as a rejection of refinements to the 1963 classification, but simply because that classification is the most familiar.

Because of the large number of languages in the Niger-Kordofanian family, it is probably impossible to make any general statements that hold true of all member languages. And even if one were to have access to a comprehensive reconstruction of Proto-Niger-Kordofanian, this would tell us relatively little about the presently attested characteristics of many (most) of the descendants of that language. For example, while most Niger-Kordofanian languages are tonal (and the proto-language surely was), there are important exceptions in languages like Fula (West Atlantic) and Swahili (Bantu; Benue-Congo). Moreover, even in the 'tonal' languages, the actual properties of the tonal systems vary considerably; languages may employ a fairly restricted system — for example, two tones and a fairly predictable distribution of the tones — or languages may employ highly articulated systems involving several distinct tones, essentially unpredictable lexical placements of the tones, complex realisation rules etc. Languages also differ, for example, as to whether tones are used for lexical and/or grammatical (e.g. tense) contrasts. In the following discussion, I will survey languages and language characteristics of Niger-Congo. Niger-Congo languages will be concentrated on since the Kordofanian group is more limited both in terms of number of speakers and in terms of geographical distribution (all the Kordofanian languages are spoken in the relatively small Kordofan area of Sudan). The languages that will be mentioned were chosen by virtue of being spoken by large numbers of people (although numbers vary from hundreds of thousands to tens of millions); topics to be discussed, however, have been chosen more in terms of anticipated interest than necessarily because they involve pan-Niger-Congo features. For example, perhaps all Niger-Congo languages have dental or alveolar stops while only an important subset of the family has doubly-articulated stops. But in such a case, the doubly-articulated stops will be discussed.

The westernmost branch of Niger-Congo is 'West Atlantic'. The languages of this group are concentrated in the extreme western portion of

West Africa, ranging basically from Senegal to Liberia. This said, the list of languages included in this group will begin with an exception. Fula (Fulani, Fulfulde, Peul, Fulbe etc.), which is perhaps the most well known language of this group, is spoken essentially throughout West Africa in a sub-Saharan belt that extends from Senegal in the west to as far east as Chad. Closely related to Fula is Serer, a language spoken predominantly in Senegal and also in Gambia. Still closely related is Wolof, centred in Senegal but also spoken in Gambia, Mali, Mauritania and Guinea. Other important languages in the West Atlantic group include Dyola (Senegal; also Gambia and Guinea), Balante (Guinea-Bissau; also Senegal), Temne (Sierra Leone), Kissi (Sierra Leone, Guinea; also Liberia), Gola (Liberia; also Sierra Leone) and Limba (Sierra Leone and Guinea).

Despite its not being a very unified group, it is typical for a West Atlantic language to have noun classes and a system of consonant mutations (Sapir 1971). Class systems of the type generally associated with Bantu languages (see for example, the chapter on Swahili and the Bantu languages in this volume) are found in languages of the West Atlantic group. Classes may have phonological, morphological, syntactic and semantic correlates. The morphological indicators of noun class membership generally involve prefixation and/or suffixation (for example, Temne has class prefixes while Fula has suffixes); in a language like Wolof, however, class membership is not morphologically marked and can only be deduced from the effect a noun has on governed elements. The important syntactic effect of noun classes is in determining properties of agreement. The various elements that can occur within a noun phrase will typically be marked to agree in class with the head of the noun phrase. Agreement can extend beyond the noun phrase to include elements such as the verb. The number of noun classes found in a particular language varies considerably within the West Atlantic group. For example, a language like Nalu has only three classes while certain dialects of Fula have up to twenty-five. While classes are generally not definable in terms of their semantics, certain generalisations can often be made. Classes are typically associated with either singular or plural nouns; classes may indicate notions such as 'augmentative' or 'diminutive'. A particularly interesting phonological property that is related to the noun class system is consonant mutation. In Fula, for example, changes in the phonological nature of the initial consonant of a stem accompany the assignment of a particular class suffix. Hence in addition to the suffix marking the appropriate singular or plural class, examples like the following involve changes in the initial stem consonant: *pul-lo* 'a Fula'; *ful-ɓe* 'Fulas'. In the singular class, the initial stem consonant must appear in its 'stop grade'; in the plural class, the initial stem consonant appears in its 'fricative' grade; other classes could require either of the above grades or a third 'nasal grade' (which for the *p*/*f* series would also be *p*, but which for many other series would be a prenasalised consonant). Although such consonant alternations correlate with noun classes in Fula, this is not always the case. In Serer, for example, the appropriate consonant grade is determined by an interaction between noun class membership and other lexical stem properties. As a final point, consonant mutation is not restricted to nouns; consonants of adjectives, verbs and even (in Fula) certain suffixes may alternate. For example, the following verbs from Fula illustrate the appearance of the fricative grade in the singular and of the nasal grade in the plural: *laamɗo warii* 'the chief came'; *laamɓe ngarii* 'the chiefs came' (*w*/*ng*).

Mande languages, the second group to be considered here, are spoken as far west as Senegal and as far east as Bourkina Fasso (Upper Volta) and Ivory Coast. The largest languages in this group are Maninka-Bambara-Dyula and Mende. Maninka-Bambara-Dyula refers to a group of very closely related dialects/languages spoken in several countries including Senegal, Gambia, Guinea, Mali, Sierra Leone, Ivory Coast and Bourkina Fasso; Mende is spoken in Sierra Leone. Other languages in the Mande group include Soninke (Mali), Vai (Sierra Leone), Susu-Yalunka (Guinea, Sierre Leone), Loma (Liberia, Guinea), Kpelle (Liberia, Guinea), Mano (Liberia, Guinea), Dan-Kweni (Ivory Coast, Liberia), Samo (Bourkina Fasso, Mali) and Busa (Benin, Nigeria). Note that Busa is exceptional geographically for Mande, occurring as far east as Nigeria.

In contrast with the West Atlantic languages, Mande languages do not have noun classes. Interestingly, however, certain Mande languages do have systems of consonant mutation. Changes in the initial consonant of a word can correlate with properties of definiteness, can occur with particular pronominal elements, can occur in particular syntactic contexts etc. (Welmers 1971: 132). Moreover, there are cases where segmental properties of consonants interact in very interesting ways with tonal properties. While it is not uncommon in general to observe that voiced consonants have a lowering effect on the pitch of an adjacent vowel while voiceless consonants have a raising effect, it is interesting that in a Mande language like Kpelle the presence or absence of a low tone actually correlates with the presence or absence of voicing. Hence a voiceless stop like *p* has a counterpart in Kpelle that is heavily voiced and bears a low tone (Welmers 1962: 71–2).

In general, the tonal properties of Mande languages are of considerable interest and importance. The observation that tone must be assigned in certain cases to morphemes rather than to some smaller phonological unit such as the syllable was first made by Welmers with respect to Kpelle (Welmers 1962: 85–6). Using examples from Mende (Leben 1978) as illustration, it can be shown that words such as the following all involve a single high-low pattern: *mbû* 'owl', *ngílà* 'dog', *félàmà* 'junction'. The high and low tones are realised on a single vowel (the only vowel) in the first example, on the first and second vowels in the second example, and in the third example, the high appears on the first vowel while the low appears on the second and third vowels. Consideration of such cases has been instrumental in determining that phonetic contour tones are best represented as involving sequences of phonologically level tones and that certain vowels that phonetically bear tones are best viewed as receiving their tones by the interaction of general principles with tonal sequences that are assigned underlyingly to morphemes rather than to specific vowels or syllables.

The Gur, or Voltaic, languages are primarily spoken in southeastern Mali, Bourkina Fasso and northern Ghana, although they extend through Togo and Benin as far east as Nigeria. The largest language of this group is Moore (also known as More, Mossi etc.), spoken in Bourkina Fasso, Ghana and Togo. Other languages include Dagari (Ghana, Bourkina Fasso), Dagomba (Ghana, Togo), Dogon (Mali, Bourkina Fasso), Gurma (Bourkina Fasso, Ghana, Togo), Lobiri (Bourkina Fasso, Ivory Coast), Bwamu (Bourkina Fasso), Senari (Ivory Coast) and Suppire-Mianka (Mali) — the two largest 'Senufo' languages —, Tem (Togo, Benin, Ghana) and Bariba (Benin, Togo, Nigeria).

Like the West Atlantic languages (and indeed typical of Niger-Kordofanian in general), Gur languages commonly manifest systems of noun classes (Bendor-Samuel 1971: 164–71). Unlike the most common Niger-Kordofanian pattern of prefixes, however, Gur languages generally have class suffixes. It should be noted, moreover, that the presence of class systems in widely diverse languages is more than simply a typological similarity. For example, it is typical of Gur that there be singular and plural person classes marked by the affixes *a* or *u* (singular) and *ba* or *bi* (plural); there is typically a class not involved in a singular/plural pairing that is used for mass/liquid nouns and generally marked by a nasal affix. Such characteristics, while typical of Gur, are widely attested throughout Niger-Kordofanian.

The morphology of Gur languages presents numerous properties of considerable phonological interest. Consider, for example, the following imperfective forms in Dagara (*rɛ́* 'imperfective'): *dɪ̀* + *rɛ́* → *dɪ̀rɛ́* (*dɪ* 'eat'); *tʊ́* + *rɛ́* → *tʊ́ʊ́r* (*tʊ́* 'insult'); *cɛ̀* + *rɛ́* → *cɪ̀ɛ́r* (*cɛ̀* 'construct'). In the first example, the imperfective suffix surfaces basically without modification. In the second example, however, the vowel of the suffix is lost while the stem vowel is lengthened. And in the third example, there is not only loss of the suffix vowel and lengthening of the stem vowel, but, in addition, the stem vowel is diphthongised. Determining the precise conditions under which these types of changes take place involves rather intricate interactions between properties of vowel quality, syllable structure and tone.

Another point concerning the morphology of Gur languages is the high frequency of compounding. For example, it is common for adjective-noun sequences to appear as a compound rather than as a syntactic sequence. In such a case, the noun stem will appear followed by the adjective followed by a single class suffix. When adjectives do appear as a syntactic constituent, there are three basic possibilities: they may be invariant; they may be marked for noun class membership just as nouns — but not participate in agreement; or they may take class affixes that agree with the head noun (Bendor-Samuel 1971: 171–2). It should be noted before leaving the topic of adjectives that this category is a very restricted one throughout Niger-Congo. Typically, the types of meanings that might be expressed by adjectives in a language like English are expressed in Niger-Congo languages by constructions involving either verbs or nouns.

Gur languages manifest some variation with respect to basic word order. For example, although the general order for subject, object and verb in Gur is SVO, certain Gur languages (e.g. Senari) have the basic order SOV. It is worth noting that Gur reflects the overall Niger-Congo patterning in this regard — in general, the Niger-Congo basic order is SVO, although in a group such as Mande it is SOV.

The Kwa languages are found in an area extending basically from Liberia in the west to Nigeria in the east. The four largest languages in the Kwa group are Akan (Ghana), Ewe (Ghana, Togo, Benin), Yoruba (Nigeria, Benin, Togo) (see the chapter on Yoruba in this volume) and Igbo (Nigeria). Other languages in this group include Bassa (Liberia), Kru (Liberia), Baule (Ivory Coast), Bete (Ivory Coast), Gã-Adangme (Ghana), Nupe (Nigeria), Gwari (Nigeria), Ebira (Nigeria), Bini (Nigeria), Igala (Nigeria), Idoma (Nigeria) and Ịjọ (Nigeria). It might be noted that there is some disagreement as to whether Ịjọ really belongs to the Kwa group or to the Benue-Congo group. Of course, such a question ceases to be an issue if it turns out that Kwa and Benue-Congo actually form a single branch of Niger-Congo (as mentioned above as a possibility).

A striking phonetic property of a typical Kwa language is the presence of doubly-articulated 'labial-velar' stops. While such segments appear in numerous non-Kwa languages, in Kwa they are commonplace. Ladefoged (1968: 9) notes that there are at least three ways for a doubly-articulated stop like [k͡p] to be produced: the labial and velar closures may be released on an air-stream that is (1) pulmonic egressive only (e.g. Guang (Ghana)); (2) pulmonic egressive and velaric ingressive (e.g. Yoruba); (3) pulmonic egressive, velaric ingressive and glottalic ingressive (e.g. Idoma).

Another typical phonetic property found in Kwa (although in no way restricted to Kwa) is tonal downstep. Although a language may contrast only two phonological tone levels, it may have a number of phonetic pitch levels that is in principle unlimited. In Igbo, for example, two adjacent high-toned syllables will normally be produced on the same pitch. If, however, a low-toned syllable intervenes between the two high tones, then the second high tone will be produced on a lower pitch than the first one. In an appropriate sequence of alternating tones (e.g. HLHLH ...), a series of gradually lowered high tones will be produced. Such completely transparent examples of phonetic downstepping are often complicated by the presence of 'floating' tones in a language's phonological representations. That is, tones may be phonologically present in certain cases even though there is no vowel available for the tone to be pronounced on. Consider again the type of HLH sequence in a downstepping language where the second high tone will be produced on a slightly lower pitch than the first. If the vowel bearing the low tone were to be deleted for some reason, then in many cases the low tone itself would remain and continue to play a role in the tonal phonology of the sequence in question — for example, by triggering the phonetic lowering of the second high tone. Hence the phonetic sequence of a high tone followed by a slightly lower tone (but not low) is in many cases the phonetic realisation of a H-L'-H sequence (where L' indicates a floating tone). In many other cases, such a slightly lower tone may of course be correctly analysed as a mid tone — phonologically distinct from either high or low. Determining the correct analysis of such non-high tones is often a major problem of tonal phonology.

With respect to syntax, one interesting construction found in a number of Kwa languages is that of the 'predicate cleft'. In this construction a predicate is focused by placing a copy of the verb in a fronted position. The following example is from Yoruba:

rírà	ni	bàbá	ra	bàtà
buying	foc.	father	buy	shoe

'Father **bought** shoes.'

In this example, the verb *rà* is focused by placing a nominalised form of the verb in the initial focus position. This construction therefore makes it possible to focus syntactically virtually any constituent of a basic Yoruba sentence — noun phrase subjects, objects etc. being typical focused constituents.

The Benue-Congo languages are distributed throughout east, central and southern Africa, extending as far west as Nigeria. Four sub-branches of Benue-Congo can be distinguished, of which the most important is Bantoid — the branch including the Bantu languages. Since a separate chapter in this volume is devoted to Bantu, the discussion here will concentrate on Benue-Congo languages other than Bantu. With respect to the number of speakers, the Bantu languages stand in marked contrast to the other languages of Benue-Congo. Whereas a large proportion of the speakers of Niger-Kordofanian languages speak Bantu languages, only relatively small groups tend to speak other Benue-Congo languages. Two exceptions to this generalisation are Efik-Ibibio (Nigeria) and Tiv (Nigeria), both spoken by large populations.

When the Bantu group is compared with the rest of the Benue-Congo group, it is striking that there is much more variation within the group not including Bantu than there is within the Bantu group itself. For example, the features that characterise the Bantu group are its systems of noun classes and agglutinative verb morphology and it is generally fairly straightforward to establish correspondences between the particular forms of one language and those of another — or between the forms of one language and the reconstructed forms of Proto-Bantu. Of course, a major reason for including Bantu in the Benue-Congo group is that the typical 'Bantu' properties can be demonstrated to occur in other languages of the Benue-Congo group. But typically, the Benue-Congo languages other than Bantu show considerable diversity in their manifestations of such properties.

Consider, for example, Benue-Congo noun class systems. While noun class systems demonstrably corresponding to Bantu are typical of Benue-Congo, there are Benue-Congo languages that have lost their class systems (e.g. Jukun). And while noun classes are morphologically marked by prefixes in Bantu, in a very closely related language like Tiv, noun classes are marked by both prefixes and suffixes.

The morphology of the Tiv noun class system is quite complex. For example, the singular person class is marked either by the absence of class marking or by a low tone prefix in conjunction with labialisation of the initial stem consonant. An example of the latter possibility is *ꜜkwásé* 'wife', where ꜜ indicates an initial downstep triggered by the low tone prefix, and labialisation of the stem *kásé* has taken place because of the singular prefix. The plural person class is marked either by a suffix *v* (e.g. *kásév* 'wives') or by one of the prefixes *ù* or *mbà*. Apart from the phonological properties of the singular affix, an interesting property of the class morphology concerns the appearance of class suffixes on nouns within prepositional phrases (Abraham 1940). One observes that class suffixes cannot occur with a preposition like *shá* 'on': *shá ꜜkwásé* 'on the wife'; *shá ùkásé* 'on the wives'. In this example, the suffix *v* that normally appears in the plural of *kásé* has been replaced by the prefix *ù* within a prepositional phrase. However, class suffixes can occur within a prepositional phrase if the relevant noun is followed by a demonstrative, possessive pronoun etc. Compare the following examples involving the stem *gèrè* 'water': *ḿgérĕm* 'water' (prefix *ḿ*; suffix *ḿ*); *shím m̀gĕr* 'in the water' (prefix *ḿ* only; final stem vowel is deleted by a regular phonological rule); *shím ḿgérĕm mèrá* 'in that water' (prefix *ḿ*; suffix *ḿ*). Not only is the suffix not present in the form *shím m̀gĕr*, but the class prefix has lost its normal high tone.

The final branch of Niger-Congo to be considered is Adamawa-Eastern or Adamawa-Ubangian. Geographically, the languages of this group are found as far west as Nigeria (although concentrated groups of Adamawa languages do not begin until Cameroon) and extend as far east as Sudan; the northern and southern extents of Adamawa-Eastern are Chad and the Congo. The largest language of this branch is Gbaya, spoken in the Central African Republic, Cameroon and the Congo. Two other Adamawa-Eastern languages are Banda (Central African Republic, Congo) and Zande (Sudan, Central African Republic, Congo).

Just as most other branches of Niger-Congo, Adamawa-Eastern shows reflexes of a Niger-Congo noun class system. Typically, the class markers in this branch are suffixes, although in some cases they can only be reconstructed through the comparison of 'stem'-final consonants in languages which have ceased to operate a synchronic class system (Boyd 1974: 56–7). Reduplication, in addition to forms of affixation, is a common morphological process in this group (and also common in other groups of Niger-Congo). As a final point concerning morphology in a broad sense (and again actually a more general point than simply relating to Adamawa-Eastern), one should take note of the class of words referred to as 'ideophones'. Although notoriously difficult to define, ideophones form an identifiable class of words in many languages (see pages 275–6 for a discussion of Yoruba ideophones). Typically, they exhibit certain morphological properties such as reduplication; phonological properties such as specific tonal patterns and the occurrence of special phonemes; syntactically, they are often used in adverbial configurations and are often idiomatically restricted to appearing with particular predicates.

With respect to phonology, this branch has a number of interesting properties (where it should be stressed that while such properties may be typical of Adamawa-Eastern, they are not restricted to it). Prenasalised segments are common; in a language like Duru (Cameroon; Boyd 1974: 24), a prenasalised stop series is attested, while in a language like Mbum (Cameroon; Hagège 1970: 54), there are both prenasalised stops and prenasalised fricatives. Evidence that such prenasalised segments belong to a single syllable — even intervocalically in a sequence such as [... aŋga ...] — can be found in the language games of a language like Gbaya (Monino and Roulon 1972: 110–11). Also with respect to nasalisation, one observes in a language like Mbum (Hagège 1970: 62) that if there are two vowels in a word, then either both will be nasal or neither will be nasal — different values for the two vowels are not attested. Also with respect to Mbum, Hagège notes (Hagège 1970: 48, 54) that glides ([y, w]) are in complementary distribution with their corresponding vowels: glides appear initially before a vowel as well as intervocalically, while the vowels appear elsewhere (e.g. *mbòì* 'follow'; *mbóyà* 'to follow'). A final general point can be made about the distribution of consonant phonemes. One typically observes that the full range of contrasts is possible only in initial position; only a restricted inventory may appear in intervocalic positions and an even more limited set is all that is possible in final position.

To close this discussion, a few brief comments will be made about the syntactic possibilities of this group, starting with a construction that is not attested: in the Adamawa-Eastern group, as in certain other groups, there is typically no morphologically marked passive construction. On the other hand, a construction that typically is found is one involving a proximate/obviative distinction between pronouns. That is, a pronoun in an embedded sentence that is coreferential to the matrix subject is distinguished morphologically from a pronoun that is disjoint in reference from the matrix subject (for Yoruba examples, see pages 281–2). Finally, one observes interesting word order properties in a language such as Duru. Boyd (1974: 52) notes that in a morphologically unmarked tense such as the past (perfective), predicates exemplify the more common pattern of this group in placing the object after the verb. But in the present (imperfective) tense, an object in Duru precedes the verb — appearing immediately after a particle that occurs in post-subject position. Hence the basic word order of a sentence depends on its tense.

Bibliography

For the establishment of the Niger-Kordofanian family, reference should be made to Greenberg (1963). Welmers (1973) is an account of a number of recurrent structural properties of sub-Saharan African languages, with emphasis inevitably on Niger-Congo languages. Ladefoged (1968) is a detailed phonetic study of some of the less usual phonetic segments occurring in West African languages. For further bibliography, reference may be made to the contributions to Sebeok (1971) and to Meier (1984).

References

Abraham, R.C. 1940. *A Dictionary of the Tiv Language* (Stephen Austin, Hertford)

Bendor-Samuel, J.T. 1971. 'Niger-Congo, Gur', in Sebeok (1971), pp. 141–78

Boyd, R. 1974. *Étude comparative dans le groupe Adamawa* (SELAF, Paris)

Elugbe, B. and K. Williamson. 1976. 'Reconstructing Nasals in Proto-Benue-Kwa', in A. Juilland (ed.), *Linguistic Studies Offered to Joseph Greenberg*, vol. 2 (Anma Libri, Saratoga, Calif.)

Greenberg, J.H. 1963. *The Languages of Africa* (Indiana University, Bloomington and Mouton, The Hague)

Hagège, C. 1970. *La Langue mbum de Nganha* (SELAF, Paris)

Ladefoged, P. 1968. *A Phonetic Study of West African Languages* (Cambridge University Press, Cambridge)

Leben, W.R. 1978. 'The Representation of Tone', in V.A. Fromkin (ed.), *Tone: A Linguistic Survey* (Academic Press, New York), pp. 177–219

Meier, W. 1984. *Bibliography of African Languages* (Otto Harrassowitz, Wiesbaden)

Monino, Y. and P. Roulon. 1972. *Phonologie du Gbaya Kara 'Bodoe* (SELAF, Paris)

Sapir, J.D. 1971. 'West Atlantic: An Inventory of the Languages, Their Noun Class Systems, and Consonant Alternation', in Sebeok (1971), pp. 45–112

Sebeok, T.A. (ed.) 1971. *Current Trends in Linguistics*, vol. 7, *Linguistics in Sub-Saharan Africa* (Mouton, The Hague)

Welmers, W.E. 1962. 'The Phonology of Kpelle', *Journal of African Languages*, vol. 1, pp. 69–93

—— 1971. 'Niger-Congo, Mande', in Sebeok (1971), pp. 113–40

—— 1973. *African Language Structures* (University of California Press, Berkeley)

15 Yoruba

Douglas Pulleyblank

1 Historical Background

Yorbua belongs to the Yoruboid group of languages, a group belonging to the Kwa branch of Niger-Congo (or belonging to the branch including both Kwa and Benue-Congo, depending on the correct classification of these larger groups see pages 255–6). Other Yoruboid languages include the group of dialects referred to collectively as the Akoko cluster, in addition to Iṣẹkiri and Igala. The vast majority of the speakers of Yoruba are found in Nigeria (upwards of 16 million), located particularly in Ọyọ, Ogun, Ondo and Kwara states — states that essentially make up the southwestern corner of the country. Speakers are also found in southeastern sections of the Republic of Benin, as well as certain sections of Togo.

It is interesting, however, that the study of Yoruba did not begin in any of the places just mentioned. In the early nineteenth century, Yorubas began to form a large percentage of the slaves being exported from West Africa. As this period also marked the beginning of the British suppression of the slave trade, it turned out that many of the freed slaves being resettled in Freetown, Sierra Leone were speakers of Yoruba. When linguistic work undertaken in Freetown was extended to include languages not indigenous to Sierre Leone, Yoruba (or 'Aku' as it was commonly called) was a natural choice for study because of the large number of speakers residing in Freetown. In fact, as early as 1831, Yoruba was selected as one of two African languages to be used as the medium of instruction in a Sierra Leone girls' school. In the 1840s, however, the study of Yoruba began to shift to Yorubaland itself. The sending of the Niger expedition by the British government signalled the beginning of CMS (Church Missionary Society) missionary activity in Yorubaland. One of the central figures in the early study of Yoruba was Samuel Crowther. Crowther was a Yoruba slave who was liberated and settled in Freetown. There he received an education and began his study of Yoruba. After accompanying the Niger expedition to Yorubaland, he both became a priest and published his first work on Yoruba (a grammar and vocabulary). The CMS established itself in Abeokuta; translation of the Bible was undertaken, primers were prepared and a

Yoruba periodical was produced (from 1859 to 1867 — perhaps the earliest such vernacular periodical to be published in West Africa).

One of the particularly important things that happened at this time was a concerted group effort aimed at establishing an efficient orthography for Yoruba. The result, which included digraphs for certain phonemes and diacritically modified letters for others, involved contributions from scholars and missionaries in Europe, Freetown and Abeokuta. Crowther's adoption of the revised orthography in conjunction with his considerable success as a translator did much to establish and promote standard Yoruba. The orthography adopted by Crowther and others in the 1850s remains essentially unmodified up to the present.

But before actually entering into a discussion of issues of Yoruba orthography and grammar, it is appropriate to note the influence that Yoruba language and culture have had in a variety of areas outside Yorubaland. Yoruba slaves were extremely influential in certain areas of Brazil and Cuba. For example, the Nagos (Yorubas) of Bahia in Brazil preserved Yoruba as a ceremonial language at least until very recently. And there are reportedly still small numbers of Yorubas in Sierra Leone. Yoruba has also undergone revivals such as that exhibited in Oyotunji village of the United States. Even where Yoruba has ceased to be spoken, it has often exerted a considerable impact on the languages that have replaced it — such as Krio in Sierra Leone.

In Yorubaland itself, Yoruba has an established and thriving literature, including books, newspapers, pamphlets etc. It is studied up to the university level in several Nigerian universities and serves as the medium of instruction for courses in Yoruba linguistics and literature. It is of course well established as a broadcasting language for both radio and television.

2 Phonology

The segmental phonemes of standard Yoruba are laid out in table 15.1. The oral vowels form a straightforward seven-vowel system. Orthographically, [ɛ] and [ɔ] are represented as *ẹ* and *ọ* respectively, while the other vowels are represented as they appear in the table (that is, *i*, *e*, *a*, *o* and *u*). Although the nasalised vowels appear to represent a fairly symmetrical subset of the oral vowels, the symmetry would perhaps better be represented as deriving from a three-way contrast between high front, high back and low nasalised vowels. This is because the vowel [ɛ̃] has an extremely limited distribution (appearing in standard Yoruba in only a few lexical items, such as *ìyẹn* 'that') and [ɔ̃] and [ɑ̃] are variants of a single phoneme. Orthographically, the nasalised vowels are represented as a vowel + *n* sequence when immediately following an oral consonant, and as a simple vowel when immediately following a nasal consonant: *sìn* [sĩ̀] 'accompany', *ìyẹn* [ìyɛ̃] 'that', *fún* [fṹ] 'give', *pọn* [kpɔ̃] 'draw (water)', *tán* [tɔ̃́] 'finish', *mọ̀* [mɔ̃̀] 'know'.

Table 15.1: Segmental Phonemes of Yoruba

Oral vowels	i		u
	e		o
	ɛ		ɔ
		a	
Nasalised vowels	ĩ		ũ
	ɛ̃		ɔ̃

	Stop		Fricative	Nasal	Lateral	Tap	Glide
Bilabial		b		m			
Labio-dental			f				
Alveolar	t	d	s		l	r	
Palato-alveolar			ʃ				
Palatal		j					y
Velar	k	g					w
Labial-velar	kp	gb					
Glottal			h				

With respect to the consonant inventory, several comments are in order. Four basic places of articulation are distinguished for Yoruba stops, namely bilabial, alveolar, palatal and velar. While alveolar and velar places of articulation include both voiced and voiceless phonemes, the bilabial and palatal positions allow only voiced ones. In addition to the four places of articulation just referred to, Yoruba has two stops that are doubly articulated — with simultaneous labial and velar closures. These labial-velar stops are orthographically represented as *p* [kp] and *gb* [gb]; the simple letter *p* suffices for the voiceless labial-velar stop since there is no voiceless bilabial stop in the language.

There are four fricatives in Yoruba, all of which are voiceless. Orthographically, the labial, alveolar and glottal fricatives are represented as *f*, *s* and *h*; the palato-alveolar fricative is represented by the dotted consonant *ṣ* [ʃ].

The remaining consonants in table 15.1 are the sonorants, *m, l, r, y* and *w*. Orthographically, these segments are written as just listed and therefore require no special comment. Phonologically, on the other hand, these segments exhibit certain interesting properties that will be discussed shortly. First, however, it is necessary to discuss two types of phonemes not included in table 15.1. The first is the syllabic nasal. Such nasals are orthographically represented as *n* or *m* but their pronunciation depends on the nature of the following segment. If the following segment is a vowel (which occurs in a fairly limited set of circumstances) then the syllabic nasal is pronounced as a velar, as in *n ò lọ* [ŋ̩̄ ò lɔ̄] 'I didn't go'. When the syllabic nasal is followed by a consonant, the nasal is homorganic to the following segment: *ḿbọ̀* [ḿ̩bɔ̀] 'is coming', *ńfọ̀* [ɱ́fɔ̀] 'is washing', *ńsùn* [ń̩sũ̀] 'is sleeping', *ńjó* [ɲ́jó] 'is dancing', *ńkà* [ŋ́kà] 'is reading'. Note that the syllabic nasal is generally only written as 'm' before 'b'. In medial position, there is potential confusion over whether an orthographic *vowel–'n'–consonant* sequence represents a phonetic *nasalised vowel–consonant* sequence or a *vowel–syllabic nasal–consonant* sequence. For example, the phonetic sequence [...ɔŋ̍k...] and [...ɔ̃k...] would both be represented orthographically as '...*ọnk*...'. Where such cases arise, they can be disambiguated by tone-marking the syllabic nasal — which, of course, bears a tone by virtue of being syllabic. This brings us to the second phoneme type not represented in table 49.1, namely tone.

Tone is of major importance in Yoruba. Three tones must be distinguished underlyingly: high, mid and low. High is orthographically represented by an acute accent '´', Low is represented by a grave accent '`' and Mid is generally left unmarked (although if it is necessary to mark it — such as with a syllabic nasal — then a macron '¯' is used). The functional load of tone is considerable in Yoruba. For example, numerous sets of lexical items are distinguished solely by tone: *igbá* 'calabash', *igba* 'two hundred', *ìgbá* 'Locustbean tree', *ìgbà* 'time', *igbà* 'climbing-rope'; *ọbẹ̀* 'soup', *ọ̀bẹ* 'knife'; *ọkọ̀* 'vehicle', *ọkọ́* 'hoe', *ọkọ* 'husband', *ọ̀kọ̀* 'spear'. The functional importance of tone is amplified when one considers how sequences of words are modified by certain phrase-level phonological rules. For example, there is a common process of vowel deletion that affects sequences of adjacent vowels in connected speech. This process takes place in a number of environments, one important one being between a transitive verb and its object. Typically in such cases, the vowel of the verb is lost: *rí aṣọ* → *ráṣọ* 'see cloth', *ra epo* → *repo* 'buy oil'. The vast majority of Yoruba verbs are monosyllabic, of the form CV. Hence if the vowel of the verb deletes, the verb's lexical content is conveyed primarily by its initial consonant and its *tone*.

Turning to matters of phonological organisation, consider first possible syllables in Yoruba. Essentially, a syllable may consist of a vowel nucleus with or without a consonant onset: V-syllable: *a* 'we', *ìwé* 'book'; CV-syllable: *rí* 'see', *gbà* 'take'. Consonant clusters are not permitted (recall that orthographic 'gb' in an example like *gbà* represents not a sequence of phonemes but a single multiply-articulated phoneme). On the other hand, long vowels are attested. Compare, for example, *oògùn* 'medicine' vs. *ògùn* '(name of a river)'; *aago* 'bell' vs. *ago* 'cup'. In many cases, long vowels can be seen to derive from disyllabic sequences that have undergone consonant deletion (for example, *agogo* ~ *aago* 'bell') or to derive from morphological juxtaposition of vowels that do not result in vowel deletion (for example, in the reduplicated form *ọ̀sọ̀ọ̀sẹ̀* 'every week' derived from *ọ̀sẹ̀* 'week'). With respect to the syllabic nasal, several observations should be made. First, when the nucleus of a syllable is a nasal, there can be no onset. That is, a syllabic nasal must constitute a syllable in its entirety. Second, a syllabic nasal may occur initially (*ńlá* 'big') and medially (*aláǹgbá* 'lizard') but not finally. Third, as mentioned above, a syllabic nasal must be homorganic with a following consonant. In fact, even in the cases where a syllabic nasal appears to occur prevocalically (such as *ñ ò lọ* 'I didn't go'), it can be argued that the nasal appears underlyingly in a preconsonantal position since *ò* '(negative)' is derived from *kò* by a rule of *k*-deletion. It is possible therefore to make the general statement that syllabic nasals appear *only* preconsonantally (at least at the relevant stage of their derivation). As a fourth and final point, one observes that in certain types of cases syllabic nasals alternate with a sequence of nasal consonant followed by [i] (for example, *ó wà nílé* ~ *ó wà ńlé* 'she is at home'). All of these observations can be accounted for if syllabic nasals are analysed as deriving from a *nasal–[i]* sequence. The place of articulation of this sequence is derived by assimilation to a following consonant; the nasality of the syllable nucleus is derived by assimilation of the nucleus to the onset. Hence a syllabic nasal cannot have an onset because it actually does have a nasal onset; to allow a phonetic onset to the syllabic nasal would require positing clusters underlyingly — and clusters are not allowed in Yoruba. Similarly, syllabic nasals cannot appear in final position since there is no following consonant to assign a place specification to such a syllable. Hence statements about syllable structure in Yoruba are almost maximally simple: syllables consist of a nucleus with an optional onset.

In the above discussion of syllabic nasals, it was suggested that the nucleus of a syllable assimilates in terms of nasality to a nasal onset. This is in fact due to a widely recognised process that applies irrespective of whether a syllabic nasal is created. Hence a vowel following the nasal consonant [m] will always be nasalised. In fact, the nasalisation process is even more general than even this suggests. As mentioned above, nasalised vowels contrast with oral vowels in Yoruba (for example, *kú* 'die' vs. *kún* [kṹ] 'be full'; *rì* 'drown' vs. *rìn* [r̃ĩ̀] 'walk'). When a nasalised vowel is preceded in a syllable by a sonorant, the sonorant itself becomes nasalised (hence *rìn* [r̃ĩ̀] 'walk', *iyán* [iỹɔ̃́] 'pounded yam', *wọ́n* [w̃ɔ̃́] 'they', *hun* [h̃ũ] 'weave'). In general, therefore, a sonorant — whether consonant or vowel — assimilates in nasality to a tautosyllabic nasal segment.

In the above discussion of nasality and syllable structure, I have left untouched the important alternation that one observes in Yoruba between [n] and [l]. These two sounds are in complementary distribution, with [n] occurring only before nasalised vowels and [l] occurring only before oral vowels. Moreover, as a result of vowel deletion, [n] and [l] alternate in various extremely common Yoruba morphemes. Consider the following examples: *ní ọjà* ~ *l'ọ́jà* 'at the market', *ní aṣọ* ~ *l'áṣọ* 'have cloth', *ó ní ó dáa* ~ *ó l'ó dáa* 'he says it's all right'. In all three cases, loss of the nasalised vowel [ĩ] entails complete loss of nasality. Hence the nasality in [n] ~ [l] cases patterns like the nasality in an example like *fún ewúrẹ́* ~ *f'éwúrẹ́* 'give (it to) the goat' in that nasality is completely lost as a result of vowel deletion. It does not pattern like a case such as *mu ẹmu* ~ *m'ẹmu* 'drink palm-wine' where loss of the nasalised vowel [ũ] has no effect on the nasality of the preceding consonant. In other words, the cases with [n] and [l] appear to pattern like the cases involving nasalised vowels — and not like the cases involving nasal consonants. Hence the general consensus has been that [n] is an allophone of the phoneme /l/ — derived when the phoneme /l/ occurs in a syllable with a nasalised vowel (see, for example, Bamgboṣe 1966). In fact, it is possible under such an analysis to assume that the rule changing /l/ into [n] is simply the general rule of syllable-internal nasalisation of sonorants that was described above.

Before leaving this topic, however, a couple of problems should be noted. First, the nasality of a nasalised vowel is sometimes retained even when the vowel itself is deleted: *pín epo* [kpĩ́ ekpo] ~ *p'énpo* [kpẽ́kpo] 'share the oil'. As far as I know, such a possibility is never observed when the *consonant–nasalised vowel* sequence is /lṼ/. That is, *ní epo* 'have oil' can be realised as *l'épo* [lékpo] but never as *n'epo* [nẽ́kpo]. The second problem is that there is a systematic exception to the first one. Whenever /lĩ/ is followed by /i/ — and the sequence undergoes vowel deletion — nasality is retained. For example, *ní ilé* 'at home' can be realised as *n'ílé* but not as *l'ílé*. Finally, the [n] ~ [l] pair patterns quite differently when it comes to certain reduplicated forms than other nasal ~ oral sonorant pairs. In forming a gerundive nominalisation, a CV prefix is attached to a verb stem. The vowel of the verb stem is invariably [í] — and whether or not the stem vowel is nasalised, the prefix vowel is oral: *rà* : *rírà* 'buy : buying', *rán* [rɔ̃́] : *rírán*[rírɔ̃́] 'sew : sewing', *wọ́* : *wíwọ́* 'pull : pulling', *wọ́n* : *wíwọ́n* 'expensive : expensiveness', *dùn* : *dídùn* 'sweet : sweetness', *pín* : *pípín* 'divide : dividing'. This pattern is broken, however, by the [n] ~ [l] pair. In stems where [n] appears — by hypothesis because the stem vowel is nasalised — [n] also appears in the reduplicative prefix: *ní* : *níní* 'have : having', *ná* : *níná* 'spend : spending'. In one way or another, nasality from the stem is transferred from the stem to the prefix with the sonorant pair [n] ~ [l] but with no others. To conclude, the distribution of [n] and [l] is rule-governed and there is therefore no reason to posit two underlying phonemes. Basically, [n] patterns simply as the nasalised variant of [l] — comparable to the nasalised variants of other sonorants in Yoruba. Nevertheless, the [n] ~ [l] pair behaves somewhat differently from other nasal-oral sonorant pairs.

There are a number of restrictions on the occurrence of vowels in Yoruba. For example, in the standard language, vowel-initial nouns cannot begin with [u] nor can they begin with a nasalised vowel. Moreover, certain vowels cannot cooccur. In three papers in volume 6 of the *Journal of African Languages*, A.O. Awobuluyi and A. Bamgboṣe show that two basic patterns of vowel harmony hold. On the one hand, the mid vowels *e* and *o* do not cooccur with the mid vowels *ẹ* and *ọ* (*ẹsẹ̀* 'foot', *ẹ̀fọ́* 'vegetable', *ọ̀sẹ̀* 'week', *ọkọ* 'husband'; *ètè* 'lips', *epo* 'oil', *òwe* 'proverb', *owó* money'; but **oCọ*,

**oCẹ*, **eCọ*, **eCẹ*, **ọCo* etc.); on the other hand, front and back vowels do not cooccur in monomorphemic ...CVCV... sequences (*ìrókò* '(kind of tree)', *àbúrò* 'younger sibling', *ìràwọ̀* 'star', *ahéré* 'hut', *òkìkí* 'fame', *àtíkè* 'make-up powder' etc.). On the whole, these harmonic restrictions operate to define possible morpheme shapes in synchronic Yoruba; there appear to be no productive morphemes manifesting alternate forms depending on the harmonic class of the stem.

It was mentioned above that Yoruba has three contrastive tones: high, mid and low. These tones are modified in a number of ways before reaching their actual phonetic manifestations. For example, although the contrastive tones are all level, phonetic contours occur in certain environments. A high tone immediately following a low tone is realised as a rising tone: *ìwé* [ìwě] 'book', *ọ̀rẹ́* [ɔ̀rɛ̌] 'friend', *ìgbá* [ìgbǎ] 'Locustbean tree'. A low tone immediately following a high tone is realised as a falling tone: *owó wà* [ōwó wâ] 'there is money', *ó dùn* [ó dû̃] 'it is tasty', *ó kéré jù* [ó kéré jû] 'it is too small'. Note that there is an asymmetry with respect to a tone's potential to create a contour tone between high and low tones on one hand and mid tones on the other. This asymmetry is also seen in other areas of Yoruba tonal phonology. For example, when a mid-toned vowel is deleted, both vowel and tone disappear. But when a high-toned vowel or a low-toned vowel is deleted, the high or low tone will generally continue to have an effect on adjacent tones (Bamgboṣe 1966, pp. 9–10). For example, in connected speech, the *i* of *ìgbá* 'garden egg' is deleted in a phrase such as the following: *fẹ́ ìgbá* [fɛ́ ìgbǎ] → *fẹ́ gbá* [fɛ́ gbǎ] 'want a garden egg'. In the phrase that has not undergone vowel deletion, the final high of *ìgbá* is realised as a rising tone because of the immediately preceding low tone; in the phrase where vowel deletion has taken place, one also observes a rising tone in spite of the apparent deletion of the low-toned vowel. Deletion of a low-toned vowel before a mid-toned vowel can actually derive a level tone that is phonetically distinct from the three basic level tones — namely, a lowered-mid tone (indicated by a vertical accent in the following example): *fẹ́ ìwo* → *fẹ́ wo̍* 'want a horn'. Orthographically, the deletion of a low-toned vowel is often indicated by including a dot where the low-toned vowel had been. A tonal rise, a lowered-mid tone etc. can then be straightforwardly inferred. For example, the two cases just discussed could be represented: *fẹ́.gbá* and *fẹ́.wo*. In cases such as these where it is a high-toned vowel that undergoes deletion, one observes that a vowel adjacent to the deleted vowel acquires a high-tone: *rí aṣọ* → *r áṣọ* 'see cloth'. As a final general point about tone, it should be noted that there is a distributional restriction for tone that is comparable to one of the restrictions on vowel types. Just as vowel-initial nouns cannot begin with *u*, so are vowel-initial nouns blocked from beginning with a high tone. Apart from this restriction, however, the co-occurrence of tones is basically free in Yoruba nouns.

3 Morphology

Word formation processes in Yoruba are for the most part derivational and not inflectional. Although certain pronominal forms do vary as a function of tense/aspect (to be discussed below), both nouns and verbs are essentially invariant — for example, nouns are neither declined for case nor inflected for number and verbs are not conjugated for person, number or gender. Word formation in Yoruba involves two basic processes: prefixation and reduplication. In the following discussion, I will begin by looking at these processes and then go on to examine certain morphological properties of pronominal forms and ideophones.

There are several ways of deriving nominal forms from verbs (for some discussion, see Rowlands (1969) pp. 182–93). These processes fall basically into two classes: an 'abstract' class and an 'agentive' class. Prefixes of the 'agentive' class include *a-*, *ò-* and *olù-*. The prefix *a-* productively attaches to verb phrases — that is, a verb plus complements. Consider the following examples: *apànìà* 'killer, murderer' (*pa* 'kill', *ènìà* 'people'); *apẹja* 'fisherman' (*pa* 'kill', *ẹja* 'fish'), *akọ̀wé* 'clerk' (*kọ* 'write', *ìwé* 'paper, book'), *akọrin* 'one who sings songs' (*kọ* 'sing', *orin* 'song'), *aṣẹ́gità* 'firewood seller' (*ṣẹ́* 'snap off ', *igi* 'wood', *tà* 'sell'), *abẹ́nilórí* 'executioner' (*bẹ́* 'cut off ', *ẹni* 'person', *ní* '(syntactic marker — see discussion in section 4)', *orí* 'head'), *abáolóńjẹkú* 'glutton' (*bá* 'accompany', *olóńjẹ* 'eater', *kú* 'die'). In all the above examples, one observes a verb with one or two objects, in certain cases with an additional verbal complement. Although the above cases all illustrate derived nouns that denote a *person* who performs the relevant action, nouns derived with *a-* can also indicate the *object* that performs the action: *abẹ* 'razor, penknife' (*bẹ* 'cut, slit'), *ata* 'that which stings' (*ta* 'sting'), *asẹ́* 'strainer' (*sẹ́* 'strain'), *abọ́máàfọ́* 'enamelled ware' (*bọ́* 'fall', *máà* 'not', *fọ́* 'break'). The last example (*abọ́máàfọ́*) illustrates another property of these derived nouns. In addition to prefixing *a-* to a single phrase, two phrases can be involved in a construction of the form *a*+[X]+*máà*+[Y] with the interpretation 'one who Xes but does not Y' (note that *máà* is the particle used syntactically to negate an imperative). The following are additional examples of this process: *alọmáàdágbére* 'one who leaves without saying goodbye' (*lọ* 'go', *dá gbére* 'bid goodbye'), *alápámáàṣiṣẹ́* 'lazybones (person who has arms but does not work)' (*ní* 'have', *apá* 'arm', *ṣiṣẹ́* 'work'), *alágbáramáàmèrò* 'person who is strong but indecisive' (*ní* 'have', *agbára* 'force, power', *mèrò* 'be sensible').

The prefix *ò-* is comparable to *a-* except that it is less productive. Phonologically, *ò-* harmonises with the base to which it attaches producing the two variants *ò-*/*ọ̀-* (although this harmony does not appear to be fully productive); in addition, this prefix induces certain tonal changes in the verb. Consider the following examples: *òṣìṣẹ́* 'workman, worker' (*ṣe* 'do', *iṣẹ́* 'work'), *ọ̀mọ̀wé* 'educated person' (*mọ̀* 'know', *ìwé* 'book'), *òjíṣẹ́* 'messenger', (*jẹ́* 'answer', *iṣẹ́* 'message'), *ọ̀mùtí* 'drunkard' (*mu* 'drink', *ọtí* 'spirits'). This prefix appears to be involved in the very large class of nouns derived from a verb phrase headed by the verb *ní* 'have, possess': *oníbàtà* 'shoe-maker' (*bàtà* 'shoes'), *onímọ́tò* 'car-owner' (*mọ́tò* 'car'), *oníbọ̀tí* 'malt-seller, owner of malt' (*bọ̀tí* 'malt'). These derived nouns have the meanings 'owner of X' or 'person who deals with X' (such as a seller of X or a person who makes X); they can also mean 'thing that has X' (for example, *aṣọ ọlọ́nà* 'cloth which has decorations on it' (*aṣọ* 'cloth', *ọnà* 'decoration'), *ọbẹ̀ ẹlẹ́ran* 'stew with meat in it' (*ọbẹ̀* 'stew', *ẹran* 'meat')). The last two examples illustrate the application of some completely regular phonological processes that affect these words. Recall from the previous section that [n] is actually an allophone of /l/. When the noun following /lĩ́/ ([nĩ́]) begins with a vowel, the vowel of /lĩ́/ deletes: /o+lĩ́+ẹrã/ → *o+l+ẹ́rã*. Since there is no longer a nasalised vowel to trigger nasalisation of /l/, /l/ surfaces in its oral form. In addition, these forms show evidence of a morphophonemic rule of vowel assimilation: the [o] of the agentive prefix completely assimilates to the following vowel when the nasality of *ní* is lost: *o+l+ẹ́rã* → *ẹ+l+ẹ́rã*. The following are some additional examples of these processes: *o+ní+aṣọ* → *aláṣọ* 'cloth-seller' (*aṣọ* 'cloth'), *o+ní+epo* → *elépo* 'oil-seller' (*epo* 'oil'). Note that if the object of *ní* begins with *i*, there is no loss of nasality and no assimilation: *o+ní+igi* → *onígi* 'wood-seller' (*igi* 'wood').

Some examples of the third agentive prefix mentioned above are as follows: *olùkọ́* 'teacher' (*kọ́* 'teach'), *olùfẹ́* 'loved one; lover' (*fẹ́* 'love'), *olùṣọ́* 'guardian' (*ṣọ́* 'watch'), *olùkórè* 'harvester' (*kórè* 'gather in the harvest').

With respect to the prefixes that form abstract nouns from verb phrases, there are basically two: *ì-* and *à-*. Both prefixes may attach to a simple verbal base: *ìmọ̀* 'knowledge' (*mọ̀* 'know'), *àlọ* 'going' (*lọ* 'go'). In such cases, however, the *à-* derivative will tend to be used in wishes and prayers (Rowlands 1969, p. 185), while the *ì-* derivative has a more neutral usage. When the base involves serial verb sequences (see section 4), the tendency is to use *à-*: *àṣejù* 'doing to excess' (*ṣe* 'do', *jù* 'exceed'), *àṣetán* 'doing to completion' (*ṣe* 'do', *tán* 'finish'), *àṣetì* 'attempting to do and failing' (*ṣe* 'do', *tì* 'fail'). Words derived with the prefix *à-* can also have a locative interpretation (for example, *àká* 'granary' (*ká* 'reap')) or a resultative interpretation (for example, *àfimọ́* 'appendix to a book' (*fimọ́* 'add thing to another thing')). Although the first example with the prefix *ì-* was with a simple verb stem, it is much more common to find *ì-* with a verb plus complements: *ìbínú* 'anger' (*bí* 'annoy', *inú* 'stomach'), *ìnáwó* 'expenditure of money' (*ná* 'spend', *owó* 'money'), *ìlọsíwájú* 'progress' (*lọ* 'go', *sí* 'to', *iwájú* 'front'), *ìfẹsẹ̀kọlẹ̀* 'walking away slowly and dejectedly' (*fi* 'put', *ẹsẹ̀* 'foot', *kọ* 'turn towards', *ilẹ̀* 'ground'). In many cases, *ì-* and *à-* can be freely substituted for each other (for example, *ìsọyé*, *àsọyé* 'explanation'). Finally, *ì-* (like *à-*) can have non-abstract interpretations in certain cases: *ìdì* 'bundle' (*dì* 'tie'), *ìránṣẹ́* 'messenger, servant' (*rán* 'send', *iṣẹ́* 'message'). One morphological difference between *ì-* and *à-* lies in their ability to appear in combination with certain other affixes. This question will be returned to below.

The two prefixes *àti-* and *àì-* are used in 'infinitival' or 'gerundive' forms; *àti-* is used in affirmative forms while *àì-* is used in negative forms: *àtilọ* 'act of going, departure' (*lọ* 'go'), *àti pa á* 'to kill him' (*pa á* 'kill him'), *àti raṣọ yẹ̀n* 'to buy that dress' (*rà* 'buy', *aṣọ* 'dress', *yẹ̀n* 'that'), *àtisùn* 'sleeping' (*sùn* 'sleep'); *àìdára* 'not being good' (*dára* 'be good'), *àìlówótó* 'not having enough money' (*ní* 'have', *owó* 'money', *tó* 'be enough'), *àìnínkan púpọ̀* 'not having many things' (*ní* 'have', *ǹkan* 'thing', *púpọ̀* 'many'), *àìmọ̀* 'ignorance' (*mọ̀* 'know').

It is possible to combine the prefixes *à-* and *àì-* as follows: *à+[X]+àì+[Y]*. Such a word will have the interpretation 'to X without Ying', 'thing that Xes but does not Y', 'thing that is Xed but not Yed', etc. (note that the phonological form of *àì* is modified by certain regular morphophonemic rules): *àjẹ̀ìjẹtán* 'eating without finishing' (*à+jẹ+àì+jẹ+tán*: *jẹ* 'eat', *tán* 'finish'), *àbùìbùtán* 'inexhaustibility, endlessness' (*à+bù+àì+bù+tán*: *bù* 'dip out', *tán* 'finish'), *àwíìgbọ́* 'disobedience' (*à+wí+àì+gbọ́*: *wí* 'speak', *gbọ́* 'listen').

Amongst the more interesting word formation processes of Yoruba are a variety of types of reduplication — both partial reduplication and complete reduplication. In some cases, the process involves the addition of affixal material while in other cases reduplication is all that is involved. Complete reduplication can be used to express intensification: *púpọ̀* 'much', *púpọ̀púpọ̀* 'very much'; *díẹ̀* 'little', *díẹ̀díẹ̀* 'very little'. Complete reduplication can also be used with numerals to mean 'a group of X' (where X is a number) or 'all X'. Cardinal numerals in Yoruba have two forms, a morphologically simple form used for counting and a prefixed form used as a noun or adjective. To obtain the 'group' interpretation, the prefix (*má*) is added prior to reduplication: *méjìméjì* 'two by two' (*èjì* 'two'), *mẹ́tàmẹ́tà* 'three by three' (*ẹ̀ta* 'three'), *mẹ́rìndínlógúnmẹ́rìndínlógún* 'sixteen by sixteen' (*ẹẹ́rìndínlógún* 'sixteen'). To obtain the universally quantified form, reduplication takes place prior to prefixation of *má*: *méjèèjì* 'both' (*má+èjì+èjì*: *èjì* 'two'), *mẹ́tẹ̀ẹ̀ta* 'all three' (*má+ẹ̀ta+ẹ̀ta*: *ẹ̀ta* 'three'), *mẹ́rẹ̀ẹ̀rìndínlógún* 'all sixteen' (*má+ẹ̀rin+ẹ̀rin+dín+ní+ogún*: *ẹẹ́rìndínlógún* 'sixteen'). Related to such cases are reduplications involving nouns of time: *ọdọọdún* 'every year' (*ọdun+ọdún*: *ọdún* 'year'), *oṣooṣù* 'every month' (*oṣu+oṣù*: *oṣù* 'month'), *ọ̀sọ̀ọ̀sẹ̀* 'every week' (*ọsẹ+ọ̀sẹ̀*: *ọ̀sẹ̀* 'week').

In addition to such cases, complete reduplication may involve the addition of a formative in between two reduplicated nouns. One common such process involves the formative *kí*: *[X]+kí+[X]*. The resulting nouns mean 'any kind of X' and often have a derogatory connotation. Consider the following examples: *ẹnikẹ́ni* 'any person' (*ẹni+kí+ẹni*: *ẹni* 'person'), *ewékéwé* 'any leaf at all; useless leaves' (*ewé+kí+ewé*: *ewé* 'leaf '), *ijókíjó* 'whatever dancing; indecent dancing' (*ijó+kí+ijó*: *ijó* 'dancing'). This type of reduplication with *kí* is extremely productive with abstract nouns derived with the prefix *ì*-: *ìnákúnǎ* 'extravagance' (*ì+ná+kí+ì+ná*: *ná* 'spend') (note that the change of [i] to [u] in these forms is fairly regular), *ìsọkúsọ̀* 'nonsense' (*ì+sọ+kí+ì+sọ*: *sọ* 'speak').

Apart from such examples of complete reduplication, Yoruba has a productive process of partial reduplication that is used to derive a nominal form from a verb. For this process, the initial consonant of a verb is copied and this copied consonant is followed by a high-toned [í]: *lílọ* 'going' (*lọ* 'go'), *sísọ* 'speaking' (*sọ* 'speak'), *rírí* 'seeing' (*rí* 'see').

It is also possible in Yoruba to derive agentive nominals by reduplicating a sequence of a verb and its object: *jagunjagun* 'warrior' (*jà* 'fight', *ogun* 'war'), *kólékólé* 'burglar' (*kó* 'steal', *ilé* 'house'), *bẹ́ríbẹ́rí* 'executioner' (*bẹ́* 'cut off', *orí* 'head'), *jẹ̀díjẹ̀dí* 'haemorrhoids' (*jẹ* 'consume', *ìdí* 'bottom').

Before leaving the topic of reduplication, it is appropriate to discuss at least briefly the phenomenon of ideophones. Ideophones are notoriously difficult to define — both in general and with respect to a single language. What is clear, however, is that there is a class of words in Yoruba which have rather distinctive and interesting properties. Reduplication is one of these properties — although as has already been seen above, reduplication is not restricted to ideophones. Consider the following examples: *kẹ́sẹkẹ́sẹ* 'of surrounding being dead quiet', *rokíroki* 'of being red', *ròdòrodo* 'of being bright', *rùbùtùrubutu* 'of round object', *kọ̀rọ̀bọ̀tọ̀kọrọbọtọ* 'of being fat', *pọ̀tọ̀pọ́tọ̀* 'soft mud', *dòdoòdò* 'of coming up brightly', *ramúramù* 'of a loud noise (e.g. lion's)', *gbàlágbàlá* 'of wobbling movement (e.g. of a fish)', *jálajàlajàlàjalà* 'of shabby appearance', *gógórogògòrogògòrògogorò* 'of several things being tall', *súúsùùsúú* 'of perching or assembling in an area'. The above ideophones involve two, three or four repetitions of a sequence. The tonal possibilities for ideophones correlate in many instances with semantic information — for example, the LHLH pattern of *gbàlágbàlá* seen above occurs in forms indicating 'lack of smoothness of activity'. Changes in the tonal pattern of an ideophone can have marked semantic consequences. For example, in the following set of ideophones, a low tone correlates with largeness or heaviness, a high tone correlates with smallness or lightness and a mid tone indicates an average value: *rògòdò* 'of a big round object', *rogodo* 'of an average round object', *rógódó* 'of a small round object'. Moreover, the quality of the vowel in such words turns out to be semantically significant in such ideophones as well. While *o* indicates roundness, replacement of *o* by *u* serves to indicate weight (with the same degree distinction possibilities correlated with tone): *rùgùdù* 'large (heavier) object', *rugudu* 'medium (heavy) object', *rúgúdú* 'small (slightly heavy) object'. In some cases, there is no obvious source for an ideophone (or at least, no semantically related source). In other cases, an ideophone can be related both semantically and phonologically to a source morpheme. For example, *kéékèèkéé* 'in small bits' can be seen to derive from *kéré* 'small' with the application of reduplication, *r*-deletion and certain tonal changes. In this respect, it should be noted that rules applying to ideophones can typically be observed to apply elsewhere in the language — to non-ideophones. For example, *r*-deletion applies in the derivation of many ideophones but also applies in many other cases — such as, in deriving the variant *Yoòbá* for *Yorùbá* (vowel assimilation in this example is triggered by *r*-deletion).

Although it was noted at the beginning of this section that Yoruba word-formation processes tend to be derivational, this section will conclude with a short discussion of certain inflectional processes observed in the pronominal system. Yoruba has two classes of pronouns (to be discussed further in section 4). While one class of pronouns is invariant (just like regular nouns), the second class of pronouns varies as a function of grammatical relation and tense/aspect/polarity. For illustration, examples will be given of first and third person singular pronominal forms: subject (for appropriate tense/aspect/polarity): *mo bínú* 'I was angry' (*mo* 'I'), *ó mọ Èkó* 'he/she knows Lagos' (*ó* 'he/she'); subject (before the negative marker *kò*): *n kò mọ̀* 'I don't know' [ŋ̍ (k)ò mɔ̃̀] (*n* 'I') or *mi kò mọ̀* [mi (k)ò mɔ̃̀] (*mi* 'I'), *kò mọ̀* 'he/she doesn't know' (Ø 'he/she'); subject (before the future marker *á*): *mà á lọ* 'I will go' (*mà* 'I'), *á á lọ* 'he/she will go' (*á* 'he/she'); object: *ó rí mi* 'he/she saw me' (*mi* 'me'), *mo rí i* 'I saw her/him/it' (*i* 'her/him/it'), *jẹ ẹ́* 'eat it' (*ẹ́* 'it'), *fà á* 'pull it' (*á* 'it'). The last three examples illustrate the fact that the form of the third person singular pronoun object is dependent on the verb that it follows: whatever the quality of the vowel of the verb, the pronoun will have the same quality. Moreover, the tone of object pronouns depends on the tone of the verb: if the verb is mid or low, then the pronoun is high; if the verb is high, then the pronoun is mid. The above examples are not exhaustive — for example, additional forms are required in possessive noun phrases. But they are representative of the morphological changes in both segmental make-up and tone that characterise the various syntactically determined pronominal forms.

4 Syntax

In this section, three basic areas of Yoruba syntax will be discussed: word order properties, clitic pronominals and serial verbs. Consider first properties of word order. Given the paucity of inflectional morphology — in particular, the absence of morphological case marking — it is relatively unsurprising that Yoruba is highly configurational. In the following discussion, word order properties of major constituents will be described and illustrated.

With respect to basic word order, Yoruba is SVO (subject–verb–object):

bàbá ra bàtà
father buy shoes
'Father bought shoes.'

If a verb takes more than one object, then both objects follow the verb. The second object in such a case is preceded by a semantically empty preposition *ní*:

Adé fún Tolú ní owó
Ade give Tolu prep. money
'Ade gave Tolu money.'

In a comparable fashion, when a verb takes a verbal complement, such a complement follows the verb:

Táíwò rò pé ó sanra
Taiwo think that he/she fat
'Taiwo thought that he/she was fat.'

Adverbials generally follow the verb (as in the first example below), but there is a small class of adverbials that precede the verb (as in the second example):

kò sanra rárá
neg. fat at all
'He/she is not fat at all.'

ó ṣẹ̀ṣẹ̀ lọ
he/she just go
'He/she has just gone.'

Tense and aspect in Yoruba are expressed by particles that appear between the subject and the verb. For example, the following sentences illustrate the placement of the perfective aspect marker *ti* and the future tense marker *á*:

ó ti kú
he/she perf. die
'He/she is/was dead.'

ọ̀rẹ́ mi á lọ
friend my fut. go
'My friend will go.'

To form a yes-no question, a particle can be added at the beginning of the sentence (*ṣé*, *ǹjẹ́*) or at the end of the sentence (*bí*):

ṣé Òjó lọ?
ǹjẹ́ Òjó lọ?
Òjó lọ bí?
'Did Ojo go?' (*lọ* 'go')

Turning our attention to the noun phrase, it can be seen that the head of the phrase appears in initial position. Hence, adjectives occur post-nominally:

ajá funfun
dog white
'white dog'

Possessive noun phrases appear after the noun possessed:

fìlà Àkàndé
cap Akande
'Akande's cap'

Determiners and demonstratives appear after the head noun:

ọmọ náà
child the
'that child' (definite determiner)

Similarly, a relative clause is placed post-nominally:

ẹni tí ó wá
person rel. he/she come
'the person who came'

As far as numerals are concerned, the appropriate word order depends on the individual case. For examples below 'one hundred and ninety', numerals that are *not* multiples of ten are placed after the noun:

ajá méjì
dog two
'two dogs'

Numerals that are multiples of ten are placed *before* the noun (starting from 'twenty'):

ogún ajá
twenty dog
'twenty dogs'

But in spite of the prenominal appearance of a numeral like 'twenty', derivatives of such a numeral appear post-nominally:

ajá méjìlélógún
dog twenty-two
'twenty-two dogs' (two over twenty)

As can be seen from the above examples, noun phrases and verb phrases are head-initial. Prepositional phrases are also head-initial (as is obvious from the terminology):

ní ọjà
at market
'at the market'

Hence in general, the head of a phrase in Yoruba comes at the beginning. While a short discussion such as this cannot even attempt to cover all important properties of word order in Yoruba, it would nevertheless be remiss to wind up without at least mentioning the extremely common 'focus' construction. This construction is derived by fronting a constituent which is marked by the morpheme *ni*. The fronted constituent can be an argument of the verb (for example, subject or object); it can be an adjunct (for example, a locative or temporal adjunct); the fronted constituent can even be the verb itself ('predicate cleft'):

èmi ni Tolú rí
me foc. Tolu see
'It's me that Tolu saw.' (object)

ní ilé ni ó ti bẹ̀rẹ̀
at house foc. it perf. start
'It was in the house that it started.' (adjunct)

rírà ni bàbá ra bàtà
buying foc. father buy shoes
'Father BOUGHT shoes.'

As can be seen in the last example, when the emphasised element is the verb, a nominalised form of the verb appears in focus position and the verb itself continues to appear in its appropriate place inside the clause. In a similar way, if the subject is focused, a pronominal form must replace the fronted noun phrase in subject position:

èmi ni ó lọ
me foc. 3 sg. go
'It's I that went'

Note that in such constructions, the 'third person singular' pronoun can be used without actually implying any qualities of person or number; in such a sentence, the pronoun serves simply to mark the subject position that the fronted constituent came from. It is possible to focus the possessor of a noun phrase. In such a case (as with subjects), a pronominal form will replace the fronted noun phrase; and as with subjects, the 'third person singular' morphological form may be used with a semantically neutral interpretation in such cases:

bàbá ni ilé rẹ̀ wó
father foc. house his collapse
'It was father whose house collapsed.'

As a final point about the focus construction, content questions are formed by placing the appropriate question word in focus position. The properties of such sentences are comparable to those of the non-interrogative focus sentences seen above. Two examples are given below:

ta ni Tolú rí ọ̀rẹ́ rẹ̀
who foc. Tolu see friend his/her
'Whose friend did Tolu see?'

ní ibo ni ó lọ
at where foc. he/she go
'Where has he/she gone?'

At several points in the above discussion, reference has been made to pronominal forms. For example, in the discussion of morphology, it was seen that pronominal forms vary as a function of their syntactic environment and it was noted above that pronominal forms fill in certain positions in focus constructions. As mentioned in the morphology section, however, there are two classes of pronouns in Yoruba — and both properties just mentioned hold of the 'weak' class. In fact, the 'weak' and 'strong' classes turn out to be distinguished on phonological, morphological and syntactic grounds. The strong pronouns behave simply like a true noun phrase. Phonologically, they fit the canonical pattern for Yoruba nouns; morphologically, they are invariant. Syntactically, their distribution parallels that of non-pronominal noun phrases. The weak pronouns, on the other hand, are systematically distinguished from non-pronominal noun phrases. Phonologically, weak pronouns are the only nominal forms that can be of a single syllable. They are also the only forms whose tonal specifications can vary depending on the context — as seen above with weak object pronouns. It has already been shown that the morphological form of weak pronouns varies — unlike regular nominals. Syntactically, the distribution of weak pronouns is quite restricted. For example, weak pronouns cannot be conjoined or modified (although strong pronouns and regular nouns can be). Weak pronouns occur only in a restricted set of syntactic positions; for example, they cannot appear in focus position and they cannot appear with interrogative particles such as *dà* 'where?' and *ńkọ́* 'what about?' (while both strong pronouns and non-pronominal noun phrases can). Such properties suggest that the strong pronouns are indeed pronominal *nouns* — and therefore show the distribution of nouns. Weak pronouns, on the other hand, can be analysed as clitics — with their morphological and phonological shape dependent on the constituent to which they are attached. By analysing them as clitics, their restricted syntactic distribution can be explained.

Apart from the properties just mentioned, there is a particularly interesting set of differences between the two pronominal sets. Consider the following sentences:

Dàda	rò	pé	ó	sanra
Dada	think	that	he	fat

'Dada thought that he (someone else) was fat.' (weak pronoun)

Dàda	rò	pé	òun	sanra
Dada	think	that	he	fat

'Dada thought that he himself was fat.' (strong pronoun)

In the sentence with the weak pronoun, the pronoun must refer to someone other than Dada; in the sentence with the strong pronoun, the pronoun must refer to Dada. This difference in interpretation involves reference to the syntactic configuration; it is not due simply to lexical properties of the strong and weak pronouns. Compare, for example, the following sentence including a strong pronoun with the sentence above that also had a strong pronoun:

Tolú	sọ	pé	òun	ni	ó	wá
Tolu	say	that	he/she	foc.	he/she	come

'Tolu said that it was he/she who came.'

In this sentence, the pronoun *òun* (a strong pronoun) may either refer to Tolu or to someone else. That is, the pronoun *òun* in the sentence with an embedded focus construction may or may not refer to the preceding subject. But the pronoun *òun* in the sentence with a simple (non-focus) embedded clause must refer to the preceding subject. Comparable syntactic considerations also determine whether a weak pronoun is interpreted as coreferential to a preceding subject. Compare the above example with a weak pronoun to the following sentence:

Dúpẹ́	ń	ta	aṣọ	bí	ó	ṣe	ń	ta	ọsàn
Dupe	prog.	sell	cloth	as	she	do	prog.	sell	orange

'Dupe sells cloth the way she sells oranges.'

In this sentence, unlike the previous one, the weak pronoun not only can be interpreted as referring to the preceding subject, but it is normally interpreted in that way. The difference in interpretation is again due to syntactic differences: the weak pronoun in the earlier sentence is contained in a clausal complement to the verb in the main clause; the weak pronoun in the later sentence is contained in a manner adjunct. The correct interpretation of a pronoun in Yoruba therefore depends on two basic factors: (1) whether the pronoun belongs to the strong class or the weak class; and (2) the nature of the syntactic configuration within which the pronoun appears.

Serial verb constructions are the final topic to be discussed in this section. In Yoruba, as in many Kwa languages, one finds sentences in which strings of verb phrases appear consecutively without any intervening conjunction or subordinator. Such sentences are extremely common and exhibit a number of interesting properties. Consider the following examples:

ó	gbé	e	wá
he/she	carry	it	come

'He/she brought it.'

wọ́n	gbé	e	lọ
they	carry	it	go

'They took it away.'

In this type of example, the second verb indicates the direction in which the first action took place. In such a case, the subject of the second verb is also the subject of the first verb. It is also possible, however, for the subject of the second verb to be the object of the first verb:

ó	tì	mí	ṣubú
he/she	push	me	fall

'He/she pushed me and I fell.'

In such a sentence, it is the object of *tì* 'push' who falls — and not the subject. Two transitive verbs can be combined in a serial verb construction. In some such examples, the serial verb sequence will have two object noun phrases:

ó	pọn	omi	kún	kete
he/she	draw	water	fill	pot

'He/she drew water and filled the pot.'

In many examples, however, a single object appears in between the two transitive verbs — and is interpreted as the object of both verbs:

ó	ra	ẹran	jẹ
he/she	buy	meat	eat

'He/she bought meat and ate it.'

ó	ra	màlúù	tà
he/she	buy	cow	sell

'He/she bought a cow in order to sell.'

In many examples syntactically comparable to the last two, the meaning of the pair of verbs ranges from being idiomatic but related to the individual verbs' meanings to being completely opaque:

ó	gba	ọ̀rọ̀	náà	gbọ́
he/she	accept	matter	the	hear

'He/she believed the matter.' (*gbà* ... *gbọ́* 'believe')

ó	ba	kẹ̀kẹ́	mi	jẹ́
he/she		bicycle	my	

'He/she spoiled my bicycle.' (*bà* ... *jẹ́* 'spoil')

Many constructions that might be thought to involve categories other than verbs can be shown to involve serial verb sequences. For example, consider the word *fún* in the following sentence:

ó	tà	á	fún	mi
he/she	sell	it	'to'	me

'He/she sold it to me.'

One might think that *fún* in such a sentence is a preposition. In fact, however, the properties of this word are verbal and not prepositional. For example, it can take object clitics such as *mi*; prepositions do not take pronominal clitics. The word *fún* can be nominalised by the process of partial reduplication: *fífún* (just like a verb). In addition, *fún* appears as a main verb meaning 'give':

ó	fún	mi	ní	owó
he/she	give	me	prep.	money

'He/she gave me some money.'

Recall that the *ní* that appears in such a sentence is a semantically empty preposition marking a second object to a verb.

The above discussion of serial verbs does not even vaguely attempt to be exhaustive. Serial verb constructions are used in many ways other than those described here — and in many cases the syntactic properties are somewhat different. Without a doubt, what are being called 'serial verb constructions' actually refer to several distinguishable syntactic types. What is probably of most interest is that various syntactic constructions use morphologically indistinguishable verbs and use them in syntactic phrases that themselves do not involve overt markers to distinguish construction types.

Bibliography

Bamgboṣe (1966) is the standard reference grammar. The grammatical notes in Rowlands (1969) are very useful; the volume includes translation exercises. Two pedagogical grammars are Bamgboṣe (1967) and Awobuluyi (1978). For the development of Yoruba orthography, see Ajayi (1960). Hair (1967) is an interesting discussion of early work on Yoruba, including a bibliography up to 1890.

References

Ajayi, J.F.A. 1960. 'How Yoruba was Reduced to Writing', *Odu: A Journal of Yoruba, Edo and Related Studies* (Ministry of Education, Ibadan) pp. 49–58

Awobuluyi, O. 1978. *Essentials of Yoruba Grammar* (Oxford University Press Nigeria, Ibadan)

Bamgboṣe, A. 1966. *A Grammar of Yoruba* (Cambridge University Press, Cambridge)

—— 1967. *A Short Yoruba Grammar* (Heinemann Educational Books (Nigeria), Ibadan)

Hair, P.E.H. 1967. *The Early Study of Nigerian Languages: Essays and Bibliographies* (Cambridge University Press, Cambridge)

Rowlands, E.C. 1969. *Teach Yourself Yoruba* (English Universities Press, London)

16 Swahili and the Bantu Languages

Benji Wald

1 Historical and Social Background

The Bantu languages dominate the southern half of the African land mass and were spoken as first languages by an estimated 157 million speakers in the early 1980s, nearly a third of Africa's total population. In their geographical extent, they come into contact with representatives of all the other major African language families: Cushitic (of Afroasiatic superstock) and Nilo-Saharan languages in the north-east, Khoisan in the south (and minimally in the north-east due to the retention of the Khoisan language Sandawe in northeastern Tanzania, surrounded by Bantu languages) and its closest relatives among the Niger-Congo languages in the north-west.

The Bantu languages are thought to have originally spread from the West African transitional area of eastern Nigeria and Cameroon, which now marks the westernmost expansion of Bantu in Africa. From this area Bantu languages were carried eastward and southward in several waves of migration, responsible for the oldest dialect divisions among the languages, and starting no later than the early centuries of the first millennium AD. It was early recognised, for example, that a major dialect division is into West and East Bantu, symptomatised by the distinction between reflexes of the lexical item 'two': Proto-West **bàdé* and Proto-East **bèdé*. West Bantu shows more syntactic diversity than East Bantu, particularly in the north-west, where the morphological richness of the majority of Bantu languages begins to give way to the more isolating syntactic tendencies of the neighbouring Benue-Congo and Kwa languages of Nigeria, e.g. the passive verbal suffix **-o-* is totally replaced by the impersonal construction, i.e. 'they saw me' replaces 'I was seen'.

The vast majority of the speakers of Bantu languages are directly involved in agricultural production. In this they contrast traditionally with the hunters and herders they came into contact with from other language families in much of their present areas, frequently effecting language shift on earlier populations, whether or not the latter maintained their modes of production. More recently, the agricultural majority also contrasts with the growing number of city dwellers involved in distribution and services, as the rapid urbanisation of Bantu Africa continues.

Map 16.1: The Bantu-speaking Area

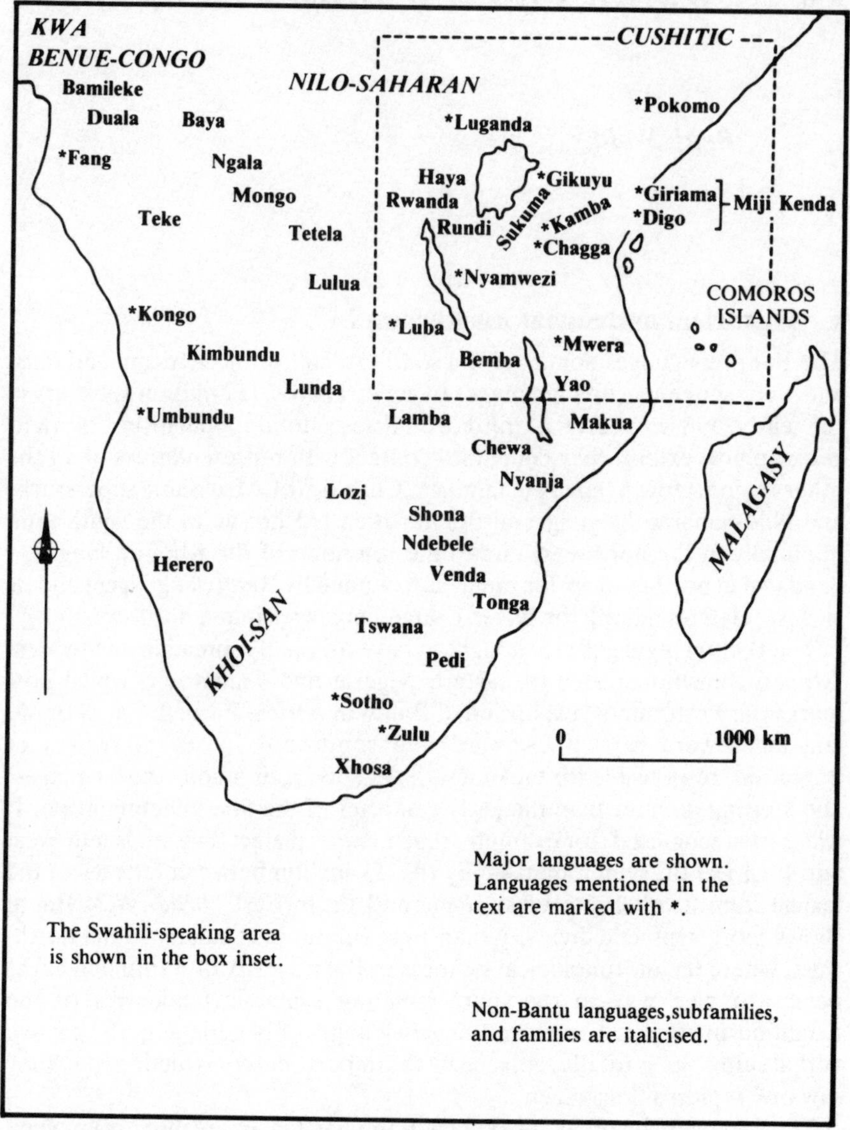

The distinctive typological nature of the Bantu languages and their close genetic relationship were recognised early by scholars. The label Bantu was established by Bleek in 1862 as the reconstructed word for 'people'; the modern Proto-Bantu reconstruction is **ba-ntò*, plural of **mo-ntò* 'person'. Bantu speakers themselves tend to recognise the essential unity of their own and neighbouring Bantu languages with which they are familiar.

Map 16.2: The Swahili-speaking Area

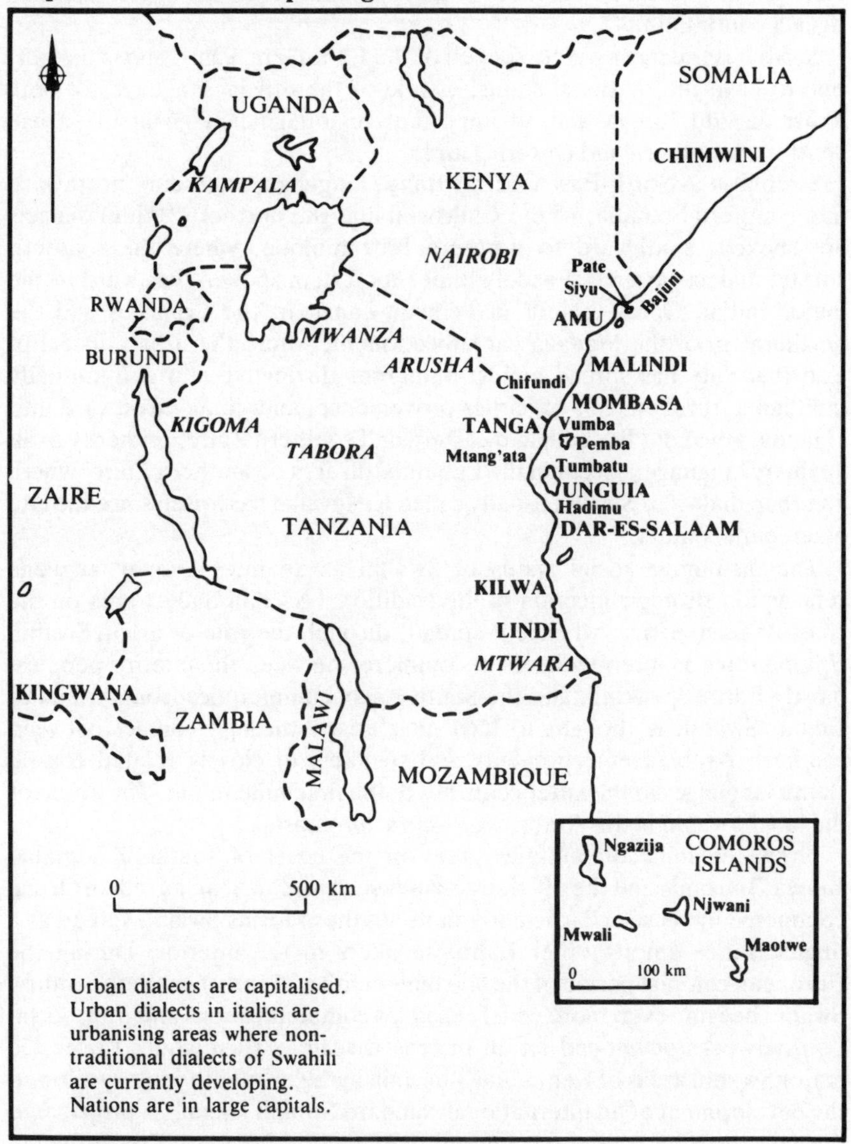

Consequent to the high degree of structural unity among most Bantu languages, together with the wide area of contact among them, a great deal of mutual influence among Bantu languages in contact renders detailed subclassification according to the tree theory of genetic relations problematic. Usually, broad areas reflecting isogloss bundles clearly circumscribe certain dialect groups despite internal diversity. Between such clear groups transitional areas are often apparent giving the appearance of a dialect continuum.

Swahili is the most widely spoken of the Bantu languages, and is the only one to have international status, as one of the official languages of both Tanzania and Kenya and an important regional language in the urban centres of southern and eastern Zaire.

Swahili is a North-East Coastal Bantu language, extending northward into southern Somalia, where ChiMwini and the northern Bajuni dialects are spoken, southward to northern Mozambique, where the southern coastal dialects are more widely understood than spoken, eastward to the major Indian Ocean islands of Pemba, Zanzibar, the Comoros and the northern tip of the Madagascar subcontinent, where the urban dialect of Zanzibar City has spread amidst numerous distinctive and non-mutually intelligible rural dialects of earlier provenience, and, finally westward into Uganda, Rwanda, Burundi and eastern and southern Zaire, primarily as an auxiliary language, except in the Lubumbashi area of southern Zaire, where an urban dialect of Swahili usually called KiNgwana has arisen since the late nineteenth century.

The distinctive social status of Swahili as an international language reflects the strategic location of the traditional Swahili dialect area on the coast of East Africa, whence it spread, through the role of urban Swahili communities as intermediaries in commerce between the interior peoples, mostly Bantu speaking, and the South Asian communities from Arabia to China. Swahili is thought to have first arisen through contact between southern Arabian entrepreneurs and speakers of closely related coastal Bantu languages in the latter centuries of the first millennium. The origin of the label *Swahili* is the Arabic word *sawa:ħil* 'coasts'.

Urban Swahili communities grew on the coast of southern Somalia, Kenya, Tanzania and the off-shore islands such as Zanzibar, as Indian Ocean commerce increased. Particularly in its southern forms Swahili spread as a lingua franca among other Bantu speakers in the interior. During the European colonial period of the late nineteenth and early twentieth century, Swahili became even more widely used, as communications and transportation networks developed on an increased scale. British control over the major Swahili areas of Kenya and Tanzania in the twentieth century allowed the development of an international standard Swahili language, propagated through the educational system and mass media, based on the cultivated southern urban dialect of Zanzibar City, a variety close to the basic form of Swahili already used as a lingua franca in precolonial times.

By the mid-1980s the estimated number of speakers of Swahili was nearly 50 million, the majority residing in Tanzania and Kenya. Most speakers use Swahili as an auxiliary language and have a different first language, also Bantu. First-language speakers traditionally tracing their ancestors back to other Swahili speakers number about two million. However, with the rapid urbanisation of East Africa and the prominence of Swahili as a lingua franca among working class East Africans, possibly another four million have come to adopt Swahili as either an only first language or simultaneously with their ethnic language, e.g. in Dar es Salaam, Mombasa, Nairobi, Lubumbashi and smaller urban centres.

Swahili, particularly the standard variety, is currently written in the Roman alphabet, using Latin vowel conventions and simplified English conventions for consonants. A modern Swahili literature has been developing since standardisation in the 1920s. Traditionally Swahili was written in a modified Arabic script, used to commit to paper verse meant to be recited. Manuscripts going back to the early eighteenth century reveal a written poetic tradition originating in the northern area and spreading southward. The literate poetic tradition is strong enough to occasion the reservation of space in standard Swahili newspapers for readers to submit poems.

Among speakers from traditional Swahili communities, Swahili is perceived as a cover term for a series of dialects among people who share a historic cultural as well as linguistic heritage. The dialects themselves are associated with local names reflecting local territoriality and ethnicity. There are three fairly distinct dialect groups:

(1) Northern: includes the sharply distinct urban dialect of ChiMwini in Brava, Somalia (not considered Swahili by its own community or other Swahili speakers); the Bajuni dialects of more southern Somalia and northern coastal Kenya; the urban island dialects of Lamu, Siyu, Pate and the transitional to Central dialect of urban Mombasa, Kenya.

(2) Central: most of these dialects are rural and spoken by relatively small communities on and off the coast of southern Kenya, northern Tanzania and the Comoros. Among these dialects are ChiFundi and Vumba of the Kenyan coast; Mtang'ata of the northern Tanzanian coast; Pemba, Tumbatu and Hadimu of the off-shore Tanzanian islands of Pemba and Zanzibar; Ngazija, Nzwani and Mwali of the Comoro Islands. These dialects are the most distinct and internally varied of the Swahili dialects.

(3) Southern: includes Zanzibar City and the urban districts of coastal Tanzania, e.g. Tanga, Dar es Salaam, Kilwa.

In some respects, the Northern and Southern dialects show more affinity to each other than they do to the Central dialects, particularly in their verbal systems, leading to the impression of a basic distinction between urban and rural dialects overlying the tripartite dialect division.

Among Bantu languages, all Swahili dialects are most striking in the adstratum of Arabic vocabulary in their lexicons while retaining the distinctive Bantu grammatical type, somewhat more extensive than the proportion of Anglo-French loanwords used in English in everyday conversation, e.g. the numerals 'six', 'seven', 'nine' and all higher multiples of 'ten' have replaced Bantu roots with Arabic loans. However, even more extreme than Swahili in its lexical borrowing is the northern Tanzanian language of Mbugu, retaining a Bantu grammar and inventory of grammatical morphemes, but almost totally non-Bantu in its lexicon (mostly of Cushitic origin). The lexical and grammatical effect of non-Bantu languages on Swahili will be discussed separately from its essential Bantu nature.

2 Phonology

The syllabic structure of the reconstructed Common Bantu word is relatively simple, consisting of CV(V) syllables only. However, the transparency of this structure is modified somewhat in various Bantu languages, where non-prominent syllables have been subject to altered glottalic and timing mechanisms which reduce their nuclei to short unvoiced vowels, or completely omit them in some cases. Apocope is most characteristic of certain North-West Bantu languages, where final consonants are found, e.g. in the Cameroonian language Fang.

Most recent reconstructions of the Common Bantu consonantal system display three manners and four points of articulation.

p	t	č	k
b	d	j	g
m	n	ny	ng'
(and		y	in some reconstructions)

Typologically the system is unusual in the absence of a distinctive phoneme /s/, but /s/ is not necessary for reconstructive purposes. This and many other phonemic fricatives exist in most Bantu languages, at least in part due to assimilatory changes caused by adjacent vowels or, through a large part of the area, the shift of the non-nasal palatals to sibilants. Southern Swahili is unusual in its area in retaining the original palatals. The Northern dialects are distinctive in the shift of the original voiceless palatal to a dental stop. Dentalisation of palatals and/or fricatives is characteristic of the Thagicu languages of interior Kenya and adjacent northern Tanzanian languages, e.g. Northern Pare, but not resulting in dental stops, cf. Thagicu [ðeka], Northern Pare [θeka], Northern Swahili [t̪eka] and Southern Swahili [čeka] for Common Bantu **čèka* 'laugh'. Alveolar affricates are the reflexes of the palatal stops among the Miji Kenda languages of the north-east coast of Kenya, relatively closely related to the adjacent forms of Swahili, e.g. [tseka] 'laugh', but in Swahili these reflexes of the palatals are only found in the isolated Comoros dialects, possibly a relic of this stage of development among the Northern dialects.

In view of their historical evolution in various Bantu languages, the prenasalised series of Common Bantu should probably be treated phonologically as an independent series rather than as a cluster of nasal + stop.

mp	nt	nč	nk
mb	nd	nj	ng

The voiceless prenasalised series shows considerable instability across many Bantu languages, e.g. with loss of nasalisation among some languages, voicing assimilation to a voiced prenasalised series in others and loss of the stop in still others, cf. *ba-ntò* 'people' > [wa-t'u] in Swahili, [a-ndũ] in the Thagicu languages of interior Kenya, [wa-nu] in Luguru (among other central coastal Tanzanian languages). The widespread areal feature of aspiration of the voiceless prenasalised consonants gave rise to a distinct opposition between an aspirated and unaspirated voiceless series upon the denasalisation of the prenasalised voiceless stops in Swahili, e.g. *kaa* 'charcoal' vs. *k'aa* 'crab' < **n-kádá*. This contrast is more typical of traditional Kenyan Swahili communities than of Southern Swahili, where the two series have merged fairly recently through the unconditioned aspiration of the original voiceless stop series.

The prenasalised voiced series is more stable and often shows behaviour parallel to or rotational with the original voiceless stops. Thus, the Common Bantu prenasalised palatal **nj* shifts parallel to **č* to dental in Northern Swahili, e.g. [nd̯aa], cf. Southern Swahili [njaa] 'hunger'. Most interesting among the Sotho group of Southern Bantu is the rotational shift of consonants, so that the Common Bantu prenasalised voiced series becomes a voiceless aspirated stop series concomitant with a shift of the Common Bantu voiceless stops to fricatives (the Common Bantu apical series is post-alveolar, resulting in a flap-like liquid *r* or *l* in the lenition processes which have affected the voiced apicals), e.g. Sotho *xo-rutha* from Common Bantu **ko-túnda* 'teach', cf. Swahili *ku-fund-isha*, with a verbal suffix added.

There is a great deal of variety in the glottalic mechanisms by which the Common Bantu stop series is realised across the current Bantu languages. In Swahili, the set of voiced stops is 'implosive' (preglottalised), rather than truly voiced. This set of voiced stops is largely of secondary origin, sometimes due to back-formations based on prenasalised forms, where the stops are truly voiced and not preglottalised. Thus, *ki-ɓovu* 'rotten' (class 7 concord) is a back-formation from *m-bovu* 'rotten' (class 9 concord), cf. *mw-ovu* 'rotten' (class 1 concord) and *-oza* 'rot (v.)' with lenition and loss of initial **b*. Lenition of the voiced non-prenasalised series to corresponding fricatives or sonorants is common in most of the Bantu area, resulting in a series:

[β/w l/r z/ž ɣ/y/Ø]

Swahili shares with a number of North-East Bantu languages a tendency towards further lenition of glides so that Common Bantu **d* is lost, primarily in the vicinity of back vowels. However, Swahili is more conservative than many of its North-East relatives in having lost *w* and *y* only before high vowels of like fronting, though also variably before *a* in vernacular speech. The Northern dialects have gone slightly further in loss of *y* (<**g*) before an unlike high vowel as well, e.g. Northern *hu-u* 'this one (anim.)' < *hu-yu*, still the Southern and standard form. Glide deletion is most advanced in the Thagicu language Kamba, e.g. *-o-* 'buy' < **-gòd-*, *-a-* 'divide' < **-gàb-*.

In some areas, e.g. in the north-east, lenition also commonly affects some or all of the members of the voiceless series, cf. Giriama *henza* for earlier North-East Bantu **pɛnja* 'love (v.)', cf. Swahili *penda*; Giriama *moho* for Common Bantu **mo-yɔ́tɔ̀* 'fire', cf. Swahili *moto*. Lenition of **p* is particularly widespread, while the velar **k* is most resistant to lenition.

A widespread tendency toward word-level manner of articulation prosody is shown in some of the more striking consonantal changes affecting large areas in the north-east and extending toward the south-west, e.g. the following dissimilatory changes: Dahl's Law, originally noted in Nyamwezi of interior Tanzania, but of a much wider area, dissimilates the voicing of the first of two consecutive voiceless stops, e.g. *-bita* < *-pita* 'pass (v.)'; the Ganda Law, originally noted for LuGanda, dissimilates the first of two consecutive voiced prenasalised stops to the corresponding nasal, e.g. *ng'ombe* 'cow' (where *ng'* is the orthographic representation of [ŋ]) < *ngɔ̀mbɛ̀*. Finally, in much of West Bantu a morphophonemic process of nasal harmony is found, changing /d/ to /n/ in verbal suffixes following a root-final nasal, e.g. Luba (southern Zaire) *-kwac-ile* 'having caught' < **kóát-edɛ*, but *-dim-ine* 'having sown' < **dèm-edɛ*.

In contrast to the consonantal system, the vowel system of Common Bantu has remained relatively stable in the various languages. The reconstructed system is a symmetrical seven-vowel system with four degrees of height:

i e ɛ
      a
u o ɔ

Prosodically, one vowel per word could be distinctively long or short and each vowel of a stem could have a high or low tone. The tonal distinctions are preserved in most of the area, with reduction of the full domain of the original tonal distinctions in large areas of the north-east and south-west. Total loss of lexical tone is unusual and confined to a few languages in the north-east, including all dialects of Swahili. The loss of distinctive vowel length is characteristic of most of the western Bantu area and a large area of the east, including Swahili along with most of the coast. Reduction of the original seven-vowel system to five vowels is characteristic of most Bantu languages, with the exception of an extreme northern band extending from the west coast almost to the east coast and the Sotho group of South-East Bantu. For the most part this five-vowel system is derived from the mergers of the highest two tiers of vowels. Unusual is the merger of Common Bantu **u* into **e* in part of the southwestern area, e.g. Umbundu *o-mbela* < **mbúdà* 'rain', cf. Swahili *mvua*.

In most of the five-vowel area, the merger of the highest two tiers of vowels did not occur before influencing the manner of articulation of the preceding consonant, generally through fricativisation of the preceding consonant before the highest original vowels **i̧* and **u*. In the largest area of this shift, reduction of point of articulation contrasts accompanied the fricativisation process. In Swahili, all fricatives became labial before **u*, e.g. *-chofu* 'tired' < **-čɔk-u*, cf. *-choka* 'tire', *fua* 'forge (v.)' < **túda*, *-ongofu* 'deceitful' < **-ɔngɔp-u*, cf. *-ongopa* 'lie (v.)'. However, the situation is much more complicated before **i*. Generally, the point of articulation of the resulting fricative is preserved, producing regular morphophonemic alternations such as the following:

-pi*k*a 'cook (v.)'	-pi*sh*-i 'cook (anim. n.)'
-fua*t*a 'follow (v.)'	-fua*s*-i 'follower'
-li*p*a 'pay'	-li*f*-i 'payer'

In the most northern dialects of Amu and Bajuni, the merger of the labials into the apicals is general, e.g. majority Swahili *fimbo* > *simbo* 'walking stick' and *vita* > *zita* 'war, battles'. A few lexical items, e.g. *mwizi* 'thief' where *mwivi* is expected (and attested, but not common), have become usual in Southern Swahili. The same merger is also characteristic of the Comoros dialects, e.g. Ngazija *-zimba* 'swell', cf. Southern Swahili *-vimba*. Otherwise, this merger is general to all urban Swahili dialects only within lexical items where **i̧* is immediately followed by another vowel, reflecting a Common Bantu double vowel, e.g. *zaa* 'bear children' < **bíáda* or *soma* 'read' < **píɔ́ma*. Many rural dialects show resistance to merger even under these conditions, as is typical of the North-East coastal Bantu languages outside of Swahili and Giriama, e.g. Vumba *vyaa, fyoma*.

Bantu vowel harmony consists of lowering **e* and **o* to **ɛ* and **ɔ* following a syllable whose nucleus is already at that degree of height. In all the Bantu languages, this is reflected in the use of this type of vowel harmony in the vowel of many verbal extensions, a morphophonemic process, e.g. Swahili *pit-i-a* 'pass by', *pand-i-a* 'climb onto', *shuk-i-a* 'come down to', but *tok-e-a* 'come from' and *end-e-a* 'go toward', where the prepositional extension *-i/e-* < **-e/ɛd-* in Common Bantu is determined by the vowel of the preceding syllable. Bantu polysyllabic roots and stems also tend to adhere to this vowel harmony, so that *C*ɛ*/*ɔ*C*ɛ*/*ɔ* is much more common than *C*ɛ*/*ɔ*C*e*/*o*.

Generally, the variety of tonal changes that have affected various Bantu languages can be traced back to a two-tone system, e.g. **-bàd-* 'count': **-bád-* 'shine' (Swahili *-waa*). The total loss of lexical tone distinctions is confined to a few languages of the north-east. Geographically intermediate are languages like LuGanda which appear to be pitch-stress languages with only one distinctive tone per word. Even among fully tonal languages, especially in the southern Bantu area, there is a tendency for one syllable per word, usually the penultimate, to have special prominence through lengthening. Swahili conforms to the penultimate stress pattern, with regular high pitch and lengthening of the penultimate vowel. Exceptions to this pattern are secondary through borrowing or clipping of reduplicated forms, e.g. *kátika* 'in' < **kàté-kàté*, reduplication of **kàté* > Swahili *káti* 'among'. While traditional Swahili communities maintain the antepenultimate stress of the clipping, second-language speakers tend to regularise stress to penultimate.

3 Morphology

Bantu languages have long been appreciated by scholars for their distinctive morphology, highly agglutinative and allowing great structural complexity to nominal and even more so to verbal forms.

Basic to Bantu nominal morphology is the division of nouns into numerous noun classes, the precise number of which varies from language to language due to syncretism and secondary developments. Traditionally, each reconstructed noun class has been assigned a number. The reconstructed Common Bantu noun classes number nineteen. Each is associated with a different class prefix preceding the noun stem. It is thought that the Bantu noun classes arose in pre-Bantu times from a system of classifiers, probably from nouns even earlier, adding content to the nouns they introduced. The semantic content of many of the classifiers is transparent due to their role in nominal derivation. Some of the noun classes specialise in marking collective or plural nouns and many of the pairings of classes into singular and plural found in the current Bantu languages are traceable to Common Bantu. The list given here presents the reconstructed Bantu noun classes with a rough indication of their semantics. Their semantics is most evident when they are used derivationally. Lexically, there is greater unpredictability for whether a noun of a particular meaning belongs to a certain class, both within and across the various languages.

Class (singular)	Class (plural)
1. *mo- 'human singular'	2. *ba- 'human plural'
3. *mo- 'thin or extended objects, trees, singular'	4. *me- 'plural of class 3'
5. *di/e- 'singular of objects that tend to come in pairs or larger groups, fruits'	6. *ma- 'collective or plural of class 5'

7. *ke- 'instrument, manner'	8. *bi- 'plural of class 7'
9. *ne- 'miscellaneous, animals'	10. *di-ne- 'plural of class 9'
11. *do- 'extended body parts'	'Use class 6/10 plural'
12. *ka- 'diminutive'	13. *to- 'plural of class 12'
14. *bo- 'abstract nouns, qualities'	
15. *ko- 'body parts'	'Use class 6 plural'
16. *pa- 'place where'	
17. *ko- 'place around which, infinitive'	
18. *mo- 'place in which'	
19. *pi- 'diminutive'	'Use class 6/8/10/13 plural'

Exemplifying from Swahili when possible: (1) *m-tu* 'person', pl. (2) *wa-tu*; (3) *m-ti* 'tree', pl. (4) *mi-ti*; (5) *ji-cho* 'eye', pl. (6) *ma-cho* (Swahili also uses this class pair for augmentatives, e.g. (5) *ji-tu* 'giant', pl. (6–5) *ma-ji-tu*); (7) *ki-tu* 'thing', pl. (8) *vi-tu* (Swahili also uses this class for diminutives, e.g. (7–5) *ki-ji-ji* 'village', pl. (8–5) *vi-ji-ji*, cf. (3) *m-ji* 'town', pl. (4) *mi-ji*); (9) *ng'ombe* 'cow', pl. (10) *ng'ombe* (**di-* is not prefixed to plural nouns in most North-East Bantu languages, cf. Zulu (9) *i-n(-)komo* 'cow', pl. (10) *i-zi-n(-)komo*); (11) *u-limi* 'tongue', pl. (10) *n-dimi*; (12) Gikuyu *ka-ana* 'small child', pl. (13) *tw-ana* (the urban Swahili dialects have lost this pair and switched their functions to (7)/(8), as shown above; *ka-* remains lexicalised in *ka-mwe* 'never' < '(not even a) little one'); (14) *u-baya* 'evil' < *-baya* 'bad'; (15) Gikuyu *kũ-gũrũ* 'leg', pl. (6) *ma-gũrũ* (Swahili has shifted this class of nouns to (3) *m-guu*, Southern pl. (4) *mi-guu*, Northern pl. (6) *ma-guu*); the locative classes (16) to (18) can be directly prefixed to nouns in most Bantu languages, cf. coastal southern Tanzanian Mwera (16) *pa-ndu* 'at a place', (17) *ku-ndu* 'around a place', (18) *mu-ndu* 'inside a place', but Swahili uses an associative construction, (16) *p-a nyumba-ni* 'at-of house-loc.', i.e. 'at home', *kw-a nyumba-ni* 'around-of house-loc.', i.e. 'at/around home', *mw-a nyumba-ni* 'in-of home', i.e. 'inside the house'; (19) Kongo (north-west Zaire) *fi-koko-koko* 'little hand', pl. (8) *vi-koko-koko* (this class is largely restricted to West Bantu and does not occur in Swahili).

Regardless of various rearrangements of the noun classes, class concord is a pervasive feature of many grammatical categories in all Bantu languages. All categories modifying a noun have concordial prefixes determined by the noun. In addition, coreferential markers in the verb phrase, such as the subject, object and relative markers, also show class concord. The form taken by the class prefix is determined by the category to which it is prefixed. A secondary set of class prefixes is general for the nasal prefixes, formed by replacing the nasal with **g* (> *y* in Swahili). Which categories take the primary vs. the secondary prefixes varies across the Bantu area. Swahili restricts the nasal class prefixes to adjectives and numerals, except for the retention of nasal class 1 for the object marker, i.e. *m(u)-* rather than *yu-*. The following examples are illustrative of the syntactic extent of class concord in Bantu languages (cp = class prefix, cc = concord):

yu-le	m-tu	*m*-moja	*m*-refu	*a*-li-	*y*-e-	*ki*-soma	*ki*-le	ki-tabu	*ki*-refu
cc-	cp-	cc-	cc-	cc-	cc-	cc-	cc-	cp-	cc-
that	person	one	tall	he past	rel.	it read	that	book	long

'That one tall (1) person who read that long (7) book.'

wa-le	wa-tu	*wa*-wili	*wa*-refu	*wa*-li	*(w)*-o-	*vi*-soma	*vi*-le	vi-tabu	*vi*-refu
cc-	cp-	cc-	cc-	cc-	(cc-)	cc-	cc-	cp-	cc-

'Those two tall (2) people who read those long (8) books.'

An interesting further development of concord has occurred among Swahili and some adjacent North-East coastal Bantu languages: animate concord. This device extends class 1/2 concord to animates, regardless of their lexical noun class. For example, most animals are class 9/10 nouns, e.g. *simba* 'lion', *njovu* 'elephant', *ndege* 'bird'. One result of animate concord is the distinction between *ndege yu-le* 'that bird' with a class 1 animate concord marking the demonstrative and *ndege i-le* 'that aeroplane' with a strictly syntactic class 9 concord on the demonstrative. It must be noted that animate concord is atypical of Bantu languages on the whole. Even in Swahili, when the class of the noun is determined by a semantic rather than a lexical process, class concord overrides animate concord. Thus, *ki-jana yu-le* 'that youth (e.g. teenager)' shows animate concord on the demonstrative, illustrating the perceived lexical arbitrariness of the class 7 prefix on the noun, but *ki-jana ki-le* 'that little-old youth' with class 7, where the class prefix to the noun functions as a diminutive. As a local innovation in North-East coastal Bantu, animate concord serves to illustrate that even though the original semantic motivation for noun class is often obscure for individual lexical items, the syntactic resources of class concord continue to be exploited for semantic purposes.

In addition to the class prefix, it is probable that Common Bantu had a preprefix marking definite and generic nouns and their modifiers. This preprefix survives in various forms and functions in the interior and south-west, usually anticipating at least the vowel of the class prefix, e.g. Zulu *u-mu-ntu* 'the person', *a-ba-ntu* 'the people'. The preprefix has been lost in much of the eastern coastal area. A relic remains in the Northern Bajuni dialects of Swahili in *i-t̪'i* 'land(s)' < **e-n(e)-čé*, Southern Swahili *nchi*. In most dialects of Swahili, the preprefix was lost earlier than voiceless nasals. With the loss of the preprefix penultimate stress was transferred to the nasal, which prevented the loss of the nasal despite its voicelessness. The opposite chronological sequence is evident for Bajuni. When removed from stress, the voiceless nasal and preprefix are lost in all dialects, cf. Bajuni *t̪'i-ni*, Southern Swahili *chi-ni* 'below' (i.e. 'on the ground').

The personal pronouns have a variety of specific forms in Bantu, according to the grammatical category to which they are attached. The chart shows the Swahili pattern, indicative of the formal variation, though not the precise shapes, of the personal pronouns in Bantu.

	Independent	*Possessive*	*Subject marker*	*Object marker*
'I'	mimi	-ngu	ni-	ni-
'you'	wewe	-ko	u-	ku-
's/he'	yeye	-ke	a-/yu-	m-
'we'	sisi	-itu	tu-	tu-
'you (pl.)'	ninyi	-inu	m(w)-	wa-
'they'	wao	-(w)o	wa-	wa-

The *k-* forms of the second and third singular are usual in Bantu and also appear as the subject markers *ku-* and *ka-* respectively in a few languages (including the central dialects of Swahili). Some Bantu languages have independent pronouns for the other classes, but Swahili uses demonstratives instead, e.g. for class 7 *hi-ki* 'this thing', *hi-ch-o* (< *hi-ky-o*) 'that thing (proximate)', *ki-le* 'that thing (distal)'.

Nominal derivational processes have already been alluded to above in the discussion of noun classes and class concord. In some Bantu languages these provide sufficient resources to nominalise verb-object predicates, e.g. Swahili *m-fanya-kazi* 'worker' with class 1 animate prefix, < *-fanya kazi* 'do work'. However, all Bantu languages also show extensive use of nominal suffixes, converting verbs to nouns, e.g. **-ɔ*: Swahili *nen-o* 'word' < *-nen-a* 'say', **-i*: Swahili *u-zaz-i* 'parenthood' < *-zaa* 'bear children' via **bo-bíád-i*, **-u*: Swahili *-bov-u* 'rotten' < *-oza* 'rot' via **-bɔd-u*. Note that the suffix *-u* derives stative qualities from process verbs and forms the basis for derived adjectives as well as nouns. Morphologically nouns and adjectives are not distinct in the Bantu languages. Among the noun derivational suffixes is the locative *-ni*, corresponding in function to the locative prefixes. Suffixed to a noun, *-ni* marks the noun as head of a locative phrase, e.g. Swahili *kazi-ni* 'at work', *mto-ni* 'at the river'. Historically, these derivational suffixes are indicative of a syntactic system quite different from the current Bantu systems and well advanced in the process of morphologising by Common Bantu times. This will be further discussed on pages 304–6.

Bantu verb morphology shows the fullest extent of Bantu agglutinative word structure. Central to the verb is the root, which may be extended to a more complex stem by the addition of derivational suffixes. Final modal suffixes **-a* and **-ɛ* distinguish the indicative and subjunctive respectively. In the indicative mode this is sufficient complexity for the imperative, e.g. Swahili *fany-a* 'do (it)'. Obligatory elsewhere is a subject marker, referring to and concording with the subject of the clause. Since lexical subjects which are inferrable in the context of discourse need not be expressed, the subject marker is often the only reference to the understood subject in a clause and thus functions as a pronoun. The independent pronouns are not obligatory in the clause. The subject marker is sufficient to form a subjunctive clause in most Bantu languages, e.g. Swahili *a-fany-e* 'he should do (it)'. In the indicative mode, at least one more element is necessary for non-imperatives: the tense/aspect marker. The tense/aspect marker may immediately follow the subject marker, preceding the verb, in which case it is called a tense prefix, or it may be suffixed to the verb stem and its extensions, depending on the particular tense/aspect marker and the language, in which case it is called a tense suffix, e.g. Gikuyu *a-gwat-ire* 'he held (today)' suffixes *-ire* 'an action which has taken place on the day of speaking' to the verb *-gwata* 'catch/hold', but *a-á-gwata* 'he just held' prefixes *-á-* 'an action taking place immediately before the time of speaking'. Most Bantu languages show a richer paradigm of tense prefixes than of tense suffixes, but all show traces of the Common Bantu tense suffix system. Thus, most Swahili dialects and the standard language retain a tense suffix only for the 'present negative' *h-a-fany-i* (neg.-he-do-pres.) 's/he doesn't do/isn't doing (it)'. The Bantu 'tense' suffix **-(n)ga*, marking 'habituality', is found among interior North-East Bantu languages, e.g. Gikuyu *a-ra-gwata-ga* 's/he kept holding' combining the tense prefix *-ra-* 'action took place no earlier than the day before the day of speaking' with the tense suffix *-ga* 'habitual'. It survives in Swahili only as a common suffix for verb nominalisation, e.g. *m-sema-ji* 'speaker' < *sema* 'speak' via **mo-sema-ga-i* (note that the root *sema* is largely restricted to Swahili and is probably not of Bantu origin).

While all of the tense suffixes are traceable to Common Bantu, some tense prefixes are traceable to other grammatical categories. For example, the urban Swahili perfect *-me-*, as in *a-me-fanya* 's/he has done it', is traceable to Bantu **-màda* 'finish' (surviving also in Swahili *mal-iza* 'bring to an end, complete') via **-màd-idɛ* > *-mez-ie* (surviving in Bajuni) with the perfect suffix **-idɛ*. Nevertheless, many of the tense/aspect prefixes are traceable to Common Bantu, showing that at that stage Bantu had already set a precedent for further development of the tense prefix system in the individual languages.

Bantu languages vary in how negation interacts morphologically with particular tenses. In the subjunctive mode the negative marker immediately follows the subject marker, e.g. Swahili *a-si-fany-e* 's/he shouldn't do (it)', where *-si-* < **-ti-* is the negative marker. In the indicative mode, both suffixation and prefixation of the negative to the subject marker are commonly found, e.g. Swahili *h-a-ta-fanya* 's/he won't do (it)' with the negative marker *h(a)-* prefixed to the complex *a-ta-fanya* 's/he will do (it)'. This absolute first position in the verb complex for the negative marker is obligatory with most tenses. With a very few tenses there is dialect division between prefixing and suffixing of a negative, e.g. with the hypothetical marker *-nge-*, Southern *h-a-nge-fanya* and Northern *a-si-nge-fanya* 's/he should/wouldn't do (it)', cf. *a-nge-fanya* 's/he would do (it)'. In a few areas, the negative is an independent particle following the entire verbal word, e.g. among the Chagga dialects (northern Tanzania) *a-le-ca fo* 's/he didn't come' beside *a-le-ca* 'he came', where *-le-* is the tense prefix for 'action took place yesterday or earlier'.

As some of the glosses above suggest, the tense/aspect systems of many

Bantu languages are quite extensive, marking a variety of tenses, aspects and moods. The fine distinction between degrees of pastness is particularly striking as unusual among world languages, e.g. Gikuyu *a-gwat-ire* 's/he held' (current (today) past), *a-ra-gwat-ire* 's/he held' (recent (yesterday) past), *a-à-gwat-ire* 's/he held' (remoter past). Among Bantu languages with such distinctions, some show tense concord between the initial tense and consecutive tense markers, e.g. Giriama *a-dza-fika a-ka-injira* 's/he arrived and entered (today)' vs. *w-a-fika a-ki-injira* 's/he arrived ... (yesterday or earlier)'. The consecutive marker, common in east coast Bantu and extending into the interior, functions as a perfective, necessarily giving a consecutive interpretation to verbs so marked with respect to the preceding verb.

A great many Bantu languages allow concatenation of particular tense/aspect markers, e.g. Gikuyu *ĩ-ngĩ-ka-na-endia* 'if I should ever sell (it)' where *-ngĩ-* is 'hypothetical', *-ka-* is 'future' and *-na-* is 'indeterminate time'. Along the east coast this degree of morphological complexity is largely reduced to a single tense prefix per verb. Thus, in Swahili 'compound tenses' allow two tenses to mark a clause through the device of an auxiliary verb *-kuwa* 'be(come)' supporting the first tense, e.g. *a-li-ku-wa a-ki-fanya* 's/he used to do it' where *-li-* is the 'past' marker and *-ki-* is 'habitual/progressive'. The construction *a-li-ki-fanya* survives in Northern Swahili with the same meaning.

Both the reduction of some of the paradigmatic complexity and the introduction of new tense-aspect markers in specific contexts have led to extensive asymmetry between affirmative and negative tense/aspect markers among the east coast languages. Swahili provides many examples. Many scholars caution against direct comparison of the semantics of the affirmative and negative tenses. Thus, the chart given here is approximative, in order to indicate differences in the affirmative and negative tenses.

Affirmative		*Negative*
-na/a-	'progressive/general'	-Ø-...-i
-me-	'perfect'	-ja- 'not yet'
-li-	'past/anterior'	-ku-
-ta-	'future'	-ta/to-
-nge/ngali-	'hypothetical'	-nge/ngali-
-ki-	'participial, progressive'	-si-po- 'unless'
-ka-	'perfective/consecutive'	(use neg. subjunctive) 'without then V-ing'

This standard Swahili paradigm is general to most urban Swahili dialects. The rural dialects show various differences, e.g. *-na-* is 'today past/perfect' in the rural coastal dialects, *-Ø-...-ie-* < **-idɛ* serves a similar function in the Bajuni dialects and ChiMwini (*-ire*), Comoros dialects use *nga-...-o* rather than a tense prefix for the 'progressive/general', e.g. *ng-u-som-o* 's/he's reading', cf. standard *a-na-soma*. In addition to the above markers standard Swahili uses *hu-*, usually considered a tense/aspect marker but not admitting a subject marker (< *ni+ku-* = copula + infinitive marker), to mark 'occasional recurrent action' (i.e. 'sometimes'). In the Northern dialects, *hu-* is generally used as the 'progressive/habitual', and *-na-* only occurs in speech to speakers of other varieties of Swahili.

An optional element of the Bantu verb is the object marker, placed immediately before the verb stem. Common to all Bantu languages is the use of an object marker anaphorically to refer to an understood second argument of the clause, not expressed in the clause itself, e.g. Swahili *a-me-vi-ona* 's/he has seen them', where *-vi-* refers to some class 8 object such as *vi-su* 'knives' (pl. of *ki-su*). The invariant reflexive object marker, *-ji-* < **gi* (many Bantu languages use a reflex of **ke-*) marks subject-object coreference, e.g. *a-me-ji-kata* 'he cut himself', *tu-me-ji-kata* 'we cut ourselves' etc.

Many Bantu languages allow multiple object markers, e.g. Umbundu *w-a-u-n-dekisa* 's/he showed him/her to me', where *-u-* is the class 1 object marker 'him/her' and *-n-* is the first person singular object marker 'me'. On the east coast and spreading inland toward the south is the restriction of the object marker to one per verb. In some languages, either of two object arguments may be represented by the object marker, the other being expressed anaphorically by an independent pronoun or demonstrative. Most investigated languages indicate that there are further restrictions on which object may be so represented. Swahili is highly developed in this respect. Animates are selected over inanimates and there is a hierarchy of roles from agent down to direct object. These roles are determined either lexically or by verbal extensions. The verbal extensions will be discussed immediately below. First, however, it is worth mentioning that Swahili is unique in gravitating toward the object marker as an obligatory verbal category, though only for reference to human objects. The use of the object marker with expressed indefinite human objects in the same clause is generally tolerated in Bantu only by those North-East coastal languages which have been in contact with Swahili for several generations (e.g. the Kenyan coastal languages Pokomo and Miji Kenda), but is obligatory in urban dialects of Swahili and the standard language, e.g. *a-li-mw-ona mtu* 's/he saw somebody', where *-m(w)-* class 1 refers to *mtu* 'person' and the referent is not yet known to the addressee. Elsewhere in Bantu the object marker must have an anaphoric reference.

The verbal extensions are verbal suffixes which define the role of one argument of the verb. They are directly suffixed to the verb root or to each other when grammatically possible. All the verbal suffixes are inherited from Common Bantu. The system has undergone little semantic change and a moderate amount of formal change in the current languages. Swahili will serve to illustrate the basic system common to all Bantu languages.

In Swahili the regular causative is *-i/esha* (the vowel determined by the

Causative	-ya, i/esha	< *-ia, *-e/ɛk-ia, respectively
Stative	-(i/e)ka	< *-(e/ɛ)ka
Prepositional	-i/ea	< *-e/ɛda
Reversive	-u/oa	< *-o/ɔda
Reciprocal	-ana	< *-a-na
Passive	-(i/e)wa	< *-(e/ɛd-)oa

vowel harmony rule discussed on page 293), e.g. *pik-isha* 'cause to cook', *chek-esha* 'make laugh'. Its origin appears to be a sequence of stative + causative. The *-ya* causative survives in a few transparent lexical items, e.g. *on-ya* 'warn', cf. *ona* 'see', *on-esha* 'show'. The causative focuses on the agent of the root verb if a specific agent referent is understood. If not, it may focus on the object of the root verb, e.g. *a-li-zi-jeng-esha* 's/he had them built', where 'them' refers to a class 10 noun such as *nyumba* 'houses'.

The stative suffix focuses on the state or potential of the subject. With the perfect *-me-* it focuses on state, e.g. *i-me-vunj-ika* 'it is broken' < *vunja* 'break', *i-me-poto-ka* 'it is twisted' < *potoa* 'twist'. With the general 'present' *-na-*, *-a-* or *hu-* it may focus on a potential, e.g. *i-na-vunj-ika* 'it is breakable' (i.e. 'it can get broken'). With some verbs the stative form is *-i/ekana* as if from stative + reciprocal, e.g. *i-na-pat-ikana* 'it is obtainable' < *pata* 'get'. Sometimes the stative interpretation remains with this tense, e.g. *i-na-jul-ikana* 'it is known' < *jua* 'know'. A number of stative verbs show lexicalisation of the stative marker, e.g. *amka* 'awaken (intr.)', *choka* 'be tired', where no simpler forms of the verb exist.

The prepositional suffix (also called applicative) covers the semantic range of the most common prepositions in English. It may be benefactive, e.g. *ni-li-m-pik-ia* 'I cooked **for** her', directive, e.g. *ni-li-lil-ia kijiko* 'I cried **over** a spoon', directional, e.g. *ni-li-m-j-ia* 'I came **to** him', instrumental, e.g. *ni-li-l-ia kijiko* 'I ate **with** a spoon', affected participant, e.g. *wa-li-m-f-ia* 'they died **on** him'. That is, the prepositional suffix focuses on the role of some argument other than the direct object. The particular role focused on in context is a matter of the lexical meaning of the verb and inference, e.g. *ni-li-mw-ib-ia* may mean either 'I stole **for** him' or 'I stole **from** him'. As with other extensions, in some cases they have lexicalised, e.g. *-ambia* 'say to' < *amb-i-a*, where the verb *-amba* 'say' survives in Swahili elsewhere only as a complementiser, e.g. *nimesikia* **kwamba** *a-me-fika* 'I heard **that** he has arrived'. Double prepositional verbs have a 'persistive' meaning, e.g. *tup-il-ia* 'throw (far) away', *end-el-ea* 'continue' < *end-e-a* 'go in a certain direction' < *enda* 'go'.

The reversive suffix functions to undo the action of the root verb, e.g. *fung-u-a* 'open, untie' < *fung-a* 'close, tie', *chom-o-a* 'pull out' < *chom-a* 'stick in, skewer'.

The reciprocal suffix indicates reciprocal roles for two subjects or a subject and the object of a *na* 'and/with' phrase, e.g. *wa-li-pig-ana* 'they fought (with each other)' < *piga* 'hit', *a-li-pig-ana na-ye* 's/he fought with him/her', where *na-ye* consists of *na* 'with/and' and a cliticised form of the independent pronoun *yeye* 'him/her'.

The passive focuses on the non-agentive status of the subject, e.g. *a-li-shind-wa* 's/he was defeated' < *shinda* 'defeat', *a-li-on-esh-wa* 's/he was shown' (...'see' + causative + passive). Only an object which can be referred to by an object marker with the active verb can be the subject of the passivised verb in Swahili. Thus, the only passive corresponding to the active sentence, *ni-sha-ku-on-esha watu* 'I already showed the people to **you**', is *u-li-on-esh-wa watu* '**you** were shown the people'. The direct object *watu* 'people' cannot be passivised over the indirect object, just as it cannot be represented by an object marker while there is an indirect object in the clause. The passive is always the last verbal extension in the Swahili verb. This appears to be quite general to Eastern Bantu. However, in the south-west the passive may precede the prepositional if the subject has the role of direct object of the active verb, e.g. Umbundu *onjo y-a-tung-iw-ila ina-hé* 'the house was built for his/her mother' < *tunga* 'build', where the subject of *tung-iw-* 'build-passive' is *onjo* 'house' and *ina-hé* 'mother-his/her' is the object of *-ila*, the prepositional suffix. A number of other verbal extensions are extant in Bantu, but are no longer productive, cf. Swahili *kama-ta* 'seize' < *kama* 'squeeze', *nene-pa* 'get fat' < *nene* 'fat (adj.)', *ganda-ma* 'get stuck' < *ganda* 'stick to'. Still further verbal extensions are recognisable through Niger-Congo reconstruction, e.g. **bí-áda* (Swahili *zaa* 'bear children') contains **bi*, a Niger-Congo root for 'child' not common in Bantu.

To complete discussion of the morphological complexity of the verb structure, the relative marker must be mentioned. In most of the Bantu area relativisation is a syntactic process which does not interfere with the verbal complex. However, among the North-East coastal languages, including Swahili, a relative marker may be infixed in the verbal complex by suffixation to the tense prefix. The relative marker in such cases is itself complex, consisting of a secondary class concord marker + the referential morpheme *-o*, e.g. *ni-li-p+o-fika* 'when I arrived'. Here the relative marker *-p+o-* consists of the concord for class 16, a locative used here as a temporal, and the referential *-o*. The form functioning as a relative marker here occurs throughout Bantu in a demonstrative series, e.g. the Swahili proximate 'that' *hu-y+o* (cl. 1), *hi-l+o* (cl. 5) etc. In the languages which have the infixed relative marker it only appears with a few tense prefixes. In all cases these tense prefixes are innovations developing later than the Common Bantu period. The origin of this infixation is postposing of the relative marker to the entire verbal complex. This process survives on the north-east coast and in the south-east, when there is no tense prefix on the verb, e.g. Swahili *mwezi u-Ø-ja-(w+)o* 'the month which is coming', i.e. 'next month', where the -Ø- marks the absence of a tense prefix and the relative marker is suffixed to the verb *ja* 'come', or Pokomo *want'u wa-Ø-j-ie-(w+)o* 'the people who came', with the addition of a tense suffix *-ie* to the verb *-ja* 'come'. The tense prefixes which allow the infixed relatives originate in auxiliaries where the relative marker was postposed, e.g. Swahili *-li-* 'past/anterior' < (*-a-* 'remote past') + *li* 'copula'. The tense prefix *-na-* 'general, progressive' regularly takes infixation in the standard and Southern dialects, but is largely resisted by the Central dialects, e.g. standard Swahili *watu wa-na-(w+)o-sema* 'the people who are speaking', while Central Swahili prefers *watu amba-(w+)o wa-na-sema* 'the people who have spoken', where the relative marker cliticises to a complementiser *amba* introducing the relative clause. This device is used for relativisation in all dialects and is the only option with tense prefixes which do not allow relative infixation.

4 Syntax

Bantu languages have a basic verb-medial word order with a strong tendency toward subject first. Auxiliaries precede the verb (itself usually in infinitive form with **ko-* prefixed). All noun modifiers follow the noun in most of the Bantu area: adjectives, numerals, demonstratives, relative clauses. However, most languages optionally allow demonstratives to precede the noun to mark definiteness. The basic possessive (or 'associative') pattern is *Possessed cc-a Possessor*, where *-a* is the associative marker 'of', and the class concord prefix concords with the possessed noun. As discussed on page 1003, the pronominalised possessor takes a special form, which is suffixed to *-a-*; thus, Swahili *ngoma z-a-mtu* '(the) drums of/for (the) man' with the class concord *z-* (class 10) concording with *ngoma* 'drums' and *ngoma z-a-ke* 'his/her drums' with the special possessive form of the pronoun suffixed to *-a-*. Most Bantu languages show concord for the class of the pronominalised possessor, but Swahili uses *-ke* for all classes except the animate plural (class 2).

With the exception of **nà* 'and/with', Common Bantu does not appear to have prepositions. Beside the prepositional extension, Swahili uses both verbs and nouns to function like English prepositions, e.g. *a-me-fika toka Dar* 'he has arrived **from** Dar', where *toka* is the verb 'come from'; *a-li-tembea* **mpaka** *Dar* 'he walked **to** Dar', where the noun *mpaka* 'boundary' is used as a vector to mean 'up to, until'. Commonly, the possessive construction is used prepositionally, e.g. *chini y-a nyumba* 'under (of) the house', where *chini* 'down, under' etymologically displays *nchi* 'ground' + *-ni*, the locative suffix. The possessed concord ignores the locative and concords directly with the root noun. The possessive construction is also used with the locative concords prefixed, especially *ku-* (class 17), to express locative, instrumental and manner relations, e.g. *kw-a Fatuma* '**at** Fatuma's (place)', *kw-a nyundo* '**with** (a) hammer', *kw-a nguvu* '**by** force'. In all cases, these preposition-like uses of constructions are noun second. In all respects, then, Swahili and the other Bantu languages are very much like the prototypical SVO language.

However, word order is not invariant. Topicalisation is possible, e.g. *kitabu ni-li-ki-kuta* 'the book, I found it'; note the usual use of the object marker (*-ki-* (class 7) in this case) in the topicalised construction. In Swahili a topicalised possessive construction is optional with animate possessors: *mtu ngoma zake* 'the man, his drums'. Some Bantu languages require a cleft construction for interrogatives, equivalent to Swahili *ni nani uliyemwona?* 'who did you see?' lit. '(it) is who that you saw?', where the interrogative pronoun *nani* 'who' is introduced as the predicate of the copula *ni*, a marker used to focus on noun phrases or entire clauses in the Bantu languages. In Swahili, topicalisation is never obligatory. The usual form of the question leaves an object interrogative in object, i.e. post-verbal, position, e.g. *ulimwona nani?* 'you saw who?'. The widespread use of Bantu interrogative pronouns ending in *-ni*, e.g. Swahili *na-ni* 'who?', *ni-ni* 'what?', *li-ni* 'when?', *ga-ni* 'what kind?' indicates the earlier prevalence of topicalisation in *wh*-questions in Bantu, still found in Bantu's Benue-Congo and Kwa relatives, where cognates of *ni* (< *ne) are suffixed to topics, whether interrogative or otherwise, e.g. in Yoruba (see page 280).

Beside its predicate-marking function, the particle *ni* (usually called a copula because of its equative function in Bantu languages, e.g. *Fatuma ni m-Swahili* 'Fatuma **is** a Swahili speaker') functions in some North-East interior languages to mark a main clause, e.g. Gikuyu *nĩ-a-gwat-ire* 'he held (it)' as main clause, but *mũndũ ũ-ria a-gwat-ire*, 'the man who held (it)', where *a-gwat-ire* is relativised by means of the demonstrative *ũ-ria* (Swahili *yu-le*) introducing the relative clause. Another Bantu 'copula' reflected in Swahili *-li* acts like a verb in taking tense prefixes and is used for both equative and locative purposes in most Bantu languages (replacing *ni* as equative with non-third persons). In Swahili, equative and locative predicates are strictly distinguished, so that *skuli ni hapa* means 'this place is a school' but *skuli i-ko hapa* (*iko* < *i-li-ko*) means 'the/a school is in/around here'.

Despite its typically verb-second syntax, much of the morphology of the Bantu languages indicates a verb-last origin, only sporadically found among the Niger-Congo languages. Signs of verb-last syntax are found in the preposing of the object marker to the verb stem (as if of OV origin), the postposing of the verbal extensions and mode markers (as if of verb–auxiliary origin), the suffixing of the locative marker *-ni* to the affected noun (as if of noun–postposition origin), the class prefix on nouns (as if of modifier–noun origin) and probably the postposing of the relative marker to the non-tense-prefixed verbal complex surviving on the north-east coast and in the south-east (as if of clause–relativiser origin). Otherwise, with its obligatory subject marker and tense prefixes in that order, and its noun–genitive possessive construction, the Bantu languages resemble the majority of their Benue-Congo and Kwa neighbours in the north-west.

The variation in position of some Bantu categories, most characteristic of the north-west, suggests an intermediate stage of evolution between an analytical verb-final syntax and the strict verbal morphology of Swahili and the east coast, with maximally a single tense prefix and object marker per verb. In particular, the morphologisation of auxiliary-like categories, both pre- and post-verbal, does not appear to have occurred uniformly over the Bantu area as the languages assumed their current verb-medial syntax. The slight ordering freedom of verbal extensions, e.g. in the Umbundu example on page 302, suggests the relatively late survival of pre-Bantu verbal extensions as a separate word class in part of the southwestern area. The prepositional verbal extension *-e/ɛda*, as well as the use of verbs for prepositional direction, e.g. Swahili *(ku)toka* 'come (from)' and *kw-enda* '(go) towards', suggest the serial verb constructions general to Niger-Congo languages, including Bantu's north-west relatives (see pages 282–3). In the process of evolution towards complex verb morphology, the attraction of these auxiliaries to the preceding verb precluded a preverbal position for the object of the 'prepositional' verb and may have precipitated verb-medial syntax. The Bantu languages which still allow multiple object-markers, the interior east and most of the west (in the north-west object markers have been partially lost in favour of post-verbal independent pronouns), indicate the retention of verb-final syntax, allowing two or more preposed objects, but only for a pronominal form of the object. That is, where O is a lexical object and o is a pronominal object, O–V O–aux. appears to have evolved into O-V+aux. O and finally V+aux. O O, but o–V o–aux. evolved into o–o–V+aux. In most contexts, languages like Swahili have gone further in reanalysing the object of the extension as the only object of the main verb. Syntactically, focusing options have been maintained in Swahili through the development of a new prepositional device, using the possessive construction for instrument discussed above, e.g. *a-li-pig-i-a nyundo msumari* 'he hit the nail with a hammer' (i.e. he used a hammer to hit the nail), with the extension focusing on the instrument, and *a-li-piga msumari kwa nyundo*, with the same meaning but use of the possessive construction, reversing the order of lexical objects. Interestingly enough, the instrumental use of the prepositional extension in Swahili still allows an object marker for the direct object despite the presence of the instrument in the clause, e.g. *a-li-u-pig-i-a nyundo msumari* (where *-u-* refers to *msumari* 'nail'). All other uses of all verbal extensions allow the object marker only to refer to the object of the extension when that object is mentioned in the clause. Amidst variation in the position of the negative marker across Bantu languages and according to tense/aspect within the languages, the widespread use of a post-verbal negative marker in the north-west (and in Chagga, as discussed above) suggests an auxiliary origin in verb-final syntax for negation: verb negative (= auxiliary). The preverbal position of the negative marker **ti* (Swahili *si*) appears to be a manifestation of the shift to verb-medial syntax. This **ti* is also the negative copula, e.g. Swahili *mnyama si mtu* 'an animal is not a person'. In the same way that there are traces of a post-predicate position for the currently prepredicate copula **ne* (Swahili *ni*) among the interrogative pronouns, as discussed earlier, the negative 'copula' appears to have shifted to a preverbal auxiliary: negative (= auxiliary) verb. The other forms of negation, which place the negative before the subject marker, appear to be even later developments within the Bantu area, evolving from verbs with inherent negation, e.g. Swahili *ha-* < *nk'a-* (still common in the Central dialects) perhaps developing from *ni* 'copula' + *kana* 'deny'.

Bantu subordination patterns are relatively consistent across languages. Relativisation is generally introduced by a demonstrative or, among languages with preprefixes, a preprefix when the subject is relativised, e.g. Zulu *a-bantu a-ba-funa-yo* 'people who want' (note the final relative marker *-yo* used with no tense prefix). The preprefix itself may derive from an earlier demonstrative in concord with the head noun and subject of the relative clause. Complement clauses and even adverbial clauses are generally introduced by verbs etymologically meaning 'say' (as generally in Niger-Congo), e.g. Swahili *kw-amba*, Southern and Central Bantu *ku-ti*, and/or 'be(come)', e.g. Swahili *ku-wa*. Thus, *-amba-* in Swahili may introduce reported speech, a relative clause and earlier introduced the protasis of conditional sentences, e.g. *na* ***kwamba*** *moyo ni chuo ningekupa ukasome* 'and **if** the heart were a book, I would give it to you for you to read' (a verse from the early nineteenth-century Mombasan poet, Muyaka). This last use of *kwamba* has been replaced by *kama*, of Arabic origin, also used as the preposition 'like'. In the rural dialect of Chifundi *ku-wa* 'be(come)' retains this function, cf. Zulu *u-ku-ba* and *u-ku-ti* which also may function like this. In Swahili *ku-wa* may also introduce reported speech and other complements of verbs of communication or mental action, e.g. 'think'.

In sum, the syntax of the Bantu languages reflects an SVO language which has evolved out of a language with both SOV characteristics and interclausal relations common to Niger-Congo languages of either basic word order. It is most distinctive among Niger-Congo languages in its noun-class system and its verb morphology. Among Niger-Congo class languages it is specifically distinctive in the complexity of its verb morphology. For example, the distantly related West Atlantic language Fula is also a class language, but the class markers follow rather than precede the noun and there are no tense prefixes or object markers preceding the verb root. Like Bantu, Fula is currently verb-medial showing the prevalence of this type of syntax throughout Niger-Congo.

5 Non-Bantu Influence on Swahili

In view of its general, even extreme, adherence to the Bantu type (extreme, for example, in the extent of its obligatory verb morphology), Swahili is usually viewed as minimally affected in its syntax by non-Bantu influence. In contrast, the Swahili lexicon shows massive borrowing from Arabic and more recently from English. In addition, as the traditional medium of communication between the Indian Ocean commercial network and the Bantu interior, it has accepted words and concepts from numerous other languages, both Bantu and foreign, e.g. Portuguese (in the sixteenth century), Persian and Hindi. Among traditional Swahili communities, words originating in Arabic often maintain some features of their Arabic pronunciation, e.g. *baxt(i)* 'luck' with a consonant cluster and the foreign phoneme /x/. However, as Swahili has spread to non-Arabicised Bantu peoples and everyday usage in traditional Swahili communities, certain Bantu processes of nativisation have taken place, e.g. *bahati* with typical Bantu syllable structure and nativisation of /x/ > /h/. In both the standard language and the traditional dialects the Arabic interdental fricatives have been adopted, e.g. *dhani* 'think', *thelathini* 'thirty'. Among the new urban Swahili communities such as Dar es Salaam in Tanzania, these interdentals are non-standardly replaced by post-alveolars, e.g. *zani, selasini*. The phonological nativisation process for loanwords from languages allowing word-final consonants consists of using the vocalic quality of the final consonant as the nucleus of a final syllable, e.g. *-jibu* 'answer' < Arabic *jib*; *-skwizi* 'hug romantically' < English *squeeze, starehe* 'relax' < Arabic *-stariħ*. An interesting detail concerning loan verbs is that they do not take the modal suffixes. Thus, the subjunctive and indicative are distinguished only by the presence or absence of a tense prefix, i.e. *a-Ø-jibu* 'he should answer' must be subjunctive because there is no tense prefix on the verb.

Bantuisation of loan nouns occurs where the loan is analysable into a class prefix + stem, thus *ki-tabu*, pl. *vi-tabu* 'book' < Arabic *kita:b*. This tendency to metanalyse also occurs within Bantu words when possible, e.g. *chupa* 'bottle' < **ne-čópà* is metanalysed in the newer urban Swahili communities as *ch-upa*, pl. *vy-upa*, by analogy with class 7/8 nouns, e.g. *ch-uma* 'iron' < **ke-ómà*, pl. *vy-uma*. This tendency is not seen in Northern Swahili communities where the reflex *t̪ʻupa* is unmistakably class 9, pl. *t̪ʻupa* (class 10).

A fuller understanding of the impact of other languages, particularly Arabic through continual contact for a millennium, awaits further examination of the semantics and rhetorical patterns of Swahili and other Bantu languages. Beside the cultural influence of Arabic reflected in Swahili's vocabulary, the use of Arabic adverbials and conjunctions is striking, e.g. *lakini* 'but, however', *au/ama* 'or', *halafu* 'then', *baada* 'after'. As rhetorical style is expressed in art, Swahili poetry has adopted numerous Arabic metres and the use of vocalic rhyme. Vocalic rhyme is unknown in traditional Bantu verse (in contradistinction to tonal rhyme), but Swahili has used the identity of word-final syllables to create a tradition of rhyme schemes far more intricate than in the Arabic source, e.g. the regular form of the Swahili quatrain (four-line stanza) has the rhyme scheme ab/ab/ab/bc, which repeats as de/de/de/ec. Note that only the final rhymes of each stanza are related. This typical pattern of stanza rhyme suggests the refrain pattern of a repeated coda line, marking the end of each stanza, commonly used in Bantu and West African song and often in Swahili song as well. This blending of Bantu and non-Bantu traditions is suggestive of more prosaic adaptations of non-Bantu rhetorical patterns which remain to be described in Swahili.

Bibliography

For Bantu as a whole, Guthrie (1967–70) is the most extensive classification and reconstruction. Nurse and Philippson (1975) presents a classification of Swahili's nearest geographical relatives.

For Swahili, Polomé (1967) is a conveniently arranged introduction to the dialects and the basic structure of the language. Ashton (1944), a pedagogical grammar, is still the most complete introduction to the standard language, while Hinnebusch (1979) presents a descriptive synopsis. Vitale (1981) is a highly comprehensive generative treatment of Swahili syntax; although it offers little in the way of new data, it relates Swahili grammar to issues in generative grammar and organises topics accordingly. Stigand (1915) is still the most extensive English-language discussion of Swahili dialects, excluding most of the Central rural dialects. Whiteley (1969) presents a sociohistorical discussion of the development of standard Swahili.

References

Ashton, E.O. 1944. *Swahili Grammar (Including Intonation)* (Longman, London)

Guthrie, M. 1967–70. *Comparative Bantu*, 4 vols. (Gregg International Publishers)

Hinnebusch, T.J. 1979. 'Swahili', in T. Shopen (ed.), *Languages and Their Status* (Winthrop, Cambridge, Mass.), pp. 204–93

Nurse, D. and G. Philippson. 1975. 'The North-Eastern Bantu Languages of Tanzania and Kenya: A Classification', *Kiswahili*, vol. 45, pp. 1–28

Polomé, E.C. 1967. *Swahili Language Handbook* (Center for Applied Linguistics, Washington DC)

Stigand, C.H. 1915. *A Grammar of Dialectic Changes in the Kiswahili Language* (Cambridge University Press, Cambridge)

Vitale, A.J. 1981. *Swahili Syntax* (Foris, Dordrecht)

Whiteley, W.H. 1969. *Swahili: The Rise of a National Language* (Methuen, London)

Language Index